EUSEBIUS

THE HISTORY OF THE CHURCH
from Christ to Constantine

EUSEBIUS

THE HISTORY OF THE CHURCH
from Christ to Constantine

Translated by
G.A.Williamson

AUGSBURG PUBLISHING HOUSE
MINNEAPOLIS, MINNESOTA

THE HISTORY OF THE CHURCH

This translation first published in 1965 by:
    Penguin Books Ltd, Harmondsworth, Middlesex, England
    Penguin Books Inc., 3300 Clipper Mill Rd., Baltimore, Maryland
    Penguin Books Pty Ltd, Ringwood, Victoria, Australia

First Augsburg Edition 1975

Library of Congress Catalog Card No. 75-22726

International Standard Book No. 0-8066-1509-5

Manufactured in the United States of America

Contents

Introduction

'THE only work of its kind, possessing a value to subsequent ages which belongs to no other uninspired work.'

'The father of ecclesiastical history – the first, the only historian of the Church bordering on primitive times.'

Such did *The History of the Church* and its author appear to the editor of the Bohn Eusebius, published nearly a century ago; and present-day readers of the book are not likely to dispute his opinion. Without this work what should we know of the progress of the early Church, its rapid extension, its glorious enthusiasm, energy, and vitality, its tribulations, persecutions, and martyrdoms, its sad divisions and astonishing heresies? The narrative books of the New Testament record nothing after the first thirty years of the Church's existence; indeed, after the first fifteen we lose sight of almost all her leading figures except one, and apart from that one we can glean little information from the rest of the New Testament about their doings or their fates. To learn a little more about those others, or to learn anything at all about their successors, we must turn to Eusebius, whose record covers three centuries and extends over many lands, whose work is on a large scale, who was himself an eyewitness of many stirring events, and who drew his information about previous generations from a remarkable number of earlier writers, enshrining in his own book most valuable materials for later historians, materials which in very many cases would otherwise have been lost for ever.

As we shall see later, Eusebius is not highly esteemed for his literary qualities, and as theologian, philosopher, orator, or historian few would call him great. Well aware of his own

limitations he describes himself as 'moderately capable', and
admits the careful preparation necessary before he could make
a public speech. But if he lacked genius he possessed a diversity
of gifts that were at least adequate: a measure of theological
and philosophical understanding, of historical grasp, of power
to express his thoughts in speech and writing, had been
granted to him; and he knew how to use all his limited gifts
in combination to produce something worth while. He possessed other qualities too – a passion for knowledge, an
immense interest in the story he was unfolding, unstinted
admiration for the heroes of the past and an ardent desire
for the limitless expansion of Christ's Kingdom in the future,
a deep interest in the writings of his predecessors both
Christian and pagan, a minute knowledge and consuming
love of the Scriptures, an unshakeable devotion to the Church,
and a burning hatred of all who injured her, either by persecution from without or by moral and doctrinal perversion from
within. He had motive enough for writing: he had, too, an
immense capacity for work. He assiduously collected Christian
documents; he devoured and assimilated their contents; and,
in spite of persecution and the heavy burdens of his episcopal
office, for nearly forty years he poured out a constant stream
of historical and other works, of which the most valuable is
The History of the Church.

There are many in these days who would find the book dull,
perhaps unreadable, as it rambles on, discoursing obscurely
on theology, arguing in minute detail about 'matters of no
consequence', relating the lives and deaths of those long since
forgotten, denouncing unintelligible heresies, and listing the
vices and brutalities of petty tyrants. But to those who do not
feel that the past is dead; that bygone struggles and calamities,
victories and defeats, successes and failures, loves and hates,
actions and reactions are irrelevant to us; that other ages and
other manners are no concern of ours – to such the book will
be full of interest. Above all, those to whom the Church is

the Body of Christ, its treasures beyond price, its agony their own, will be held fast as they read its pages. If they value the message that has come down to their generation they will be moved as they read of those who laboured to take that message from a tiny country to the whole known world, and of the countless 'champions of Christ' who faced appalling tortures without flinching and endured to the end. Have we not all wondered what the early Christians were like, and whether we could stand firm in similar trials? Here we shall find them revealed in all their strength and in all their weakness, and to become acquainted with them will prove a salutary experience.

Many of us in this land grew up in the conviction that the early Christians had very simple beliefs, the most primitive organization, and an almost complete lack of ceremonial. A study of Eusebius's pages will satisfy us that we have been greatly deceived. Not only in his own statements, but in the testimonies of the earliest authorities on which he draws, we shall find inescapable proof that the Church of the first generations of Christians was one in which an Anglican of our own day would recognize most of the ideas and practices to which he is accustomed. We shall find the same line drawn between clergy and laity, the same division of the clergy into the three orders of bishops, presbyters, and deacons, the same practice of episcopal ordination and consecration, the same insistence on the Apostolic Succession and on the establishment by Christ of One Holy Catholic and Apostolic Church. We shall find Christendom partitioned up into dioceses and archdioceses, presided over and ruled by bishops who are held in the highest esteem. Did not James, the Lord's brother, within a few years of the Saviour's death sit on the episcopal throne of Jerusalem and officiate clad in sacerdotal vestments? Was not John the beloved disciple 'a sacrificing priest wearing the mitre'? There may have been a short period when services were held in private houses, but as soon as possible churches began to rise, then cathedrals, and on these the builders lavished all their loving artistry, to the delight and sublimation of the beholder. No one can read Eusebius's account of how the cathedral of Tyre, with all its elaborate symbolism, rose from the ashes, without thinking of Coventry. Truly, that generation and this are one.

Within the house of God, then as now, was a sanctuary, and within the sanctuary an altar, at which the priest celebrated the Eucharist, and when they had pledged themselves to keep the commandments of God and had sung hymns and antiphons to His divine Son, administered to the faithful the Body and Blood of the Lord. From the Sacrament notable sinners were excluded till they had shown themselves penitent and received absolution; but the sick were not forgotten and the Reserved Sacrament was taken to them. Baptism, too, was regarded as of the highest importance, and credal declarations were required of the candidates: immersion was general but affusion was permitted. Then as now, after Baptism came Confirmation by the bishop. The laity were required to hear sermons, and though these were normally delivered by the clergy lay preachers were sanctioned, and their audiences might include bishops. As to the doctrines taught, we shall find little to distinguish them from our own, though of course emphasis changes with every generation. But dogmas which those who are not members of the Roman communion reject we shall not find in the pages of Eusebius. Papal Infallibility, the Immaculate Conception, and the Bodily Assumption of the Virgin Mary belong to a later age. The word Pope is applied only to the Bishop of Alexandria, which shares with Rome the primacy of the churches and is no whit inferior to her. If the Bishop of Rome tried to put others in their place, his brother-bishops 'sternly rebuked' him. Nor is Peter regarded as the founder of the Roman see: the language used of him is used of Paul as well, and Linus is the first Bishop of Rome 'after Paul and Peter'. Nor is Peter associated exclusively with Rome; for Ignatius was 'the second to be appointed to the Bishopric of Antioch in succession to Peter'. Observe also that the title 'the Apostle' is used frequently by one writer after another to indicate Paul and no one else.[1] Mary is mentioned less than half a dozen times, and though the doctrine of the Virgin Birth is stoutly maintained, no title of honour is applied to her, nor is it ever suggested that she or any other saint can be the recipient or channel of prayer. Finally, we note that so far from celibacy being imposed on bishops or clergy, such imposition is regarded as rank heresy.[2] It is clear that for those who are interested in the history, character, and doctrines of the Church a study of Eusebius's great work is essential: for those who have no such interest, it will at least provide a fund of stories of heroic endurance and soul-stirring courage.

Born about A.D. 260, Eusebius was probably a native of Caesarea, the limestone city which Herod the Great had built on the coast of Palestine where Strato's Tower had been, adorning it with magnificent temples and masterpieces of sculpture, and equipping it with an immense harbour that was a triumph of engineering skill.[3] This city became his capital, and was later that of Archelaus and Pilate, of Felix and Festus. It was of this city that Eusebius was one day to be bishop.

As a young man he became the disciple and close friend of Pamphilus, a teacher whose influence over his receptive pupil was profound. Pamphilus was dedicated to the spread of sound learning. He established at Caesarea a school of theology, and built up a large and well stocked library, thus largely contributing to the vast erudition later displayed by

1. Clement of Rome, after referring to Peter and Paul as 'the good apostles', praised Peter in two sentences, Paul in ten.

2. Protestants should note that Eusebius, like Paul, repudiates Sabbatarianism.

3. For a description see Josephus: *Jewish War* (Penguin Classics), pp. 76–7.

the younger man. Eusebius had already published several books, but for a time he gave up his original work to assist his tutor in the composition of a *Defence of Origen*. In the year 309 they were both imprisoned as confessors of Christ, but they continued their combined labours until Pamphilus was put to death for the Faith – a martyrdom which made an immense impact on his disciple. Eusebius, released from prison, withdrew to Tyre, where he honoured his friend's memory by taking the name of Eusebius (son) of Pamphilus, and himself contributing the sixth and last book to the *Defence*. To complete his tribute, he wrote a *Life of Pamphilus*, which, like his part of the *Defence*, is lost.

In 311 Eusebius left Caesarea for Egypt, where he was again consigned to prison. But his confinement was brief and the next year he was back in Palestine. When he was ordained to the diaconate and presbyterate we do not know, but in 314 he was consecrated Bishop of Caesarea, a position which he occupied for the rest of his life. The library of Caesarea was open to him once more, and he was able also to visit Jerusalem and there to avail himself of the library founded by Bishop Alexander. Possessed of a most retentive memory he acquired an immense store of learning; and for that and also for his great common sense he was highly esteemed by the last emperor whom we shall meet in his pages, Constantine the Great. They had first become acquainted when as a youth of eighteen Constantine had been invited to assume the imperial purple: from then until death parted them the bishop enjoyed the emperor's confidence and protection.

The common sense of Eusebius, which prevented him from going to any extremes and from becoming a rigid party man in the theological disputes which divided the Church, made him always ready to compromise when compromise did not conflict with the principles which he held dear. This became evident at the Council of Nicaea, over which the emperor himself presided in 325. Placed at his side Eusebius led the central group; and, anxious that the Church should not shed either of its wings, he submitted a draft creed, intended to be acceptable to both. But when he realized the true character of the teaching propounded by Arius, with whom he had hitherto felt himself inclined to sympathize, he voted with the Alexandrian party for a creed directed against Arian beliefs. But at no time did he become an extremist himself. Alas! Nicaea did not bring a cessation of quarrels between the bishops, some of whom behaved despicably. Indeed, at the Synod of Tyre ten years later Eusebius was to see Athanasius convicted on perjured evidence of cutting off the hand of another bishop, subsequently found to be still in possession of two!

A leading figure at the Synod of Jerusalem (which also was held in 335), at Constantinople a year later Eusebius was called on to deliver a panegyric on the emperor who had built this new capital of the Empire, and whom he so profoundly admired. The admiration was mutual; for Constantine had called on him to deliver the opening address at Nicaea, and six years later, declaring that he was fitted to become bishop of the whole world, he had desired to translate him from Caesarea to the much more important see of Antioch, an offer which Eusebius was humble enough to decline. Moreover, it was to Eusebius that Constantine had confided the story of the heavenly vision which had inspired him to throw off his habitual caution and take the dangerous step from which there was no turning back; it was from the hands of another Eusebius that the all-powerful monarch received Christian baptism.

Like his father Constantius, Constantine was not destined to live long, and a year after the panegyric was delivered he died a natural death – a most unusual end for a Roman emperor – while still in his forties. His friend survived him for two or three years, dying in 339 or 340, not much less than eighty years old.

Eusebius had lived a very full life. He had experienced the disasters which had in successive reigns befallen the Church. He had known the bitterness of seeing recantation followed by renewed persecution, the destruction of places of worship, the martyrdom of thousands who dared to proclaim the name of Christ, whose agonies in many cases he had witnessed with his own eyes. He had himself twice been confined within prison walls; yet he had toiled all his life for his beloved Master, and not the least of his toils had been the out-pouring of books to inform and edify his fellow-Christians. His output was truly amazing: he is credited with no less than forty-six works, some of them in ten, fifteen, twenty, and even twenty-five volumes. Nor was he content to write books and fling them at the public; they must be revised and enlarged, and new and better editions issued.

The modern reader should pause to think what a task the production of a book was in ancient days. If research was necessary, libraries were few and copies of old books scarce; it was hardly possible to obtain them from a bookseller. If passages had to be looked up for copying or summarizing they had to be ferreted out of an awkward roll; the reader could not find them in an index and then turn quickly to a numbered page. And how much more difficult the search must have been when there were no spaces between words, no paragraphs, no inverted commas, and no stops! When the necessary information had been collected, the author had to pen his book laboriously on papyrus with a reed and periodically turn back and search for any passages he might wish to emend or rewrite. Having finished the book, how was he to obtain copies for publication? They must be produced by hand, and he must either entrust the original to a scribe, who could turn out only one copy at a time, or read it aloud to a number of scribes, who would take it down at his dictation. Even that method was slow, and either method, as all students of ancient manuscripts know, resulted in numerous mistakes.

Yet the prolific and voluminous writers of imperial times overcame all these difficulties.

But, unless a book was an outstanding success, few copies would get into circulation, and fewer still would survive. We have many manuscripts of Virgil's poems, but none at all of those of his contemporary Varius. As for Eusebius, of his forty-six works fifteen have disappeared entirely, ten are represented by a few short quotations, four are incomplete, one survives only in a Syriac version, and one in Armenian and Latin versions, while fifteen have come down to us seemingly intact. Though Eusebius wrote only on religious subjects, his works fall into distinct groups – epistolary, oratorical, dogmatic, polemical, biblical, and historical. Of the letters, only the one addressed to his own diocese has survived. Of the speeches, we have the *Festival Oration* (incorporated in Book 10 of the present work), the *Panegyric on Constantine*, and the *Panegyric on the Martyrs*. The dogmatic and polemical works are of little interest to English readers. One lost dogmatic work bore the strange title *The Numerous Progeny of the Ancients*; the polemical include the lost *Defence of Origen*, the rest being directed against Hierocles, Marcellus, Porphyry, and the Manichees. Of the Biblical works, many were commentaries on books of the two Testaments, containing much sound sense but too many allegorical interpretations. Others dealt with Biblical place-names, the geography of the Holy Land, discrepancies in the Gospels, and the like. We have unfortunately lost the 'fifty sumptuous copies' of the Bible which the Emperor directed Eusebius to produce for his new capital. It is the historical works that are of most value to us, and though two have disappeared – the *Life of Pamphilus* and the *Collection of Martyrs* – we are fortunate enough to possess four. The *Martyrs of Palestine* is an account of martyrdoms which had taken place over a period of eight years: of most of them Eusebius could write from personal knowledge; for he had risked his life to be there as a witness. The *Life of Constantine*, written after the Emperor's death and when the writer himself had only a year or two to live, is an important though biased historical document, particularly valuable for its account of the proceedings at Nicaea. The *Chronological Tables* are an epitome of events in various countries, arranged side by side in dated sequence. Most important of all is our present work, *The History of the Church*, a 'monumental work', as F. J. Bacchus wrote, 'for which it would be difficult to overestimate the obligation which posterity is under to Eusebius'.

Regarding the order in which these numerous books were written there is much uncertainty. It has already been mentioned that some of them were revised more than once, and where additions have been made at the end of a historical work references to late events do not prove that the whole book was written at a late date. Suffice it to say here that at least five books were written before *The History of the Church*, for they are mentioned in that work, namely, *Chronological Tables* (p. 32), *Selections from the Prophets* (pp. 40, 53), *Collection of Martyrs* (pp. 192, 206), *Defence of Origen* (pp. 263, 270, 272), and *Life of Pamphilus* (pp. 270, 325). Conversely, *Martyrs of Palestine* is referred to (p. 345) as still to be written.

In contrast to the New Testament, which has come down to us in thousands of manuscripts, many of them very ancient indeed, most Greek and Latin works have survived in a very few copies, written many centuries after the publication of the originals. This is the case with *The History of the Church*, of which we possess only seven primary copies, the rest, if Schwartz is right, being derived from them. These seven, which fall into two groups, are thought to have been written in the tenth, eleventh, and twelfth centuries – far nearer to the invention of printing than to the composition of the book. We have also a Syriac version and a Latin paraphrase by Rufinus. There are numerous differences between these authorities, but the total effect is small, and there is no need to trouble the reader with such variations. Printed editions of the Greek text began with that of Stephanus, based on two very late manuscripts and published in Paris in 1544. Many others followed, mostly in Germany, culminating in that of Schwartz (Leipzig, 1903).

In this country the importance of the work has long been recognized, and a number of translations have been published, the first being that of Hanmer (1584). The translator is faced with many problems; for the Greek of Eusebius is by no means easy. He employs an enormous vocabulary, and some of his words have meanings not met with in classical Greek. These meanings are not always to be found even in the largest lexicons and have to be deduced from the context; and some of the Greek words do not appear in lexicons at all. Other words vary in meaning, and it is not always clear which meaning is intended. Are *martyres* martyrs or witnesses? Are *presbyteroi* presbyters, priests, elders, or old-timers? Is *philosophia* philosophy, science, love of wisdom, profound study, earnest inquiry, or asceticism? And does *logos* mean word, message, book, system, doctrine, or the pre-existent Word? Other words are by their nature ambiguous. Do *theophiles* and *theomises* mean God-loving and God-hating, or God-loved and God-hated? Or do the words denote reciprocity of emotion – mutual attraction and mutual repulsion between God and individual men? These difficulties are due to defects in the Greek language: another difficulty is the fault of Eusebius himself; for he is guilty of quite needless obscurity. He is inordinately fond of long and involved sentences, and he lacks the skill of a Demosthenes to keep them under control. The first sentence of Book 1 is 166 words long, and we have to plough through 153 of them before we reach the one and only main verb. Sometimes there is no main verb at all, or the sentence is an anacoluthon, beginning in one way and ending in another. The reader may well lose his way in the morass!

In this translation I have endeavoured above all things to make clear what the writer is trying to say. I have broken up the huge sentences into fragments, as anyone must do who professes to be writing the English of today, and I have omitted numbers of the superfluous 'padding' words with which Eusebius fills out his lines. The multitude of quotations from the Bible presented a problem. Should I follow the example of my predecessors, and copy the wording of the Authorized or Revised Version? This would have saved trouble and have made it easy for the reader to recognize the passages quoted. But there were several objections. The difference between the language of 1611 and that of three hundred and fifty years later is very great; the difference between the Greek of Eusebius and that of the Septuagint and the New Testament is comparatively small. Again, while some of his quotations are set out as such, many are worked into his sentences and adapted to his constructions. Thirdly, the wording of the passages as he quotes them often differs from that of the Hebrew and Greek texts on which our standard versions are based, so that an accurate translation would involve the use of synthetic 'old' English. I therefore resolved that the Scriptural quotations must be put into the same kind of English as the rest; in other words, they must be translated afresh. I have however used the customary 'Thou' in prayers, as this usage is still generally followed, and in verse passages I have used conventional 'poetic' language. When Eusebius copies a long passage from a non-Scriptural work, he often indicates omissions by such formulae as 'a little later he adds'; I have substituted a row of dots.

The division of the work into ten books was made by the author: the headings in capitals are mine. A list of contents appears in the manuscripts at the beginning of each book. Some of these lists are so long that no English reader would read them through, or remember them if read. I have thought it better to insert them at appropriate places in the narrative, and to distinguish them by the use of italics. Some that are inordinately long I have shortened, and where they come in too rapid succession I have grouped two or three together, hoping thus to divide each book into manageable sections.

Finally, I have tried to give intelligible titles to the works quoted by Eusebius: I have replaced the *Apology*, *Stromateis*, *Hypotyposes*, and *Hexaemeron* of earlier versions by *Defence*, *Miscellanies*, *Outlines*, and *The Six Days*. On the other hand, as genuinely foreign words in an original text should never be translated, I have retained (in italics) all the Latin words transliterated by Eusebius, explaining them in footnotes where this appeared necessary. I have added many other footnotes, in the hope of making the book more intelligible to the reader. The student who requires fuller information must turn to the admirable and most scholarly notes of Dr Lawlor in the S.P.C.K. edition of Eusebius.

How and when was *The History of the Church* written? The generally accepted theory is that the first edition consisted of eight books only, that Book 9 was added later, and Book 10 later still. Schwartz pointed out that the summary of the work with which Eusebius begins Book 1 covers the contents of Books 1 to 8. He promises that the culmination of his work shall be 'the martyrdoms of later days down to my own time, and at the end of it all the kind and gracious deliverance accorded by our Saviour'; and in Book 8, after describing the persecutions of his time, he ends with the Imperial Recantation, which he introduces with the words: 'It became evident that we were in the kindly, beneficent keeping of divine and heavenly grace.' At the time he believed that persecution had ended for ever. But it was resumed, and he was compelled to add a ninth book, to be followed later by a tenth, when Constantine had triumphed over his last enemy and Christianity had triumphed too. The Recantation was published in 311, so that Eusebius's summary could not have been written before that year, and Schwartz concluded that the work was not planned till then. It cannot have been finished until 325, since Book 10 records the fall of Licinius towards the end of 324. On the other hand a later date is unlikely, as Crispus, 'an emperor most dear to God and in every way resembling his father', was in 326 executed by that father as a traitor.

Dr Lawlor holds that the work was begun six years earlier, in 305, on the ground that *Pilate's Memoranda*, mentioned in Book 1 as a recent forgery, had appeared in that year. He thus allows twenty years for the composition of the ten books, and suggests that five of them were written before the author was imprisoned in 309, and two more after his release; and that the eighth was written in Egypt when news had reached him of the Recantation. The prefatory summary was then written and placed at the beginning of Book 1. The last two books were added later, as in Schwartz's theory.

I cannot say that I feel sure that the arguments of these scholars are unquestionably correct. As regards the author's summary, the theory that it was added later implies that Eusebius started his work without any plan, and leaves us to guess what can have been the original opening of Book 1. Again, I cannot see that the words quoted from Book 8 in praise of God correspond with the words in Book 1 about 'the kind and gracious deliverance accorded by our Saviour' any more closely than do the ascription of praise to God and to the Saviour with which Book 10 opens and the paean of thankfulness with which it closes. As to *Pilate's Memoranda*, I suggest that 'recent' is a very vague word indeed.[1] I also find it difficult to believe that Books 7 and 8 were written

1. When applied to our Saviour's advent it means 'three centuries ago'. And is it not plain from Book 9 that, as Dr Eisler saw, the *Memoranda* were not published till 311?

as early as has been suggested, for they contain many allusions to events later than 311, forcing Dr Lawlor to give a long list of scattered passages which he regards as later insertions – a convenient but dangerous supposition. In all humility I submit that, as Schwartz thought, the summary was written first and was indeed the plan of the work, but that it was to be a work in ten books – 'a perfect number', as the author himself calls it, and much more likely than eight, to judge by the practice of Eusebius and other writers. Secondly, I submit that in the absence of textual evidence that they are after-thoughts we ought to treat all references to late events as proof of late writing, and ought not to suppose years to have elapsed between the composition of the first eight books and that of the last two, or picture Eusebius as writing a series of scraps punctuated by the production of a score of other works. Lastly, I suggest that we need not assume that a work of this size would take so prolific a writer fourteen or twenty years to produce. Livy may have taken thirty-five years to write his History of Rome; but *The History of the Church* is only as long as four books of that history, and Livy wrote 142! Writing at Livy's speed Eusebius would need only a twelve-month.

A history of the Church might comprise no more than an accurate account of the things that Christians did and suffered during the period covered by the writer. Such an account Eusebius does in fact give us, but the prefatory summary makes it clear that his intention is more complex, and that the book is to be no mere chronicle of events. He is going to give us the succession of bishops, because, as Kirsopp Lake points out, that succession includes the whole intellectual, spiritual, and institutional life of the Church, and is the guarantee of the preservation of one unchanging God-given doctrine. He is going to do justice to the great men of the Church – its rulers, its teachers, and above all its martyrs; and he is going to expose its enemies – persecuting emperors

21

and demon-inspired heretics. He is going to recount the calamities of the Jews, and so demonstrate the way in which God punishes sin. Eusebius's purpose, no less than Milton's, is to justify the ways of God to men – and the final justification is the overthrow of God's enemies and the triumph of the Church. To understand the book we must bear in mind that from first page to last the writer's theme is the working of Providence, to be demonstrated not by moral tales but by historical facts.

Owing to the annalistic arrangement of the book – and the author's earlier *Chronological Tables* show that such an arrangement was natural to him – his special interests are treated not in separate chapters but sporadically throughout the book. To assist the reader to study them separately if he so desires, I have collected Eusebius's references to them in a series of Appendices; but a few comments on them at this point will not be out of place. No one can fail to observe the importance which he attaches to episcopacy and the Apostolic Succession, to martyrs and confessors, to heresies and schisms, to historical sources, and to the canon of Holy Scripture. He refers to at least fifty-eight episcopal sees, naming forty-seven of them, along with 175 bishops. Dioceses differed in importance, and he quotes Dionysius as appending to a list of the churches in the East – Antioch, Caesarea, Aelia, Tyre, Laodicea, Tarsus, Cappadocia – the comment 'I have named the more distinguished bishops only', while he himself reveals the prominence of Caesarea, Tyre, and (Syrian) Laodicea by naming more of their bishops than of those of any dioceses other than the 'big four' – Rome, Alexandria, Jerusalem, Antioch. Of these four alone he gives complete succession-lists, and among them he indicates the pre-eminence of the first two by frequently coupling them together, by dating the successive bishops, and by quoting the report on Paul of Samosata addressed to the bishops of Rome and Alexandria. The world of Eusebius is limited, and he names no bishoprics west of

Carthage and Arles; and though he implies the existence of
churches in Numidia and Mauretania he never once mentions
Spain.

Of martyrs he informs us that the number was immense;
he describes the ordeals of no fewer than 146, naming ninety-
seven of them. Of these he clearly held Polycarp, 'that
wonderful and apostolic man', in the highest regard, as the
supreme martyr of the post-apostolic age, while outstanding
among those of Palestine was 'Pamphilus, the holy martyr of
my own day . . . the most wonderful man of my time'.

Heresies caused him a great deal of indignation and distress.
He traced them back to Simon the Magus – in other words
to the first ten years of the Church's existence. It is indeed
true that heresy was present from the start: it distressed the
apostles themselves, as is evident from the Prologue of the
Fourth Gospel and from the much earlier Epistle to the
Colossians, where we find the Gnostics and Docetics put
firmly in their place. These and eight other groups are
assailed in the pages of Eusebius, who names forty-seven
individual heretics who operated in a period of less than two
centuries. They divided the Church and corrupted both faith
and morals. Some were sexually perverted, and either in-
dulged in vice themselves or impudently tried to forbid holy
matrimony to others. At times the civil authority had to be
called on to deal with them, as in the case of Paul of Samosata.
Those to whom 'orthodoxy' suggests unthinking conformity,
and 'heterodoxy' freedom of conscience and perhaps intellectual superiority, may be inclined to accept the dictum of
Ivan Yates that a heresy is merely the distortion of a neglected
truth. But in the heresies that afflicted the early Church and
endangered its survival it would be hard to find that truth.
Many of them indeed did not originate within the Church or
represent legitimate differences of opinion among Christians;
they were imported from without, some from Judaism, some
(notably Gnosticism, Montanism, and Manicheism) from

heathendom. And since every heresy, even if it can be supported by some isolated passage of Scripture, can be refuted by Scripture as a whole, the different heresiarchs were obliged either to 'correct' the sacred text or to reject whatever books of the Bible conflicted with their doctrines: in the case of Cerinthus, who upheld several heresies at once, this meant the greater part of the New Testament.

It has already been mentioned that *The History of the Church* is extremely well documented, that the author draws his information from a great number of sources. Chief of these is, of course, the Holy Bible – the Old Testament in the form in which it was known to our Lord and to all the New Testament writers, namely the Greek version of the Seventy, and the New Testament very much in the form in which we ourselves know it. From the Bible he quotes constantly. Twenty-six – just half – of the Old Testament and Apocryphal books and all twenty-seven of the New Testament books are laid under contribution, between them contributing nearly six hundred quoted passages. With Eusebius, as with Christ and St Paul, the favourite Old Testament book is Psalms, followed by Isaiah. Of New Testament books he finds Acts the most useful. Of the Gospels he quotes Matthew the most often and Mark very rarely, in spite of his belief in its Petrine origin. His quotations, when set out formally to substantiate his argument, are so accurately worded as to prove that he verified his references; when worked more or less casually into his own sentences the freedom of their wording seems to indicate reliance on memory. In the case of non-Biblical authorities he rarely if ever relied on his memory. Of these he quotes or summarizes over a hundred books, letters, or decrees by forty-nine different authors. Seventeen other authors are mentioned without being quoted, together with some fifty of their works. Seven authors he found particularly valuable – Josephus, Irenaeus, Clement and Dionysius of Alexandria, Justin Martyr, Origen, and Hegesippus, in that order. Between them they contributed many pages to his work. But he did not confine himself to Jewish and Christian writers: he made use of Homer, of Herodotus and Thucydides, of Plato and Aristotle, of Demosthenes, and of Hippocrates.

In his quotations from earlier writers Eusebius twice reproduces lists of the Old Testament books. But he shows much more interest in those of the New, discussing which books should be included in the Canon as 'recognized' and which should be regarded as 'disputed' or as 'rejected'. He is deeply interested in their authenticity and authorship and in the circumstances of their production. He gives special attention to the second Gospel and to the Revelation of John, and seems to have given us every scrap of information that he could derive from earlier writers. All serious students of the New Testament should look up and study the passages listed in the last Appendix.

What were our author's qualifications for his task? To fashion such a work as he planned he needed to be an effective writer, a trained thinker, a sound theologian, and a scientific historian. Was Eusebius any of these things? Greek is a language capable of great precision and, when handled by an artist in words, of wonderful beauty. But Eusebius was not an artist in words, and his style and diction have been universally condemned. 'His greatness,' says one recent writer, 'rests upon his vast erudition and his sound judgement. The value of his work does not lie in its literary merit, but in the wealth of the materials which it furnishes for the knowledge of the early Church.' Or, as another writer puts it: 'It is not a literary work which can be read with any pleasure for the sake of its style.' Or as Photius the Lexicographer wrote eleven centuries ago, 'His diction is never pleasant or clear.' Greek was no longer the language it had been in the time of Demosthenes, with whose works Eusebius was familiar, but he need not have handled it as clumsily as he did. His immense and ill-constructed sentences were mentioned some pages back, and a further difficulty is the frequent ambiguity which puzzles translators. He loves to jumble his sentences, placing his words in the most unusual order and separating as widely as possible those that must be taken together. Like those decadent speakers of today to whom things are 'awfully sweet' or 'frightfully nice' or 'simply gorgeous', he cannot be content with simple adjectives but substitutes the strongest epithets he can lay his hand on, and constantly indulges in superlatives. He uses strings of unnecessary words: 'Josephus writes somewhat thus word for word.' Pleonasm and tautology abound: 'They were of necessity compelled'; 'topsy-turvy head downwards'; 'raised aloft towering up to a height'; 'most solid in the highest degree'. A cleric is not made Bishop of Rome but 'appointed to the presidency of the church of the Romans'. In my translation I have seen no reason to inflict such language upon my readers.

As a thinker Eusebius has no claim to be considered original, but philosophy was not beyond his grasp: he appreciated the greatness of Plato, and valued highly the contribution made to Christian thought by such philosophers as Justin Martyr. Like Origen, he knew that philosophy could lead men to Christ, and that those who employed philosophy as a weapon against the Church must be fought on their own ground. In his own mind philosophy could not be detached from theology and revelation. Hence his realization that the true principle underlying punishment was not deterrence but retribution was tied up with the conviction that the prosperity and misery of men were the direct results of God's pleasure or anger with his creatures. Like Josephus he was obsessed with the ideas of vengeance and divine justice, and was certain that the destruction of Jerusalem was God's visitation upon the wicked. Sometimes these ideas take the form of a delight in 'poetic justice', as when he relates the appropriate fates that destroyed the enemies of Narcissus; sometimes of sheer vindictiveness, as in his exultation over the miserable ends of Herod and Agrippa, Galerius and Maxentius. But it was a lofty vindictiveness: like Elijah he was 'very jealous for the Lord, the God of hosts'. Nowadays we regard our troubles as due to the working of natural laws, or to mere chance, or perhaps as the automatic consequences of human folly, not as the direct and deliberate punitive action of an indignant Deity. But let us not forget how modern such a view is. The belief of Eusebius was the belief that pervades the Old Testament, and in the New is clearly expressed by Pharisees and disciples alike. It was the belief enshrined in our Prayer-book thanksgivings for fair weather and for deliverance from the plague. It was the belief that caused Restoration preachers to attribute the Fire of London to the sin of gluttony (did it not start in Pudding Lane?), and within living memory led newspapers to suggest that Messina was destroyed by earth-quake because of its extreme wickedness. Few Christians have realized how revolutionary were our Lord's words about the needle's eye and the Tower of Siloam.

Again, we must not be too ready to condemn Eusebius for his attribution of evil to the devil. The present generation has abolished the devil, and finds evil, if it finds it at all, in the mind and nature of man. But the devil was as real to Eusebius and to the authors whom he quotes as he was to Luther, and has been to many a good man besides. And after all, the Son of God declared that it was Satan who had tempted Him, Satan who took away the seed from the souls of men, Satan who asked to have Simon and his fellow-disciples, Satan who had bent the woman's back.

As a historian Eusebius has been the target of many barbed shafts, but not all of them have stuck. Gibbon's notorious sneer – 'He indirectly confesses that he has related whatever might redound to the glory, and has suppressed all that could tend to the disgrace, of religion' – was effectively disposed of by Lightfoot, who fully vindicated Eusebius's honour as a narrator 'against this unjust charge'. Nor can the accusation that he quoted sources which he knew to be false, or wilfully tampered with their text, be sustained. Nor does the fact that he exhibits bias and sees men as either black or white imply any falsification of the truth. Nor again is it fair to accuse him of credulity because he reproduces 'tall stories'. More observant critics would have noticed his careful insertion of the words 'they say'. Of course, he was not a scientific historian in the modern sense. But with the possible exception of Thucydides how many of the ancients were? Was he as cruelly unfair to the worst of the emperors as was Livy to Hannibal? Did he show more enmity towards the later autocrats of Rome than Suetonius and Tacitus had shown towards the earlier? Did any previous writer in so few pages justify his statements by quoting two hundred and fifty passages from the best available authorities? Again, we must appreciate the fact that Eusebius had a much harder task than the modern historian. When he sat down to write, he had not on his desk half a dozen histories which other men had written about the same period, nor had he a bibliography, an encyclopedia, and an atlas and gazetteer at his elbow; he had nothing but a vast quantity of scrappy materials which he himself had laboriously collected, and which he himself must reduce to order as best he could. Nor could he consult a handy list of dates such as we possess: he had to base his chronology on the lives of emperors and bishops, and this he did with painstaking care.

Having said this we may readily admit that he was too prone to dogmatize about the motives of men's actions; that he gives us too much subjective opinion; and that he makes too sweeping generalizations, often failing to support them by any adequate citing of instances, and is too vehement, too certain that he is right.

One fact is beyond question. *The History of the Church* is a mine of valuable information given to us by no other writer;

and, as Guy Schofield puts it, 'Eusebius – the dependable, the scholarly, the shrewd discarder of the dubious – was by far the most important and reliable historian of the ancient church'. Imperfect as it is, puzzling as it is, irritating as it is, his book is one of the treasures of Christendom; and we may thank God that amidst all the dangers and tribulations of that unhappy time this brave and devoted servant of Christ was both moved to take his ambitious task in hand and spared to bring it to fruition.

G.A.W.

1962

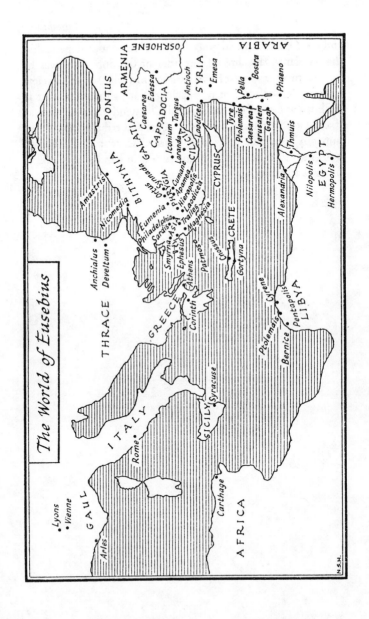

The World of Eusebius

Book 1

Plan of the projected work

1. The chief matters to be dealt with in this work are the following:

a. The lines of succession from the holy apostles, and the periods that have elapsed from our Saviour's time to our own; the many important events recorded in the story of the Church; the outstanding leaders and heroes of that story in the most famous Christian communities; the men of each generation who by preaching or writing were ambassadors of the divine word.

b. The names and dates of those who through a passion for innovation have wandered as far as possible from the truth, proclaiming themselves the founts of Knowledge falsely so called[1] while mercilessly, like savage wolves, making havoc of Christ's flock.[2]

c. The calamities that immediately after their conspiracy against our Saviour overwhelmed the entire Jewish race.

d. The widespread, bitter, and recurrent campaigns launched by unbelievers against the divine message, and the heroism with which when occasion demanded men faced torture and death to maintain the fight in its defence.

1. 1 Tim. vi. 20.   2. Acts xx. 29.

31

e. The martyrdoms of later days down to my own time, and at the end of it all the kind and gracious deliverance accorded by our Saviour.

Could I do better than start from the beginning of the dispensation of our Saviour and Lord, Jesus the Christ of God?

I trust that kindly disposed readers will pardon the deficiencies of the work, for I confess that my powers are inadequate to do full justice to so ambitious an undertaking. I am the first to venture on such a project and to set out on what is indeed a lonely and untrodden path; but I pray that I may have God to guide me and the power of the Lord to assist me. As for men, I have failed to find any clear foot-prints of those who have gone this way before me; only faint traces, by which in differing fashions they have left us partial accounts of their own lifetimes. Raising their voices like warning lights far ahead and calling out as from a distant watchtower perched on some hill, they make clear to me by what path I must walk and guide the course of my book if I am to reach my goal in safety. Thus from the scattered hints dropped by my predecessors I have picked out whatever seems relevant to the task I have undertaken, plucking like flowers in literary pastures the helpful contributions of earlier writers, to be embodied in the continuous narrative I have in mind. If I can save from oblivion the successors, not perhaps of all our Saviour's apostles but at least of the most distinguished, in the most famous and still pre-eminent dioceses, I shall be content. It is, I think, most necessary that I should devote myself to this project, for as far as I am aware no previous Church historian has been interested in records of this kind; records which those who are eager to learn the lessons of history will, I am confident, find most valuable. It is true that in the *Chronological Tables* that I compiled some years ago I provided a summary of this material; but in this new work

I am anxious to deal with it in the fullest detail. As I said before, my book will start with a conception too sublime and overwhelming for man to grasp – the dispensation and divinity of our Saviour Christ. Any man who intends to commit to writing the record of the Church's history is bound to go right back to Christ Himself, whose name we are privileged to share, and to start with the beginning of a dispensation more divine than the world realizes.

The pre-existence and divinity of our Saviour

2. The nature of Christ is twofold; it is like the head of the body in that He is recognized as God, and comparable to the feet in that for our salvation He put on manhood as frail as our own.[1] My account of what follows will therefore be complete if I begin my exposition of His entire story with the basic and essential points of the doctrine. By this means, both the antiquity and the divine character of Christian origins will be demonstrated to those who imagine them to be recent and outlandish, appearing yesterday for the first time.

To explain the origin and worth, the very essence and nature of Christ, no language could be adequate. The Holy Spirit Himself says in prophecy: 'His generation who shall declare?'[2] For no one has known the Father, except the Son; nor again has anyone ever known the Son fully, except only the Father who begot Him.[3] As for the Light that existed before the world, the intellectual and essential Wisdom that was before time itself, the living Word that in the beginning was with the Father and was God – who but the Father could clearly conceive of Him?[4] Before anything was created and fashioned, visible or invisible,[5] He was the first and only begotten of God; the commander-in-chief of the spiritual and immortal host of heaven;[6] the angel of mighty

1. Acts xiv. 15 and Jas v. 17.   2. Is. liii. 8.   3. Matt. xi. 27.
4. John i. 1, 2, 9 and Prov. viii. 23.   5. Col. i. 15–16.   6. Josh. v. 14.

counsel;[1] the agent of the ineffable purpose of the Father; the fashioner, with the Father, of all things; the second cause, after the Father, of the universe; the Child of God, true and only-begotten; of all begotten the Lord and God and King, who has received from the Father lordship and dominion, godhead, power, and honour.[2] To His divinity the Scriptures bear mystic witness:

> In the beginning was the Word,
> And the Word was with God,
> And the Word was God.
> All things came into being through Him,
> And apart from Him came into being not one thing.[3]

This again is the teaching of the great Moses, the earliest prophet of all, when by the Holy Spirit he described the coming into being and marshalling of the whole: the Marshal and Fashioner of the universe gave up to Christ Himself – and to no one, it is plain, but the divine Word, His first-begotten, the making of subordinate beings, and discussed with Him the creation of man:

> For God said, 'Let us make man in our image and likeness.'[4]

This saying is confirmed by another of the prophets, who in hymns deifies him thus:

> He spoke, and they were begotten:
> He commanded, and they were created.[5]

---

1. Is. ix. 4.   2. Rev. v. 12–13.   3. John i. 1, 3.

4. Gen. i. 26. The author, whom Eusebius assumes to have been Moses, probably used the plural because the Hebrew word for God (Elohim) is plural. But Christians have always seen in this passage an indication of plurality in the unity of the Godhead.

5. A conflation of Ps. xxxiii. 9, and cxlviii. 5. Eusebius accepts the traditional Christian identification of 'the word of the Lord' in Ps. xxxiii. 6 with the Word of John's theology, and takes the 'He' of verse 9 as referring to 'the word', not to 'the Lord'.

The Father and Maker he introduces as giving commands like
a supreme ruler by an imperial fiat; the divine Word, who
holds the second place to Him – none other than the One
whom we proclaim – as subserving His Father's behests.

Ever since man was first created, all who are said to have
been distinguished for righteousness and the purity of their
religion – the great servant Moses and his companions; before
him Abraham, the very first, and his children; and all the
righteous men and prophets who have since appeared –
recognized Him in visions seen with the pure eyes of the
mind, and paid due honour to Him as God's Son. He for
His part, showing no slackness in His veneration of the
Father, made Himself for all mankind the teacher of knowledge of the Father. Thus the Lord God is stated to have
appeared as an ordinary human being to Abraham as he sat
by the oak of Mamre. Abraham fell down at once, and
though he saw a human being with his eyes he worshipped
Him as God, besought Him as Lord, and owned that he knew
who He was; for these were his very words:

O Lord, the Judge of all the world, wilt Thou not do justice?[1]

Reason would never allow that the uncreated and immutable
substance of Almighty God should be changed into the form
of a man, or, alternatively, that by the illusion of any created
thing it should deceive the eyes of the beholder, or that
Scripture should falsely invent such a tale. Who then could
be spoken of as God, and the Lord who is the judge of all
the world and does justice, appearing in human shape? As it
is not permissible to suggest the First Cause of the universe,
there is only one answer – His pre-existent Word. Of Him
it is written in the Psalms:

He sent His Word and healed them,
And rescued them from their corruptions.[2]

1. Gen. xviii. 1–2, 25.   2. Ps. cvii. 20.

Of Him Moses is unmistakably speaking, as second Lord after the Father, when he says:

The Lord rained on Sodom and Gomorrah brimstone and fire from the Lord.[1]

To Him, when He later appeared to Jacob in a man's shape, Holy Scripture again refers as God – when He said to Jacob:

No longer shall your name be called Jacob,
But Israel shall be your name;
For you have prevailed with God.

Then too:

Jacob called the name of that place The Form of God, saying: 'For I saw God face to face, and my life was spared.'[2]

It is clearly not permissible to regard the recorded theophanies as visitations by subordinate angels and ministers of God; for whenever one of these appears to human beings Scripture makes no secret of the fact, but explicitly declares that they are called not God or Lord, but angels, as can easily be proved by any number of instances.

The name which Moses' successor Joshua gave to Him, as Leader of the heavenly angels and archangels and of the celestial powers, and as the Power and Wisdom of the Father, entrusted with the second place in the kingship and rule over all things, was Commander-in-chief of the army of the Lord; yet Joshua like the others saw Him only in human form and shape. Here is the passage:

When Joshua was in Jericho, he raised his eyes and saw a man standing facing him, his sword drawn in his hand. Joshua went up to him and said, 'Are you for us or for our opponents?' He replied, 'It is as Commander-in-chief of the army of the Lord that I have now come.' Then Joshua fell face downwards on the ground and asked Him, 'Master, what do you command your servant?' The Commander-in-chief of the Lord replied, 'Take your sandals off your feet: the place where you are standing is a holy place.'[3]

1. Gen. xix. 24.   2. Gen. xxxii. 28, 30.   3. Josh. v. 13–15.

36

Here, too, you will gather from the actual words that this was the very Person who had instructed Moses; for in his case too the words of Scripture are the same:

When the Lord saw that he was coming near to see, He called out to him from the bush, 'Moses, Moses!' He replied, 'What is it?' The Lord answered, 'Do not come this way: take your sandals off your feet; for the place where you are standing is holy ground.' Then He continued: 'I am the God of your father, the God of Abraham, the God of Isaac, and the God of Jacob.'[1]

That this is in truth a Being, living and subsisting before the world, who assisted the Father and God of the universe in the fashioning of all created things, named the Word of God and Wisdom, the evidence goes beyond the proofs given above: one may hear it from the person of Wisdom herself, who by the mouth of Solomon initiates us most fully into her secret:

I, Wisdom, have made counsel my dwelling,
I have invoked knowledge and thought.
By me kings reign,
And princes decree justice;
By me the great achieve greatness,
And monarchs by me are masters of the earth.

To this she adds:

The Lord created me the beginning of His ways for His works;
Before time began He established me;
In the beginning, before He made the earth,
Before the springs of water issued forth,
Before the mountains were fixed in place,
And before all hills he begot me.
When He prepared the heaven, I was at His side;
And when He made safe the springs under heaven,
I was with Him, setting them in order.
I was she in whom He delighted every day,
And I rejoiced before Him at every time,
When He rejoiced that He had finished the world.[2]

1. Ex. iii. 4–6.   2. Prov. viii. 12–31 (with omissions).

Such in outline are the proofs that the divine Word pre-existed and showed Himself to some, if not to all.[1]

Why He was not preached long ago, as He is now, to all men and to every nation, what follows will make clear. It was impossible for the teaching of Christ in all its wisdom and virtue to be grasped by the human race in its former state. At the very beginning, after the original life of blessed-ness, the first man disregarded the divine command and fell into this mortal, transitory state, receiving this earth with its curse in place of the former heavenly delights.

His descendants, who peopled all our world, showed them-selves much worse, apart from one or two, plunging into a beastly existence and a life not worth living. City and state, arts and sciences meant nothing to them; laws and statutes, morality and philosophy were not even names; they lived a nomadic life in the desert like wild and savage creatures; nature's gift of reason and the germs of thought and culture in the human soul were destroyed by the immensity of their deliberate wickedness. Unholy practices of every kind had taken complete possession of them, so that at one time they corrupted, at another they murdered each other, at yet another they became cannibals; they dared to join battle with God and to fight those battles of the giants that are everywhere famous; they planned to fortify earth against heaven, and in the madness of a deranged mind prepared for war against the Ruler of all things Himself.

While they followed this reckless course God, from whom nothing is hidden, visited them with cataclysms and con-flagrations as if they had been a wild forest stretching across

1. It seems surprising that Eusebius in attempting to prove an essential Christian doctrine should make so much use – and such strange use – of the O.T., quoting only one passage from the New, and that not from our Lord's own words. It is surprising also that he describes the relationship between Father and Son in such strange terms; but the theologically-minded will see why in the Arian controversy he found it difficult to come down on the side of orthodoxy.

the whole world. With continual famines and pestilences, and again with wars and with thunderbolts from the sky, He cut them off, making His punishments more and more drastic as if to check some terrible and well-nigh fatal sickness of the soul. So at that crisis, when nearly all mankind had been submerged by a vast surfeit of wickedness, which like complete intoxication overshadowed and darkened almost every human soul, the first-begotten and first-created[1] Wisdom of God, the pre-existent Word Himself in His measureless love for mankind showed Himself, now by a vision of angels to His subjects, now in person as God's saving power to one or two of God's beloved servants of old; but always, always in human form, since in no other way could He appear to them. When these in turn had sown the seeds of true religion in numbers of men, a whole nation, sprung from the ancient Hebrews and devoted to true religion, arose in the world. On these – a mass of men still tied and bound by ancient habits – He bestowed, through the prophet Moses, images and symbols of a mystical sabbath and of circumcision, and instruction in other spiritual principles; but without actual, open initiation. Their Law became famous and like a fragrant breeze penetrated to every corner of the world. From the Jews the movement spread, and soon the characters of most heathen races began to grow gentler, thanks to the lawgivers and thinkers in every land. Savage and cruel brutality changed to mildness, so that profound peace, friendship, and easy intercourse were enjoyed.

Then at last, when all mankind and every race throughout the world had already received help and by now were fitted to receive knowledge of the Father, once again that same Teacher of virtue, the Father's Minister in all that is good, the divine and heavenly Word of God, in a human body which in all essentials shared our own nature, appeared in the early years of the Roman Empire. What He did and what He

1. So Milton: 'first of created things'.

suffered accorded with the prophecies, which foretold that a
man who was also God would live in the world as a worker of
miracles and would be revealed to all nations as a teacher of
the worship due to the Father. They foretold also the miracle
of His birth, the new teaching, and the marvels of His works,
and furthermore the manner of His death, His resurrection
from the dead, and last of all His restoration to heaven by the
power of God. His final kingdom was shown by the Holy
Spirit to Daniel the prophet, who thus inspired described the
vision of God in human terms:

I watched until thrones were placed and an Ancient of Days was
seated. His clothing was white like snow, and the hair of his head like
pure wool. His throne was a flame of fire, its wheels flaming fire;
a river of fire flowed before Him. A thousand thousand ministered to
Him, and ten thousand times ten thousand stood before Him. The
court of judgement sat, and the books were opened. . . . I watched,
and lo, with the clouds of heaven came One like a Son of Man, who
came quickly to the Ancient of Days and was brought face to face
with Him. To Him was given the dominion, the glory, and the
kingdom; and all the peoples, tribes, and languages shall serve Him.
His authority is an everlasting authority, which shall not pass away,
and His kingdom shall not be destroyed.[1]

Such words clearly, would never be applied to anyone but
our Saviour, the Word who was in the beginning with God
and was God, called Son of Man because ultimately He
became a man.[2] However, I have collected in special pamphlets
the *Selections from the Prophets* that concern our Saviour Jesus
Christ, and in other works have provided a fuller explanation
of the statements about Him; so in the present work I shall
add nothing to what has been said.

1. Dan. vii. 9–10, 13–14.
2. There can be no doubt that our Lord habitually claimed this title in order
to identify Himself with the almighty Potentate of Daniel's vision and the
Final Judge of Enoch's, not, as is often thought, hiding the fact that He was the
Messiah, but insisting that He was something far greater.

The names Jesus and Christ known and honoured
from the first

3. Both Jesus and Christ were names honoured even by God's beloved prophets of old, as I must now make clear. The extreme sanctity and glory of the name Christ was first proclaimed by Moses himself, who, in obedience to the oracle that said to him, 'See that you make everything according to the pattern shown you in the mount',[1] communicated patterns and symbols of heavenly things, and mystical images. For in describing God's high priest, the most powerful of men, he called him Christ, and on this high-priestly office, which in his eyes surpassed all pre-eminence among men, he bestows as a mark of honour and glory the name of Christ.[2] It is clear then that he understood the divine import of the word Christ.

Moses again was enabled by the Holy Spirit to foresee quite plainly the title Jesus: it too, he felt to be worthy of special privilege. Never yet heard by human ears till it was made known to Moses, the title Jesus was bestowed by him for the first and only time on the man who – again as a pattern and symbol – he knew would after his own death succeed to the supreme authority.[3] His successor had not hitherto used the designation Jesus, but was known by another name, Hoshea, which his parents had given him;[4] but Moses calls him Jesus, conferring the name on him as a priceless honour, far greater than a kingly crown; for Joshua the son of Nun himself bore the image of our Saviour, who alone, after Moses and the completion of the symbolic worship given to men by him, succeeded to the authority over the true and most pure religion.

1. Ex. xxv. 40 (Heb. viii. 5).
2. In Lev. iv. 5, 16 and vi. 22 the high priest is described as anointed. It must be remembered that while in English this does not suggest the name Christ, in Greek the two words are the same. Similarly in Hebrew Messiah = anointed.
3. Num. xxvii. 15–20: Jesus is the Greco-Latin transliteration of Joshua.
4. Num. xiii. 16.

Moses thus bestows on the two men who in his time surpassed all the people in merit and glory – the high priest
and the man chosen to follow him as leader – the name of our
Saviour Jesus Christ as a signal honour.

With equal clarity the prophets who came later named
Christ in their prophecies, witnessing beforehand alike to the
intrigue destined to be levelled against Him by the Jewish
people, and to the calling of the Gentiles through Him. At one
time Jeremiah says:

> The Spirit of our face, Christ the Lord, was caught in their
> corruptions;
> Of whom we said, 'In His shadow we shall live among the
> Gentiles.'[1]

At another David in his perplexity asks:

> Why did the Gentiles rage,
> And the peoples imagine vain things?
> The kings of the earth ranged themselves,
> And the rulers gathered themselves together,
> Against the Lord and against His Christ.

Later, speaking in the person of Christ Himself, he continues:

> The Lord said to Me, 'You are my Son;
> I have today begotten you.
> Ask me, and I will give you the Gentiles as your inheritance,
> And as your possession the limits of the world.'[2]

Thus, it was not only those honoured with the high priesthood, anointed with prepared oil for the symbol's sake, who
were distinguished among the Hebrews with the name of
Christ, but the kings too; for they, at the bidding of God,
received the chrism from prophets and were thus made
Christs in image, in that they, too, bore in themselves the
patterns of the kingly, sovereign authority of the one true

---

1. Lam. iv. 20.   2. Ps. ii. 1–2, 7–8.

Christ, the divine Word who reigns over all. Again, some of
the prophets themselves by chrism became Christs in pattern,
as the records show, so that they all stand in relation to the
true Christ, the divine and heavenly Word who is the sole
High Priest of the universe, the sole King of all creation,
and of prophets the sole Archprophet of the Father. This is
proved by the fact that none of those who of old received the
symbolical chrism, whether priest, king, or prophet, ever
obtained such power of inspired virtue as our Saviour and
Lord, Jesus the only veritable Christ, has revealed.

None of those men, however outstanding in dignity and
honour among their own people in the course of so many
generations, ever made their being in imagery entitled Christ
the justification for calling their subjects Christians. None of
them was honoured by his subjects with worship, or held in
such affection after his death that anyone was ready to die
for the person honoured. No one in those days caused such a
stir among all the nations throughout the world, since the
power of the symbol could not produce in them any effect
comparable to that of the truth presented and revealed by our
Saviour. He did not receive the symbols and patterns of the
high priesthood from anyone; He did not trace his physical
descent from the acknowledged priests; He was not promoted
by the soldiers' weapons to a kingdom; He did not become a
prophet in the same way as those of old; He did not receive
from the Jews any rank or pre-eminence whatever. Yet with
all these, not indeed in symbols but in very truth, He had
been adorned by the Father. He may not have obtained the
same honours as those mentioned above, yet He is more
entitled than any of them to be called Christ. And being
Himself the one true Christ of God He has filled the whole
world with Christians – His own truly venerated and holy
name. No longer does He communicate to His followers
patterns or images but fully revealed virtues and a heavenly
life with the very doctrines of truth; and He has received the

chrism, not that prepared with physical materials, but the divine chrism with the spirit of God, by sharing in the unbegotten divinity of the Father.

This very point, moreover, is driven home by Isaiah, who, as if from Christ's own lips, cries out:

> The spirit of the Lord is upon me;
> For He anointed me to bring good tidings to the poor.
> He has sent me to proclaim deliverance to captives,
> And new sight to the blind.[1]

And not only Isaiah but David too addresses Him in person:

> Thy throne, O God, is for ever and ever:
> A sceptre of uprightness is the sceptre of Thy kingdom.
> Thou hast loved righteousness and hated iniquity;
> Therefore God, Thy God, has anointed Thee
> With the oil of gladness beyond Thy fellows.[2]

In the first line the passage calls Him God; in the second it honours Him with a royal sceptre; then next, after divine and royal power, it goes on in the third place to portray Him as having become Christ, anointed not with oil made of physical substance but with the divine oil of gladness. Furthermore, it signifies the special distinction that makes Him far superior to and quite different from those who in earlier ages had received in imagery a more physical chrism.

Elsewhere, the same writer makes His status clear:

> The Lord said to my Lord, 'Sit at my right hand,
> Till I make Thine enemies the footstool of Thy feet. . . .
> From the womb before the daystar I begat Thee.'
> The Lord swore and will not repent:
> 'Thou art a priest for ever
> Of the order of Melchizedek.'[3]

---

1. Is. lxi. 1 (Luke iv. 18).
2. Ps. xlv. 6–7 (Heb. i. 8–9).
3. Ps. cx. 1, 3–4 (Heb. v–vii *passim*).

This Melchizedek is introduced in the sacred record as priest of God Most High, though not consecrated with any prepared chrism or even belonging by birthright to the Hebrew priesthood. That is why it is according to his order, not that of the others who received symbols and patterns, that our Saviour has been called Christ and Priest with the backing of an oath. And so the record does not state that He received physical chrism from the Jews, or even that He belonged to the same tribe as the acknowledged priests, but that before the daystar, that is, before the construction of the world, He had His being, and holds His priesthood deathless and ageless to all eternity.

That in His case the chrism was non-physical and divine is clearly and amply proved by the fact that of all who have ever lived till this day He alone is known to all men throughout the entire world as Christ; that He is acknowledged and witnessed to by all men under this title, and is spoken of thus by Greeks and non-Greeks alike; and that to this day He is honoured by His devotees throughout the world as King, revered more than a prophet, and glorified as the true and only High Priest of God, and in addition to all this as the Word of God, pre-existent, having His being before all ages and having received from His Father the right to be worshipped; and that He is adored as God. But the greatest marvel of all is that it is not only with voices and the sound of words that we who are dedicated to Him do Him honour, but with all the affection of our soul, so that we care less for life itself than for our testimony to Him.

Nothing novel or strange in the religion preached by Him

4. This must suffice as introduction to my story proper: it was necessary in order to guard against any inclination to think of our Saviour and Lord, Jesus Christ, as novel, because of the date of His sojourn in the flesh. But to prevent anyone

from imagining that His teaching either was new and strange, as being put together by a man of recent date no different from his fellows, let us now deal briefly with this point.

When the advent of our Saviour Jesus Christ recently shed its light on all men, it was admittedly a new people – not small or weak or established in some remote corner of the earth, but the most numerous and God-fearing of all peoples, indestructible and invincible in that for all time it receives God's help – that at the mystically appointed time all at once appeared, a people honoured by all with the name of Christ. This so amazed one of the prophets, when with the eye of the Holy Spirit he foresaw what was to be, that he burst out:

> Who ever heard such things?
> And who ever spoke thus?
> Was the earth in travail but one day?
> And was a people born at once?[1]

The same writer also hinted at its future title:

> Those who serve Me shall be called by a new name,
> Which shall be blessed on the earth.[2]

But although we certainly are a youthful people and this undeniably new name of Christians has only lately become known among all nations, nevertheless our life and mode of conduct, together with our religious principles, have not been recently invented by us, but from almost the beginnings of man were built on the natural concepts of those whom God loved in the distant past, as I shall proceed to show. The Hebrews are not a youthful people, but are respected by all men for their antiquity and are known to all. Now the spoken and written records of this people embrace men of a very early age, scarce and few in number, but at the same time outstanding in religious devotion, righteousness, and all other virtues. Several of these lived before the flood, others after it

1. Is. lxvi. 8.　　2. Is. lxv. 15-16.

– some of Noah's sons and descendants, but especially Abraham, whom the children of the Hebrews boast as their own founder and ancestor. All these, whose righteousness won them commendation, going back from Abraham himself to the first man, might be described as Christians in fact if not in name, without departing far from the truth. For the name means this, that the Christian man, through the knowledge and teaching of Christ, excels in self-discipline and righteousness, in firmness of purpose and manly courage, and in an acknowledged devotion to the one, sole God over all; and for all this they showed no less enthusiasm than do we.[1] They cared nothing for bodily circumcision – nor do we; or for the keeping of Sabbaths – nor do we; nor for abstentions from certain foods or distinctions between others (all that Moses was the first man ever to hand down, for later generations to carry out, in symbols) – nor do these things matter to Christians now. But it is obvious that they knew God's Christ Himself, since He appeared to Abraham, instructed Isaac, spoke to Israel,[2] and conversed freely with Moses and the prophets who came later, as I have already shown. Hence, you will find that those men, God's beloved, were even honoured with the appellation of Christ, according to the word which says of them:

> Touch not my Christs,
> And among my prophets commit no mischief.[3]

Obviously we must regard the religion proclaimed in recent years to all nations through Christ's teaching as none other than the first, most ancient, and most primitive of all religions, discovered by Abraham and his followers, God's beloved.

---

1. We may think it absurd to give the name of Christians to those who lived before Christ, but the same line of thought will be found in Heb. xi and 1 Cor. x; and Christ equated His own moral teaching with that of the time before Moses, at least as regards marriage. See Mark x. 1–12.

2. i.e. Jacob.   3. Ps. cv. 15.

If it is argued that long afterwards Abraham received the ordinance of circumcision, I reply that before this, as we are informed, he had been commended for righteousness through faith, as the sacred record tells us:

Abraham believed God, and it was counted to him for righteousness.[1]

Such he was before his circumcision, and it was then that an oracle was announced to him by God – Christ Himself, the Word of God – who showed Himself to him.[2] This concerned those who in later days were to be justified in the same way as himself. It runs as follows:

In you shall be blessed all the races of the world.[3]

Again:

He shall become a great and mighty nation, and in him shall be blessed all the nations of the world.[4]

That, as we can see, has been fulfilled in us, for it was by faith in Christ the Word of God who appeared to him that he was justified, abandoning the superstition of his fathers and the old error of his ways, acknowledging one God, the God over all, and serving Him with right actions, not with the worship of the Law of Moses, who came later. Such he was when he was told that all the races of the world and all the nations would be blessed in him. And in actions more convincing than words at the present time Christians alone can be seen throughout the world practising religion in the very form in which Abraham practised it.

What then is to prevent us from admitting that we, Christ's followers, share one and the same life and form of religion

1. Gen. xv. 6 and Rom. iv. 3.
2. Eusebius's view that the O.T. theophanies were appearances of Christ (in human form though not yet born a man) seems impossible to us. But have we yet solved the problem of reconciling the stories of encounters between men and the Deity with St John's assertion that no man has ever seen God?
3. Gen. xii. 3.   4. Gen. xviii. 18.

with those who were dear to God so long ago? Thus the practice of religion as communicated to us by Christ's teaching is shown to be not modern and strange but, in all conscience, primitive, unique, and true. There we will leave the matter.

The date of Christ's appearance to men

5. So now, after this necessary introduction to my proposed *History of the Church*, let me begin my journey with the appearance of our Saviour in the flesh, first calling on God, the Father of the Word, and Jesus Christ Himself of whom I am speaking, our Saviour, the heavenly Word of God, to be my helper and co-worker in producing a truthful record.

It was the forty-second year of Augustus's reign, and the twenty-eighth after the subjugation of Egypt and the deaths of Antony and Cleopatra, the last of the Ptolemaic rulers of Egypt,[1] when our Saviour and Lord, Jesus Christ, at the time of the first registration, while Quirinius was governor of Syria,[2] in accordance with the prophecies about Him, was born in Bethlehem, in Judaea.[3] This registration in Quirinius's time is mentioned also by the most famous of Hebrew historians, Flavius Josephus, who gives in addition an account of the Galilean sect which appeared on the scene at the same period, and to which our own Luke refers in the Acts:

After him came the rising of Judas the Galilean at the time of the registration. He persuaded a number of people to revolt under

1. Augustus's reign is reckoned from the death of Julius in 44 B.C. Antony and Cleopatra died in 30 B.C. Counting these dates as the first year in accordance with 'inclusive reckoning', we arrive in each case at 3 B.C. This is too late for the birth of our Lord, which must have preceded by many months the death of Herod early in 4 B.C. and may well have been in 7 B.C. If it is remembered that Eusebius wrote centuries before the invention of the B.C.–A.D. system, when chronological exactitude was extraordinarily difficult, we shall give him credit for a very near approximation.

2. Luke ii. 2.   3. Matt. ii. 1, 5–6.

his leadership; but he too perished, and all his followers were dispersed.[1]

This statement is supported by the historian referred to above, in *Antiquities* Book XVIII:

Quirinius, a member of the senate who had filled the minor offices and passed through them all to become consul, and in other ways was a man of great distinction, arrived with a few officials in Syria. He had been sent by Caesar to be supreme judge of the nation and to assess the value of their property ... Judas, a Gaulonite from a city called Gamala, took Zadok, a Pharisee, with him and instigated a revolt. They alleged that the valuation would lead to nothing but complete slavery, and summoned the nation to the defence of their freedom.[2]

And in the *History of the Jewish War*, Book II, he writes this about the same man:

In his[3] time a Galilean named Judas tried to stir the natives to revolt, saying that they would be cowards if they submitted to paying taxes to the Romans, and after serving God accepted human masters.[4]

Extinction of the native Jewish dynasty: Herod, the first foreign king

6. At this time Herod became the first foreigner to be king of the Jewish nation, fulfilling the words of Moses:

There shall not be wanting a ruler from Judah,
Nor a leader sprung from his loins,
Until he come for whom it is reserved.[5]

1. Acts v. 7: Eusebius has identified this registration (thought to have taken place in A.D. 6–7) with that of Herod's time, which an inscription places in 8 B.C.
2. *Antiquities* XVIII, 1, 4.
3. Coponius, procurator 6–9.
4. *Jewish War* (Penguin Classics), p. 126: Josephus is inconsistent in calling Judas both a Galilean and a Gaulonite; Gamala was east of the Sea of Tiberias.
5. Gen. xlix. 10.

Moses adds that he will be the expectation of the Gentiles. There could be no fulfilment of the prediction as long as they were free to live under rulers of their own race, beginning with Moses himself and continuing to Augustus's reign; in his time the first foreigner, Herod, was entrusted by the Romans with the government of the Jews.[1] Josephus informs us that he was an Idumaean on his father's side and an Arab on his mother's;[2] but according to Africanus[3] – and he was no ordinary historian – the best authorities[4] say that Antipater, Herod's father, was son of a certain Herod of Ascalon, one of the 'temple-slaves' of Apollo. This Antipater was taken prisoner by Idumaean bandits when a small child, and remained in their hands because his father was too poor to put down his ransom. He was brought up in their ways and later befriended by Hyrcanus, the Jewish high priest. His son was the Herod of our Saviour's time.

When a man of such antecedents came to be king of the Jews, at the door already, in accordance with the prophecy, was the expectation of the Gentiles, for with him the succession from Moses of Jewish rulers and governors came to an end. Before their captivity and removal to Babylon they were ruled by kings, Saul and David being the first. Before the kings the government was in the hands of rulers known as judges, who came to the fore after Moses and his successor Joshua. After the return from Babylon they maintained continuously an aristocratic and oligarchic constitution, priests being in complete control. This lasted till Pompey, the Roman commander, arrived and besieged Jerusalem with the utmost vigour. He defiled the holy places, going right into the innermost sanctuary of the temple.[5] The man who

1. In 37 B.C. Herod displaced the last native ruler, Antigonus. Augustus was, of course, not yet reigning, but, as we have seen, Eusebius dates his reign from 44 B.C.
2. In *Antiquities* XIV, 16 we are told that both parents were Idumaean.
3. Julius Africanus, A.D. *c.* 170–243; see p. 269.
4. See p. 55.   5. 63 B.C.

had continued the succession of his ancestors till that time and was both king and high priest, Aristobulus by name, he dispatched as a prisoner to Rome together with his children. To Hyrcanus, Aristobulus's brother, he transferred the high priesthood, and he made the whole Jewish nation from then on tributary to Rome. As soon as Hyrcanus, the last to whom fell the high-priestly succession, was taken prisoner by the Parthians,[1] Herod, as I have said, was the first foreigner to be entrusted by the Roman senate and the Emperor Augustus with the Jewish nation. It was without question in his time that the advent of Christ occurred; and the expected salvation and calling of the Gentiles followed at once, in accordance with the prophecy.

As soon as the rulers and leaders from Judah – those of Jewish stock – came to an end, not surprisingly the high priest-hood, which had passed in regular succession, generation by generation, was plunged into immediate confusion. For this, too, you have a reliable witness in Josephus, who informs us that when entrusted with the kingdom by the Romans Herod no longer appointed high priests of the ancient stock but assigned the office to nonentities, and that a policy similar to Herod's regarding the appointment of priests was adopted by his son Archelaus, and after him by the Romans, when they took over the government of Judaea. The same writer informs us that Herod actually locked up the sacred vestment of the high priest and kept it under his own seal, no longer permitting the high priests to have charge of it. His example was followed by his successor Archelaus, and after him by the Romans.[2]

This evidence I have put forward as proof that in the appearing of our Saviour Jesus Christ another prophecy was fulfilled. It is perfectly clear that in Daniel Scripture specifies the exact number of weeks till the rule of Christ – I have

1. See *Jewish War*, pp. 41, 55.
2. *Antiquities*, various passages.

dealt with the subject elsewhere[1] – and prophesies that after the completion of these weeks the anointing of Jews will be brought to an end.[2] There can be no doubt that at the time of the birth of our Saviour Jesus Christ this prophecy was fulfilled. In order to establish the truth of the date it was necessary to make these preliminary points.

The alleged discrepancy in the gospels as to Christ's genealogy

7. The genealogy of Christ has been differently recorded for us in the gospels of Matthew and Luke. Most people see a discrepancy in this, and through ignorance of the truth each believer has been only too eager to dilate at length on these passages. So I feel justified in reproducing an explanation of the difficulty that has come into my hands. This is to be found in a letter which Africanus, to whom I referred a little while back, wrote to Aristides on the harmony of the gospel genealogies. Having first refuted other people's theories as forced and demonstrably false, he sets out the explanation he had himself received. I will quote his actual words:

The names of the families in Israel were reckoned either by nature or by law; by nature, when there was genuine offspring to succeed; by law, when another man fathered a child in the name of a brother who had died childless. For as no clear hope of being raised from the dead had yet been given, they portrayed the promise of the future with a mortal 'raising up', in order that the name of the deceased might be preserved for all time.[3] These genealogies therefore comprise some who succeeded their actual fathers, and some who were the children of one father but were registered as children of another. Thus the memory of both was preserved – of the real and nominal fathers. Thus neither of the gospels is in error, since they take account of both nature and law. For the two families, descended from Solomon and Nathan respectively, were so interlocked by the

1. *Selections from the Prophets.*   2. Daniel ix. 25–6.
   3. See Matt. xxii. 24, where the word for 'raising up' seed is, as here, the same as is used for 'resurrecting'. The passage is quite ruined in the *New English Bible.*

re-marriage of childless widows[1] and the 'raising up' of offspring, that the same persons could rightly be regarded at different times as the children of different parents – sometimes the reputed fathers, sometimes the real. Thus both accounts are perfectly true, bringing the line down to Joseph in a manner complex perhaps but certainly accurate.

What I am trying to say will become clear if I explain the interrelation of the families. If we reckon the generations from David through Solomon, we find that the third from the end is Matthan, who begot Jacob, Joseph's father;[2] if we follow Luke and reckon from David's son Nathan, the corresponding third from the end is Melchi, Joseph being the son of Heli, Melchi's son.[3] Joseph then being the subject of our study, I have to explain how each appears in the records as his father, Jacob tracing his descent from Solomon and Heli from Nathan. Before that I must explain how these two, Jacob and Heli, were brothers, and before that how their fathers, Matthan and Melchi, members of different families, are stated to have been Joseph's grandfathers. Well now, Matthan and Melchi, successive husbands of the same wife, fathered half-brothers, for the law allows a woman who has been either divorced or widowed to marry again. The wife in question, whose name is given as Estha, first married Matthan the descendant of Solomon, and bore him Jacob; then on the death of Matthan the widow married Melchi, whose line went back to Nathan, and who belonged to the same tribe, though not to the same family, and by him had a son Heli. Thus though the families were different, we shall find that Jacob and Heli had the same mother. When Heli died childless, his brother Jacob took his wife and by her became father of Joseph in the third generation. According to nature Joseph was his son – and according to reason, so that Scripture says, 'Jacob begot Joseph'; but according to law he was Heli's son; for Jacob as a good brother 'raised up' offspring to him. It follows that the genealogy in which he finds a place cannot be invalidated, though Matthew the evangelist in his account says, 'Jacob begot Joseph', whereas Luke says, 'Who was, as people imagined' – note this comment – 'the son of Joseph, the son of Heli, the son of Melchi'.[4] It was impossible to express legal descent more

1. The Greek is corrupt: this seems to be what Africanus means.
2. Matt. i. 15–16.   3. Luke iii. 23–4, 31.
4. It is impossible to say why Africanus omits two generations.

explicitly, and never once from beginning to end did he use the word 'begot' with reference to this type of fatherhood, as he traced the line, in the reverse direction, to 'Adam, the son of God'.[1]

This is not dogmatic assertion or mere guesswork: the Saviour's human relations, either in an ostentatious spirit or simply to give information, but in either case telling the truth, have handed down this tradition too. When Idumean bandits swooped on Ascalon, a city in Palestine, along with the other spoil from the temple of Apollo, which was built close to the walls, they carried away captive Antipater, the child of a certain Herod, a temple slave. As the priest was unable to put down the money for his son's ransom, Antipater was brought up in Idumean ways and later befriended by Hyrcanus, the Judean high priest. Sent to Pompey as ambassador for Hyrcanus, he secured from him the freedom of his kingdom – freedom which his brother Aristobulus had filched away. This brought high office to Antipater himself, who was given the title of superintendent of Palestine. When envy of his high office caused him to be treacherously assassinated, he was succeeded by his son Herod, who later was chosen by Antony and Augustus and by decree of the senate to be king of the Jews. His sons were Herod[2] and the other tetrarchs. This information is confirmed by the Greek historians.

But in the archives were still inscribed the Hebrew families and those descended from proselytes, e.g. Achion the Ammonite[3] and Ruth the Moabitess, and the persons of mixed blood who had fled with them from Egypt.[4] So Herod, who had no drop of Israelitish blood in his veins and was stung by the consciousness of his base origin, burnt the registers of their families, thinking that he would appear nobly born if no one else was able by reference to public documents to trace his line back to the patriarchs or proselytes, or to the 'sojourners' of mixed blood.[5] A few careful people had private records of their own, having either remembered the names or recovered them from copies, and took pride in preserving the memory of their aristocratic origin. These included the people mentioned above, known as Desposyni[6] because of their relationship to the Saviour's family. From the Jewish villages of Nazareth and Cochaba they passed through the rest of the country, expounding the

1. Luke iii. 38.   2. Antipas.   3. Judith v. 5 and xiv. 10.
4. Ex. xii. 38.   5. Ex. xii. 19.   6. 'The Master's People.'

genealogy discussed above, quoting from the books of Chronicles as
far as they could trace it. This may or may not be the truth of the
matter; but in my opinion and that of every fair-minded person no
one else could give a clearer exposition, and we must content ourselves with it even if unconfirmed, as we are not in a position to
suggest a better or truer one. In any case the gospel record is true.

Africanus concludes his letter as follows:

Matthan, Solomon's descendant, begot Jacob. On Matthan's
death Melchi, Nathan's descendant, begot Heli by the same woman.
Thus Heli and Jacob had the same mother. When Heli died childless,
Jacob 'raised up' offspring to him, begetting Joseph – by nature his
own son, by law Heli's. Thus Joseph was the son of both.

In tracing thus the genealogy of Joseph, Africanus has
virtually proved that Mary belonged to the same tribe as her
husband, in view of the fact that under the Mosaic law inter-
marriage between different tribes was forbidden, for the rule
is that a woman must wed someone from the same town and
the same clan, so that the family inheritance may not be
moved from tribe to tribe.[1] Let us leave it at that.

1. This paragraph is illogical and inaccurate. The genealogy does nothing to
prove that Mary belonged to the same tribe as Joseph; nor does the Mosaic
regulation (Num. xxxvi. 8–9) make any mention of towns or clans, or apply to
any women except heiresses. If Mary was an heiress, it might be presumed that
she belonged to the same tribe (Judah) as Joseph; but could we reconcile her
membership of Joseph's tribe with the statements of St Luke that Elisabeth was
descended from Aaron (and therefore belonged to the tribe of Levi), and that
Mary was her kinswoman?

On the other hand the argument of Africanus must be treated with respect.
Joseph's pedigree may not matter to us, but Christians have always been
troubled, as he was, by the apparent discrepancy between the two gospel
accounts, which seemed to cast doubts on the reliability of one writer or both.
Nor is Africanus's solution to be ruled out. He clearly derived his information
from relatives of the Holy Family, and it must be remembered that in the
Near East family trees were, and still are, most carefully preserved; and that
the 'raising up' of offspring to a childless brother must often have occurred.

Those who find the problem interesting will find it admirably discussed in
F. W. Farrar's St Luke, *Cambridge Bible*. The one certainty is that the discrepancy cannot be explained away by the absurd suggestion that one genealogy
is that of our Lord's mother.

Herod's plot against the children, and his terrible end

8. When Christ was born, in accordance with prophecy, at Bethlehem in Judaea at the time already stated, Herod was asked by the magi from the East where they could find the one who was born king of the Jews, for they had seen his star and for that reason had made this long journey in their eagerness to worship as God the child that had been born. Herod was badly shaken by the inquiry, thinking that his throne was in danger. So he consulted the teachers of the Law among the people and asked them where they expected the Christ to be born. When he heard Micah's prophecy foretelling the birth at Bethlehem he issued a single decree ordering the destruction in Bethlehem and all its neighbourhood, of the male infants, of two years and under, in accordance with the time he had found out from the magi, naturally supposing that Jesus would certainly suffer the same fate as those of his own age. However, the plot was forestalled by the removal of the Child to Egypt, as by the appearance of an angel His parents had learnt in time what was to come. The story may be studied in the sacred gospel record.[1]

In this connexion it is worth while to recall the price paid by Herod for his crime against Christ and the other babies. Instantly, without the shortest delay, divine justice overtook him while still alive, giving him a foretaste of what awaited him in the next world. This is not the place to list the ways in which he dimmed the supposed glories of his reign by the successive calamities that befell his house, the revolting murder of wife, children, and all who were bound to him by the closest ties of blood and affection. No tragic drama is as dark as their story, of which Josephus has given a full account in his *Histories*.[2] How, from the moment of the plot against

1. Matt. ii. 1–16.
2. For the murder of Mariamme, Alexander, and Aristobulus see *Jewish War*, pp. 80–95.

our Saviour and the other helpless infants, a scourge wielded
by the hand of God struck Herod and drove him to death,
we should do well to hear from the lips of that historian. In
Jewish Antiquities Book xvii he describes his terrible end in
these words:

Herod's sickness grew steadily worse as God exacted punishment
for his iniquities. He was consumed by a slow fire which gave no
clear indication to the touch of the burning heat that added so much
to his internal miseries. He had an overpowering desire for food,
which it was impossible to satisfy, ulceration of the intestines with
agonizing pains in the lower bowel, and a clammy transparent
humour covering the feet. The abdomen was in the same miserable
state, and in the genitals mortification set in, breeding worms.
Breathing was constricted and only possible when sitting upright,
and it was most offensive because of the heavy stench and feverish
respiration. He suffered in every part convulsions that were un-
bearably severe. Those who practised divination and had the gift
of foretelling such things declared that God was exacting a penalty
from the king for his continual wickedness.[1]

Such is the story as told by Josephus in the *Antiquities*. In
Book ii[2] of the *Histories* he gives a very similar account of
Herod's last days:

From then on the sickness spread through his entire body, accompanied by a variety of painful symptoms. He had a mild fever, an
unbearable itching all over his body, constant pains in the lower
bowel, swellings on the feet as in dropsy, inflammation of the
abdomen, and mortification of the genitals, producing worms; as
well as difficulty in breathing, especially when lying down, and
spasms in all his limbs. The diviners said that his diseases were a
punishment. But though he was wrestling with so many disorders
he hung on to life, hoped for recovery, and planned his own treatment. He crossed the Jordan and tried the hot baths at Callirrhoe,
which empty their water into the Dead Sea – water sweet enough to
drink. The doctors there decided to warm up his whole body with
hot oil by lowering him into a bathful of it, but he fainted and

1. *Antiquities* xvii, vi, 5.   2. Book i in our texts.

turned up his eyes as if in a faint.[1] The noise of his attendants beating their breasts[2] brought him back to consciousness; but having no further hope of recovery he ordered the distribution of £15[3] a head to the soldiers, and large gratuities to the officers and to his gentle-men.

By the time he arrived at Jericho on the return journey he was melancholy-mad, and in a virtual challenge to death itself he pro-ceeded to devise a monstrous outrage. He brought together the most eminent men of every village in the whole of Judaea and had them locked up in the Hippodrome. Then he sent for his sister Salome and her husband Alexas and said: 'I know the Jews will greet my death with wild rejoicings; but I can be mourned on other people's account and make sure of a magnificent funeral if you will do as I tell you. These men under guard: as soon as I die, kill them all – let loose the soldiers amongst them; then all Judaea and every family will weep for me willy-nilly. . . .'

Later he was so tormented by lack of food and a racking cough that his sufferings mastered him and he made an effort to anticipate his appointed end. He took an apple and asked for a knife, it being his habit to cut up apples when he ate them; then looking round to make sure there was no one to stop him he raised his hand to stab himself.

Josephus goes on to relate that just before he died Herod gave orders for the execution of yet a third of his lawful sons[4] in addition to the two already executed, and that his life was instantly broken off, to the accompaniment of agonizing pains.[5] Such was the final end of Herod; he paid a just penalty for the children he had put to death in Bethlehem and its neighbourhood in his attempt against our Saviour.

After this an angel appeared in a dream to Joseph while he was staying in Egypt, and ordered him to leave for Judaea with the Child and His mother, informing him that those who

1. In Josephus, 'as if dead'.
2. In Josephus, 'crying aloud'.
3. The rough purchasing power of Josephus's 50 drachmas.
4. Antipater.
5. *Jewish War*, p. 111.

sought the death of the little Child were dead. The evangelist
proceeds:

> But hearing that Archelaus had succeeded his father Herod as
> king, he was afraid to go there; and being warned in a dream, he
> withdrew into the district of Galilee.[1]

Pilate's date; high priests at the time of Christ's mission

9. The accession to power of Archelaus after Herod is confirmed by Josephus, who describes how in accordance with
the will of Herod his father and the decision of Caesar
Augustus he succeeded to the Judaean kingdom; and how after
his fall from power ten years later his brothers Philip and the
younger Herod,[2] together with Lysanias, continued to rule
their tetrarchies.[3]

In *Antiquities* Book XVIII,[4] the same writer informs us
that in the twelfth year of Tiberius, who had mounted the
imperial throne after the fifty-seven-year reign of Augustus,[5]
Judaea was entrusted to Pontius Pilate, and that Pilate remained
there ten years,[6] almost till Tiberius's death. This clearly
proves the forged character of the *Memoranda* so recently
published, blackening our Saviour;[7] at the very start the
note of time proves the dishonesty of the forgers. If they are
to be believed the crime of the Saviour's Passion must be
referred to Tiberius's fourth consulship, i.e. the seventh year
of his reign, but at that time it is clear that Pilate was not yet
in charge of Judaea, if we may accept the testimony of
Josephus, who explicitly declares, in the passage already
quoted, that it was in the *twelfth* year of his reign that
Tiberius appointed Pilate procurator of Judaea.

1. Matt. ii. 19–22.   2. Antipas.
3. *Jewish War*, pp. 111, 122, 124, 131.   4. XVIII, ii, 2, and iv, 2.
5. March 44 B.C. to August A.D. 14.   6. A.D. 26–36.
7. Not the extant Acta Pilati but a heathen forgery published *c.* 311.

10. In their time, when, according to the evangelist, Tiberius
Caesar was in the fifteenth year of his reign and Pontius
Pilate in the fourth of his governorship, and Herod, Lysanias,
and Philip were tetrarchs of the rest of Judaea,[1] our Saviour and
Lord, Jesus the Christ of God, beginning His mission at the
age of about thirty,[2] came to John's baptism and then and
there set to work preaching the gospel. Holy Scripture
further tells us that He completed the whole period of His
teaching when Annas and Caiaphas were high priest,[3] showing
that the years covering their ministry include the whole
period of His teaching. Since, then, He began His mission in
the high priesthood of Annas and continued till the reign of
Caiaphas, the period covered does not stretch to four complete years. For, at that time the ordinances of the Law were
already obsolescent and the rule was no longer operative
under which the duties of God's service were hereditary and
lasted for life; the Roman governors bestowed the high
priesthood first on one, then on another, and the office was
held for not more than a single year. In fact, Josephus records
that after Annas there were four successive high priests,
Caiaphas being the last. I quote from the book of *Antiquities*:

Valerius Gratus, after depriving Ananus[4] of the priesthood,
appointed as high priest Ishmael son of Phabi; but a little later he
removed him and nominated as high priest Eleazar, son of the high
priest Ananus. When a year had gone by he removed him in turn
and transferred the high priesthood to Simon son of Camithus. He
too remained in office no more than a year: he was succeeded by
Joseph, also known as Caiaphas.[5]

Thus the whole period of our Saviour's teaching is shown
to be actually less than four complete years, four high priests
in four years, from Annas to the appointment of Caiaphas,

1. An inaccurate paraphrase of Luke iii. 1.
2. Luke iii. 23. It is plain from this sentence and the next but one that
Eusebius interpreted the words correctly, as did R.V.
3. Luke iii. 2.   4. Annas.   5. *Antiquities* XVIII, ii, 2.

having held office for a twelvemonth. Naturally, the gospel narrative named Caiaphas as high priest in the year in which the events of our Saviour's Passion were enacted; it also shows that the period of Christ's teaching harmonizes with the foregoing line of inquiry.[1]

Not very long after the start of His preaching our Saviour and Lord called the twelve apostles, to whom alone of all His disciples He gave, as a special privilege, the name of apostles.[2] Furthermore, He appointed seventy others; these, too, He sent out two and two ahead of Him to every town or place to which He Himself intended to come.[3]

Evidence regarding John the Baptist and Christ

11. Not long afterwards John the Baptist was beheaded by the younger Herod, as we learn from the inspired gospel narrative.[4] Confirmation comes from Josephus, who mentions Herodias by name and tells how though she was his brother's wife Herod married her, discarding his existing lawful wife – daughter of King Aretas of Petrea – and separating Herodias from her husband, who was still alive. For her sake, too, he put John to death and was involved in war with Aretas, whose daughter he had slighted. The war ended, as Josephus records, with a pitched battle in which Herod's

1. Eusebius's argument is by no means satisfactory. It is, of course, true that Christ's ministry lasted less than four years; few scholars would suggest that it went beyond two and a half. But Eusebius has misrepresented both Josephus, who clearly states that the four successors of Annas held office for eleven years in all, and Luke, who says not that the ministry began in the time of Annas and ended in that of Caiaphas, but that it began when Annas and Caiaphas were the high priest, i.e. when Annas was still high priest in Jewish eyes, the office being held for life, though Caiaphas had as a political expedient been appointed by the Romans to replace him. The situation was exactly the same at the end of our Lord's life, as we see from John xviii. 13–24, where the writer informs us that He was examined by Annas before being sent to Caiaphas, and within the compass of five lines refers to each as the high priest.

2. Matt. xi and Luke vi. 13.   3. Luke x. 1.   4. Mark vi. 14–29.

army was totally destroyed, the direct result of his outrageous treatment of John. The same writer acknowledges that John was a man of unimpeachable virtue, and a baptist, confirming the description of him contained in the gospel narrative. He also records the fact that Herod was deprived of his throne on account of the same woman, with whom he was driven into exile and condemned to live in Vienne, a city in Gaul.[1] The story will be found in *Antiquities* Book XVIII, from which I quote verbatim what he has to say about John:

Some of the Jews believed that Herod's army had been destroyed by God, as a richly deserved punishment for his treatment of John who was called the Baptist. For Herod killed him, a good man who urged the Jews to train themselves in virtue, to be just to each other and pious towards God, and to come together for baptism: on one condition only would their baptism be acceptable to Him – if it was undergone not to escape the penalty of sins but to purify the body, since the soul had been already purged by righteousness. When crowds assembled, very excited on hearing his words, Herod was afraid that his extraordinary hold over the people would lead to some revolt, as they seemed prepared to do anything at his suggestion. So he thought it much better to forestall any revolutionary movement prompted by John by putting him out of the way, rather than wait for an outbreak to occur and reproach himself when it was too late. Because of Herod's suspicion John was sent in chains to Machaerus, the fortress mentioned above, and there executed.[2]

After giving this account of John, in the same part of his work he goes on to speak as follows of our Saviour:

At this time appeared Jesus, a very gifted man – if indeed it is right to call him a man; for he was a worker of miracles, a teacher of such men as listened with pleasure to the truth, and he won over many of the Jews and many of Gentile origin as well. This was the Christ; and when at the instigation of our leading men he had been condemned to the cross by Pilate, those who had loved him at the first

1. According to *Antiquities* XVIII, vii, 2, Lyons; according to *Jewish War*, p. 128, Spain.
2. *Antiquities* XVIII, v, 2.

did not cease to do so; for on the third day he appeared to them alive again, the inspired prophets having foretold this and countless other wonderful things about him. Even now the group of people called Christians after him has not died out.[1]

When a historian sprung from the Hebrews themselves has furnished in his own writing an almost contemporary record of John the Baptist and our Saviour too, what excuse is there left for not condemning the shameless dishonesty of those who forged the *Memoranda* blackening them both? And there we will leave the matter.

Our Saviour's disciples

12. The names of our Saviour's apostles are in the gospels for all to read: of the seventy disciples no list has ever been found. It is stated[2] that one of them was Barnabas, who is mentioned several times in the Acts of the Apostles, and notably by Paul in writing to the Galatians.[3] Another is said to have been Sosthenes, joint author with Paul of one Epistle to the Corinthians.[4] Then there is Clement's story (*Outlines* Book v) in which he says that Cephas – of whom Paul writes: 'When Cephas came to Antioch I withstood him to his face'[5] – was one of the seventy disciples, who happened to have the same name as Peter the Apostle.[6] There is evidence also that Matthias, who took Judas's place in the list of apostles, and the other man honoured like him in the drawing of lots,[7] had both been called to be among the seventy. Thaddaeus,

1. *Antiquities* XVIII, ii, 3. In defiance of the unanimous testimony of the MSS., sceptics have asserted that this famous paragraph, at least in its present form, is a Christian forgery. It is, however, defended by more recent critics, e.g. Burkitt, Harnack, and Barnes. The same problem arises with passages in *The Jewish War* found only in the Slavonic version. See Penguin Classics edition pp. 403–8.

2. See p. 72.   3. Gal. ii. 1, 9, 13.   4. I Cor. i. 1.   5. Gal. ii. 11.

6. An absurd suggestion in view of Gal. ii. 9; no doubt Clement wished to save the face alluded to by Paul.

7. Joseph Barsabbas; Acts i. 23–6.

again, is said to have been one of them; about him a story has come to my notice which I shall very shortly recount.

In addition to the Seventy there were other disciples of the Saviour, as you would find if you considered the matter and accepted the testimony of Paul, who states that after His resurrection from the dead He was seen first by Cephas, then by the Twelve, and after them by more than five hundred brethren at once, of whom some, he says, have fallen asleep, but most remain alive at the time of writing. Next, he says, He was seen by James – one of the reputed brothers of the Lord; then, as if in addition to these there had been, on the pattern of the Twelve, a large number of apostles such as Paul himself,[1] he adds: 'Later He was seen by all the apostles.'

A story about the Prince of Edessa

13. The story about Thaddaeus is as follows: Because of His power to work miracles the divinity of our Lord and Saviour Jesus Christ became in every land the subject of excited talk and attracted a vast number of people in foreign lands very remote from Judaea, who came in the hope of being cured of diseases and disorders of every kind. Thus it happened that when King Abgar, the brilliantly successful monarch of the peoples of Mesopotamia, who was dying from a terrible physical disorder which no human power could heal, heard continual mention of the name of Jesus and unanimous tribute to His miracles, he sent a humble request to Him by a letter-carrier, begging for relief from his disease. Jesus did not immediately accede to his request, but honoured him with a personal letter, promising to send one of His disciples to cure his disease, and at the same time to bring salvation to him

1. An astonishing suggestion. It is plain from all accounts of the Ascension that our Lord's final appearance was to the Eleven; there is no hint of the existence of any other apostles (apart from Matthias) before the time of the missionary journeys, and it is inconceivable that Paul himself should have cheapened the title of which he was so proud.

and all his kin. In a very short time the promise was fulfilled. After His resurrection and ascent into heaven, Thomas, one of the twelve apostles, was moved by inspiration to send Thaddaeus, himself in the list of Christ's seventy disciples,[1] to Edessa as preacher and evangelist of the teaching about Christ. Through him every word of our Saviour's promise was fulfilled.

Written evidence of these things is available, taken from the Record Office at Edessa, at that time the royal capital. In the public documents there, embracing early history and also the events of Abgar's time, this record is found preserved from then till now; and the most satisfactory course is to listen to the actual letters, which I have extracted from the archives and translated word for word from the Syriac as follows:

COPY OF A LETTER WRITTEN BY ABGAR THE TOPARCH TO
JESUS AND SENT TO HIM AT JERUSALEM BY
THE COURIER ANANIAS

Abgar Uchama the Toparch[2] to Jesus, who has appeared as a gracious saviour in the region of Jerusalem – greeting.

I have heard about you and about the cures you perform without drugs or herbs. If report is true, you make the blind see again and the lame walk about; you cleanse lepers, expel unclean spirits and demons, cure those suffering from chronic and painful diseases, and raise the dead.[3] When I heard all this about you, I concluded that one of two things must be true – either you are God and came down from heaven to do these things, or you are God's Son doing them. Accordingly I am writing to beg you to come to me, whatever the inconvenience, and cure the disorder from which I suffer. I may add that I understand the Jews are treating you with contempt and

1. The only Thaddaeus in the Bible was one of the Twelve, called by Luke 'Judas son of James', and by Matthew and Mark 'Thaddaeus', according to the best MSS., 'Lebbaeus' according to some others.

2. A.D. 13–50.

3. Similar to, but not identical with, the list in Matt. xi. 5 and Luke vii. 2.

desire to injure you: my city is very small, but highly esteemed, adequate for both of us.

[He wrote this letter when the heavenly light had shone on him only a little while. It is desirable also to hear the letter which Jesus sent him by the same letter-carrier. It is only a few lines long, but very impressive. Here it is.[1]]

JESUS'S REPLY TO THE TOPARCH ABGAR BY THE COURIER ANANIAS

Happy are you who believed in me without having seen me![2] For it is written of me that those who have seen me will not believe in me, and that those who have not seen will believe and live.[3] As to your request that I should come to you, I must complete all that I was sent to do here, and on completing it must at once be taken up to the One who sent me. When I have been taken up I will send you one of my disciples to cure your disorder and bring life to you and those with you.

To these letters is subjoined the following in Syriac:

After Jesus was taken up, Judas, also known as Thomas, sent to him as an apostle[4] Thaddaeus, one of the Seventy, who came and stayed with Tobias, son of Tobias. When his arrival was announced [and he had been made conspicuous by the wonders he performed], Abgar was told: 'An apostle has come here from Jesus, as He promised you in His letter.' Then Thaddaeus began in the power of God to cure every disease and weakness, to the astonishment of everyone. When Abgar heard of the magnificent and astonishing

1. The bracketed passages are wanting in some MSS. Possibly they were added by Eusebius to his final edition.
2. See John xx. 29. The whole letter bears a resemblance to that gospel.
3. This sentence is somewhat like Is. vi. 9.
4. The word 'apostle', meaning 'an emissary', is not used in the narrow sense, but simply to denote a person sent by Christ: the Greek word is the noun corresponding to the verb 'send', used in this sentence, in Jesus's reply, and in John *passim*.

things that he was doing, and especially his cures, he began to suspect that this was the one to whom Jesus referred when He wrote in His letter: 'When I have been taken up I will send you one of my disciples who will cure your disorder.' So summoning Tobias, with whom Thaddaeus was staying, he said: 'I understand that a man with unusual powers has arrived and is staying in your house [and is working many cures in the name of Jesus.' Tobias answered: 'Yes, sir. A man from foreign parts has arrived and is living with me, and is performing many wonders.' Abgar replied:] 'Bring him to me.'

So Tobias went to Thaddaeus and said to him: 'The Toparch Abgar has summoned me and told me to bring you to him so that you can cure him.' Thaddaeus answered: 'I will present myself, since the power of God has sent me to him.' The next day Tobias got up early and escorted Thaddaeus to Abgar. As he presented himself, with the king's grandees standing there, at the moment of his entry a wonderful vision appeared to Abgar on the face of Thaddaeus. On seeing it Abgar bowed low before the apostle, and astonishment seized all the bystanders; for they had not seen the vision, which appeared to Abgar alone. He questioned Thaddaeus.

'Are you really a disciple of Jesus the Son of God, who said to me, "I will send you one of my disciples who will cure you and give you life"?'

'You wholeheartedly believed in the One who sent me, and for that reason I was sent to you. And again, if you believe in Him, in proportion to your belief shall the prayers of your heart be granted.'

'I believed in Him so strongly that I wanted to take an army and destroy the Jews who crucified Him, if I had not been prevented by the imperial power of Rome from doing so.'

'Our Lord has fulfilled the will of His Father: after fulfilling it He was taken up to the Father.'

'I too have believed in Him and in His Father.'

'For that reason I lay my hand on you in His name.'

When he did this, Abgar was instantly cured of the disease and disorder from which he suffered. It surprised Abgar that the very thing he had heard about Jesus had actually happened to him through

His disciple Thaddaeus, who had cured him without drugs or herbs – and not only him but also Abdus son of Abdus, who had gout. He too came, and falling at his feet found his prayer answered through the hands of Thaddaeus, and was cured. Many other fellow-citizens of theirs Thaddaeus restored to health, performing many wonders and preaching the word of God.

After this Abgar said: 'It is by the power of God that you, Thaddaeus, do these things; and we ourselves were amazed. But I have a further request to make: explain to me about the coming of Jesus and how it happened, and about His power – by what power did He do the things I have heard about?'

Thaddaeus replied: 'For the time being I shall say nothing; but as I was sent to preach the word, be good enough to assemble all your citizens tomorrow, and I will preach to them and sow in them the word of life – about the coming of Jesus and how it happened; about His mission and the purpose for which His Father sent Him; about His power and His deeds, and the mysteries He spoke in the world, and the power by which He did these things; about His new preaching; about His lowliness and humility, and how He humbled Himself and put aside and made light of His divinity, was crucified and descended into Hades,[1] and rent asunder the partition which had never been rent since time began, and raised the dead; how He descended alone, but ascended with a great multitude to His Father [; and how He is seated on the right hand of God the Father with glory in the heavens; and how He will come again with power to judge living and dead].'

So Abgar instructed his citizens to assemble at daybreak and hear the preaching of Thaddaeus. After that he ordered gold and silver to be given to him. But Thaddaeus refused them and asked, 'If we have left our own property behind, how can we accept other people's?'

All this happened in the year 340.[2]

1. It is worthy of note that this phrase should occur in an early Syriac document. The doctrine can be found in a number of N.T. passages, but nowhere in these words, which appear nowhere else at such an early date. They form, of course, a clause of the Apostles' Creed, a much later document produced in the West and never yet adopted by Eastern Christendom.

2. of the Seleucid era – apparently A.D. 30, the probable year of the Ascension.

Here we may leave for the present this valuable document, literally translated from Syriac.[1]

1. The authenticity of this circumstantial story presents an interesting problem. It is generally regarded as mere legend, designed to create the belief that Christianity reached Mesopotamia very early indeed. But if, as scholars tell us, there is no other evidence that missionaries arrived there till a century later, there is equally no evidence that they did not. It would, indeed, be surprising if Christianity, which spread over almost the whole Empire with such remarkable rapidity, should have been withheld from an area so near Palestine, and one where a similar dialect was spoken. Let us not forget that while Edessa is only 180 miles from Antioch, the starting-point of all Paul's journeys, Ephesus is 500, Rome over 1,000, and Spain 2,000. Moreover, as Josephus tells us (*Jewish War*, p. 21), there was close contact between Jerusalem and the Jewish inhabitants of northern Mesopotamia, for whom he wrote the Aramaic original of his book.

It should be noted that the original Syriac, of which we possess a copy, does not say that Jesus wrote the letter, but that He gave a verbal message to Ananias, who wrote it down. In other respects Eusebius's version is more reliable than our text of the Syriac, which has been corrupted by the copyists.

Book 2

(*Compiled by me from the works of Clement, Tertullian, Josephus, and Philo*)

TIBERIUS TO NERO: THE WORK OF THE APOSTLES FROM THE CHOICE OF MATTHIAS TO THE DEATHS OF PAUL AND PETER

THOSE facts about the story of the Church that needed to be explained by way of preface – the divinity of the saving Word, the early history of our teaching, the antiquity of the Christian way of life in accordance with the gospel, and especially the details of Christ's recent advent, the events before His Passion, and the choice of the apostles – I discussed in the previous book, outlining the arguments. Let us now in the present book inquire into the events following His Ascension, drawing on Holy Writ for some, and deriving others from outside sources which I shall name as occasion demands.

How the apostles lived after the Ascension

1. The first, then, to be chosen by lot for the apostleship in place of the traitor Judas was Matthias,[1] who, as has been mentioned,[2] had been one of the Lord's disciples. By prayer and the laying-on of the apostles' hands there were appointed to the diaconate for the service of the community men of proved worth to the number of seven.[3] These were headed by Stephen, who was the first after the Lord – almost as soon as he was ordained, as if this was the real purpose of his advancement – to be put to death, stoned by the Lord's

1. Acts i. 15–26.   2. p. 64.   3. Acts vi. 1–6.

murderers.[1] Thus he was the first to win the crown called by the same name as he,[2] and reserved for Christ's worthily victorious martyrs.

Then there was James, who was known as the brother of the Lord; for he, too, was called Joseph's son, and Joseph Christ's father, though in fact the Virgin was his betrothed, and before they came together she was found to be with child by the Holy Ghost, as the inspired gospel narrative tells us.[3] This James, whom the early Christians surnamed the Righteous because of his outstanding virtue, was the first, as the records tell us, to be elected to the episcopal throne of the Jerusalem church. Clement, in *Outlines* Book VI, puts it thus:

> Peter, James, and John, after the Ascension of the Saviour, did not claim pre-eminence because the Saviour had specially honoured them, but chose James the Righteous as Bishop of Jerusalem.

In Book VIII of the same work the writer makes this further statement about him:

> James the Righteous, John, and Peter were entrusted by the Lord after his resurrection with the higher knowledge. They imparted it to the other apostles, and the other apostles to the Seventy, one of whom was Barnabas. There were two Jameses, one the Righteous, who was thrown down from the parapet and beaten to death with a fuller's club, the other the James who was beheaded.[4]

James the Righteous is also mentioned by Paul when he writes:

> Of the other apostles I saw no one except James the Lord's brother.[5]

It was at this time that our Saviour's promise to the king of the Osrhoenes[6] was receiving its fulfilment. Thomas was

1. Acts vii. 59.
2. In Greek 'Stephen' and 'crown' are identical. So in the medieval hymn:
> Glitters now the crown above thee,
> Figured in thy sacred name.
3. Matt. i. 18.   4. Acts xii. 2.   5. Gal. i. 19.
6. Osrhoene was the district round Edessa.

moved by inspiration to send Thaddaeus to Edessa as preacher and evangelist of the teaching about Christ, as I showed a little way back from the document found there. When he arrived in the country Thaddaeus restored Abgar to health by the word of Christ, and amazed all the inhabitants by his wonderful miracles. By his actions he exerted such an influence on them that he led them to reverence the power of Christ, and made disciples of the saving doctrine. From that day to this the whole city of Edessa has been devoted to the name of Christ, providing most convincing proof of our Saviour's goodness to them also.

After this excursion into early history let us return once more to the inspired record.

Stephen's martyrdom was followed by the first and greatest persecution by the Jews themselves of the Jerusalem church. All the disciples except the Twelve alone were dispersed about Judaea and Samaria.[1] Some, as the inspired record says, travelled as far as Phoenicia, Cyprus, and Antioch; but they could not yet venture to share the message of the Faith with Gentiles, and proclaimed it to Jews alone.[2] At that time also Paul was still raging against the Church, entering the houses of the faithful, dragging off men and women, and handing them over for imprisonment.[3] But Philip, one of the men already ordained with Stephen to the diaconate, was among the dispersed. He went down into Samaria,[4] and filled with divine power was the first to preach the word there. So great was the divine grace working with him that even Simon the Magus with very many others was won over by his words. Such a name had Simon obtained at that time by the sorceries with which he got his dupes into his power that he was believed to be the Great Power of God, but now even he was struck dumb by the miracles that Philip performed by divine

1. Acts viii. 1.   2. Acts xi. 19.   3. Acts viii. 3.
4. In the O.T. Samaria is a city, in the N.T. a district. The city (Sebaste) is nowhere named in the N.T.

power, and slipped in: he actually received baptism, in his
hypocritical pretence of belief in Christ. It is an astonishing
fact that this is still the practice of those who to the present
day belong to his disgusting sect. Following in their pro-
genitor's footsteps they slip into the Church like a pestilential
and scabby disease, and do the utmost damage to all whom
they succeed in smearing with the horrible, deadly poison
concealed on them. By now, however, most of these have
been expelled – just as Simon himself, when his real character
had been exposed by Peter, paid the appropriate penalty.[1]

While every day the saving message spread farther afield,
some providence brought from Ethiopia, a country tradi-
tionally ruled by a woman, one of the queen's principal
officers. The first Gentile to receive from Philip by revelation
the mysteries of the divine word, and the first-fruits of the
faithful throughout the world, he is believed to have been the
first to go back to his native land and preach the gospel of the
knowledge of the God of the universe[2] and the life-giving
sojourn of our Saviour among men. Through him came the
actual fulfilment of the prophecy:

> Ethiopia shall stretch out her hand to God.[3]

The next stage began when Paul, the chosen vessel – neither
from men nor through men, but through revelation of Jesus
Christ Himself and God the Father who raised Him from the
dead – was appointed an apostle, receiving his call through a
vision and the heavenly voice that accompanied the revelation.[4]

1. Summarized from Acts viii. 5–23.
2. A favourite phrase with Eusebius, who appreciated the gulf separating
Christianity from the cult of local and numerous deities; see Paul's speeches at
Lystra and Athens.
3. Ps. lxvii. 31.
4. Acts ix. 3–4 and Gal. i. 1.

*Tiberius's reaction on learning Christ's story, which soon sped
to every part of the world*

2. Our Saviour's marvellous resurrection and ascension into
heaven were by now everywhere famous, and it had long
been customary for provincial governors to report to the
holder of the imperial office any change in the local situation,
so that he might be aware of all that was going on. The
story of the resurrection from the dead of our Saviour Jesus,
already the subject of general discussion all over Palestine,
was accordingly communicated by Pilate to the Emperor
Tiberius.[1] For Pilate knew all about Christ's supernatural
deeds, and especially how after death He had risen from the
dead and was now generally believed to be a god. It is said
that Tiberius referred the report to the senate, which rejected
it. The apparent reason was that they had not gone into the
matter before, for the old law still held good that no one
could be regarded by the Romans as a god unless by vote and
decree of the senate; the real reason was that no human
decision or commendation was required for the saving teaching of the divine message. In this way the Roman council
rejected the report sent to it about our Saviour, but Tiberius
made no change in his attitude and formed no evil designs
against the teaching of Christ.

These facts were noted by Tertullian, an expert in Roman
law and famous on other grounds – in fact one of the most
brilliant men in Rome. In his *Defence of the Christians*, written
in Latin and translated into Greek, he has this to say:

To go back to the origin of such laws, there was an old decree
that no one should be consecrated a god by an emperor till he had
been approved by the senate. Marcus Aemilius followed this procedure in the case of a false god, Alburnus. This reinforces my argument that among you godhead is conferred by human approval. If a

1. It can hardly be doubted that Pilate sent such a report, but none of the
various extant versions is regarded as genuine.

god does not satisfy man, he does not become a god; so according to this it is for man to show favour to God. Tiberius then, in whose time the name of Christian came into the world, when a report of this doctrine reached him from Palestine where it originated, communicated it to the senate, making it clear to them that he favoured the doctrine. The senate however, because they had not examined the doctrine for themselves, rejected it; but Tiberius stuck to his own view, and threatened to execute any who accused the Christians.[1]

Heavenly providence had purposefully put this in the emperor's mind, in order that the gospel message should get off to a good start and speed to every part of the world.

3. Thus with the powerful cooperation of Heaven the whole world was suddenly lit by the sunshine of the saving word. At once, in accordance with the Holy Scriptures, the voice of its inspired evangelists and apostles went forth into all the earth, and their words to the ends of the world.[2] In every town and village, like a well-filled threshing-floor, churches shot up bursting with eager members. Men who through the error they had inherited from generations of ancestors were in the grip of the old spiritual sickness of idol-worship, by the power of Christ and through the teaching of His followers and the miracles they wrought were freed, as it were, from cruel masters and found release from galling fetters. They turned their backs on devilish polytheism in all its forms, and acknowledged that there was one God only, the Fashioner of all things. Him they honoured with the ordinances of true religion through that divine, reasonable worship of which our Saviour sowed the seed in the life of men.

The divine grace was now being poured on the other nations too. First, at Palestinian Caesarea Cornelius with his entire household, through divine revelation and the agency of Peter, embraced the Christian faith.[3] He was followed by many other Gentiles at Antioch, who had heard the preaching

1. *Defence* v.　　　2. Ps. xix. 4.　　　3. Acts x.

of those dispersed by the persecution of Stephen's time. The Antioch church was now flourishing and growing rapidly, and a large number of the prophets from Jerusalem were there, accompanied by Barnabas and Paul and another group of brethren as well. It was at that time and in that city that the name of Christian first appeared, as if from a copious and life-giving fountain. Agabus again, one of the prophets staying with them, foretold the coming famine, and Paul and Barnabas were sent to do everything possible for the relief of the brethren.[1]

Agrippa appointed king and Herod banished: sufferings of the Jews: suicide of Pilate

4. After a reign of about twenty-two years[2] Tiberius died, and the principate passed to Gaius,[3] who at once had Agrippa crowned ruler of the Jews.[4] He made him king of the tetrarchies of Philip and Lysanias, to which a little later he added the tetrarchy of Herod, having sentenced that monarch – the Herod of our Saviour's Passion – to banishment for life, along with his wife Herodias, because of a long list of offences. The details will be found in Josephus.[5]

In Gaius's reign Philo became widely known as one of the greatest scholars, not only among our own people but also among those brought up as pagans. By descent a Hebrew, he could hold his own with any of the eminent occupants of official positions in Alexandria. The constant and conscientious labour that he bestowed on theological and traditional studies is plain for all to see, while of his proficiency in the philosophical and liberal thought of the pagan world there is no need to speak, since it is on record that in his enthusiasm for the systems of Plato and Pythagoras he surpassed all his contemporaries.

1. Acts xi. 19–30.   2. August A.D. 14 to March A.D. 37.
3. Caligula.   4. His subjects were certainly not Jews.
5. *Jewish War*, pp. 127–8.

5. What happened to the Jews in Gaius's reign Philo has related in five books.[1] In these he describes the emperor's insanity and how he proclaimed himself a god and over and over again abused his position; the sufferings of the Jews in his time; the mission to Rome that Philo undertook on behalf of his compatriots in Alexandria;[2] his appearance before Gaius, when his defence of their ancestral laws met with nothing but derisive laughter and well nigh cost him his life.

These facts are mentioned also by Josephus, who in *Antiquities* Book XVIII writes as follows:

> When a clash took place in Alexandria between the Jewish colony and the Greeks, three men were chosen by each faction to represent them before Gaius. One of the Alexandrian representatives was Apion, who brought many damaging accusations against the Jews, alleging in particular that they neglected the honours due to Caesar – all the subjects of the Roman government raised altars and temples to Gaius, and in every other respect accepted him as they did the gods: the Jews alone thought it improper to honour him with statues and swear by his name. When Apion had brought many serious charges, by which he hoped with good reason that Gaius would be roused, Philo, the leading Jewish representative, rose to reply. A man highly esteemed on every ground, brother of Alexander the alabarch,[3] and a skilled philosopher, he was quite capable of rebutting the charges; but he was cut short by Gaius, who ordered him to clear out, being so infuriated that he was obviously on the point of taking drastic action against them. Out went Philo, grossly insulted, and told his Jewish colleagues they need have no fear: Gaius might be furious with them, but in reality he was already taking the field against God.[4]

So much we learn from Josephus. Philo himself, in his historical work *The Mission*, gives us a detailed and precise

1. Evidently a much larger work than the pamphlet *The Mission* that we possess.
2. A.D. 40.
3. Originally a commander of Arabs, later a controller of customs.
4. *Antiquities* XVIII, viii, 1.

account of his actions at that time. I shall omit the greater
part, quoting only those points that will make abundantly
clear to my readers the calamities which befell the Jews so
promptly and after so short an interval, in consequence of
their crimes against Christ. In the first place he relates that in
Tiberius's reign, at Rome, Sejanus, then most influential at
the emperor's court, took energetic steps to exterminate the
entire race. Meanwhile, in Judaea, Pilate, in whose period of
office the crime against our Saviour was committed, made
an attempt on the temple (then still standing) at Jerusalem in
defiance of Jewish privileges, goading the people to absolute
frenzy.

6. After the death of Tiberius, he continues, Gaius ascended
the throne, and among the many victims of his numerous
outrages the whole Jewish race suffered to a peculiar and
extreme degree. This we may learn in brief from his own
words, which I reproduce exactly as written:

> So incalculable was the behaviour of Gaius towards everyone,
> especially the Jewish race. He hated them so bitterly that in city after
> city, beginning with Alexandria, he seized the synagogues and filled
> them with images and statues of himself – for as he gave permission
> for them to be erected, it was really he who put them there – and in
> the Holy City he tried to change the sanctuary, which was still
> untouched and regarded as inviolable, and transform it into a temple
> of his own, to be called the Temple of Jupiter the Glorious, the
> Younger Gaius.[1]

Countless other atrocities that beggar description, inflicted
on the Jews at Alexandria in the same reign, are related by
Philo in a second short work, entitled *The Virtues*. His statements are confirmed by Josephus, who similarly points out
that the calamities which overtook the whole nation began
with the time of Pilate and the crimes against the Saviour.

1. The elder Gaius being Julius Caesar.

Listen to what he has to say in *The Jewish War* Book II. Here are his actual words:

> As procurator of Judaea Tiberius sent Pilate, who during the night, secretly and under cover, conveyed to Jerusalem the images of Caesar known as *signa*. When day dawned this put the Jews into a frenzy; for those who were near were amazed at the sight, which meant that their laws had been trampled on – they do not permit any portrait-image to be set up in the city.[1]

If you compare this with the gospel account, you will see that it was not long before they paid the penalty for the cry they uttered before Pilate himself, when they shouted that they had no other king than Caesar alone.[2] Josephus goes on to relate a second calamity that overtook them soon after:

> After this he stirred up further trouble by expending the sacred treasure known as Corban[3] on an aqueduct thirty-five miles long. This roused the populace to fury, and when Pilate visited Jerusalem they surrounded the tribunal and shouted him down. But he had foreseen this disturbance, and had made the soldiers mix with the mob, wearing civilian clothing over their armour, and with orders not to draw their swords but to use clubs on the obstreperous. He now gave the signal from the tribunal and the Jews were cudgelled, so that many died from the blows, and many as they fled were trampled to death by their friends. The fate of those who perished horrified the crowd into silence.[4]

Besides this, the same writer shows that in Jerusalem itself a great many other revolts broke out, making it clear that from then on the city and all Judaea were in the grip of faction, war, and an endless succession of criminal plots, until the final hour overtook them – the siege under Vespasian. Such was the penalty laid upon the Jews by divine justice for their crimes against Christ.

1. *Jewish War*, p. 126.   2. John xix. 15, reworded.
3. See Mark vii. 11, where 'Corban' is retained in English Bibles, and Matt. xxvii. 6, where it is translated 'treasury' or 'temple fund'.
4. *Jewish War*, p. 127.

7. It is worthy of note that, as the records show, in the reign of Gaius, whose times I am describing, Pilate himself, the governor of our Saviour's day, was involved in such calamities that he was forced to become his own executioner and to punish himself with his own hand: divine justice, it seems, was not slow to overtake him. The facts are recorded by those Greeks who have chronicled the Olympiads[1] together with the events occurring in each.

The famine in Claudius's time: martyrdom of James: punishment of Agrippa

8. The reign of Gaius had not yet lasted four years when he was succeeded as emperor by Claudius. In his time famine descended on the whole world, a fact which writers whose point of view is very different from ours have recorded in their histories.[2] Thus, the prediction of Agabus in the Acts of the Apostles about the famine that was to occur all over the world received its fulfilment. The famine in Claudius's time is indicated in the Acts by Luke, who relates how by Paul and Barnabas the Christians in Antioch, each according to his means, sent help to those in Judaea.[3] He continues:

9. At that time [obviously that of Claudius] King Herod made a determined attack on certain members of the Church, killing James the brother of John with the headsman's sword.

Referring to this James, Clement in *Outlines* Book VII tells an interesting story, on the strength of an authentic tradition. It appears that the man who brought him into court was so moved when he saw him testify that he confessed that he, too, was a Christian:

So they were both taken away together, and on the way he asked James to forgive him. James thought for a moment; then he said,

1. Four-year periods, the basis of Greek chronology.
2. Tacitus and Dio Cassius.   3. Acts xi. 28–9.

'I wish you peace', and kissed him. So both were beheaded at the same time.

Then, as we read in the sacred record, Herod, seeing that his action in putting James to death had given satisfaction to the Jews, laid hands on Peter as well, clapped him in prison, and was on the very point of perpetrating his murder too, but for divine intervention: in the night an angel stood by him, and he was miraculously released from his fetters and set free for the ministry of preaching. It was in this way that Peter's life was ordained by heaven.[1]

10. The king's attempt on the apostles brought swift retribution: the avenging minister of divine justice overtook him at once, immediately after his action against the apostles, as the narrative of the Acts records. He had set out for Caesarea, and there on an important feast day, adorned with magnificent royal robes, he mounted on a dais, and standing in front of his throne delivered a harangue which the entire audience received with thunderous applause, as the utterance of a god, not a man; and the inspired record tells us that instantly he was struck by an angel of the Lord, was eaten by worms, and expired.[2] It is remarkable how in the case of this miracle also the sacred record is borne out by the account in Josephus, who clearly testifies to the truth in *Antiquities* Book xix, where he tells us the amazing story in these words:

He had reached the end of his third year as king of all Judaea;[3] and he came to the city of Caesarea, formerly known as Strato's Tower. There he was celebrating public games in Caesar's honour, knowing that this was a festival for his safety.[4] It was attended by a great number of provincial officials and other leading men. On the

1. Condensed from Acts xii. 3–10.
2. Compressed from Acts xii. 19–23.
3. Agrippa became king of Judaea in A.D. 41.
4. The four-yearly festival *pro salute Caesaris* was due to be celebrated in A.D. 44.

second day of the games he put on a robe made entirely of silver, remarkable in texture, and at daybreak entered the theatre. There the silver was lit up by the first glint of the sun's rays, and shone dazzlingly, glittering in such a way that those who gazed at it trembled with fear. At once his flatterers shouted aloud from every side – little good did it do him – and hailed him as a god, adding: 'Be gracious! Hitherto we have reverenced you as a man; henceforth we acknowledge you as of more than mortal nature.' The king did not rebuke these people or repudiate their blasphemous flattery.

A moment later he looked up, and sitting over his head he saw an angel. This, as he at once realized, was the bringer of evil, as he had once been of good. He felt a pang in his breast, and all at once a violent pain gripped his belly, agonizing from the start. So looking hard at his friends, he murmured: 'I, your god, am now commanded to depart this life, for fate has instantly disproved the lies you have just told about me. You called me immortal, and now I am being taken away to die. I must bow to destiny, as God has willed it. Anyway my life has not been a poor one, but has reached the length that people envy.'

As he said this, the severity of his pain got the better of him; so no time was lost in carrying him into the palace, and soon the news reached all ears that he was bound to die in a matter of hours. By ancestral custom the crowd at once sat down, women and children as well, on sackcloth, and began to supplicate God for the king, and wailing and lamentation resounded everywhere. Lying in a top-floor room and looking down at them as they fell on their faces, the king could not restrain his own tears. For five days without intermission he was tortured by the pain in his belly; then he passed away in the fifty-fourth year of his life and the seventh of his reign.[1] He had reigned four years in the time of Gaius Caesar, ruling Philip's tetrarchy for three years, and in the fourth receiving Herod's too, and three more while Claudius Caesar was emperor.[2]

1. He had become tetrarch in A.D. 37.
2. *Antiquities* XIX, viii, 2. The quotation presents us with a baffling problem. According to the extant MSS. of Josephus, Agrippa saw not an angel (*angelos*), the bringer of evil, but an owl, a messenger (*angelos*) of evil. Eusebius is so accurate in his quotations that we have no right to suspect him of altering the text to bring it into line with Acts. If the text had been altered before it reached Eusebius, this need not be due to deliberate falsification; Dr Lawlor ingeniously

On these and other matters Josephus confirms the truth of Holy Scripture in a way that surprises me. If regarding the king's name some consider that there is a discrepancy, the answer is that the date and the facts prove that he is the same: either the name has been changed by a copyist's error, or else, like many others, the same man had two names.[1]

Theudas the impostor: Queen Helen of Adiabene

11. In the Acts, again, Luke introduces Gamaliel as saying at the examination of the apostles that at the time referred to Theudas rose in revolt, claiming to be somebody, and that he was killed and his entire following dispersed.[2] Well now, let us compare this with what Josephus writes about him. Here is his account, quoted verbatim from the work just referred to:

> When Fadus was procurator of Judaea, an impostor called Theudas persuaded a vast crowd to take their belongings and follow him to the River Jordan; for he claimed to be a prophet, and promised to divide the river by his command and provide them with an easy crossing. A great many people were deceived by this talk. Fadus however did not allow them to enjoy their folly, but sent a troop of cavalry against them. These attacked them without warning,

suggests that a copyist, puzzled by the author's use of the Latin word for owl, omitted it, and to make sense inserted 'bringer'. The point of Josephus's account is that he has already told us that when in prison Agrippa had seen an owl, and a German soldier had told him that though this time it indicated coming prosperity, the next time it appeared he would have but five days to live. That prophecy is now fulfilled. This story, so unconvincing to us, would delight the heart of Josephus. Apart from the owl, his account, with its emphasis on Agrippa's failure to repudiate the blasphemy, is so like Luke's that we can hardly doubt that both drew on the same written source, which certainly laid stress on the 'angelos'. It should be remembered that Josephus wrote fifty years after the event, Luke perhaps only twenty.

1. No difficulty here: Luke calls him 'Herod', Josephus 'Agrippa': both are right.

2. Compressed from Acts v. 34–6.

killed many, and took many alive, capturing Theudas himself, whose head they cut off and conveyed to Jerusalem.[1]

Immediately after this he mentions the famine that took place in Claudius's time:

12. It was just after this that the great famine took place in Judaea, in which Queen Helen at great expense bought corn from Egypt and distributed it among those in want.

You will find that this too agrees with the account in the Acts of the Apostles, which tells how the disciples at Antioch, each in proportion to his means, resolved to send relief to those living in Judaea. This they did, sending to the presbyters by Barnabas and Paul.[2] To this day splendid monuments of the Helen referred to by the historian are pointed out in the suburbs of what is now called Aelia.[3] She was said to have been Queen of Adiabene.[4]

Simon the Magus and Peter at Rome

13. As faith in our Saviour and Lord Jesus Christ was now spreading in all directions, the enemy of man's salvation, in a wily attempt to capture the imperial city in time, brought there Simon who was mentioned earlier,[5] and by lending his own weight to the man's artful impostures took possession

1. *Antiquities* xx, v, 1. Eusebius evidently did not realize that, as Fadus was not procurator till A.D. 44, the events recorded by Josephus could not have been known to Gamaliel a dozen years before. The difficulty has led many to believe that Luke put an impossible speech into Gamaliel's mouth and is therefore not to be trusted. But there is no evidence that the two writers are referring to the same Theudas; the two accounts bear little resemblance to each other; Luke expressly puts Theudas before Judas, who revolted as early as A.D. 6; and Josephus himself tells us that in the period before Judas there were innumerable disorders in Judaea, and that every rebel leader was at once created a king.

2. Acts xi. 29–30.
3. See p. 158.
4. Beyond the Tigris near the site of Nineveh.
5. p. 73.

of many people in Rome and led them astray. This we learn from Justin, an ornament of our Faith soon after the apostles' time. I shall state the essential facts about him in due course. In his first *Defence* of our doctrines to Antoninus he writes:

After the Lord was taken up into heaven the demons put forward a number of men who claimed to be gods. These not only escaped being persecuted by you, but were actually the objects of worship – for example Simon, a Samaritan from a village called Gittho, who in Claudius Caesar's time, thanks to the art of the demons who possessed him, worked wonders of magic, and in your imperial city of Rome was regarded as a god, and like a god was honoured by you with a statue in the River Tiber between the two bridges. It bears this inscription in Latin, SIMONI DEO SANCTO.[1] Almost all Samaritans, and a few from other nations too, acknowledge him as their principal god, and worship him. And a woman named Helen, who travelled around with him at that time and had previously lived in a brothel, they call the First Emanation from him.[2]

This is Justin's version, and it is supported by Irenaeus, who in Book I of his *Heresies Answered* gives a brief account of the man and his unholy, sordid teaching. To reproduce the latter in the present work would be superfluous: those who wish can learn all about the origins and lives of the heresiarchs who followed him, the bases of their false doctrines and the practices they introduced, for they are most carefully described in the work of Irenaeus mentioned above.

Simon, we are given to understand, was the prime author of every heresy. From his time to our own those who follow his lead, while pretending to accept that sober Christian philosophy which through purity of life has won universal fame, are as devoted as ever to the idolatrous superstition

1. i.e. 'to Simon the Holy God'.
2. *Defence* 1. 26: it is generally thought that Justin misread the inscription SEMONI SANCO DEO, Semo Sancus being a Sabine deity. But as he lived only six miles from Simon's village, his other statements may well be correct. It is, of course, not he but Eusebius who identifies this impostor with the Simon of Acts.

from which they seemed to have escaped: they prostrate themselves before pictures and images of Simon himself and his companion, the Helen already mentioned, and give themselves to worshipping them with incense, sacrifices, and libations. Their more secret rites, which they claim will so amaze a man when he first hears them that, in their official jargon, he will be wonderstruck, are indeed something to wonder at, brim-full of frenzy and lunacy, and of such a kind that not only can they not be put down in writing; they involve such appalling degradation, such unspeakable conduct, that no decent man would let a mention of them pass his lips. For whatever could be imagined more disgusting than the foulest crime known has been outstripped by the utterly revolting heresy of these men, who make sport of wretched women, burdened indeed with vices of every kind.[1]

14. Of such vices was Simon the father and contriver, raised up at that time by the evil power which hates all that is good and plots against the salvation of mankind, to be a great opponent of great men, our Saviour's inspired apostles. Nevertheless, divine and celestial grace worked with its ministers, by their advent and presence speedily extinguishing the flames of the Evil One before they could spread, and through them humbling and pulling down every lofty barrier raised against the knowledge of God.[2] Consequently, neither Simon nor any of his contemporaries managed to form an organized body in those apostolic days, for every attempt was defeated and overpowered by the light of the truth and by the divine Word Himself who had so recently shone from God on men, active in the world and immanent in His own apostles.

The impostor of whom we have been speaking, as though his mind's eye had been struck by a divine miraculous flash of light when earlier, in Judaea, his mischievous practices had

1. A reminiscence of 2 Tim. iii. 6.   2. 2 Cor. x. 5.

been exposed by the apostle Peter,[1] promptly undertook a very long journey overseas from east to west, and fled precipitately, thinking that only so could he live according to his inclinations. He arrived in Rome, where he was greatly helped by the power that awaited its opportunity there, and in a short time his efforts met with such success that the citizens actually set up a statue of him and honoured him as a god. However, this success of his was short-lived. Close on his heels, in the same reign of Claudius, the all-gracious and kindly providence of the universe brought to Rome to deal with this terrible threat to the world, the strong and great apostle, chosen for his merits to be spokesman for all the others, Peter himself. Clad in the divine armour,[2] like a noble captain of God, he brought the precious merchandise of the spiritual light from the East to those in the West, preaching the good news of light itself and the soul-saving word, the proclamation of the Kingdom of Heaven. 15. Thus, when the divine word had made its home among them, Simon's power was extinguished and destroyed at once with the man himself.

So brightly shone the light of true religion on the minds of Peter's hearers that, not satisfied with a single hearing or with the oral teaching of the divine message, they resorted to appeals of every kind to induce Mark (whose gospel we have), as he was a follower of Peter, to leave them in writing a summary of the instruction they had received by word of mouth, nor did they let him go till they had persuaded him, and thus became responsible for the writing of what is known as the Gospel according to Mark. It is said that, on learning by revelation of the spirit what had happened, the apostle was delighted at their enthusiasm and authorized the reading of the book in the churches. Clement quotes the story in *Outlines* Book VI, and his statement is confirmed by Bishop Papias of Hierapolis, who also points out that Mark is

---

1. Acts viii. 18–23: Samaria formed part of the Roman province of Judaea.
2. A loose reference to Eph. vi. 11.

mentioned by Peter in his first epistle, which he is said to have composed in Rome itself, as he himself indicates when he speaks of the city figuratively as Babylon:

> The church in Babylon, chosen like yourselves, sends you greeting, and so does my son Mark.[1]

16. Mark is said to have been the first man to set out for Egypt and preach there the gospel which he had himself written down, and the first to establish churches in Alexandria itself. So large was the body of believers, men and women alike, built up there at the first attempt, with an extremely severe rule of life, that Philo decided that he must record in writing their activities, gatherings, meals, and everything else about their way of living.

Philo's account of the Egyptian ascetics

17. It is also recorded that under Claudius Philo came to Rome to have conversations with Peter, then preaching to the people there. This would not be improbable, as the short work to which I am referring, and which he produced at a considerably later date, clearly contains the rules of the Church still observed in our own day. And again, when he describes the life of our ascetics with the greatest precision, it is plain enough that he not only knew but welcomed with whole-hearted approval the apostolic men of his day, who it seems were of Hebrew stock and therefore, in the Jewish manner, still retained most of their ancient customs. In the work that he entitled *The Contemplative Life, or The Suppliants*, he first assures us that he will add nothing that goes beyond the truth, nothing of his own invention, to the account he is about to give. Then he says that they are called *Therapeutae*

---

1. 1 Peter v. 13.

and their womenfolk *Therapeutrides,* and goes on to explain this title. It was conferred either because like doctors they rid the souls of those who come to them from moral sickness and so cure and heal[1] them, or in view of their pure and sincere service[2] and worship of God. Whether he invented this designation and applied it to them, fitting a suitable name to their mode of life, or whether they were actually called this from the very start, because the title Christian was not yet in general use, need not be discussed now.

This much is certain. He lays special emphasis on their renunciation of property, saying that when they embark on the philosophic life[3] they hand over their possessions to their relations, then, having renounced all worldly interests, they go outside the walls and make their homes on lonely farms and plantations well aware that association with men of different ideas is unprofitable and harmful. That, apparently, was the practice of the Christians of that time, who with eager and ardent faith disciplined themselves to emulate the prophetic way of life. Similarly, in the canonical Acts of the Apostles it is stated that all the disciples of the apostles sold their possessions and belongings and shared them out among the others in accordance with individual needs, so that no one was in want among them; all who were owners of land or houses, Scripture tells us, sold them and brought the price they fetched and laid it at the apostles' feet, so that it was distributed to everyone in accordance with individual needs.[4] Having testified to practices very similar to these, Philo goes on:

The community is to be found in many parts of the world, for it was right that what is perfectly good should be shared by both Greek and foreign lands. It is very strong in Egypt in each of the *nomes,* and especially in the Alexandrian area. The best men in each region set out as colonists for a highly suitable spot, regarding it as

1. Greek *therapeuo.*   2. Greek *therapeia.*   3. See p. 242 n.
4. Loosely quoted from Acts iv. 34–5.

the homeland of the *Therapeutae*. It is situated above Lake Mareotis[1]
on a low hill, very convenient in view of its security and the mildness
of the climate.

Next, after describing the character of their dwellings, he
has this to say about the churches in the area:

In every house there is a holy chamber called a sanctuary or
'monastery', where they celebrate in seclusion[2] the mysteries of the
sanctified life, bringing in nothing – drink, food, or anything else
required for bodily needs – but laws and inspired oracles spoken by
prophets, hymns, and everything else by which knowledge and true
religion are increased and perfected. ... The whole period from
dawn to dusk is given up to spiritual discipline.[3] They read the sacred
scriptures, and study their ancestral wisdom philosophically, allegoriz-
ing it, since they regard the literal sense as symbolic of a hidden reality
revealed in figures. They possess also short works by early writers,
the founders of their sect, who left many specimens of the allegorical
method, which they take as their models, following the system on
which their predecessors worked.

It seems likely that Philo wrote this after listening to their
exposition of the Holy Scriptures, and it is very probable
that what he calls short works by their early writers were the
gospels, the apostolic writings, and in all probability passages
interpreting the old prophets, such as are contained in the
Epistle to the Hebrews and several others of Paul's epistles.
He then goes on to write this about their composing new
psalms:

Thus they not only practise contemplation but also compose
songs and hymns to God in all kinds of metres and melodies, setting
them, as might be expected, to solemn measures.

A great many other points relevant to our subject are
discussed in the same book, but it seemed necessary to pick

---

1. Lake Mariut, adjoining Alexandria on the south.
2. 'Monastery' means a place of seclusion.
3. The word from which 'ascetic' is derived.

out those in which the characteristics of Church life are displayed. If anyone does not agree that what has been described is peculiar to the gospel way of life but thinks it applicable to other people too, he will surely be convinced by Philo's next paragraph, in which, if he is reasonable, he will find the evidence on this point beyond dispute:

Having first laid down self-control as a foundation for the soul, they build the other virtues on it. None of them would take food or drink before sundown, as they hold that philosophy deserves daylight but darkness is good enough for bodily needs. So to the one they assign the day, to the others a small part of the night. Some think of food only once in three days – those in whom a greater passion for knowledge is rooted; others so delight and luxuriate as they feast on the wisdom that richly and ungrudgingly supplies their doctrines that they hold out even for twice that time, and scarcely taste necessary food once in six days, having accustomed themselves to this.

These statements of Philo seem to me to refer plainly and unquestionably to members of our Church. But, if after this someone insists on denying it, he will surely abandon his scepticism and be convinced by still clearer evidences which cannot be found anywhere but in the religious practices of Christians who follow the gospel. For Philo states that among the people in question there are women also, most of them elderly spinsters

who have remained single, not of necessity, like some priestesses of pagan cults, but of their own free will, through their passionate craving for wisdom, with which they were so eager to live that they scorned bodily pleasures, and set their hearts not on mortal children but on immortal, which only the soul that loves God can bring into the world.

A little farther on he adds this, in his vivid way:

Their explanations of the sacred scriptures are expressed figuratively in allegories. For the whole Law seems to them to resemble a living being, which for body has the literal precepts, for soul the meaning that is hidden in the words out of sight. This community was the first to make such meaning the object of special investigation, the words providing a mirror in which thoughts of extraordinary beauty are revealed.

Need I add to this an account of their meetings, or of the segregation of men and women living in the same place, or of the regular spiritual discipline still practised among us, especially during the commemoration of our Saviour's Passion, when it is our habit to abstain from food, spend whole nights in prayer, and devote ourselves to the word of God? All this is described, in precise accordance with the practice observed by us and us alone to this day, in Philo's own writings. He describes the all-night vigils of the great festival, the spiritual discipline in which they are spent, the hymns that we always recite, and how while one man sings in regular rhythm the others listen silently and join in singing the refrains of the hymns; how on the appointed days they lie on straw mattresses on the ground and – as he expressly writes – absolutely refuse to touch wine or any flesh food, drinking nothing but water and seasoning their bread with salt and hyssop. He further writes about the comparative status of those entrusted with the ministries of the Church, from the diaconate to the highest and most important office, the episcopate. Anyone who is anxious to gain precise knowledge of these things can learn them from Philo's account: anyone can see that when he wrote it he had in mind the first preachers of the gospel teaching and the customs handed down by the apostles from the beginning.

Philo's extant works

18. A copious writer and a thinker of wide range, studying Holy Writ from a lofty and elevated viewpoint, Philo expounded the sacred books from many different angles. At

one stage he carried out his detailed examination of Genesis in systematic order, in the books which he entitled *Allegories of the Sacred Laws*. At another he carefully arranged under chapter headings the difficulties in the Scriptures, stating them and offering his solutions in the books to which he gave the titles of *Questions and Answers in Genesis* and *Questions and Answers in Exodus*. In addition to these, there are authoritative works by him on special problems, e.g. two on *Farming*, two on *Drunkenness*, and others with various appropriate titles such as *What the Sober Mind Desires and Detests; The Confounding of Tongues; Flight and Discovery; Study Groups; Who Inherits the Treasures of God? or The Division into Equivalents and Opposites;* and again, *The Three Cardinal Virtues Propounded by Moses*. In addition to these, there is his *New Names and Why They were Given*, in which he states that he also composed *Covenants* Books I and II. There are also works of his on *Emigration; Life of a Wise Man Perfected in Righteousness, or Unwritten Laws; Giants, or The Immutability of the Godhead;* and *The Mosaic Conviction that Dreams are Sent from God*, Books I–V.

These are the books that have come into my hands dealing with Genesis. On Exodus I am acquainted with *Questions and Answers* Books I–V; *The Tabernacle; The Ten Commandments; Laws Classified under the Appropriate Headings of the Decalogue* Books I–IV; *Sacrificial Animals and Varieties of Sacrifice;* and *How the Law Rewards Virtue and Punishes and Denounces Vice*. His extant writings also include single volumes, e.g. *The Statesman*; the essay on *Providence*; and another work, *The Jews*; also *Alexander, or Rational Behaviour in Irrational Animals*. Nor must we forget *Every Bad Man is a Slave*, followed by *Every Good Man is Free*. Then came *The Contemplative Life, or Suppliants*, from which I have quoted passages describing life in the apostolic community. *Interpretations of Hebrew Names in the Law and the Prophets* is also said to be his work.

In Gaius's time he came to Rome and wrote an account of that monarch's revolting conduct, with characteristic irony entitling it *Virtue*. It is stated that when Claudius came to the throne Philo read this work from end to end at a full meeting of the Roman senate, and that his writings were so greatly admired that they were honoured with a place in libraries.

At this time, while Paul was completing his journey from Jerusalem by a roundabout route as far as Illyricum,[1] Claudius expelled the Jews from Rome, and Aquila and Priscilla with the other Jews left Rome and sailed to Asia Minor, where they stayed with Paul the Apostle, who was busy strengthening the foundations of the churches, foundations laid by himself not long before. Our source of information is the inspired narrative of the Acts.[2]

Disaster in Jerusalem at the Passover, and events there in Nero's reign

19. While Claudius was still on the throne, during the Passover Feast so riotous a tumult broke out in Jerusalem that of those Jews alone who were forcibly crushed together round the temple exits 30,000 trampled each other to death.[3] Thus the Feast ended in distress to the whole nation and bereavement to every household. Josephus goes on to say that Claudius made Agrippa the son of Agrippa king of the Jews,[4] and sent Felix as procurator of the whole country, including Samaria, Galilee, and the district known as Peraea in

1. Rom. xv. 9; see also Acts xx. 2.
2. See Acts xviii. 2, 18–19, 23; xix. 1–7; of which Eusebius gives a garbled summary. Aquila and Priscilla had gone from Rome to Corinth, where Paul stayed with them. Later they accompanied him to Ephesus; his visit to Illyricum was probably later still.
3. Loosely quoted from *Jewish War*, p. 132.
4. Josephus does not mention the Jews. For Agrippa II, see Acts xxv–xxvi; for Felix, Acts xxiii–xxiv.

addition. He himself, having ruled the empire for thirteen years and eight months, died, leaving his throne to Nero.[1]

20. In Nero's reign, when Felix was procurator of Judaea, Josephus relates the quarrel between the priests, writing as follows in *Antiquities* Book xx:

> A quarrel broke out between the chief priests on the one side and the priests and leaders of the Jerusalem populace on the other. Each of them recruited a band of the most reckless revolutionaries and put himself at their head, and when collisions occurred they greeted each other with abuse and stone-throwing. There was not a single person to reprimand them; the scandal went on with impunity, as though in a city without a government. Such impudence and audacity possessed the chief priests that they actually sent slaves to the thresh-ing-floors to seize the tithes that were the priests' by right, so that destitute priests could be seen perishing of want. So completely was justice obliterated by the violence of the warring parties.[2]

Josephus also records that at the same period a type of bandits sprang up in Jerusalem. These, he says, in broad daylight and in the middle of the city murdered those who met them. Their favourite trick was to mingle with festival crowds, concealing under their garments small daggers with which they stabbed their opponents. When their victims fell the assassins melted into the indignant crowd, and through their plausibility entirely defied detection. First to have his throat cut by them was Jonathan the high priest, and after him many were murdered every day. More terrible than the crimes themselves was the fear they aroused, every man, as in war, hourly expecting death.[3]

21. A little later he goes on:

> A greater blow than this was inflicted on the Jews by the Egyptian false prophet. Arriving in the country this man, a fraud who posed

1. Loosely quoted from *Jewish War*, p. 134.
2. *Antiquities* xx, viii, 8.
3. *Jewish War*, p. 135. Josephus calls these assassins by the Latin name *sicarii*, employed by Luke in Acts xxi. 38, quoted below.

as a seer, collected about 30,000 dupes,[1] led them round by the wild
country to the Mount of Olives, and from there was ready to force
an entry into Jerusalem, overwhelm the Roman garrison, and seize
supreme power, with his fellow-raiders as bodyguard. But Felix
anticipated his attempt by meeting him with the Roman heavy
infantry, the whole population rallying to the defence, so that when
the clash occurred the Egyptian fled with a handful of men and
most of his followers were killed or captured.[2]

This passage comes from Book 11 of the *Histories*.[3] It is
worth while to note what is stated about the Egyptian there
and in the Acts of the Apostles, where in the time of Felix
the military tribune at Jerusalem said to Paul, when the Jewish
mob was rioting against him: 'Then you're not the Egyptian
who a little while back started a revolt and led the 4,000
Assassins out in the wilds?'[4]

Paul sent as a prisoner to Rome and there acquitted

22. As successor to Felix, Nero sent Festus. It was in his time
that Paul was put on trial, and then conveyed in fetters to
Rome.[5] With him went Aristarchus, to whom somewhere in
the epistles he naturally refers as a fellow-prisoner.[6] And Luke,
who committed to writing the Acts of the Apostles, ended his
story at this point, after informing us that Paul spent two
complete years at Rome under no restraint and preached the
word of God without hindrance. There is evidence that,
having then been brought to trial, the apostle again set out
on the ministry of preaching, and having appeared a second
time in the same city found fulfilment in his martyrdom. In
the course of this imprisonment he composed the second
Epistle to Timothy, referring both to his earlier trial and to

1. Note the figure given by Luke in the next paragraph.
2. *Jewish War*, p. 135.
3. Josephus does not use this title.   4. Acts xxi. 38.
5. See Acts xxiv. 27 to xxv. 27.   6. Col. iv. 10.

his impending fulfilment.[1] Listen to his testimony on this point:

At my first trial nobody supported me: they all left me to my fate – may God forgive them! But the Lord stood by me and gave me strength, that through me the message might be fully proclaimed in the hearing of the whole pagan world. Thus I was rescued out of the lion's mouth.[2]

This passage proves beyond question that on the first occasion, in order that the message proclaimed through him might be fully preached, he was rescued out of the lion's mouth, the reference being apparently to Nero, because of his bestial cruelty.[3] He does not go on to add anything like 'he *will* rescue me out of the lion's mouth', for he saw by the Spirit that his death was imminent. And so after the words 'and I was rescued out of the lion's mouth' he goes on to say 'The Lord will rescue me from every evil attempt and keep me safe for His heavenly kingdom',[4] indicating his forthcoming martyrdom. This he foretells more clearly still in the same letter, when he says: 'For I am already being offered as a sacrifice, and the time for my departure has come.'[5] In this second Epistle to Timothy he remarks that only Luke is with him as he writes, and at his first trial not even he: presumably that is why Luke concluded the Acts of the Apostles at that point, having traced the course of events throughout the time he was with Paul. I have said this to show that it was not during the stay in Rome described by Luke that Paul's martyrdom was accomplished. The probability is that since at first Nero's disposition was

1. There is no satisfactory English equivalent for the word which Eusebius uses here and constantly applies to the martyrs. It seems to combine all the meanings given to it in various passages of the English N.T., viz. *'fulfil'*, *'accomplish'*, *'perfect'*, *'finish'*, *'consecrate'*.

2. 2 Tim. iv. 16–17.

3. More probably Paul is speaking of danger in general, like the Psalmist whom he is quoting (Ps. xxii. 21).

4. 2 Tim. iv. 18.   5. 2 Tim. iv. 6.

milder,[1] it was easier for Paul's defence of the Faith to be received, but that when he had gone on to commit abominable crimes, above all else he launched his attack on the apostles.

The martyrdom of James 'the Lord's brother'

23. When Paul appealed to Caesar and was sent to Rome by Festus, the Jews were disappointed of the hope in which they had devised their plot against him and turned their attention to James the Lord's brother, who had been elected by the apostles to the episcopal throne at Jerusalem. This is the crime that they committed against him. They brought him into their midst and in the presence of the whole populace demanded a denial of his belief in Christ. But when, contrary to all expectation, he spoke as he liked and showed undreamt-of fearlessness in the face of the enormous throng, declaring that our Saviour and Lord, Jesus, was the Son of God, they could not endure his testimony any longer, since he was universally regarded as the most righteous of men because of the heights of philosophy and religion which he scaled in his life. So they killed him, seizing the opportunity for getting their own way provided by the absence of a government, for at that very time Festus had died in Judaea, leaving the province without governor or procurator.[2] How James died has already[3] been shown by the words quoted from Clement, who tells us that he was thrown from the parapet and clubbed to death. But the most detailed account of him is given by Hegesippus, who belonged to the first generation after the apostles.[4] In his fifth book he writes:

Control of the Church passed[5] to the apostles, together with the Lord's brother James, whom everyone from the Lord's time till our

1. Nero's tyranny did not begin till A.D. 62, when Paul's first imprisonment was over.

2. Until late in A.D. 62.   3. p. 72.

4. He was born about the time that John died.

5. Presumably from Christ Himself.

own has called the Righteous,[1] for there were many Jameses, but this one was holy from his birth; he drank no wine or intoxicating liquor and ate no animal food; no razor came near his head;[2] he did not smear himself with oil, and took no baths.[3] He alone was permitted to enter the Holy Place, for his garments were not of wool but of linen.[4] He used to enter the Sanctuary[5] alone, and was often found on his knees beseeching forgiveness for the people, so that his knees grew hard like a camel's from his continually bending them in worship of God and beseeching forgiveness for the people. Because of his unsurpassable righteousness he was called the Righteous and *Oblias*[6] – in our own language 'Bulwark of the People, and Righteousness' – fulfilling the declarations of the prophets regarding him.[7]

Representatives of the seven popular sects already described by me asked him what was meant by 'the door of Jesus', and he replied that Jesus was the Saviour.[8] Some of them came to believe that Jesus was the Christ: the sects mentioned above did not believe either in a resurrection or in One who is coming to give every man what his deeds deserve,[9] but those who did come to believe did so because of James. Since therefore many even of the ruling class believed,[10] there was an uproar among the Jews and Scribes and Pharisees, who said there was a danger that the entire people would expect Jesus as the Christ. So they collected and said to James: 'Be good enough to restrain the people, for they have gone astray after Jesus in the belief that he is the Christ. Be good enough to make the facts about Jesus

1. Whenever the word 'righteous' occurs it must be remembered that to the Jew righteousness was a compound of morality, justice, and strict observance of the Law. It was the third of these that won James his title; his attitude to the Law was very different from Paul's; see Gal. i. 1–21.

2. See Num. iv. 1–5, where the Nazirite rules are laid down; see also Luke i. 15.

3. These two forms of self-denial are nowhere enjoined in Holy Writ.

4. i.e. he was authorized to wear priestly robes.

5. The Sanctuary, comprising Holy Place and Holy of Holies, was an oblong building replacing the original temple of Solomon. It stood within a series of courts, with which it formed the temple. The Sanctuary might only be entered by priests of Aaron's family, and, if we may trust Hegesippus, by Nazirites granted priestly privileges.

6. A Hebrew or Aramaic word, as yet unexplained.

7. Reference unknown.   8. John x. 9.

9. Rev. xxii. 12.   10. John xii. 42.

clear to all who come for the Passover Day. We all accept what you say: we can vouch for it, and so can all the people, that you are a righteous man and take no one at his face value.[1] So make it clear to the crowd that they must not go astray as regards Jesus: the whole people and all of us accept what you say. So take your stand on the Temple parapet, so that from that height you may be easily seen, and your words audible to the whole people. For because of the Passover all the tribes have forgathered, and the Gentiles too.'

So the Scribes and Pharisees made James stand on the Sanctuary parapet and shouted to him: 'Righteous one, whose word we are all obliged to accept, the people are going astray after Jesus who was crucified; so tell us what is meant by "the door of Jesus".' He replied as loudly as he could: 'Why do you question me about the Son of Man? I tell you, He is sitting in heaven at the right hand of the Great Power, and He will come on the clouds of heaven.'[2] Many were convinced, and gloried in James's testimony, crying: 'Hosanna to the Son of David!' Then again the Scribes and Pharisees said to each other: 'We made a bad mistake in affording such testimony to Jesus. We had better go up and throw him down, so that they will be frightened and not believe him.' 'Ho, ho!' they called out, 'even the Righteous one has gone astray!' – fulfilling the prophecy of Isaiah:

'Let us remove the Righteous one, for he is unprofitable to us.'
Therefore they shall eat the fruit of their works.[3]

So they went up and threw down the Righteous one. Then they said to each other 'Let us stone James the Righteous', and began to stone him, as in spite of his fall he was still alive. But he turned and knelt, uttering the words: 'I beseech Thee, Lord God and Father, forgive them; they do not know what they are doing.'[4] While they

---

1. See Luke xx. 21; not a quotation but a cliché.

2. Matt. xxvi. 64. The name 'The Son of Man' suggests that James was thinking of Stephen's words in Acts vii. 56, the only recorded case of our Lord's favourite title for Himself being used by anyone else. As this title implied that Jesus, crucified like a criminal, was the final judge of all mankind foretold by Daniel and Enoch, when used by Stephen and James it was as deliberately provocative as when hurled at Caiaphas by our Lord Himself.

3. Is. iii. 10.

4. Luke xxiii. 34: Stephen had echoed his Master's forgiving spirit; James His very words.

pelted him with stones, one of the descendants of Rechab the son of Rachabim[1] – the priestly family to which Jeremiah the Prophet bore witness,[2] called out: 'Stop! what are you doing? the Righteous one is praying for you.' Then one of them, a fuller, took the club which he used to beat out the clothes, and brought it down on the head of the Righteous one. Such was his martyrdom. He was buried on the spot, by the Sanctuary, and his headstone is still there by the Sanctuary. He has proved a true witness to Jews and Gentiles alike that Jesus is the Christ.

Immediately after this Vespasian began to besiege them.[3]

This is the full account which, in agreement with Clement, is given by Hegesippus. So remarkable a person must James have been, so universally esteemed for righteousness, that even the more intelligent Jews felt that this was why his martyrdom was immediately followed by the siege of Jerusalem, which happened to them for no other reason than the wicked crime of which he had been the victim. And indeed Josephus did not hesitate to write this down in so many words:

These things happened to the Jews in requital for James the Righteous, who was a brother of Jesus known as Christ, for though he was the most righteous of men, the Jews put him to death.[4]

Josephus has also recounted his death in *Antiquities* Book xx:

Caesar sent Albinus to Judaea as procurator, when he was informed of the death of Festus. But the younger Ananus, who as I said had received the high priesthood, was headstrong in character and

1. Not really a person, but the Rechabites, a foreign tribe which had intermarried with the Levites and so acquired priestly status.

2. Jer. xxxv.

3. As Vespasian's invasion began in A.D. 67, this sentence has been thought to indicate a later date for James's martyrdom than A.D. 62, the date implied by Josephus, who was in Palestine at the time. But it is not necessary to interpret so strictly the word 'immediately'as used by a second-century writer, or fair to accuse Eusebius of inconsistency because he reproduces both Josephus and Hegesippus.

4. Not in our MSS. of Josephus but quoted by Origen too.

audacious in the extreme. He belonged to the sect of the Sadducees, who in judging offenders are cruel beyond any of the Jews, as I have already made clear. Being a man of this kind, Ananus thought that he had a convenient opportunity, as Festus was dead and Albinus still on the way. So he assembled a council of judges and brought before it James, the brother of Jesus, known as Christ, and several others, on a charge of breaking the law, and handed them over to be stoned. But those who were considered the most fair-minded people in the City, and strict in their observance of the Law, were most indignant at this, and sent secretly to the king imploring him to write to Ananus to stop behaving in this way: his conduct had been wrong from the first. Some of them, too, waylaid Albinus on the road from Alexandria, and explained that it was illegal for Ananus to assemble a council without his authority. Convinced by their arguments, Albinus wrote an angry letter to Ananus, threatening to punish him; in consequence King Agrippa deprived him of the high priesthood, which he had held for three months only, and appointed Jeshua son of Dammaeus.[1]

Such is the story of James, to whom is attributed the first of the 'general' epistles. Admittedly its authenticity is doubted, since few early writers refer to it, any more than to 'Jude's', which is also one of the seven called general. But the fact remains that these two, like the others, have been regularly used in very many churches.[2]

Annianus bishop of Alexandria

24. In the eighth year of Nero's reign Annianus was the first after Mark the evangelist to take charge of the see of Alexandria.[3]

---

1. *Antiquities* xx, ix. 1.

2. There is no reason to doubt that the two epistles were written by James and Jude, 'brothers' of the Lord. In calling James's the first Eusebius is referring to its position in the canon, but it was also probably the first to be written, and possibly the first of all N.T. books.

3. Eusebius here implies that Mark died before Peter and Paul, but in Book v (p. 198) he quotes Irenaeus as saying that he wrote his gospel after Peter's death.

The Neronian persecution, in which Paul and Peter died

25. When Nero's power was now firmly established he gave himself up to unholy practices and took up arms against the God of the universe. To describe the monster of depravity that he became lies outside the scope of the present work. Many writers have recorded the facts about him in minute detail, enabling anyone who wishes to get a complete picture of his perverse and extraordinary madness, which led him to the senseless destruction of innumerable lives, and drove him in the end to such a lust for blood that he did not spare even his nearest and dearest but employed a variety of methods to do away with mother, brothers, and wife alike, to say nothing of countless other members of his family, as if they were personal and public enemies. All this left one crime still to be added to his account – he was the first of the emperors to be the declared enemy of the worship of Almighty God. To this the Roman Tertullian refers in the following terms:

Study your records: there you will find that Nero was the first to persecute this teaching when, after subjugating the entire East, in Rome especially he treated everyone with savagery.[1] That such a man was author of our chastisement fills us with pride. For anyone who knows him can understand that anything not supremely good would never have been condemned by Nero.

So it came about that this man, the first to be heralded as a conspicuous fighter against God, was led on to murder the apostles. It is recorded that in his reign Paul was beheaded in Rome itself, and that Peter likewise was crucified, and the record is confirmed by the fact that the cemeteries there are still called by the names of Peter and Paul, and equally so by a churchman named Gaius, who was living while Zephyrinus was Bishop of Rome. In his published *Dialogue* with Proclus,

1. In A.D. 64 the Parthians were defeated, Rome was burnt, and the Christians were persecuted.

the leader of the Phrygian heretics,[1] Gaius has this to say about the places where the mortal remains of the two apostles have been reverently laid:

> I can point out the monuments of the victorious apostles. If you will go as far as the Vatican or the Ostian Way, you will find the monuments of those who founded this church.

That they were both martyred at the same time Bishop Dionysius of Corinth informs us in a letter written to the Romans:

> In this way by your impressive admonition you have bound together all that has grown from the seed which Peter and Paul sowed in Romans and Corinthians alike. For both of them sowed in our Corinth[2] and taught us jointly: in Italy too they taught jointly in the same city, and were martyred at the same time.[3]

These evidences make the truth of my account still more certain.

Beginning of the last Jewish war against Rome

26. In the course of his very long account of the catastrophe that overwhelmed the entire Jewish nation Josephus expressly states that, in addition to very many others, innumerable Jews in high positions were flogged with scourges and crucified in Jerusalem itself by Florus,[4] and that he was procurator of Judaea at the time when the beginning of the war blazed up in the twelfth year of Nero's reign.[5] Then he says that throughout Palestine the revolt of the Jews was followed by hopeless confusion, and that on every side the members of

---

1. Montanists.
2. 1 Cor. i. 12.
3. Letter to Soter, written c. A.D. 170.
4. *Jewish War*, p. 140; Florus was procurator A.D. 64–6.
5. *Jewish War*, p. 138, Nero's twelfth year was A.D. 66.

the nation were mercilessly destroyed, as if they were enemies, by the inhabitants of the various cities:

The cities could be seen full of unburied corpses, the dead bodies of the aged flung down alongside those of infants, women without a rag to conceal their nakedness, and the whole province full of indescribable horrors. Even worse than the atrocities continually committed were the threats of terrors to come.[1]

Such is the account of Josephus, and such was the plight of the Jews.

1. *Jewish War*, p. 156.

Book 3

VESPASIAN TO TRAJAN: THE DISTRIBUTION AND
WRITINGS OF THE APOSTLES AND THEIR
SUCCESSORS: ENEMIES WITHIN THE
CHURCH: PERSECUTIONS

*Countries evangelized by the apostles: the first Bishop of Rome:
apostolic epistles: the apostles' first successors*

1. Such then was the plight of the Jews. Meanwhile the
holy apostles and disciples of our Saviour were scattered
over the whole world. Thomas, tradition tells us, was chosen
for Parthia, Andrew for Scythia, John for Asia, where he
remained till his death at Ephesus. Peter seems to have
preached in Pontus, Galatia and Bithynia, Cappadocia and
Asia, to the Jews of the Dispersion.[1] Finally, he came to Rome
where he was crucified, head downwards at his own request.
What need be said of Paul, who from Jerusalem as far as
Illyricum preached in all its fulness the gospel of Christ,[2]
and later was martyred in Rome under Nero? This is exactly
what Origen tells us in Volume III of his *Commentary on
Genesis*.

2. After the martyrdom of Paul and Peter[3] the first man to
be appointed Bishop of Rome was Linus. He is mentioned

1. Peter i. 1: Peter does not say that he had preached in these areas; the Dispersion means Jews outside Palestine.
2. Romans xv. 19.
3. Believing that Paul died before Peter (pp. 104, 110), Eusebius puts Paul first whenever he has their deaths in mind. But we find Peter put first in quotations from Dionysius and Irenaeus, who are referring to his arrival in Rome, which they believed to be prior to Paul's, as did Eusebius (p. 88).

by Paul when writing to Timothy from Rome, in the saluta-
tion at the end of the epistle.[1]

3. Of Peter one epistle, known as his first, is accepted, and
this the early fathers quoted freely, as undoubtedly genuine,
in their own writings. But the second Petrine epistle we
have been taught to regard as uncanonical; many, however,
have thought it valuable and have honoured it with a place
among the other Scriptures. On the other hand, in the case
of the 'Acts' attributed to him, the 'Gospel' that bears his
name, the 'Preaching' called his, and the so-called 'Revelation', we have no reason at all to include these among the
traditional Catholic Scriptures, for neither in early days nor
in our own has any Church writer made use of their testimony.[2] In the course of my narrative I shall take care to
indicate in each period which of the Church historians of the
time used the various disputed books; their comments on the
canonical and recognized Scriptures; and their remarks about
the other sort.

These then are the works attributed to Peter, of which I
have recognized only one epistle as authentic and accepted
by the early fathers. Paul on the other hand was obviously
and unmistakably the author of the fourteen epistles, but
we must not shut our eyes to the fact that some authorities
have rejected the Epistle to the Hebrews, pointing out that
the Roman Church denies that it is the work of Paul: what
our predecessors have said about it I will quote at the proper
time. As for the 'Acts' attributed to him, no one has ever
suggested to me that they are genuine.

As the same apostle, in the salutations that conclude the
Epistle to the Romans, has referred among others to Hermas,
the reputed author of the 'Shepherd',[3] it is to be noted that

1. 2 Tim. iv. 21.   2. Eusebius is in error here.
3. The 'Shepherd' finds a place in Codex Sinaiticus, one of the great fourth-
century MSS.

this, too, has been rejected by some authorities and therefore cannot be placed among the accepted books. Others, however, have judged it indispensable, especially to those in need of elementary instruction. Hence we know that it has been used before now in public worship, and some of the earliest writers made use of it, as I have discovered.

4. That by his preaching to the Gentiles Paul had laid the foundations of the churches from Jerusalem by a round-about route as far as Illyricum is obvious from his own words and from Luke's account in the Acts. Similarly, from Peter's language we can gather the names of the provinces in which he preached the gospel of Christ to the circumcised, proclaiming the message of the New Covenant. It is clearly stated in the epistle which, as I said, is accepted as his, in which he writes to the Hebrews of the Dispersion in Pontus and Galatia, Cappadocia, Asia, and Bithynia. But how many of them and which ones became genuine enthusiasts, and were judged fit to shepherd the churches founded by the apostles, is not easy to determine, except for those whose names can be extracted from the statements of Paul. For he had innumerable fellow-workers or – as he himself called them – fellow-soldiers.[1] Most of these he has honoured with an imperishable memory, paying them constant tribute in his own letters. Again Luke in the Acts, in listing Paul's disciples, mentions them by name. We may instance Timothy, stated to have been the first bishop appointed to the see of Ephesus, as was Titus to the churches of Crete.

Luke, by birth an Antiochene and by profession a physician, was for long periods a companion of Paul and was closely associated with the other apostles as well. So he has left us examples of the art of healing souls which he learnt from them in two divinely inspired books, the Gospel and the Acts of the Apostles. The former, he declares, he wrote in accordance

---

1. Phil. ii. 25, Philem. 2.

with the information he received from those who from the
first had been eyewitnesses and ministers of the word, information which, he adds, he had followed in its entirety from the
first.[1] The latter he composed not this time from hearsay but
from the evidence of his own eyes.[2] It is actually suggested
that Paul was in the habit of referring to Luke's gospel
whenever he said, as if writing of some Gospel of his own:
'According to my gospel.'[3]

Of his other followers, Paul informs us that Crescens had
set out for Gaul.[4] Linus, who is mentioned in the Second
Epistle to Timothy as being with Paul in Rome, as stated
above was the first after Peter to be appointed Bishop of
Rome.[5] Clement again, who became the third Bishop of
Rome, was, as the Apostle himself testifies, Paul's fellow-
worker and fellow-combatant.[6] Besides these there was the
Areopagite, Dionysius by name, who was, as Luke related
in the Acts, the first convert after Paul's address to the
Athenians in the Areopagus.[7] He became the first Bishop of
Athens, a fact recorded by a very early writer, another
Dionysius, pastor of the see of Corinth. As we go on our way
I shall take the opportunity to set out the details of the
chronological sequence from the apostles. For the moment I
had better proceed to the next stage in the story.

The final siege of the Jews after Christ: the crushing weight
of famine

5. When Nero had been master of the empire for thirteen
years, the business of Galba and Otho occupied a year and

1. Luke i. 2–3.   2. Certainly true of the 'we' passages at least.
3. Rom. ii. 16, xvi. 25; 2 Tim. ii. 8.

4. 2 Tim. iv. 10, where our oldest M S. agrees with Eusebius that Paul wrote
'Gaul', not 'Galatia'.

5. The mention of Peter without Paul clearly implies that he outlived his
fellow-apostle.

6. Phil. iv. 3, where the translation should run: 'They were fellow-com-
batants with me in the gospel, with Clement also.'   7. Acts xvii. 34.

a half; and then Vespasian, after his dazzling success in the campaigns against the Jews, was proclaimed emperor while still in Judaea, after being hailed as *Imperator* by the armies there. He at once set out for Rome, entrusting the war against the Jews to his son Titus.[1]

After the Ascension of our Saviour, the Jews had followed up their crime against Him by devising plot after plot against His disciples. First they stoned Stephen to death; then James the son of Zebedee and brother of John was beheaded; and finally James, the first after our Saviour's Ascension to be raised to the bishop's throne there, lost his life in the way described, while the remaining apostles, in constant danger from murderous plots, were driven out of Judaea. But to teach their message they travelled into every land in the power of Christ, who had said to them: 'Go and make disciples of all the nations in my name.'[2] Furthermore, the members of the Jerusalem church, by means of an oracle given by revelation to acceptable persons there, were ordered to leave the City before the war began and settle in a town in Peraea called Pella. To Pella those who believed in Christ migrated from Jerusalem; and as if holy men had utterly abandoned the royal metropolis of the Jews and the entire Jewish land, the judgement of God at last overtook them for their abominable crimes against Christ and His apostles, completely blotting out that wicked generation from among men.

The calamities which at that time overwhelmed the whole nation in every part of the world; the process by which the inhabitants of Judaea were driven to the limits of disaster; the thousands and thousands of men of every age who together with women and children perished by the sword, by starvation, and by countless other forms of death; the number

1. Eusebius omits Vitellius, who reigned eight months, and Vespasian's visit to Alexandria, where he stayed till Rome had been won for him.

2. Matt. xxviii. 19, in a simpler, perhaps a more primitive form.

of Jewish cities besieged and the horrors they endured –
especially the terrible and worse than terrible sights that met
the eyes of those who sought refuge in Jerusalem itself as an
impregnable fortress; the character of the whole war and the
detailed events at all its stages; the last scene of all when the
Abomination of Desolation announced by the prophets was
set up in the very Temple of God, once world-renowned,
when it underwent utter destruction and final dissolution by
fire – all this anyone who wishes can gather in precise detail
from the pages of Josephus's history.[1] I must draw particular
attention to his statement that the people who flocked
together from all Judaea at the time of the Passover Feast and –
to use his own words – were shut up in Jerusalem as if in a
prison, totalled nearly three million.[2] It was indeed proper
that in the very week in which they had brought the Saviour
and Benefactor of mankind, God's Christ, to His Passion,
they should be shut up as if in a prison and suffer the destruction that came upon them by the judgement of God.

Passing over the details of the successive disasters that
befell them from the sword and in other ways, I think it
necessary to mention only the miseries they suffered from
starvation, so that readers of this book may have some knowledge at least of how their crime against the Christ of God
a very little time later brought on them God's vengeance.

6. Come then, pick up once more Book v of Josephus's
Histories, and go through the tragic story of what then
happened.

For the wealthy it was just as dangerous to stay in the city as to
leave it, for on the pretext that he was a deserter many a man was
killed for the sake of his money. As the famine grew worse, the
frenzy of the partisans increased with it, and every day these two
terrors strengthened their grip. For as nowhere was there corn to be
seen, men broke into the houses and ransacked them. If they found

1. *Jewish War*, pp. 321–6.   2. *Jewish War*, p. 337.

some, they maltreated the occupants for saying there was none; if they did not, they suspected them of having hidden it more carefully, and tortured them. Proof that they had or had not food was provided by the appearance of the unhappy wretches. If they still had flesh on their bones, they were deemed to have plenty of stores; if they were already reduced to skeletons they were passed over, for it seemed pointless to dispatch those who were certain to die of starvation before long. Many secretly exchanged their possessions for a measure of corn – wheat if they happened to be rich, barley if they were poor. Then they shut themselves up in the darkest corners of their houses, where some through extreme hunger ate their grain as it was, and others made bread, necessity and fear being the only guides. Nowhere was a table laid – they snatched the food from the fire while still uncooked, and ate like wolves.

The sight of such misery would have brought tears to the eyes, for while the strong had more than enough, the weak were in desperate straits. All human feelings, alas, yield to hunger, of which decency is always the first victim; for when hunger reigns, restraint is abandoned. Thus it was that wives robbed their husbands, children their fathers, and – most horrible of all – mothers their babes, snatching the food out of their very mouths; and when their dearest ones were dying in their arms, they did not hesitate to deprive them of the morsels that might have kept them alive. This way of satisfying their hunger did not go unnoticed: everywhere the partisans were ready to swoop even on such pickings. Wherever they saw a locked door, they concluded that those within were having a meal, and instantly bursting the door open, they rushed in and hardly stopped short of squeezing their throats to force out the morsels of food. They beat old men who held on to their crusts, and tore the hair of women who hid what was in their hands. They showed no pity for grey hairs or helpless babyhood, but picked up the children as they clung to their precious scraps and dashed them on the floor. If anyone anticipated their entry by gulping down what they hoped to seize, they felt themselves defrauded and retaliated with worse savagery still.

Terrible were the methods of torture they devised in their quest for food. They stuffed bitter vetch up the genital passages of their victims, and drove sharp stakes into their seats. Torments horrible

even to think about they inflicted on people, to make them admit
possession of one loaf or reveal the hiding-place of a single handful of
barley. It was not that the tormentors were hungry – their actions
would have been less barbarous had they sprung from necessity – but
rather they were keeping their passions exercised, and laying in
stores for use in the coming days. Again, when men had crawled
out in the night as far as the Roman guardposts to collect wild
plants and herbs, just when they thought they had got safely away
from the enemy lines these marauders met them and snatched their
treasures from them. Piteous entreaties and appeals to the awful
Name of God could not secure the return of even a fraction of what
they had collected at such risk: they were lucky to be only robbed,
and not killed as well. . . .

The Jews, unable now to leave the city, were deprived of all hope
of survival. The famine became more intense, and devoured whole
houses and families. The roofs were covered with women and
infants too weak to stand, the streets full of old men already dead.
Young men and boys, swollen with hunger, haunted the squares like
ghosts and fell wherever faintness overcame them. To bury their
kinsfolk was beyond the strength of the sick, and those who were fit
shirked the task because of the number of the dead and uncertainty
about their own fate; for many while burying others fell dead themselves, and many set out for their graves before their hour struck.
In their misery no weeping or lamentation was heard; hunger stifled
emotion; with dry eyes those who were slow to die watched those
whose end came sooner. Deep silence enfolded the city, and a darkness burdened with death. Worse still were the bandits, who broke
like tomb-robbers into the houses of the dead and stripped the bodies,
snatching off their wrappings, then came out laughing. They tried
the points of their swords on the corpses, and even transfixed some of
those who lay helpless but still alive, to test the steel. But if any begged
for a sword-thrust to end their sufferings, they contemptuously left
them to die of hunger. Everyone as he breathed his last fixed his
eyes on the Temple, turning his back on the partisans he was leaving
alive. The latter at first ordered the dead to be buried at public
expense, as they could not bear the stench; later, when this proved
impossible, they threw them from the walls into the valleys. When
in the course of his rounds Titus saw them choked with dead, and a

putrid stream trickling from under the decomposing bodies, he groaned, and uplifting his hands called God to witness that this was not his doing. . . .

I cannot refrain from saying what my feelings dictate. I think that if the Romans had delayed their attack on these sacrilegious ruffians, either the ground would have opened and swallowed up the city, or a flood would have overwhelmed it, or lightning would have destroyed it like Sodom. For it produced a generation far more godless than those who perished thus, a generation whose mad folly involved the nation in ruin.[1]

In Book VI he writes:

In the city famine raged, its victims dropping dead in countless numbers, and the horrors were unspeakable. In every home, if the shadow of something to eat was anywhere detected, war broke out and the best of friends came to grips with each other, snatching away the wretchedest means of support. Not even the dying were believed to be in want; at their last gasp they were searched by the bandits, in case some of them had food inside their clothes and were feigning death. Open-mouthed with hunger like mad dogs, the desperadoes stumbled and staggered along, hammering at the doors like drunken men, and in their helpless state breaking into the same houses two or three times in a single hour. Necessity made them put their teeth in everything; things not even the filthiest of dumb animals would look at, they picked up and brought themselves to swallow. In the end they actually devoured belts and shoes, and stripped off the leather from their shields and chewed it. Some tried to live on scraps of old hay, for there were people who collected the stalks and sold a tiny bunch for fifteen shillings!

But why should I speak of the inanimate things that hunger made them shameless enough to eat? I am now going to relate a deed for which there is no parallel in the annals of Greece or any other country, a deed horrible to speak of and incredible to hear. For myself I am so anxious that future ages should not suspect me of grotesque inventions that I would gladly have passed over this calamity in silence, had there not been countless witnesses of my own generation to bear me out; and besides, my country would have little

1. *Jewish War*, pp. 290–1, 297–8, 302.

reason to thank me if I drew a veil over the miseries that were so
real to her.

There was a woman, Mary the daughter of Eleazar, who lived
east of Jordan in the village of Bathezor ('House of Hyssop'). She
was of good family and very rich, and had fled with the rest of the
population to Jerusalem, where she shared in the horrors of the
siege. Most of the property that she had packed up and moved from
Peraea into the city had been plundered by the party chiefs; the
remnants of her treasures, and any food she had managed to obtain,
were being carried off in daily raids by their henchmen. The wretched
woman was filled with uncontrollable fury, and let loose a stream of
abuse and curses that enraged the looters against her. When neither
resentment nor pity caused anyone to kill her, and she grew tired of
finding food for others – and whichever way she turned it was almost
impossible to find – and while hunger was eating her heart out and
rage was consuming her still faster, she yielded to the suggestions of
fury and necessity, and in defiance of all natural feeling laid hands on
her own child, a babe at the breast. 'Poor little mite!' she cried. 'In
war, famine, and civil strife, why do I keep you alive? With the
Romans there is only slavery, even if we are alive when they come;
but famine is forestalling slavery, and the partisans are crueller than
either. Come, you must be food for me, to the partisans an avenging
spirit, and to the world a tale, the only thing left to fill up the measure
of Jewish misery.' As she spoke she killed her son, then roasted him
and ate one half, concealing and saving up the rest.

At once the partisans appeared, and sniffing the unholy smell,
threatened that if she did not produce what she had prepared they
would kill her on the spot. She replied that she had kept a fine helping
for them, and uncovered what was left of her child. They, overcome
with instant horror and amazement, could not take their eyes off the
sight. But she went on: 'This child is my own, and the deed is mine
too. Help yourselves: I have had my share. Don't be softer than a
woman or more tender-hearted than a mother! But if you are
squeamish, and don't approve of my sacrifice – well, I have eaten
half, so you may as well leave me the rest.' That was the last straw,
and they went away quivering. They had never before shrunk from
anything, and did not much like giving up even this food to the
mother. From that moment the entire city could think of nothing

else but this abomination; everyone saw the tragedy before his own eyes, and shuddered as if the crime was his. The one desire of the starving was for death: how they envied those who had gone before seeing or hearing of these appalling horrors![1]

Christ's predictions: warnings before the war

7. Such was the reward of the Jews' iniquitous and wicked treatment of God's Christ. It is worth while to set alongside it our Saviour's absolutely true prediction, in which He reveals those very things in this prophecy:

Alas for those who have a child unborn or at the breast in those days! Pray that your flight may not take place in winter or on a sabbath. For then there will be great distress, such as there has never been from the beginning of the world till now, and will never be again.[2]

In computing the whole number of those who lost their lives, the historian says that famine and the sword destroyed 1,100,000 persons; that those who had taken part in sedition and terrorism informed against each other after the capture of the city and were put to death; that the tallest and handsomest of the youngsters were kept for the triumphal procession; that of the rest, those over seventeen were put in irons and sent to hard labour in Egypt, and still more were distributed among the provinces to perish in the theatres by sword or by wild beasts, while those under seventeen were carried off captive and sold, the number of these alone reaching 90,000.[3]

These things happened in the second year of Vespasian's reign,[4] in exact accordance with the prophetic predictions of our Lord and Saviour Jesus Christ, who by divine power had foreseen them as though already present, and wept and mourned over them, as we learn from the holy evangelists,

1. *Jewish War*, pp. 318–20.   2. Matt. xxiv. 19–21.
3. *Jewish War*, p. 337.   4. A.D. 70.

who have set down His very words. On one occasion He said,
as if to Jerusalem herself:

> If only you, even you, had known today the way to your peace!
> But now it has been hidden from your sight. For a time will come
> upon you when your enemies will throw up an earthwork round you
> and encircle you and hem you in on every side, and bring to the
> ground both you and your children.[1]

On another occasion, with the people in mind, He said:

> For there will be great distress in the land, and indignation against
> this people: they will fall at the point of the sword, and they will be
> carried into captivity in every heathen land; and Jerusalem will be
> trampled on by heathen, till the day of the heathen is over.[2]

And again:

> When you see Jerusalem encircled by armies, then you may be
> sure that her desolation has drawn near.[3]

Anyone who compared our Saviour's words with the rest of the
historian's account of the whole war could not fail to be astonished, and to acknowledge as divine and utterly marvellous
the foreknowledge revealed by our Saviour's prediction.

After the Saviour's Passion, and the cries with which the
Jewish mob clamoured for the reprieve of the bandit and
murderer and begged that the Author of Life should be
removed from them,[4] disaster befell the entire nation. There
is no need to add anything to the historical records. But it
would be right to mention, too, certain facts which bring
home the beneficence of all-gracious Providence, which for
forty years after their crime against Christ delayed their
destruction. All that time most of the apostles and disciples,
including James himself, the first Bishop of Jerusalem, known
as the Lord's brother, were still alive, and by remaining in the
city furnished the place with an impregnable bulwark. For
the overruling power of God was still patient, in the hope

---

1. Luke xix. 42–4, with minor variations.   2. Luke xxi. 23–4.
3. Luke xxi. 20.   4. Acts iii. 14–17.

that at last they might repent of their misdeeds and obtain pardon and salvation; and besides this wonderful patience, it granted miraculous warnings from God of what would happen to them if they did not repent. These occurrences were thought worthy of mention by the historian whom I have been quoting, and I cannot do better than make them available to readers of this work.

8. Turn then to Book VI of the *Histories*, and read what he says:

The unhappy people were beguiled at that stage by cheats and false messengers of God, while the unmistakable portents that foreshadowed the coming desolation they treated with indifference and incredulity, disregarding God's warnings as if they were moonstruck, blind, and senseless. First a star stood over the city, very like a broadsword, and a comet that remained a whole year. Then before the revolt and the movement to war, while the people were assembling for the Feast of Unleavened Bread, on the 8th of April at three in the morning so bright a light shone round the Altar and the Sanctuary that it might have been midday. This lasted half an hour. The inexperienced took it for a good omen, but the sacred scribes at once gave the true interpretation, before the events. During the same feast a cow brought by the high priest to be sacrificed gave birth to a lamb in the middle of the Temple courts, while at midnight it was observed that the east gate of the inner Sanctuary had opened of its own accord – a gate made of bronze, and so solid that every evening twenty strong men were required to shut it, fastened with iron-bound bars and secured by bolts which went down a long way.

A few days after the Feast, on the 21st of May, a supernatural apparition was seen, too amazing to be believed. What I have to relate would have been dismissed as an invention had it not been vouched for by eyewitnesses and followed by disasters that bore out the signs. Before sunset there were seen in the sky over the whole country chariots and regiments in arms speeding through the clouds and encircling the towns. Again, at the Feast of Pentecost, when the priests had gone into the Temple at night to perform the usual ceremonies, they declared that they were aware, first of a violent movement and a loud crash, then of a concerted cry: 'Let us go hence!'

An incident more alarming still had occurred four years before the war, at a time of exceptional peace and prosperity for the city. One Jeshua son of Ananias, a very ordinary yokel, came to the feast at which every Jew is expected to set up a tabernacle for God. As he stood in the Temple he suddenly began to shout: 'A voice from the east, a voice from the west, a voice from the four winds, a voice against Jerusalem and the Sanctuary, a voice against bridegrooms and brides, a voice against the whole people!' Day and night he uttered the cry as he went through the streets. Some of the more prominent citizens, very annoyed at these ominous words, laid hold of the fellow and beat him savagely. Without saying a word in his own defence or for the private information of his persecutors, he persisted in shouting the same warning as before. The Jewish authorities, rightly concluding that some supernatural force was responsible for the man's behaviour, took him before the Roman procurator. There, though scourged till his flesh hung in ribbons, he neither begged for mercy nor shed a tear, but lowering his voice to the most mournful of tones answered every blow with: 'Woe to Jerusalem!'[1]

A still more astonishing story follows a paragraph later, where it is stated that an oracle was found in their sacred writings to the effect that at that time a man from their country would become monarch of the whole world: this oracle the historian himself believed to have been fulfilled in Vespasian.[2] But Vespasian did not reign over the entire world, but only the part under Roman rule: it would be more justly applied to Christ, to whom the Father had said,

> Ask of me, and I will give you the heathen world for your in-
> heritance,
> And for your possession the ends of the earth.[3]

At that very time it was true of His apostles that

> Their speech went out to the whole earth,
> And their words to the ends of the world.[4]

1. *Jewish War*, pp. 326–8.   2. *Jewish War*, p. 328.
3. Ps. ii. 8.   4. Ps. xix. 4.

Josephus and the writings that he left: his allusions to the sacred books

9. Besides all this it is well that the origin and ancestry of Josephus himself, who has provided so much material for this present history, should be generally known. He furnishes this information himself:

I, Josephus, son of Matthias, am a priest from Jerusalem; in the early stages I myself fought against the Romans, and of the later events I was an unwilling witness.[1]

Of the Jews at that time he was the most famous, not only among his fellow-countrymen but among the Romans too, so that he was honoured with the erection of a statue in the city of Rome, and the labours of his pen found a place in the Library. He has set out the whole of *Ancient Jewish History*[2] in twenty books, and the story of the Roman war of his own day in seven.[3] The latter work he committed not only to Greek but also to his native language, as he himself testifies[4] – and in view of his general truthfulness, we may accept this. Two other worth-while books of his are extant, entitled *The Antiquity of the Jews*,[5] his reply to Apion the grammarian, who had recently published an attack on the Jews, and to others who had made similar attempts to misrepresent the ancestral customs of the Jewish people. In the first of these he gives the number of the canonical scriptures forming the Old Testament, as it is called, showing which of them are undisputed among the Hebrews as being backed by ancient tradition:

10. We do not have vast numbers of books, discordant and conflicting, but only twenty-two, containing the record of all time

1. *Jewish War*, p. 21.
2. The author's own title; we have unfortunately adopted the Latin substitute *Antiquities*.
3. The author's own title is *The Jewish War*.   4. *Jewish War*, p. 21.
5. Needlessly renamed in Latin *Against Apion*.

and with reason believed to be divine. Of these five are books of Moses, containing the Laws and the tradition of[1] the origin of mankind up to his death. This period covers nearly 3,000 years. From Moses' death to that of Artaxerxes, who followed Xerxes as King of Persia, the prophets after Moses recorded the events of their own time in thirteen books. The remaining four contain hymns to God and precepts for human conduct. [2] From Artaxerxes to the present day the whole story has been written down, but does not command the same belief as the earlier narrative because there was not an unbroken succession of prophets. It is evident from our actions what is our attitude to our own scriptures; for though so many centuries have gone by, no one has presumed to add, take away, or alter anything in them,[3] but it is innate in every Jew from the day of his birth to regard them as the ordinances of God, to abide in them, and if need be to die for them gladly.[4]

This quotation from the historian is of obvious value. He produced yet another work of considerable merit, *The Supremacy of Reason*, entitled *Maccabees*[5] by some, because it deals with the struggles of those Hebrews who, as related in the books bearing the same name *Maccabees*, fought so manfully for the worship of Almighty God. And at the end of Book xx of *Antiquities* he announces that he has decided to write a work in four books on the traditional beliefs of the Jews about God and His nature, and about the reasons why the Laws permit certain things and forbid others.[6] Other books, already published, are also referred to in his surviving works.

Finally, it would be appropriate to reproduce the words

1. Josephus probably wrote 'from'.

2. The familiar Talmudic division of the scriptures into twenty-four books, eleven of them in the third group, belongs to a later period; Josephus has included in that group only the books without historical content – presumably Ps., Prov., Song, and Eccles.

3. On the contrary, till A.D. *c.* 100 additions, deletions, and alterations seem to have been freely made.

4. *Against Apion* I, 8.

5. 4 *Maccabees* (no longer attributed to Josephus).

6. *Antiquities*, last sentence.

attached to the end of *Antiquities* and so confirm the testimony of the passages I have borrowed from him. In impugning the historical accuracy of Justus of Tiberias, who had attempted to record the events of the same period as himself, after bringing many other charges against him he adds the following:

> I had no such apprehensions as yourself with regard to what I myself had written: I submitted the work to the emperors themselves,[1] when the events had hardly passed out of sight. For, conscious that I had observed absolute truthfulness in my account, I expected to receive testimony to my accuracy, and was not disappointed. I also submitted my history to many others, some of whom had actually seen service in the war, including King Agrippa[2] and several of his relations. For the Emperor Titus was so anxious that from my work alone should men derive their knowledge of the events, that he wrote with his own hand an order for its publication, while King Agrippa wrote sixty-two letters testifying to the truthfulness of my account.[3]

Two of these letters he quotes. And there we may leave Josephus and go on to the next stage.

11. After the martyrdom of James and the capture of Jerusalem which instantly followed, there is a firm tradition that those of the apostles and disciples of the Lord who were still alive assembled from all parts together with those who, humanly speaking, were kinsmen of the Lord – for most of them were still living. Then they all discussed together whom they should choose as a fit person to succeed James,[4] and voted unanimously that Symeon, son of the Clopas mentioned in the gospel narrative,[5] was a fit person to occupy the throne of the Jerusalem see.[6] He was, so it is said, a cousin of the

---

1. Vespasian and Titus, on whom in *The Jewish War* he had lavished compliments.
2. Herod Agrippa II.   3. *Life of Josephus*, pp. 361–4.
4. No *congé d'élire* in those days.   5. John xix. 25; perhaps Luke xxiv. 18.
6. Eusebius has repeatedly referred to the throne of this see, and of no other.

Saviour, for Hegesippus tells us that Clopas was Joseph's brother.[1]

12. Hegesippus also records that after the capture of Jerusalem Vespasian issued an order that, to ensure that no member of the royal house should be left among the Jews, all descendants of David should be ferreted out; and that this resulted in a further widespread persecution of the Jews.

13. When Vespasian had reigned for ten years he was succeeded as emperor by his son Titus.[2] In the second year of Titus's reign Linus, Bishop of Rome, after holding his office for twelve years yielded it to Anencletus.

Titus was succeeded by his brother Domitian[3] after reigning for two years and as many months.

14. In the fourth year of Domitian the first Bishop of Alexandria, Annianus, after completing twenty-two years, passed away, and was succeeded by the second, Avilius.

15. In the twelfth year of the same principate Anencletus, after twelve years as Bishop of Rome, was succeeded by Clement, who is described by the Apostle in his Epistle to the Philippians as a fellow-worker:

With Clement and the rest of my fellow-workers, whose names are in the book of life.[4]

16. Clement has left us one recognized epistle, long and wonderful, which he composed in the name of the church at Rome and sent to the church at Corinth, where dissension had recently occurred. I have evidence that in many churches

1. The passage is quoted on p. 181.
2. 23 June A.D. 79.
3. 13 Sept. A.D. 81.
4. Phil. iv. 3: the identification (by Origen) of the bishop with Paul's fellow-worker rests on no certain evidence, but cannot be disproved.

this epistle was read aloud to the assembled worshippers in early days, as it is in our own. That it was in Clement's time that the dissension at Corinth broke out is plain from the testimony of Hegesippus.

Domitian's persecution: John the apostle and our Saviour's relatives

17. Many were the victims of Domitian's appalling cruelty. At Rome great numbers of men distinguished by birth and attainments were executed without a fair trial, and countless other eminent men were for no reason at all banished from the country and their property confiscated. Finally, he showed himself the successor of Nero in enmity and hostility to God. He was, in fact, the second to organize persecution against us, though his father Vespasian had had no mischievous designs against us.

18. There is ample evidence that at that time the apostle and evangelist John was still alive, and because of his testimony to the word of God was sentenced to confinement on the island of Patmos.[1] Writing about the number of the name given to antichrist in what is called the Revelation of John, Irenaeus has this to say about John in Book v of his *Heresies Answered*:

Had there been any need for his name to be openly announced at the present time, it would have been stated by the one who saw the actual revelation. For it was seen not a long time back, but almost in my own lifetime, at the end of Domitian's reign.

Indeed, so brightly shone at that time the teaching of our faith that even historians who accepted none of our beliefs unhesitatingly recorded in their pages both the persecution and the martyrdoms to which it led. They also indicated the

1. Rev. xiii. 18.

precise date, noting that in the fifteenth year of Domitian[1] Flavia Domitilla, who was a niece of Flavius Clemens, one of the consuls at Rome that year, was with many others, because of their testimony to Christ, taken to the island of Pontia[2] as a punishment.

19. The same emperor ordered the execution of all who were of David's line, and there is an old and firm tradition that a group of heretics accused the descendants of Jude – the brother, humanly speaking, of the Saviour – on the ground that they were of David's line and related to Christ Himself. This is stated by Hegesippus in so many words:

20. And there still survived of the Lord's family the grandsons of Jude, who was said to be His brother, humanly speaking. These were informed against as being of David's line, and brought by the *evocatus*[3] before Domitian Caesar, who was as afraid of the advent of Christ as Herod had been.[4] Domitian asked them whether they were descended from David, and they admitted it. Then he asked them what property they owned and what funds they had at their disposal. They replied that they had only £1,500[5] between them, half belonging to each; this, they said, was not available in cash, but was the estimated value of only twenty-five acres of land, from which they raised the money to pay their taxes and the wherewithal to support themselves by their own toil.

Then, the writer continues, they showed him their hands, putting forward as proof of their toil the hardness of their bodies and the calluses impressed on their hands by incessant labour. When asked about Christ and His Kingdom – what it was like, and where and when it would appear – they explained that it was not of this world or anywhere on earth but angelic and in heaven, and would be established at the end

---

1. A.D. 96.   2. Ponza in the Gulf of Gaeta.
3. Latin for 'veteran': the meaning here is unknown.
4. Matt. ii. 3–4.
5. 9,000 denarii: the denarius was a silver coin nominally worth 8*d*, but equivalent to about 3*s* 4*d* at the present day.

of the world, when He would come in glory to judge the quick and the dead and give every man payment according to his conduct. On hearing this, Domitian found no fault with them, but despising them as beneath his notice let them go free and issued orders terminating the persecution of the Church.[1] On their release they became leaders of the churches, both because they had borne testimony and because they were of the Lord's family; and thanks to the establishment of peace they lived on into Trajan's time.

So much we learn from Hegesippus. Tertullian, again, has this to say about Domitian:

A similar attempt had once been made by Domitian, who almost equalled Nero in cruelty; but – I suppose because he had some common sense – he very soon stopped, even recalling those he had banished.[2]

After fifteen years of Domitian's rule Nerva succeeded to the throne. By vote of the Roman senate Domitian's honours were removed, and those unjustly banished returned to their homes and had their property restored to them. This is noted by the chroniclers of the period. At that time too[3] the apostle John, after his exile on the island, resumed residence at Ephesus, as early Christian tradition records.

Bishops of Alexandria and Antioch

21. When Nerva had reigned a little more than a year he was succeeded by Trajan. It was in his first year that Avilius, after heading the church of Alexandria for thirteen years, was succeeded by Cerdo: he was the third bishop of the see, Annianus having been the first. At that time Clement was still head of the Roman community, occupying in the same

1. Hegesippus was referring to the Jerusalem church only.
2. The recall took place under Nerva, as stated in the next sentence.
3. A.D. 96.

way the third place among the bishops who followed Paul and Peter.[1] Linus was the first and Anencletus the second.

22. At Antioch, where Euodius had been the first bishop, Ignatius was becoming famous at this time; his contemporary Symeon was similarly the next after our Saviour's brother to be in charge of the church at Jerusalem.

A story about John the apostle

23. In Asia, moreover, there still remained alive the one whom Jesus loved, apostle and evangelist alike, John, who had directed the churches there since his return from exile on the island, following Domitian's death. That he survived so long is proved by the evidence of two witnesses who could hardly be doubted, ambassadors as they were of the orthodoxy of the Church – Irenaeus and Clement of Alexandria. In Book II of his *Heresies Answered*, Irenaeus writes:

> All the clergy who in Asia came in contact with John, the Lord's disciple, testify that John taught the truth to them; for he remained with them till Trajan's time.

In Book III of the same work he says the same thing:

> The church at Ephesus was founded by Paul, and John remained there till Trajan's time; so she is a true witness of what the apostles taught.

Clement, in addition to indicating the date, adds a story that should be familiar to all who like to hear what is noble and helpful. It will be found in the short work entitled *The Rich Man Who Finds Salvation*. Turn up the passage, and read what he writes:

> Listen to a tale that is not just a tale but a true account of John the apostle, handed down and carefully remembered. When the tyrant was dead, and John had moved from the island of Patmos to

1. See p. 107 n.

Ephesus, he used to go when asked to the neighbouring districts of the Gentile peoples, sometimes to appoint bishops, sometimes to organize whole churches, sometimes to ordain one person of those pointed out by the Spirit. So it happened that he arrived at a city not far off, named by some,[1] and after settling the various problems of the brethren, he finally looked at the bishop already appointed, and indicating a youngster he had noticed, of excellent physique, attractive appearance, and ardent spirit, he said: 'I leave this young man in your keeping, with all earnestness, in the presence of the Church and Christ as my witness.' When the bishop accepted him and promised everything, John addressed the same appeal and adjuration to him a second time.

He then returned to Ephesus, and the cleric took home the youngster entrusted to his care, brought him up, kept him in his company, looked after him, and finally gave him the grace of baptism. After this he relaxed his constant care and watchfulness, having put upon him the seal of the Lord as the perfect protection. But the youngster snatched at liberty too soon, and was led sadly astray by others of his own age who were idle, dissolute, and evil-livers. First they led him on by expensive entertainments; then they took him with them when they went out at night to commit robbery; then they urged him to take part in even greater crimes. Little by little he fell into their ways; and like a hard-mouthed powerful horse he dashed off the straight road, and taking the bit between his teeth rushed down the precipice the more violently because of his immense vitality. Completely renouncing God's salvation, he was no longer content with petty offences, but, as his life was already in ruins, he decided to commit a major crime and suffer the same fate as the others. He took these same young renegades and formed them into a gang of bandits of which his was the master mind, surpassing them all in violence, cruelty, and bloodthirstiness.

Time went by, and some necessity having arisen, John was asked to pay another visit. When he had dealt with the business for which he had come, he said: 'Come now, bishop, pay me back the deposit which Christ and I left in your keeping, in the presence of the Church over which you preside as my witness.' At first the bishop was taken aback, thinking that he was being dunned for money he had never

1. Smyrna.

received. He could neither comply with a demand for what he did not possess, nor refuse to comply with John's request. But when John said 'It is the young man I am asking for, and the soul of our brother', the old man sighed deeply and shed a tear.

'He is dead.'

'How did he die?'

'He is dead to God: he turned out wicked and profligate, in short, a bandit; and now, instead of the Church, he has taken to the mountain with an armed gang of men like himself.'

The apostle rent his garment, groaned aloud, and beat his head. 'A fine guardian,' he cried, 'I left of our brother's soul! However, let me have a horse immediately, and someone to show me the way.' He galloped off from the church, then and there, just as he was. When he arrived at the place, and was seized by the bandits' sentry-group, he made no attempt to escape and asked no mercy, but shouted: 'This is what I have come for:[1] take me to your leader.' For the time being the young man waited, armed as he was; but as John approached he recognized him, and filled with shame, turned to flee. But John ran after him as hard as he could, forgetting his years and calling out: 'Why do you run away from me, child – from your own father, unarmed and very old? Be sorry for me, child, not afraid of me. You still have hopes of life. I will account to Christ for you. If need be, I will gladly suffer your death, as the Lord suffered death for us; to save you I will give my own life. Stop! believe! Christ sent me.'

When he heard this, the young man stopped and stood with his eyes on the ground; then he threw down his weapons; then he trembled and began to weep bitterly. When the old man came up he flung his arms round him, pleading for himself with groans as best he could, and baptized a second time with his tears, but keeping his right hand out of sight. But John solemnly pledged his word that he had found pardon for him from the Saviour: he prayed, knelt down, and kissed that very hand as being cleansed by his repentance. Then he brought him back to the church, interceded for him with many prayers, shared with him the ordeal of continuous fasting, brought his mind under control by all the enchanting power of words, and did not leave him, we are told, till he had restored him

1. A reminiscence of John xviii. 37.

to the Church, giving a perfect example of true repentance and a perfect proof of regeneration, the trophy of a visible resurrection.

This story from Clement I have included both for its historical interest and for the benefit of future readers.

The order of the gospels

24. Now let me indicate the unquestioned writings of this apostle. Obviously his gospel, recognized as it is by all the churches in the world, must first be acknowledged. That the early fathers had good reason to assign it the fourth place after the other three can easily be seen. Those inspired and wonderful men, Christ's apostles, had completely purified their lives and cultivated every spiritual virtue, but their speech was that of every day. The divine wonder-working power bestowed on them by the Saviour filled them with confidence; and having neither the ability nor the desire to present the teachings of the Master with rhetorical subtlety or literary skill, they relied only on demonstrating the divine Spirit working with them, and on the miraculous power of Christ fully operative in them.[1] Thus they proclaimed the knowledge of the Kingdom of Heaven through the whole world, giving very little thought to the business of writing books. The reason for this practice was the ever-present help of a greater, superhuman ministry. We may instance Paul, who though he surpassed all others in the marshalling of his arguments and in the abundance of his ideas, committed to writing nothing but his very short epistles; and yet he had countless unutterable things to say, for he had reached the vision of the third heaven, had been caught up to the divine paradise itself, and had been privileged to hear there unspeakable words.[2]

Similar experiences were enjoyed by the rest of our

1. See 1 Cor. ii. 4.   2. See 2 Cor. xii. 2–4.

Saviour's pupils – the twelve apostles, the seventy disciples, and countless others besides. Yet of them all Matthew and John alone have left us memoirs of the Lord's doings, and there is a firm tradition that they took to writing of necessity. Matthew had begun by preaching to Hebrews; and when he made up his mind to go to others too, he committed his own gospel to writing in his native tongue, so that for those with whom he was no longer present the gap left by his departure was filled by what he wrote. And when Mark and Luke had now published their gospels, John, we are told, who hitherto had relied entirely on the spoken word, finally took to writing for the following reason. The three gospels already written were in general circulation and copies had come into John's hands. He welcomed them, we are told, and confirmed their accuracy, but remarked that the narrative only lacked the story of what Christ had done first of all at the beginning of His mission.

This tradition is undoubtedly true. Anyone can see that the three evangelists have recorded the doings of the Saviour for only one year, following the consignment of John the Baptist to prison, and that they indicated this very fact at the beginning of their narrative. After the forty days' fast and the temptation that followed Matthew shows clearly the period covered by his narrative when he says: 'Hearing that John had been arrested, He withdrew from Judaea into Galilee.'[1] In the same way, Mark says: 'After the arrest of John, Jesus went into Galilee.'[2] Luke too, before beginning the acts of Jesus, makes a similar observation, saying that Herod added one more to his other crimes by shutting up John in gaol.[3]

We are told, then, that for this reason the apostle John was urged to record in his gospel the period which the earlier evangelists had passed over in silence and the things done during that period by the Saviour, i.e. all that happened

1. Matt. iv. 12.   2. Mark i. 14.   3. Luke iii. 19–20.

before the Baptist's imprisonment; that this is indicated, first by his words 'Thus did Jesus begin His miracles',[1] and later by his mentioning the Baptist, in the middle of his account of Jesus's doings, as then still baptizing at Aenon near Salim; and that he makes this plainer when he adds 'for John had not yet been thrown into gaol'.[2]

Thus John in his gospel narrative records what Christ did when the Baptist had not yet been thrown into gaol, while the other three evangelists describe what happened after the Baptist's consignment to prison. Once this is grasped, there no longer appears to be a discrepancy between the gospels, because John's deals with the early stages of Christ's career and the others cover the last period of His story; and it seems natural that as the genealogy of our Saviour as a man had already been set out by Matthew and Luke, John should pass it over in silence and begin with the proclamation of His divinity, since the Holy Spirit had reserved this for him, as the greatest of the four.

This is all that I propose to say about the composition of John's gospel: the origin of Mark's has already been explained. Luke's work begins with a preface in which the author himself explains the reason for its composition. Many others had somewhat hastily undertaken to compile an account of things of which he himself was fully assured;[3] so, feeling it his duty to free us from doubts as to our attitude to the others, he furnished in his own gospel an authentic account of the events of which, thanks to his association and intercourse with Paul and his conversations with the other apostles, he had learnt

1. John ii. 11: 'Miracles' represents a non-Biblical word common in Eusebius and here substituted for 'sign', the word always used by John, as the R.V. makes plain.

2. John iii. 23–4.

3. Luke i. 1: Eusebius, in agreement with the R.V. margin, took the second half of the verse to mean, 'those matters which have been fully established among us'. Reference to all other N.T. passages where the same Greek verb or the corresponding noun is used shows that (*pace* the *New English Bible*) he was right.

the undoubted truth.[1] This is how I see the matter: at a more appropriate moment I shall endeavour to show, by quoting early writers, what others have said about it.

Of John's writings, besides the gospel, the first of the epistles has been accepted as unquestionably his by scholars both of the present and of a much earlier period: the other two are disputed. As to the Revelation, the views of most people to this day are evenly divided. At the appropriate moment, the evidence of early writers shall clear up this matter too.[2]

Writings accepted as sacred, and those not accepted

25. It will be well, at this point, to classify the New Testament writings already referred to. We must, of course, put first the holy quartet of the gospels, followed by the Acts of the Apostles. The next place in the list goes to Paul's epistles, and after them we must recognize the epistle called 1 John; likewise 1 Peter. To these may be added, if it is thought proper, the Revelation of John, the arguments about which I shall set out when the time comes. These are classed as Recognized Books. Those that are disputed, yet familiar to most, include the epistles known as James, Jude, and 2 Peter, and those called 2 and 3 John, the work either of the evangelist or of someone else with the same name.[3]

Among spurious books must be placed the 'Acts' of Paul, the 'Shepherd', and the 'Revelation of Peter'; also the alleged 'Epistle of Barnabas',[4] and the 'Teachings of the Apostles',[5] together with the Revelation of John, if this seems the right place for it: as I said before, some reject it, others include it among the Recognized Books. Moreover, some have found a

1. Luke i. 3–4.
2. Not in the work as we have it.
3. The name John appears nowhere in the three epistles.
4, 5. These works are extant, but authorship and dates are unknown.

place in the list for the 'Gospel of the Hebrews',[1] a book which has a special appeal for those Hebrews who have accepted Christ. These would all be classed with the Disputed Books, but I have been obliged to list the latter separately, distinguishing those writings which according to the tradition of the Church are true, genuine, and recognized, from those in a different category, not canonical but disputed, yet familiar to most churchmen; for we must not confuse these with the writings published by heretics under the name of the apostles, as containing either Gospels of Peter,[2] Thomas,[3] Matthias, and several others besides these, or Acts of Andrew,[4] John,[5] and other apostles. To none of these has any churchman of any generation ever seen fit to refer in his writings. Again, nothing could be farther from apostolic usage than the type of phraseology employed, while the ideas and implications of their contents are so irreconcilable with true orthodoxy that they stand revealed as the forgeries of heretics. It follows that so far from being classed even among Spurious Books, they must be thrown out as impious and beyond the pale.

Menander the impostor

26. Let us now return to the course of our story. Simon the Magus was succeeded by Menander, a second tool of the devil's ingenuity as bad as his predecessor, as he showed by his conduct. He too was a Samaritan, and having risen to the same heights of imposture as his master, he poured out a stream of still more marvellous tales. He actually claimed to be the saviour sent down from somewhere aloft to save

1. Fragments survive; the work was written before A.D. 150.
2. A large fragment survives: the work was probably written early in the 2nd century.
3. The extant Gospel of Thomas may consist of the orthodox parts of this work.
4. A third-century list of miracles, of which a summary survives.
5. A second-century work, of which large portions survive.

mankind from invisible aeons,[1] and taught that there was no
way by which a man could get the better even of the angels
who made the world, unless he had first been taken through
the magical skills transmitted by himself and the baptism
which he bestowed: those who were admitted to this baptism
would share in everlasting immortality in this present world,
no longer subject to death but destined to continue here for
ever, ageless and immortal. All this is clearly stated in the
writings of Irenaeus. Justin, too, follows up his comments on
Simon with an account of his successor:

Another Samaritan, called Menander, from the village of Caparat-
taea, became a disciple of Simon and like him was driven mad by the
demons. It is known that he arrived in Antioch and deluded many
by magical trickery. He even persuaded his followers that they
would not die: and there are still some who on the strength of his
assertion maintain this belief.[2]

It was certainly characteristic of the devil's ingenuity to
make use of such impostors, who usurped the name of
Christian, in his determination to misrepresent in the interests
of magic the great mystery of religion,[3] and to make a
mockery of the Church's teaching on the immortality of the
soul and the resurrection of the dead. But those who have
entitled these men 'saviours' have fallen from the true hope.[4]

The Ebionite sect: the heresies of Cerinthus and Nicolaus

27. There were others whom the evil demon, unable to shake
their devotion to the Christ of God, caught in a different
trap and made his own. Ebionites they were appropriately

1. In Gnostic language 'aeons' were major supernatural powers: the world
had been created by lower angels, evil and hostile, of which the soul, if it
was to be saved, could get the better only by sacramental initiation and
esoteric knowledge.

2. Justin Martyr, *Defence.*   3. 1 Tim. iii. 16.

4. Eusebius is right in his belief that Gnosticism did not begin as a Christian
movement, but soon drew Christians into it.

named by the first Christians, in view of the poor and mean opinions they held about Christ. They regarded Him as plain and ordinary, a man esteemed as righteous through growth[1] of character and nothing more, the child of a normal union between a man and Mary;[2] and they held that they must observe every detail of the Law – by faith in Christ alone, and a life built upon that faith, they would never win salvation.

A second group went by the same name, but escaped the outrageous absurdity of the first. They did not deny that the Lord was born of a virgin and the Holy Spirit, but nevertheless shared their refusal to acknowledge His pre-existence as God the Word and Wisdom. Thus the impious doctrine of the others was their undoing also, especially as they placed equal emphasis on the outward observance of the Law. They held that the epistles of the Apostle ought to be rejected altogether, calling him a renegade from the Law; and using only the 'Gospel of the Hebrews', they treated the rest with scant respect. Like the others, they observed the Sabbath and the whole Jewish system; yet on the Lord's Day they celebrated rites similar to our own in memory of the Saviour's resurrection. It is then because of such practices that they have been dubbed with their present name: the name of Ebionites hints at the poverty of their intelligence, for this is the way in which a poor man is referred to by the Hebrews.[3]

28. At the time under discussion, tradition tells us, another heretical sect was founded by Cerinthus.[4] Gaius, whose words

1. The word used in Luke ii. 52.

2. The fact that these very early heretics denied the Virgin Birth implies its general acceptance.

3. Both these wild guesses at the origin of the name are derived from Origen. A more likely explanation is that it was applied to the earliest Jewish Christians in reference to their voluntary poverty.

4. A Judaizing gnostic, whose views are rebutted in the prologue of John's gospel.

I quoted earlier,[1] in the *Disputation* attributed to him writes this about him:

> Then there is Cerinthus, who by revelations purporting to have been written by a great apostle presents us with tales of wonder falsely alleged to have been shown to him by angels. He declares that after the Resurrection the Kingdom of Christ will be on earth, and that carnal humanity will dwell in Jerusalem, once more enslaved to lusts and pleasures.[2] And in his enmity towards the Scriptures of God, and his anxiety to lead men astray, he foretells a period of a thousand years given up to wedding festivities.

Dionysius again, who held the bishopric of the Alexandrian see in my own time, in Book 11 of his *Promises* makes certain statements about the Revelation of John on the basis of very ancient tradition. He then refers to Cerinthus in the following terms.

> Cerinthus: the founder of a sect called Cerinthian after him, who wished to attach a name commanding respect to his own creation. This, they say, was the doctrine he taught – that Christ's Kingdom would be on earth; and the things he lusted after himself, being the slave of his body and sensual through and through, filled the heaven of his dreams – unlimited indulgence in gluttony and lechery at banquets, drinking-bouts, and wedding-feasts, or (to call these by what he thought more respectable names) festivals, sacrifices, and the immolation of victims.[3]

That is how Dionysius puts it. Irenaeus in Book 1 of his *Heresies Answered* set out some of his more revolting errors, and in Book 111 has placed on record a memorable story. He states on the authority of Polycarp that one day John the apostle went into a bath-house to take a bath, but when he found that Cerinthus was inside he leapt from the spot and

---

1. p. 105.   2. Titus iii. 3.
3. An excerpt from the passage quoted on p. 309; Cerinthus and the Nicolaitans tried to import into Christianity the notorious licentiousness of western Asia Minor.

ran for the door, as he could not endure to be under the same roof. He urged his companions to do the same, calling out: 'Let us get out of here, for fear the place falls in, now that Cerinthus, the enemy of the truth, is inside.'[1]

29. In their day, too, the very short-lived sect of the Nicolaitans came into existence. It is mentioned in the Revelation of John.[2] These sectaries laid claim to Nicolaus, who like Stephen was one of the deacons appointed by the apostles to assist those in want.[3] Clement of Alexandria in Book III of his *Miscellanies* gives this account of him:

> This man, we are told, had an attractive young wife. After the Saviour's Ascension the apostles accused him of jealousy, so he brought his wife forward and said that anyone who wished might have her. This action, we are told, followed from the injunction 'the flesh must be treated with contempt'; and by following example and precept crudely and unquestioningly the members of the sect do in fact practise utter promiscuity. But my own information is that Nicolaus had no relations with any woman but his wife; and that, of his children, his daughters remained unmarried till the end of their days and his son's chastity was never in doubt. Such being the case, his bringing the wife whom he loved so jealously into the midst of the apostles was the renunciation of desire, and it was mastery of the pleasures so eagerly sought that taught him the rule 'treat the flesh with contempt'. For in obedience to the Saviour's command, I imagine, he had no wish to serve two masters, pleasure and Lord. It is believed that Matthias also taught this, that we must fight against the flesh and treat it with contempt, never yielding to it for pleasure's sake, but must nourish the soul through faith and knowledge.

So much for those who during that period endeavoured to twist the truth, only to be extinguished completely, in less time than it takes to tell.

1. The story in Irenaeus's own words will be found on p. 167.
2. Rev. ii. 16.   3. Acts vi. 5.

Apostles who were married men

30. Clement, whose words we have just been reading, goes on from the passage I have quoted to rebut those who deprecated marriage, by listing the apostles known to have been married men. He says:

> Or will they condemn even the apostles? For Peter and Philip had families, and Philip gave his daughters in marriage, while Paul himself does not hesitate in one of his epistles to address his yoke-fellow,[1] whom he did not take round with him[2] for fear of hindering his ministry.

While I am on the subject, I may as well quote another of Clement's interesting stories, to be found in Book VII of his *Miscellanies*:

> We are told that when blessed Peter saw his wife led away to death he was glad that her call had come and that she was returning home, and spoke to her in the most encouraging and comforting tones, addressing her by name: 'My dear, remember the Lord.' Such was the marriage of the blessed, and their consummate feeling towards their dearest.

These quotations, relevant as they are to this section of my work, must suffice for the moment.

The deaths of John and Philip

31. When and how Paul and Peter died, and where after their departure from this life their mortal remains were laid, I have already explained.[3] The date of John's death has also been roughly fixed:[4] the place where his mortal remains lie

1. It would seem from 1 Cor. vii. 8 that Paul was either a widower or a bachelor. The 'true yokefellow' of Phil. iv. 3 may mean 'loyal comrade', as in the *New English Bible*.
2. 1 Cor. ix. 5 does not say that Paul had a wife, only that he was entitled to have one. Why did not Clement quote the rest of the verse, which says that all the twelve and the Lord's brothers had wives?
3. pp. 104–5.   4. p. 128.

can be gathered from a letter of Polycrates, Bishop of Ephesus, to Victor, Bishop of Rome. In it he refers not only to John but to Philip the apostle and Philip's daughters as well:

> In Asia[1] great luminaries sleep who shall rise again on the last day, the day of the Lord's advent, when He is coming with glory from heaven and shall search out all His saints – such as Philip, one of the twelve apostles, who sleeps in Hierapolis with two of his daughters, who remained unmarried to the end of their days, while his other daughter lived in the Holy Spirit and rests in Ephesus. Again there is John, who leant back on the Lord's breast, and who became a sacrificing priest wearing the mitre, a martyr and a teacher; he too sleeps in Ephesus.[2]

So much Polycrates tells us about their deaths. And in the *Dialogue* of Gaius of whom I spoke a little while ago, Proclus, with whom he was disputing, speaks thus about the deaths of Philip and his daughters, in agreement with the foregoing account:

> After him there were four prophetesses at Hierapolis in Asia, daughters of Philip. Their grave is there, as is their father's.

That is Gaius's account. Luke in the Acts of the Apostles refers to Philip's daughters as then living with their father at Caesarea in Judaea and endowed with the prophetic gift. His words are:

> We arrived at Caesarea, where we went to the house of Philip the Evangelist, one of the Seven, and stayed with him. He had four unmarried daughters who were prophetesses.[3]

1. The Roman province, as always.
2. An excerpt from the passage quoted on p. 231; Polycrates was born *c.* A.D. 125 and wrote his letter *c.* A.D. 190. Both John and James the Lord's brother are stated to have worn the mitre (derived from the Jewish high priest), presumably in their archiepiscopal capacity. The word 'martyr' does not imply that John was put to death, but only that his witness cost him dear.
3. Acts xxi. 8–9: there seems ample evidence in ancient documents that both Philip the Apostle and Philip the Evangelist came to Hierapolis. Unfortunately Eusebius thought they were the same.

In these pages I have set down all the facts that have come to my knowledge regarding the apostles and the apostolic period; the sacred writings they have left us; the books which though disputed are nevertheless constantly used in very many churches; those that are unmistakably spurious and foreign to apostolic orthodoxy. Let us now go on to the story of what followed.

The martyrdom of Symeon, Bishop of Jerusalem

32. After Nero and Domitian, under the emperor whose times I am now describing,[1] there is a firm tradition that persecution broke out against us sporadically in one city at a time as a result of popular risings. In the course of it Symeon, son of Clopas, the second to be appointed Bishop of Jerusalem, as already stated,[2] is known to have ended his life by martyrdom. The authority for this statement is the writer to whose history I have appealed several times already, Hegesippus. When writing of certain heretics he goes on to explain how at this time they brought an accusation against Symeon, and how after being subjected for days on end to a variety of tortures for being a Christian, to the utter amazement of the judge and his assessors, he won the prize of an end like that suffered by the Lord. But we cannot do better than listen to the writer's own version of the story:

Some of these [heretics] charged Simon son of Clopas with being a descendant of David and a Christian; as a result he suffered martyrdom at the age of 120, when Trajan was emperor and Atticus consular governor.[3]

The same writer tells us that in the sequel, when members of the royal house of Judah were being hunted, Symeon's accusers were arrested too, on the ground that they belonged to it. And it would be reasonable to suggest that Symeon was

1. Trajan: there was no persecution in Nerva's short reign.
2. p. 123.   3. A.D. 106 or 107.

an eyewitness and earwitness of the Lord, having regard to the length of his life and the reference in the gospel narrative to Mary, wife of the Clopas whose son he was, as explained in an earlier section.[1]

The same historian tells us that other descendants of one of the 'brothers' of the Saviour named Jude lived on into the same reign, after bravely declaring their faith in Christ, as already recorded,[2] before Domitian himself. He writes:

> Consequently they came and presided over every church, as being martyrs and members of the Lord's family, and since profound peace came to every church they survived till the reign of Trajan Caesar – till the son of the Lord's uncle, the aforesaid Simon son of Clopas, was similarly informed against by the heretical sects and brought up on the same charge before Atticus, the provincial governor. Tortured for days on end, he bore a martyr's witness, so that all, including the governor, were astounded that at the age of 120 he could endure it; and he was ordered to be crucified.

In describing the situation at that time Hegesippus goes on to say that until then the Church had remained a virgin, pure and uncorrupted, since those who were trying to corrupt the wholesome standard of the saving message, if such there were, lurked somewhere under cover of darkness. But when the sacred band of the apostles had in various ways reached the end of their life, and the generation of those privileged to listen with their own ears to the divine wisdom had passed on, then godless error began to take shape, through the deceit of false teachers, who now that none of the apostles was left threw off the mask and attempted to counter the preaching of the truth by preaching the knowledge falsely so called.

Christian-hunting stopped by Trajan

33. So great was the intensification of the persecution directed against us in many parts of the world at that time, that

1. p. 123.   2. pp. 126–7.

Plinius Secundus,[1] one of the most distinguished governors, was alarmed by the number of martyrs and sent a report to the emperor about the number of those who were being put to death for the faith. In the same dispatch he informed him that he understood they did nothing improper or illegal: all they did was to rise at dawn and hymn Christ as a god, to repudiate adultery, murder, and similar disgraceful crimes, and in every way to conform to the law. Trajan's response was to issue a decree that members of the Christian community were not to be hunted, but if met with were to be punished.[2] This meant that though to some extent the terrifyingly imminent threat of persecution was stifled, yet for those who wanted to injure us there were just as many pretexts left. Sometimes it was the common people, sometimes the local authorities, who devised plots against us, so that even without open persecution sporadic attacks blazed up in one province or another, and many of the faithful endured the ordeal of martyrdom in various forms.

I have taken this story from a book referred to above, Tertullian's Latin *Defence*. The translation is as follows:

And yet we have found that even hunting us is forbidden. For Plinius Secundus, as governor of a province, after condemning several Christians and depriving them of their status, was at a loss because of their numbers; and not knowing what to do in the future, he sent a report to the Emperor Trajan to the effect that except for their refusal to worship idols he had detected nothing improper in their behaviour. He also informed him that the Christians got up at dawn and hymned Christ as a god, and in order to uphold their principles were forbidden to commit murder, adultery, fraud, theft, and the like. In response, Trajan sent a rescript ordering that members of the Christian community were not to be hunted, but if met with were to be punished.

1. Pliny the younger, governor of Bithynia.
2. These famous letters were exchanged in A.D. 112; though we possess copies, apparently Eusebius did not.

Bishops of Rome and Jerusalem

34. In the bishopric of Rome, in the third year of Trajan's reign, Clement departed this life, yielding his office to Evarestus. He had been in charge of the teaching of the divine message for nine years in all.

35. When Symeon had found fulfilment in the manner described, his successor on the throne of the Jerusalem bishopric was a Jew named Justus, one of the vast number of the circumcision who by then believed in Christ.

Ignatius and his epistles

36. Pre-eminent at that time in Asia was a companion of the apostles, Polycarp, on whom the eyewitnesses and ministers[1] of the Lord had conferred the episcopate of the church at Smyrna. Famous contemporaries of his were Papias, bishop of the see of Hierapolis, and one who to this day is universally remembered – Ignatius, the second to be appointed to the bishopric of Antioch in succession to Peter.

There is evidence that Ignatius was sent from Syria to Rome and became food for wild animals because of his testimony to Christ. He made the journey through Asia under the strictest military guard, encouraging the Christian community, by homilies and exhortations, in every city where he stayed. In particular he warned them to guard most carefully against the heresies which were then first becoming prevalent, and exhorted them to hold fast to the apostolic tradition, which, as he was now on his way to martyrdom, he thought it necessary for safety's sake to set down clearly in writing. Thus, when he arrived at Smyrna where Polycarp was, he wrote one epistle to the church at Ephesus referring to their pastor Onesimus, another to the church at Magnesia

1. Luke i. 2.

on the Maeander, where he refers to Bishop Damas, and a
third to the church at Tralles, which, as he states, was then
under the rule of Polybius. In addition he wrote to the
church at Rome; in his letter he implores them not to beg
him off from his martyrdom and so rob him of his longed-
for hope.

In support of these statements it will be well to quote
some very short passages from these letters:

All the way from Syria to Rome I am fighting with wild animals
on land and sea, by night and day, fettered to ten leopards – a squad
of soldiers – whom kindness makes even worse. Their disgraceful
conduct makes me still more a disciple, but that does not justify me.[1]
May it be for my good that the wild animals are ready for me: I
pray that I may find them prompt. I shall coax them to devour me
promptly, unlike some whom they have been afraid to touch; if
they are unwilling and refuse, I will compel them to do it. Pardon
me: I know what is best for me, and now I am beginning to be a
disciple. May nothing seen or unseen grudge my attaining to Jesus
Christ! Let fire and cross, encounters with wild animals, tearing
apart of bones, hacking of limbs, crushing of the whole body, tortures
of the devil come upon me, if only I may attain to Jesus Christ![2]

These letters he wrote from Smyrna to the churches named.
At a further stage of his journey he communicated in writing
from Troas with the Christians at Philadelphia and the
church at Smyrna, along with a personal letter to the head of
that church, Polycarp. He was well aware that Polycarp was
an apostolic man, so like a true and kind shepherd he commended to him the flock at Antioch, asking him to take great
care of it. In his letter to Smyrna he quotes a saying from an
unknown source to support what he is saying about Christ:

I know and am convinced that even after the Resurrection He was
in the flesh. When He came to Peter and his companions He said to

1. 1 Cor. iv. 4.   2. Ignatius: *Romans*.

them: 'Take hold, handle me, and see that I am not a bodiless phantom.' And they at once touched Him and were convinced.[1]

His martyrdom was well known to Irenaeus, who draws on his epistles:

As one of our people said, when because of his witness he was condemned to the beasts: 'I am God's wheat, ground by the teeth of beasts, that I may be found pure bread.'

Polycarp also alludes to these same epistles in the letter to the Philippians that bears his name:

I urge you all to be obedient and to practise the unfailing endurance that you saw before your eyes, not only in blessed Ignatius, Rufus, and Zosimus, but in others from your own number, and in Paul himself and the rest of the apostles: satisfied that all these did not run in vain[2] but in faith and righteousness, and that they are in the place that is their due, by the side of the Lord whose sufferings they shared. For they did not love this present world[3] but the One who died on our behalf and for our sakes was raised by God. ... You wrote to me as did Ignatius, requesting that if anyone was going to Syria he should take your letters with him. I will do so, if I find a convenient opportunity, either personally or by sending an agent on our joint behalf. The epistles which Ignatius sent us, and any others I have by me, I am sending you as requested: they are enclosed with this letter. You will find them most helpful, for they contain faith, endurance, and all the edification that concerns our Lord.

There we must leave Ignatius. As Bishop of Antioch he was succeeded by Heros.

Evangelists still eminent at that time

37. Among the shining lights of the period was Quadratus, who according to the written evidence was, like Philip's

---

1. Ignatius may be quoting from some lost gospel, but is probably giving a loose paraphrase of Luke xxiv. 40, borrowing the word 'convinced' from John xx. 29.

2. Phil. ii. 16.   3. 2 Tim. iv. 10.

daughters, eminent for a prophetic gift. Besides them many others were well known at the time, belonging to the first stage in the apostolic succession. These earnest disciples of great men built on the foundations of the churches everywhere laid by the apostles,[1] spreading the message still further and sowing the saving seed of the Kingdom of Heaven far and wide through the entire world. Very many of the disciples of the time, their hearts smitten by the word of God with an ardent passion for true philosophy, first fulfilled the Saviour's command by distributing their possessions among the needy; then, leaving their homes behind, they carried out the work of evangelists,[2] ambitious to preach to those who had never yet heard the message of the faith[3] and to give them the inspired gospels in writing. Staying only to lay the foundations of the faith in one foreign place or another, appoint others as pastors, and entrust to them the tending of those newly brought in, they set off again for other lands and peoples with the grace and cooperation of God, for even at that late date many miraculous powers of the divine Spirit worked through them, so that at the first hearing whole crowds in a body embraced with whole-hearted eagerness the worship of the universal Creator.[4]

Clement's Epistle: works mistakenly attributed to him

As it is impossible for me to enumerate by name all who in the first succession from the apostles became pastors or evangelists in the churches of all the known world, I have naturally included in my account the individual stories only of those whose transmission of the apostolic teaching can still be studied in their writings.   38. Obvious instances are Ignatius, in the epistles already listed, and Clement in the

---

1. 1 Cor. iii. 10.   2. 1 Tim. iv. 5.   3. A reminiscence of Rom. xv. 20–21.
4. The aim of these evangelists, as of Paul at Lystra and Athens, was to wean pagans from polytheism to belief in one beneficent Creator.

one universally recognized, which he indited in the name of the church at Rome to that at Corinth. In this he echoes many thoughts from the Epistle to the Hebrews, and indeed makes many verbal quotations from it, proving beyond a doubt that the document was not of recent origin, and making it seem quite natural to include it with the rest in the list of the Apostle's writings. Paul had communicated with the Hebrews by writing to them in their native tongue; and some say that the evangelist Luke, others that this same Clement translated the original text. The second suggestion is the more convincing, in view of the similarity of phraseology shown throughout by the Epistle of Clement and the Epistle to the Hebrews, and of the absence of any great difference between the two works in the underlying thought.

It must not be overlooked that there is a second epistle said to be from Clement's pen, but I have no reason to suppose that it was well known like the first one, since I am not aware that the early fathers made any use of it. A year or two ago other long and wordy treatises were put forward as Clement's work. They contain alleged dialogues with[1] Peter and Apion, but there is no mention whatever of them by early writers, nor do they preserve in its purity the stamp of apostolic orthodoxy.

The writings of Papias

39. I have now made it clear what is the acknowledged work of Clement, and have discussed the works of Ignatius and Polycarp. Papias has left us five volumes entitled *The Sayings of the Lord Explained*. These are mentioned by Irenaeus as the only works from his pen:

> To these things Papias, who had listened to John and was later a companion of Polycarp, and who lived at a very early date, bears written testimony in the fourth of his books; he composed five.

1. Or 'between'.

That is what Irenaeus says; but Papias himself in the preface to his work makes it clear that he was never a hearer or eye-witness of the holy apostles, and tells us that he learnt the essentials of the Faith from their former pupils:

> I shall not hesitate to furnish you, along with the interpretations, with all that in days gone by I carefully learnt from the presbyters and have carefully recalled, for I can guarantee its truth. Unlike most people, I felt at home not with those who had a great deal to say, but with those who taught the truth; not with those who appeal to commandments from other sources but with those who appeal to the commandments given by the Lord to faith and coming to us from truth itself. And whenever anyone came who had been a follower of the presbyters, I inquired into the words of the presbyters, what Andrew or Peter had said, or Philip or Thomas or James or John or Matthew, or any other disciple of the Lord, and what Aristion[1] and the presbyter John, disciples of the Lord, were still saying. For I did not imagine that things out of books would help me as much as the utterances of a living and abiding voice.[2]

Here it should be observed that he twice includes the name of John. The first John he puts in the same list as Peter, James, Matthew, and the rest of the apostles, obviously with the evangelist in mind; the second, with a changed form of expression, he places in a second group outside the number of the apostles, giving precedence to Aristion and clearly calling John a presbyter. He thus confirms the truth of the story that two men in Asia had the same name, and that there were two tombs in Ephesus, each of which is still called John's. This is highly significant, for it is likely that the second – if we cannot accept the first – saw the Revelation that bears the name of John. Papias, whom we are now discussing, owns that he learnt the words of the apostles from their former followers, but says that he listened to Aristion and the presbyter John with his own ears. Certainly

1. The reputed author of the present ending of Mark's gospel.
2. A reminiscence of 1 Peter i. 23.

he often mentions them by name, and reproduces their teachings in his writings.[1]

I hope that these suggestions are of some value. Now we must go on, from the remarks of Papias already quoted, to other passages in which he tells us of certain miraculous events and other matters, on the basis, it would seem, of direct information. It has already been mentioned that Philip the Apostle resided at Hierapolis with his daughters: it must now be pointed out that their contemporary Papias tells how he heard a wonderful story from the lips of Philip's daughters. He describes the resurrection of a dead person[2] in his own lifetime, and a further miracle that happened to Justus, surnamed Barsabas, who swallowed a dangerous poison and by the grace of the Lord was none the worse. After the Saviour's ascension, this Justus was put forward with Matthias by the holy apostles, who prayed over them before drawing lots for someone to fill up their number in place of the traitor Judas. This incident is described in the Acts:

And they put forward two men, Joseph called Barsabas and surnamed Justus, and Matthias. Then they prayed and said . . .[3]

Papias reproduces other stories communicated to him by word of mouth, together with some otherwise unknown

1. Eusebius's reasoning is unsatisfactory. The fact that the second John is called a presbyter does not distinguish him from the first John, who like Peter, Andrew, and the rest is expressly referred to as a presbyter, nor does the precedence given to Aristion: Philip and Thomas are similarly put before the first John. Nor does the fact that he is mentioned twice: he is first included in the list of presbyters (which, as Eusebius saw, is here equivalent to apostles); then he is mentioned with Aristion, because these two long survived the others. Eusebius has failed to notice the change of tense from 'had said' to 'were saying'. His only authority for the belief that there were two tombs is Dionysius's cautious statement, written nearly two centuries after John's death: 'There are said to have been two tombs in Ephesus, each reputed to be John's.' Nor would two tombs prove that there were two Johns, any more than the five cities each claiming to possess the head of John the Baptist prove that there were five Baptists.

2. Named by Papias as the wife of Manaen.

3. Acts i. 23.

parables and teachings of the Saviour, and other things of a more allegorical character. He says that after the resurrection of the dead there will be a period of a thousand years, when Christ's kingdom will be set up on this earth in material form. I suppose he got these notions by misinterpreting the apostolic accounts and failing to grasp what they had said in mystic and symbolic language. For he seems to have been a man of very small intelligence, to judge from his books. But it is partly due to him that the great majority of churchmen after him took the same view, relying on his early date; e.g. Irenaeus and several others, who clearly held the same opinion.[1]

In his own book Papias gives us accounts of the Lord's sayings obtained from Aristion or learnt direct from the presbyter John. Having brought these to the attention of scholars, I must now follow up the statements already quoted from him with a piece of information which he sets out regarding Mark, the writer of the gospel:

This, too, the presbyter used to say. 'Mark, who had been Peter's interpreter, wrote down carefully, but not in order, all that he remembered of the Lord's sayings and doings. For he had not heard the Lord or been one of His followers, but later, as I said, one of Peter's. Peter used to adapt his teaching to the occasion, without making a systematic arrangement of the Lord's sayings, so that Mark was quite justified in writing down some things just as he remembered them. For he had one purpose only – to leave out nothing that he had heard, and to make no misstatement about it.'

Such is Papias's account of Mark. Of Matthew he has this to say:

Matthew compiled the *Sayings* in the Aramaic language, and everyone translated them as well as he could.[2]

1. We shall need more evidence before accepting this contemptuous dismissal of Papias and so many others as unintelligent. Did they misinterpret the apostolic accounts, or did Eusebius misinterpret theirs?
2. There seems no reason to doubt this statement, but what the *Sayings* (i.e. divine pronouncements) were is uncertain. Probably they were a collec-

Papias also makes use of evidence drawn from 1 John and 1 Peter, and reproduces a story about a woman falsely accused before the Lord of many sins. This is to be found in the Gospel of the Hebrews.[1]

This is all that it is necessary to add to the passages I have quoted.

---

tion of our Lord's authoritative utterances, later translated into Greek and fitted, perhaps by another hand, into a framework of narrative to make the complete gospel that we possess.

1. Is this the story of the woman taken in adultery (which appears in our Bibles on the strength of one good MS. only, and is there clearly out of place)?

Book 4

*Bishops of Rome and Alexandria in Trajan's reign:
the Jewish tragedy*

1. About the twelfth year of Trajan's reign[1] the Bishop of
Alexandria mentioned a few pages back[2] departed this life,
and Primus, the fourth from the apostles, was chosen to hold
office there. Meanwhile at Rome, when Evarestus had completed his eighth year, Alexander took up the bishopric as fifth
successor to Peter and Paul.

2. While our Saviour's teaching and His Church were
flourishing and progressing further every day, the Jewish
tragedy was moving through a series of disasters towards its
climax. When the emperor was about to enter his eighteenth
year another rebellion broke out and destroyed vast numbers
of Jews. In Alexandria and the rest of Egypt, and in Cyrene
as well, as if inflamed by some terrible spirit of revolt they
rushed into a faction fight against their Greek fellow-citizens,
raised the temperature to fever heat, and in the following
summer started a full-scale war, Lupus being at that time
governor of all Egypt. From the first encounter they emerged
victorious. But the Greeks fled to Alexandria, where they
killed or captured the Jews in the city. But though deprived
of their aid, the Jews of Cyrene went on plundering the territory of Egypt and ravaging the various districts, led by Lucuas.

1. A.D. 109.   2. Cerdo.

Against them the emperor sent Marcius Turbo with land and sea forces, including a contingent of cavalry. He pursued the war against them relentlessly in a long series of battles, destroying many thousands of Jews, not only those from Cyrene but others who had come from Egypt to assist Lucuas their king.

The emperor, suspecting that the Jews in Mesopotamia also would attack the people there, instructed Lucius Quietus to clear them out of the province. Lucius deployed his forces and slaughtered great numbers of the people there – a success for which the emperor appointed him governor of Judaea. These events were recorded in similar terms by the Greek authors who wrote histories of the same period.[1]

Hadrian's reign: defenders of the Faith, and Bishops of Rome and Alexandria

3. When Trajan had ruled for six months short of twenty years Aelius Hadrianus succeeded to the throne.[2] To him Quadratus addressed and sent a pamphlet which he had composed in defence of our religion, because unscrupulous persons were trying to get our people into trouble. Many of the brethren still possess copies of this little work; indeed, I have one myself. In it can be found shining proofs of the author's intellectual grasp and apostolic correctness. He reveals his very early date by the wording of his composition.

Our Saviour's works were always there to see, for they were true – the people who had been cured and those raised from the dead, who had not merely been seen at the moment when they were cured or raised, but were *always* there to see, not only when the Saviour was among us, but for a long time after His departure; in fact some of them survived right up to my own time.[3]

---

1. e.g. Appian and Dio Cassius.   2. 8 August A.D. 117.
3. They might well survive till the nineties, when Quadratus was presumably a young man.

Aristides again, a loyal and devoted Christian, has like Quadratus left us a *Defence of the Faith* addressed to Hadrian. Many people still preserve copies of his work also.

4. In the third year of the same reign[1] Alexander Bishop of Rome died, after completing the tenth year of his ministry: Xystus was his successor. In the diocese of Alexandria at about the same time Primus passed away in the twelfth year of his rule and was succeeded by Justus.

Bishops of Jerusalem up to Hadrian's time

5. Of the dates of the bishops at Jerusalem I have failed to find any written evidence – it is known that they were very short lived – but I have received documentary proof of this, that up to Hadrian's siege of the Jews there had been a series of fifteen bishops there. All are said to have been Hebrews in origin, who had received the knowledge of Christ with all sincerity, with the result that those in a position to decide such matters judged them worthy of the episcopal office. For at that time their whole church consisted of Hebrew believers who had continued from apostolic times down to the later siege in which the Jews, after revolting a second time from the Romans, were overwhelmed in a full-scale war.

As that meant the end of bishops of the Circumcision,[2] this is the right moment to list their names from the first. The first, then, was James 'the Lord's brother'. Second came Symeon, third Justus, fourth Zacchaeus, fifth Tobias, sixth Benjamin, seventh John, eighth Matthias, ninth Philip, tenth Seneca, eleventh Justus, twelfth Levi, thirteenth Ephres, fourteenth Joseph, fifteenth and last Judas. That was the number of bishops in the city of Jerusalem from apostolic times to the date mentioned, all of them of the Circumcision.[3]

1. A.D. 119.   2. In A.D. 135 Hadrian banished all Jews from Jerusalem.
3. There must therefore have been thirteen bishops between A.D. 106 and 135.

In Hadrian's twelfth year, Xystus, Bishop of Rome for a decade, was succeeded by the seventh from the apostles, Telesphorus. A year and some months later the see of Alexandria came under the rule of Eumenes, the sixth to be appointed, his predecessor having been in office eleven years.

The final siege of the Jews

6. When the Jewish revolt again grew to formidable dimensions, Rufus governor of Judaea, on receiving military reinforcements from the emperor, took merciless advantage of their crazy folly and marched against them, destroying at one stroke unlimited numbers of men, women, and children alike, and – as the laws of war permitted – confiscating all their lands. The Jews at that time were under the command of a man called Bar Cochba, which means a star – a bloodthirsty bandit who on the strength of his name,[1] as if he had slaves to deal with, paraded himself as a luminary come down from heaven to shine upon their misery.

The climax of the war came in Hadrian's eighteenth year, in Betthera, an almost impregnable little town not very far from Jerusalem.[2] The blockade from without lasted so long that hunger and thirst brought the revolutionaries to complete destruction, and the instigator of their crazy folly paid the penalty he deserved. From that time on, the entire race has been forbidden to set foot anywhere in the neighbourhood of Jerusalem, under the terms and ordinances of a law of Hadrian which ensured that not even from a distance might Jews have a view of their ancestral soil. Aristo of Pella tells the whole story. When in this way the city was closed to the Jewish race and suffered the total destruction of its former inhabitants, it was colonized by an alien race, and the Roman city which subsequently arose changed its name, so

1. Which implied Messiahship: see Num. xxiv. 17.
2. Probably Bittir, seven miles s.w. of Jerusalem.

that now, in honour of the emperor then reigning, Aelius Hadrianus, it is known as Aelia. Furthermore, as the church in the city was now composed of Gentiles, the first after the bishops of the Circumcision to be put in charge of the Christians there was Mark.

Leaders at that time of Knowledge falsely so called

7. Like dazzling lights the churches were now shining all over the world, and to the limits of the human race faith in our Saviour and Lord Jesus Christ was at its peak, when the demon who hates the good, sworn enemy of truth and in- veterate foe of man's salvation, turned all his weapons against the Church. In earlier days he had attacked her with persecu- tions from without; but now that he was debarred from this, he resorted to unscrupulous impostors as instruments of spiritual corruption and ministers of destruction, and em- ployed new tactics, contriving by every possible means that impostors and cheats, by cloaking themselves with the same name as our religion, should at one and the same time bring to the abyss of destruction every believer they could entrap, and by their own actions and endeavours turn those ignorant of the Faith away from the path that leads to the message of salvation.

Thus it was that from Menander – who was mentioned above as successor to Simon – proceeded a power with the two mouths and twin heads of a snake, which set up the originators of two heresies, Saturninus, an Antiochene by birth, and Basilides of Alexandria, who – one in Syria and one in Egypt – established schools of detestable heresies. For the most part Saturninus taught the same false doctrines as Menander, as Irenaeus makes clear; but Basilides, under the pretence of deeper mysteries, extended his fantasies into the infinite, inventing monstrous fictions to support his impious heresy. Consequently, while a great number of churchmen were busy at that time fighting for the truth and eloquently championing the beliefs of the apostles and the Church, some also set down on paper for the benefit of later generations the means of defence against these very heresies.

I have in my hands, from the pen of a very well-known writer of the day, Agrippa Castor, a most effective refutation of Basilides, which unmasks the man's clever imposture. In laying bare his mysteries he says that Basilides compiled twenty-four books on the gospel and that he named as his prophets Barcabbas and Barcoph, inventing for himself several others, creatures of his imagination, and calling them by barbarous names to amaze those who gape at such things. He taught that there was no objection to eating meat offered to idols, or to cheerfully forswearing the Faith in times of persecution. Like Pythagoras he enjoined on his neophytes a five-year silence. Other facts of the same sort about Basilides are catalogued by Agrippa, who thus admirably exposed the erroneous character of this heresy.

Irenaeus also writes that contemporary with these was Carpocrates, father of another heresy known as that of the Gnostics.[1] These claimed to transmit Simon's magic arts, not secretly like Basilides but quite openly, as if this was something marvellous, preening themselves as it were on the spells which they cast by sorcery, on dream-bringing familiar spirits, and on other goings-on of the same sort. In keeping with this they teach that all the vilest things must be done by those who intend to go through with their initiation into these 'mysteries' or rather abominations; for in no other way can they escape the 'cosmic rulers' than by rendering to them all the due performance of unspeakable rites.

Thus it came about that with the help of these ministers the demon that delights in evil enslaved their pitiable dupes and brought them to ruin, furnishing the unbelieving heathen with ample grounds for speaking ill of the divine message, since

1. There had been other gnostics many years earlier.

the talk to which they gave rise circulated widely and involved the whole Christian people in calumny. This was the main reason why that wicked and outrageous suspicion regarding us was current among the unbelievers of that time – the suspicion that we practised unlawful intercourse with mothers and sisters and took part in unhallowed feasts.[1]

But this propaganda brought Carpocrates no lasting success, for Truth asserted herself, and with the march of time shone with increasing light. For by her activity the machinations of her foes were promptly shown up and extinguished, though one after another new heresies were invented, the earlier ones constantly passing away and disappearing, in different ways at different times, into forms of every shape and character. But the splendour of the Catholic and only true Church, always remaining the same and unchanged, grew steadily in greatness and strength, shedding on every race of Greeks and non-Greeks alike the majestic, spotless, free, sober, pure light of her inspired citizenship and philosophy. Thus the passage of time extinguished the calumnies against the whole of our doctrine, and our teaching remained alone, everywhere victorious and acknowledged as supreme in dignity and sobriety, in divine and philosophic doctrines, so that no one today could dare to subject our Faith to vile abuse or to any such misrepresentation as in the past those who conspired against us were in the habit of using.

Church writers

However, at the time of which I am speaking Truth again put forward many to do battle for her, and they, not only with spoken arguments but also with written demonstrations, took the field against the godless heresies. Among these Hegesippus was prominent.   8. I have already quoted him on numerous occasions, using information gained from him to establish

1. The reference is to cannibalism.

facts about the apostolic age. In five short books, written in
the simplest style, he gave an authentic account of the apostolic preaching. His *floruit* is indicated by his remarks on those
who first set up idols:

> In their honour they erected cenotaphs and temples, as they still
> do. One of these was Antinous, a slave of Hadrian Caesar's, in memory
> of whom the Antinoian Games are held. He was my own contem-
> porary. Hadrian even built a city called after him, and appointed
> prophets.[1]

In his time also Justin, a genuine lover of the true philosophy, was still busy studying Greek learning. He too indicates this date, when in his *Defence* to Antoninus he writes:

> I think it not out of place at this point to mention Antinous who
> died so recently. Everyone was frightened into worshipping him as
> a god, though everyone knew who he was and where he came from.

Again, speaking of the war which had just been fought
against the Jews, Justin remarks:

> In the recent Jewish war, Bar Cochba, leader of the Jewish insur-
> rection, ordered the Christians alone to be sentenced to terrible pun-
> ishments if they did not deny Jesus Christ and blaspheme Him.

In the same volume he also shows that his change from
Greek philosophy to true religion was not made hastily but
after mature reflection:

> I myself found satisfaction in Plato's teaching, and used to hear
> the Christians abused, but when I found them fearless in the face of
> death and all that men think terrible, it dawned on me that they could
> not possibly be living in wickedness and self-indulgence. For how
> could a self-indulgent or licentious person who took pleasure in de-
> vouring human flesh greet death with a smile, as if he wanted to be
> deprived of the things he loved most? Would he not rather strive by
> all means to prolong his present existence indefinitely, and keep out

1. Antinous, a favourite slave who was drowned, was deified in A.D. 130
or 131.

of sight of the secular authorities, rather than give himself up to certain death?

Justin also notes that when Hadrian received from His Excellency the Governor Serennius Granianus an appeal on behalf of the Christians, maintaining that it was not right when no charge had been brought to gratify popular clamour by putting them to death without a trial, he sent a rescript to Minucius Fundanus, proconsul of Asia, forbidding him to try anyone unless properly charged and prosecuted in a reasonable manner. He appends a copy of the letter, retaining the original Latin and prefacing it with the following:

> Though on the strength of a letter from the great and glorious Caesar Hadrian, your father, I might have petitioned you to carry out my request and order the trials to be held, I am basing this request not on the command of Hadrian but on my awareness that in my address I am requesting what is just. However I am appending a facsimile of Hadrian's letter, that you may know that on this point also I am speaking the truth. Here it is.

To this the writer appends the actual Latin rescript: I have rendered it into Greek as well as I can.

Hadrian's letter forbidding persecution without trial

9. To Minucius Fundanus. I have received a letter written to me by His Excellency Serennius Granianus, your predecessor. It is not my intention to leave the matter uninvestigated, for fear of causing the men embarrassment and abetting the informers in their mischief-making. If then the provincials can so clearly establish their case against the Christians that they can sustain it in a court of law, let them resort to this procedure only, and not rely on petitions or mere clamour. Much the most satisfactory course, if anyone should wish to prosecute, is for you to decide the matter. So if someone prosecutes them and proves them guilty of any illegality, you must pronounce sentence according to the seriousness of the offence. But if anyone

starts such proceedings in the hope of financial reward, then for goodness sake arrest him for his shabby trick, and see that he gets his deserts.

Such were the terms of Hadrian's rescript.

Bishops of Rome and Alexandria in Antoninus's reign: the heresiarchs

10. When Hadrian, after twenty-one years, paid the debt of nature, Antoninus called Pius succeeded to the Roman Empire.[1] In his first year, Telesphorus departed this life in the eleventh year of his ministry, and Hyginus took over the office of Bishop of Rome. Irenaeus notes that Telesphorus died nobly as a martyr. In the same chapter he states that while Hyginus was bishop, Valentinus, who introduced a heresy of his own, and Cerdo, who was responsible for the Marcionite error, were both prominent in Rome. He writes:

11. Valentinus arrived in Rome in the time of Hyginus, reached his heyday under Pius, and remained till Anicetus. Cerdo, who preceded Marcion, also joined the Roman church and declared his faith publicly, in the time of Hyginus, the ninth bishop;[2] then he went on in this way – at one time he taught in secret, at another he again declared his faith publicly, at another he was convicted of mischievous teaching and expelled from the Christian community.

This comes from Book III of *Heresies Answered*. In Book I we find this additional information about Cerdo:

One Cerdo, whose notions stemmed from the followers of Simon, had settled in Rome in the time of Hyginus, who held the ninth place in the episcopal succession from the apostles. He taught that the God proclaimed by the Law and the Prophets was not the Father of our Lord Jesus Christ; for the one was known, the other unknown; the one was righteous, the other gracious. He was succeeded by Marcion of Pontus, who inflated his teaching, blaspheming unblushingly.

1. 10 July A.D. 138.   2. The eighth, unless Irenaeus counts Peter.

In another passage Irenaeus most effectively exposes the limitless depths of Valentinus's most erroneous system, and brings his wickedness, hidden out of sight like a reptile lurking in a hole, to the light of day. He further tells us about a contemporary of theirs, Marcus by name, a past-master in magical trickery, and writes of their senseless ceremonies and misbegotten mysteries, explaining them thus:

Some of them fit out a bridal chamber, and celebrate a mystery with invocations on those being initiated, declaring that what they are doing is a spiritual marriage on the pattern of the unions above; others take the candidates to water and baptize them, reciting this formula: 'Into the name of the unknown Father of the universe, into Truth the Mother of all things, into Him who came down into Jesus.' Others recite Hebrew words, in order to cause still more astonishment to those being initiated.

After four years as Bishop of Rome Hyginus died, and Pius was chosen for the office. At Alexandria Mark was appointed pastor when Eumenes had completed thirteen years in all; ten years later, when Mark rested from his ministry, Celadion took over the ministry of the church at Alexandria. In Rome Pius passed away in the fifteenth year of his episcopate and Anicetus took charge of the community there. In his time Hegesippus settled in Rome, as he tells us himself, staying there till the episcopate of Eleutherus.

In their time Justin was at his most active; wearing the garb of a philosopher he proclaimed the divine message, and contended by means of his writings on behalf of the Faith. In a pamphlet which he wrote against Marcion he mentions that at the time when he was composing it the man was alive and in the public eye:

There was one Marcion of Pontus, who is still busy teaching his adherents to believe in some other god greater than the Creator. All over the world, with the help of the demons, he has induced many to speak blasphemously, denying that the Maker of this universe is the Father of Christ, and declaring that the universe was made by

another, greater than He. All who base their belief on such doctrines
are, as I said, called Christians, just as philosophers, even if they have
no common principles, yet have one thing in common – the name
'philosopher'.

He adds a further note:

I have also written a book in answer to all the heresies that have
appeared: if you would care to read it, I will present it to you.

Justin's Defence: *Antoninus's letter to the Council of Asia*

Justin, in addition to his admirable work *Against the Greeks*,
addressed other compositions containing *A Defence of our
Faith* to the Emperor Antoninus, surnamed Pius, and to the
Roman Senate: he had made his home in the capital. In the
Defence he explains who he was and where he came from:

12. To the Emperor Titus Aelius Hadrianus Antoninus Pius Caesar
Augustus, to Verissimus his son the philosopher,[1] to Lucius,[2] son by
nature of the philosopher Caesar and by adoption of Pius, a passionate seeker after knowledge, and to the holy Senate and the entire
People of Rome, on behalf of the men of every nation who are unjustly hated and abused, I, Justin, son of Priscus and grandson of
Bacchius, of Flavia Neapolis[3] in Palestine, being one of their number,
have composed this address and petition.

Petitioned also by Christians in Asia who were labouring
under injuries of every kind at the hands of the local population, the same emperor[4] was pleased to address this decree to
the Council of Asia:

13. The Emperor Caesar Marcus Aurelius Antoninus Augustus
Armenius, Pontifex Maximus, holding Tribunician Power the

1. Later the Emperor Marcus Aurelius.
2. Later joint ruler with Marcus Aurelius.
3. The New City of Flavius (i.e. Vespasian), now Nablus.
4. Eusebius, confused by the multiple names of the Antonines, seems not to
have realized that Antoninus Pius was not called Marcus Aurelius.

fifteenth time, Consul the third, to the Council of Asia, greeting. I know that the gods also take care that such persons should not go undetected: they are far more likely to punish those who will not worship them than you are. You get them into serious trouble by your accusations of atheism, and thereby strengthen their existing determination: and if accused they would choose apparent death rather than life, for the sake of their own god. And so they are the real winners, when they part with their lives rather than agree to carry out your commands. As regards the earthquakes which have been and still are occurring, it will not be out of place to draw your attention to the fact that whenever they happen your courage fails you, providing a painful contrast between our morale and theirs. They gain increased confidence in their god; whereas you, the whole of the time that you appear to be ignorant, neglect the other gods and the worship of the Immortal.[1] But when the Christians worship Him you bully them and persecute them to death. On behalf of these people many of the provincial governors at an earlier date wrote to our most divine father,[2] who sent them a reply forbidding them to take any action against these people unless it was clear that they were scheming against the Roman government. I too have received information about them from many quarters: I have replied in accordance with my father's wishes. But if anyone persists in starting legal proceedings against one of these people, simply because he is one of them, the accused shall be acquitted of the charge even if it is plain that he is one, and the accuser shall be liable to penalty. Published at Ephesus in the Council of Asia.[3]

That this is how things happened we also gather from Melito, the eminent Bishop of Sardis at that time. So much is clear from what he says in the *Defence of our Doctrine* which he sent to the Emperor Verus.

1. The Greek is hardly intelligible.
2. The previous emperor.
3. This rescript, or the Latin of which it is a clumsy translation, is thought by many scholars to be a forgery, but is in the main defended by Harnack. It is always possible for genuine documents to be corrupted, like many passages in A.V., by the innocent incorporation of marginal glosses.

The story of Polycarp, the pupil of the apostles

14. At this period, while Anicetus was head of the Roman church, Polycarp, who was still living, came to Rome and discussed with Anicetus some difficulty about the date of Easter. This we gather from Irenaeus, who tells us another story about Polycarp which must be included in the account of him that I am giving. Here it is:

FROM BOOK III OF HERESIES ANSWERED, BY IRENAEUS

Polycarp was not only instructed by apostles and conversant with many who had seen the Lord, but was appointed by apostles to serve in Asia as Bishop of Smyrna. I myself saw him in my early years, for he lived a long time and was very old indeed when he laid down his life by a glorious and most splendid martyrdom. At all times he taught the things which he had learnt from the apostles, which the Church transmits, which alone are true. These facts are attested by all the churches of Asia and by the successors of Polycarp to this day – and he was a much more trustworthy and dependable witness to the truth than Valentinus and Marcion and all other wrong-headed persons. In the time of Anicetus he stayed for a while in Rome, where he won over many from the camp of these heretics to the Church of God, proclaiming that the one and only truth he had received from the apostles was the truth transmitted by the Church. And there are people who heard him describe how John, the Lord's disciple, when at Ephesus went to take a bath, but seeing Cerinthus inside rushed out of the building without taking a bath, crying: 'Let us get out of here, for fear the place falls in, now that Cerinthus, the enemy of truth, is inside!' Polycarp himself on one occasion came face to face with Marcion, and when Marcion said 'Don't you recognize me?' he replied: 'I do indeed: I recognize the firstborn of Satan!' So careful were the apostles and their disciples to avoid even exchanging words with any falsifier of the truth, in obedience to the Pauline injunction: 'If a man remains heretical after more than one warning, have no more to do with him, recognizing that a person of that type is a perverted sinner, self-condemned.'[1]

1. Titus iii. 10.

There is also a most forceful epistle written by Polycarp to the
Philippians, from which both the character of his faith and his
preaching of the truth can be learnt by all who wish to do so and care
about their own salvation.

Such is Irenaeus's account. Polycarp in his letter to the
Philippians, referred to above and still extant, has supported
his views with several quotations from the First Epistle of
Peter.

Martyrdom of Polycarp and others at Smyrna

Antoninus Pius, after a reign of twenty-two years, was succeeded[1] by his son Marcus Aurelius Verus (or Antoninus) in
association with his brother Lucius.   15. In this period[2] Asia
was thrown into confusion by the most savage persecutions,
and Polycarp found fulfilment in martyrdom. As a written
account of his end has come down to us, I am in duty bound
to enshrine it in my pages. I refer to the letter, sent on behalf
of the church over which he himself had presided, to inform
the Christian communities everywhere of what happened to
him. It begins thus:

The church of God at Smyrna to the church of God at Philo-
melium[3] and to all communities of the Holy Catholic Church everywhere – may mercy, peace, and love from God the Father and our
Lord Jesus Christ be yours in abundance. We are writing, brethren,
to tell you the story of those who have suffered martyrdom, especially
blessed Polycarp, who as though he had set his seal on it by his
martyrdom, brought the persecution to an end.

After this, before giving an account of Polycarp's death,
they relate what happened to the other martyrs, vividly describing the heroism with which they faced their torments, to
the amazement of the spectators on every side. Sometimes

1. 7 March A.D. 161.
2. Five years earlier, most scholars think.
3. In Phrygia.

they were torn with scourges to the innermost veins and
arteries, so that even the secret hidden parts of the body, the
entrails and internal organs, were laid bare; sometimes they
were forced to lie on pointed seashells and sharp spikes. After
going through every kind of punishment and torture, they
were finally flung to the beasts as food.

Special mention is made of the noble Germanicus, who by
divine grace overcame his natural physical fear of death. The
proconsul tried to dissuade him, stressing his youth and begging him as one still in the very prime of life to spare himself;
but without a moment's hesitation he drew the savage beast
towards him, wellnigh forcing and goading it on, the more
quickly to escape from their wicked, lawless life. After his
glorious death the whole crowd were so astounded by the
heroism of God's beloved martyr, and the courage of Christian people everywhere, that a shout went up from all sides:
'Away with the godless! Fetch Polycarp!' The uproar that
followed these shouts was so tremendous that a man named
Quintus, newly arrived from Phrygia, on seeing the beasts
and the threatened torments to follow broke down completely and ended by throwing away his salvation. It is plain
from the text of the letter I have quoted that along with others
this man dashed towards the tribunal with too much haste
and without due thought, but when seized he gave everyone
clear proof that it is fatal to risk such ventures in a reckless
and thoughtless spirit. So ends the story of these men.

As for the wonderful Polycarp, when he first heard the
news he remained unperturbed, preserving a firm and unshakeable demeanour, and wished to stay on in the city; but
when his friends begged and besought him to make good his
escape he was persuaded to go as far as a farm only a little
distance away. There he remained with a few companions,
devoting himself night and day to constant prayer to the
Lord, pleading and imploring as he had always done that God
would grant peace to the churches throughout the world.

Three nights before his arrest, while at prayer he saw in a trance the pillow under his head burst into flames and burn to a cinder. He awoke at once and interpreted the vision to those present, opening the book of things to come and leaving his friends in no doubt that for Christ's sake he was to depart this life by fire. As the efforts of his pursuers went on relentlessly, the love and devotion of the brethren compelled him to move on to yet another farm. There he was soon overtaken: two of the farm servants were seized, and under torture one of them revealed Polycarp's quarters. Late in the evening they arrived and found him in bed upstairs. He might easily have moved to another house but he had refused, saying: 'God's will be done.' Indeed, when he heard that they had come, the account informs us, he came down and talked to them in the most cheerful and gentle manner, so that, never having seen him before, they could hardly believe their eyes when confronted with his advanced years and dignified confident bearing. Why, they wondered, was there such anxiety to arrest an old man of this kind? He meanwhile ordered the table to be laid for them immediately, and invited them to eat as much as they liked, asking in return a single hour in which he could pray unmolested. Leave being given, he stood up and prayed, full of the grace of the Lord, to the amazement of those who were present and heard him pray, many of them indeed distressed now by the coming destruction of an old man so dignified and so godlike.

From that point the letter tells us the rest of the story as follows:

At last he ended his prayer, after mentioning all with whom at any time he had been associated, whether small or great, famous or unknown, and the whole Catholic Church throughout the world. The hour for departure had come, so they set him on an ass and brought him to the city. The day was a Great Sabbath.[1] He was met

1. Either Purim or the Passover Saturday.

by Herod the chief of police and his father Nicetes, who after trans-
ferring him to their carriage sat beside him and tried persuasion.
'What harm is there in saying "Lord Caesar" and sacrificing? You
will be safe then.' At first he made no answer, but when they persisted he replied: 'I have no intention of taking your advice.' Persuasion having failed they turned to threats, and put him down so
hurriedly that in leaving the carriage he scraped his shin. But without
even looking round, as if nothing had happened, he set off happily
and at a swinging pace for the stadium. There the noise was so deafen-
ing that many could not hear at all, but as Polycarp came into the
arena a voice from heaven came to him: 'Be strong, Polycarp, and
play the man.' No one saw the speaker, but many of our people heard
the voice.

His introduction was followed by a tremendous roar as the news
went round: 'Polycarp has been arrested!' At length, when he stepped
forward, he was asked by the proconsul if he really was Polycarp.
When he said yes, the proconsul urged him to deny the charge.
'Respect your years!' he exclaimed, adding similar appeals regularly
made on such occasions: 'Swear by Caesar's fortune; change your
attitude; say: "Away with the godless!"' But Polycarp, with his face
set, looked at all the crowd in the stadium and waved his hand towards them, sighed, looked up to heaven, and cried: 'Away with the
godless!' The governor pressed him further: 'Swear, and I will set
you free: execrate Christ.' 'For eighty-six years,' replied Polycarp,
'I have been His servant,[1] and He has never done me wrong: how
can I blaspheme my King who saved me?' When the other persisted: 'Swear by Caesar's fortune,' Polycarp retorted: 'If you
imagine that I will swear by Caesar's fortune, as you put it, pretending not to know who I am, I will tell you plainly, I am a Christian.
If you wish to study the Christian doctrine, choose a day and you
shall hear it.' The proconsul replied, 'Convince the people.' 'With
you,' rejoined Polycarp, 'I think it proper to discuss these things;
for we have been taught to render as their due to rulers and powers
ordained by God such honour as casts no stain on us: to the people I
do not feel it my duty to make any defence.' 'I have wild beasts,'
said the proconsul. 'I shall throw you to them, if you don't change
your attitude.' 'Call them,' replied the old man. 'We cannot change

1. Does this imply infant baptism?

our attitude if it means a change from better to worse. But it is a splendid thing to change from cruelty to justice.' 'If you make light of the beasts,' retorted the governor, 'I'll have you destroyed by fire, unless you change your attitude.' Polycarp answered: 'The fire you threaten burns for a time and is soon extinguished: there is a fire you know nothing about – the fire of the judgement to come and of eternal punishment, the fire reserved for the ungodly. But why do you hesitate? Do what you want.'

As he said this and much besides, he was filled with courage and joy, and his features were full of grace, so that not only did he not wilt in alarm at the things said to him, but on the contrary the pro-consul was amazed, and sent the crier to stand in the middle of the arena and announce three times: 'Polycarp has confessed that he is a Christian.' At this announcement the whole mass of Smyrnaeans, Gentiles and Jews alike, boiled with anger and shouted at the tops of their voices: 'This fellow is the teacher of Asia, the father of the Christians, the destroyer of our gods, who teaches numbers of people not to sacrifice or even worship.' So saying, they loudly demanded that the Asiarch Philip should set a lion on Polycarp. He objected that this would be illegal, as he had closed the sports. Then a shout went up from every throat that Polycarp must be burnt alive. For it was inevitable that the vision which appeared to him about the pillow should be fulfilled: he had seen it burning as he prayed, and turning to the faithful with him had said prophetically: 'I must be burnt alive.'

The rest followed in less time than it takes to describe: the crowds rushed to collect logs and faggots from workshop and public baths, the Jews as usual joining in with more enthusiasm than anyone. When the pyre was ready, he took off all his outer garments, loosened his belt, and even tried to remove his shoes, though not used to doing this, because each of the faithful strove at all times to be the first to touch his person. Even before his hair turned grey he had been honoured in every way because of his virtuous life. There was no hesitation now. The instruments prepared for the pyre were put round him, but when they were going to nail him too, he cried: 'Leave me as I am: He who enables me to endure the fire will enable me, even if you don't secure me with nails, to remain on the pyre without shrinking.' So they bound him without nailing him. He

put his hands behind him and was bound like a noble ram presented
from a great flock as a whole burnt offering acceptable to God Almighty. Then he prayed: 'O Father of Thy beloved and blessed Son,
Jesus Christ, through whom we have come to know Thee, the God
of angels and powers and all creation, and of the whole family of the
righteous who live in Thy presence, I bless Thee for counting me
worthy of this day and hour, that in the number of the martyrs I
may partake of Christ's cup, to the resurrection of eternal life of both
soul and body in the imperishability that is the gift of the Holy Ghost.
Among them may I be received into Thy presence today, a rich and
acceptable sacrifice as Thou has prepared it beforehand, foreshadow-
ing it and fulfilling it, Thou God of truth that canst not lie. Therefore
for every cause I praise Thee, I bless Thee, I glorify Thee, through
the eternal High Priest, Jesus Christ Thy beloved Son, through whom
and with whom in the Holy Ghost glory be to Thee, both now and
in the ages to come. Amen.'

When he had offered up the Amen and completed his prayer, the
men in charge lit the fire, and a great flame shot up. Then we saw a
marvellous sight, we who were privileged to see it and were spared
to tell the others what happened. The fire took the shape of a vaulted
room, like a ship's sail filled with wind, and made a wall round the
martyr's body, which was in the middle not like burning flesh but
like gold and silver refined in a furnace. Indeed, we were conscious
of a wonderful fragrance, like a breath of frankincense or some other
costly spice. At last, seeing that the body could not be consumed by
the fire, the lawless people summoned a *confector*[1] to come forward
and drive home his sword. When he did so there came out a stream
of blood that quenched the fire, so that the whole crowd was astonished at the difference between the unbelievers and the elect. To
the elect belonged this man, the most wonderful apostolic and prophetic teacher of our time, bishop of the Catholic Church in Smyrna.
For every word that he uttered was and shall be fulfilled.

But when the evil one, the enemy of the household of the righteous,
saw the greatness of Polycarp's martyrdom and the blamelessness of
his entire life, and how he had been crowned with the crown of imperishability and had carried off a prize beyond gainsaying, in
jealousy and envy he saw to it that not even his poor body should

1. An official whose duty was to dispatch the victim.

173

be taken away by us, though many longed to do this and to have communion with his holy flesh. So Nicetes, Herod's father and Alce's brother, was induced to request the governor not to give up the body 'lest they should abandon the Crucified and start worshipping this fellow'. These suggestions were made under persistent pressure from the Jews, who watched us when we were going to take him out of the fire, not realizing that we can never forsake Christ, who suffered for the salvation of those who are being saved in the entire world, or worship anyone else. For to Him, as the Son of God, we offer adoration; but to the martyrs, as disciples and imitators of the Lord, we give the love that they deserve for their unsurpassable devotion to their own King and Teacher: may it be our privilege to be their fellow-members and fellow-disciples.

When the centurion saw that the Jews were determined to make trouble, he brought him into their midst in the usual way and burnt him. So later on we took up his bones, more precious than stones of great price, more splendid than gold, and laid them where it seemed right. When, if it proves possible, we assemble there, the Lord will allow us to celebrate with joy and gladness the birthday of his martyrdom, both to the memory of those who have contended in the past, and for the training and preparation of those whose time is yet to come.

Such was the story of blessed Polycarp. Counting those from Philadelphia, he was the twelfth to endure martyrdom at Smyrna, but he alone is specially remembered by all, so that even the heathen everywhere speak of him.

And such was the conclusion granted to the story of that wonderful and apostolic man.[1] The record was set down by the brethren of the church at Smyrna in the letter which I have reproduced.

The document which tells us about Polycarp contains accounts of other martyrdoms which also took place at Smyrna at about the same period as his. Among them Metrodorus, who in Marcion's heretical sect passed for a presbyter, was consigned to the flames and put to death. One of the best-known and most celebrated martyrs of that time was

1. i.e. pupil of an apostle (John).

Pionius.[1] His repeated declarations of belief, his outspoken-
ness, his defences of the Faith before the people and the
authorities, his public lectures, as well as his friendly aid to
those who had yielded to temptation in the persecution, and
the encouraging words that he addressed in prison to the
brother-Christians who visited him; the tortures that he later
suffered, the agonies that these involved, the nailings, his
endurance on the pyre, and to crown all his marvellous deeds
his death – all these are described very fully in the *Martyrdom
of Pionius*, which is included in my collection of *Early Martyrdoms* and which I can recommend to those interested.

Extant also are memoirs of others who were martyred in
Pergamum, a city in Asia, Carpus and Papylus and a woman,
Agathonice, who after many noble declarations of their be-
lief found glorious fulfilment.

Justin the Philosopher martyred in Rome

16. At the same period, Justin, whom I mentioned a little way
back, after presenting a second book in defence of our doctrines to the rulers already named, was honoured with a divine
martyrdom, owing to the philosopher Crescens, a man who
strove to make his life and conduct conform to his title of
Cynic.[2] It was he who devised the plot against Justin; for
Justin had repeatedly refuted him in debate with an audience
present, and now at the last by his martyrdom bound on his
brow the trophies of victory of the truth he ever proclaimed.
That martyrdom he himself, truly the most philosophical of
men, clearly foretold in the *Defence* referred to above, exactly
as it was so soon to happen to him. This is what he wrote:

I too expect to be plotted against and clapped in the stocks[3] by one
of those I have named, or maybe by Crescens, who calls himself a

1. Pionius is thought to have died nearly a century later.
2. Meaning 'like a dog'.   3. Meaning doubtful.

philosopher yet is a lover not of wisdom but of showing off. He does not deserve the name of philosopher, seeing that he publicly criticizes what he does not understand, alleging that Christians are godless and impious, his object being to win the favour and applause of the deluded masses. For if he lashes out at us without studying Christ's teaching he is most unscrupulous and much worse than simple people, who as a rule refrain from arguing and making false statements on subjects they know nothing about: if he has studied it and failed to understand its greatness, or has understood it but for fear of being suspected behaves in this shameful way, there is all the more reason to call him ignoble and unscrupulous, yielding as he does to ignorant and senseless prejudice and suspicion. I would like you to know that by putting certain questions of this kind for him to answer I found out – in fact, proved – that he really is totally ignorant: to show that I am speaking the truth, if you have not been informed of our discussions, I am prepared even in your presence to discuss the questions again. This would be a task worthy of emperors.[1] But if you are already acquainted with my questions and his answers, it must be obvious to you that he knows nothing of what we stand for: if he does know, but dare not say so for fear of the audience, then, as I said before, he is shown up as a lover not of wisdom but of glory; for he does not even honour the admirable precept of Socrates.[2]

These are Justin's words. That in accordance with his own prediction he was entrapped by Crescens, and found his fulfilment, is recorded by Tatian – a man who in his early years acquired a considerable reputation by his lectures on Greek philosophy and science, and left a number of works for which he will long be remembered – in his work *The Greeks Answered*:

That wonderful man, Justin, rightly declared that these people were no better than bandits.

1. The plural is used throughout, because Justin is addressing the emperor and his 'sons'.
2. Eusebius has unaccountably failed to transcribe Justin's quotation. 'A man is not to be reverenced more than the truth.'

Then, after further comments on the philosophers, he goes on:

Crescens, for instance, who made his lair in the great city, went beyond everyone in his offences against boys, and was passionately devoted to money-making. He urged others to despise death, but was so afraid of it himself that he did his best to compass the death of Justin – as though death was a calamity – simply because by preaching the truth Justin convicted the philosophers of gluttony and fraud.

Such was the cause of Justin's martyrdom.

The martyrs mentioned in Justin's own writings

17. Before his own ordeal Justin, in his first *Defence*, refers to others martyred before him. His account bears on our subject:

There was a woman who lived with a dissolute husband. At first she was as dissolute as he was, but when she came to know Christ's teaching, she reformed her ways and tried to persuade her husband to reform his, passing on what she had learnt and warning him that there will be punishment in eternal fire for those who do not reform and order their lives aright. But he remained as dissipated as ever and by his actions estranged his wife. For she thought it wrong to go on sharing the bed of a man who in defiance of natural law and of morality tried to obtain the satisfaction of his desires in every possible way; so she planned to end the union. When, however, she was implored by her family, who urged her to remain with him still, in the hope that one day her husband would change, she forced herself to stay. But when her husband went off to Alexandria, and news came that he was behaving still worse, she determined not to be involved in his abominable misconduct by maintaining the marriage bond as sharer of his board and bed; so she gave him what you call the *repudium*, and regained her freedom.

That splendid fellow, her husband, ought to have been glad that she had finished with all that in the old days she had done so recklessly with servants and hirelings, delighting in drunken revels and vice of every kind, and that she wanted him to finish with them too. But no. She had left him against his wish, so he brought an accusation

against her on the ground that she was a Christian. She then filed a
petition with you, the Emperor, asking that she might be allowed
first to put her affairs in order, and when that was done to answer
the accusation. To this you agreed. Her former husband was no
longer in a position to attack her,[1] so he turned his attention to a man
called Ptolemy, who had been her instructor in Christian doctrine
and was punished by Urbicius.[2] His method was simple. He persuaded
a centurion friend to manacle Ptolemy, hold him tight, and ask him
one question only – was he a Christian? When Ptolemy, a truthful
man who hated deceit and falsehood, confessed himself a Christian,
the centurion kept him manacled and tortured him for a long time
in the prison. Finally, the poor fellow was brought before Urbicius
and questioned as before on one point only – was he a Christian?
Again, fully conscious of the benefits that came to him through
Christ's teaching he confessed his schooling in divine virtues. For a
man who denies anything either denies it because he condemns it, or
avoids confession because he knows that he is unworthy and incapable of it. Neither of these is true of the real Christian.

When Urbicius ordered him to be led to execution, one Lucius,
a Christian like Ptolemy, seeing the utter unreasonableness of the
verdict said to Urbicius: 'Why have you punished this man, who is
neither an adulterer, a fornicator, a homicide, a thief, nor a robber,
and has not been found guilty of any offence, but merely confesses the
name of Christian? Your verdict is discreditable to the Emperor Pius,
to Caesar's philosopher son, and to the sacred Senate, Urbicius.'
Urbicius made no reply except to say to Lucius: 'I think you're one
of them yourself.' And when Lucius answered 'Indeed I am', he
ordered him also to be led to execution. 'Thank you very much,'
said Lucius. 'Now I'm free from such iniquitous masters, and I'm
going to God, my gracious Father and King.' Then a third man
stepped forward, and was condemned to the same punishment.

From this Justin naturally goes on to add the words I
quoted above:

I too expect to be plotted against by one of those I have named,
etc.

1. Because he would first have had to return her dowry.
2. City Prefect between A.D. 150 and 160.

The works of Justin that have come into my hands

18. Justin has left us many short works, the products of a cultured mind deeply versed in theology. They are full of good things, and I can recommend them to students, indicating those that have come usefully to my knowledge. There is one work of his championing our doctrines, addressed to Antoninus Pius, his sons, and the Roman Senate, and another containing *A Second Defence of our Faith*, written for the enlightenment of that emperor's successor and namesake, Antoninus Verus, whose period I am dealing with at present. A third work is *The Greeks Answered*, in which, after a very lengthy discussion of numerous questions debated both by ourselves and by the Greek philosophers, he expatiates on the nature of demons: these arguments there is no pressing need to quote at present. A second treatise of his in answer to the Greeks has come into my hands: this he entitled *A Refutation*. Then there is one called *The Sovereignty of God*, compiled not only from our own scriptures but from Greek books as well. Besides these there is a work entitled *The Harpist*, and a disputation on *The Soul*, in which he propounds various questions regarding the problem involved, and cites the opinions of the Greek philosophers: he promises to answer these and state his own opinion in a further treatise. Finally, he composed a *Dialogue in Answer to the Jews*, reproducing the argument that he had had in Ephesus with Trypho, one of the most eminent Hebrews of the day. In it he shows how God's grace guided him into the doctrine of the Faith, how keen he had once been on philosophic studies, and how fanatically he had striven to learn the truth.

Describing in the same work how the Jews contrived a plot against the teaching of Christ, he hurls these reproaches at Trypho:

Not only did you feel no remorse for your crimes, but you chose picked men at that time and dispatched them from Jerusalem to all parts of the world, saying that a godless sect of Christians had appeared, and retailing all the accusations which those who do not know us invariably bring against us, so that you corrupt not only yourselves but the entire human race.

He also tells us that right up to his own time prophetic gifts were a conspicuous feature of the Church. He refers to the Revelation of John, stating explicitly that it was the work of the apostle. He also cites some passages from the prophets, proving against Trypho that the Jews had actually cut them out of the Scriptures.

Numerous other books on which he laboured are in the possession of many Christian scholars, and so worthy of study did even the earlier writers think his writings that Irenaeus quotes passages from him. In Book iv of *Heresies Answered*, he makes this comment:

> Justin puts it neatly in his treatise against Marcion: 'I would not have believed the Lord Himself, if He had preached another god beside the Creator.'

And in Book v of the same work he writes:

> Justin puts it neatly: 'Before the Lord's advent Satan never dared blaspheme God, since he did not yet know his condemnation.'

All this had to be said to encourage students to pay careful attention to his books, and there we will leave him.[1]

Prelates of Rome, Alexandria, and Antioch: Church writers of the time

19. When this reign was now in its eighth year[2] Anicetus, who had completed eleven years as Bishop of Rome, was succeeded by Soter, and when Celadion had headed the see of

---

1. In the above list of Justin's works, no mention is made of his pamphlet against heresies, referred to on p. 165.

2. A.D. 168.

Alexandria for fourteen years [20] Agrippinus took up the succession; while in the diocese of Antioch Theophilus, sixth from the apostles, was eminent. The fourth, appointed there after Hero, had been Cornelius, and after him in the fifth place Eros had succeeded to the bishopric.

21. It was at this period that a number of writers flourished in the Church. Hegesippus we have met already. There was also Bishop Dionysius of Corinth and Bishop Pinytus of Crete, as well as Philip, Apolinarius, Melito, Musanus, Modestus, and above all Irenaeus. In every case writings which show their orthodoxy and unshakable devotion to the apostolic tradition have come into my hands.

22. Hegesippus in the five short works that have come into my hands has left a very full account of his own beliefs. In them he describes how when travelling as far as Rome he mixed with a number of bishops and found the same doctrine among them all. Listen to what he appends to some remarks about Clement's *Epistle to the Corinthians*:

> The Corinthian church continued in the true doctrine until Primus became bishop. I mixed with them on my voyage to Rome and spent several days with the Corinthians, during which we were refreshed with the true doctrine. On arrival at Rome I pieced together the succession down to Anicetus, whose deacon was Eleutherus, Anicetus being succeeded by Soter and he by Eleutherus. In every line of bishops and in every city things accord with the preaching of the Law, the Prophets, and the Lord.

The same writer sketches the origins of the heresies of his day:

> When James the Righteous had suffered martyrdom like the Lord and for the same reason, Symeon the son of his uncle Clopas was appointed bishop. He being a cousin of the Lord, it was the universal demand that he should be the second. They used to call the Church

a virgin for this reason, that she had not yet been seduced by listening
to nonsense. But Thebuthis, because he had not been made bishop,
began to seduce her by means of the seven sects (to which he himself
belonged) among the people. From these came Simon and his Simon-
ians, Cleobius and his Cleobienes, Dositheus and his Dositheans,
Gorthaeus and his Gorathenes, and the Masbotheans. From these were
derived the Menandrianists, Marcionists, Carpocratians, Valentians,
Basilidians, and Saturnilians, every man introducing his own opinion
in his own particular way. From these in turn came false Christs, false
prophets, false apostles, who split the unity of the Church by poisonous suggestions against God and against His Christ.[1]

Hegesippus also names the sects that once existed among
the Jews:

There were various groups in the Circumcision, among the
Children of Israel, all hostile to the tribe of Judah and the Christ.
They were these – Essenes, Galilaeans, Hemerobaptists, Masbotheans,
Samaritans, Sadducees, and Pharisees.[2]

He wrote much else besides, to parts of which I have already referred, quoting his narrative whenever it was to the
point. He also draws occasionally on the Gospel of the Hebrews, on the Syriac Gospel,[3] and particularly on works in
Aramaic,[4] showing that he was a believer of Hebrew stock,
and he mentions other matters as coming from Jewish oral
tradition. And not only he but Irenaeus too, and the whole
group of early writers, used to call Solomon's Proverbs the
'All-virtuous Wisdom'. And in discussing the apocryphal
books, as they are called, he states that some of them were
fabricated by heretics in his own time. But now I must move
on to another writer.

1. This passage is somewhat obscure; perhaps Eusebius has omitted sentences.
2. The Galilaeans were possibly followers of Judas (see p. 50); the Hemerobaptists practised daily rebaptism; the Masbotheans were atheistic materialists;
the Samaritans rejected the O.T. prophets, and with them the Davidic Messiah.
3. Otherwise unknown.   4. Or 'Hebrew'.

The epistles of Bishop Dionysius of Corinth

23. First it must be said of Dionysius that when he had been enthroned as Bishop of Corinth he lavished his inspired industry without stint, not only on those under him but also on those in foreign lands, rendering the greatest service to all in the general epistles which he indited to the churches. Of these the one to the Spartans contains instruction in ortho-doxy[1] and an exhortation to peace and unity; the one to the Athenians is a rousing call to faith and to life according to the gospel. For their scorn of such a life, he takes them to task as virtual apostates from the word, since Publius their bishop had died a martyr's death in the persecutions of the time. He mentions that after Publius's martyrdom Quadratus was appointed their bishop, and testifies that through his endeav-ours they were brought together and their faith rekindled. He further informs us that Dionysius the Areopagite who, as related in the Acts,[2] was converted to the Faith by the apostle Paul, was the first to be appointed Bishop of Athens.

Another extant epistle of his is addressed to the Nico-medians. In this he joins battle with Marcion's heresy in defence of the standard of truth.

He also wrote to the church at Gortyna and the other com-munities in Crete, congratulating Philip, their bishop, on the many courageous acts credited to the church under him, but warning him to guard against the distortions of the heretics.

In a similar letter to the church at Amastris and to those in Pontus he mentions that Bacchylides and Elpistus had pressed him to write it. He then gives explanations of Holy Scripture, and refers by name to their bishop Palmas. The letter also

1. i.e. the true doctrine; of the implication of stodginess which the word has unfortunately acquired there is of course no trace in Eusebius.
2. Acts xvii. 34.

contains a great deal of advice about marriage and celibacy,[1] and a directive that those who returned to the fold after any kind of lapse, whether improper conduct or heretical error, should be warmly received.

Next on the list is an epistle to the Cnossians, in which he urges Pinytus, the bishop of the diocese, not to put on the brethren a heavy burden as being essential[2] – the rule of celibacy – but to remember that most people were weak creatures. To this Pinytus replies that he admires and esteems Dionysius, but urges him in his turn to provide more solid food in the near future and nourish his flock with a further letter, this time a more advanced one, so that they may not be kept all their lives on a diet of milky words and treated like babes till they grow old without knowing it. In this letter Pinytus's orthodoxy regarding the Faith, his anxiety to help those under him, his learning and grasp of theology, are mirrored to perfection.

There is also extant an epistle of Dionysius to the Romans, addressed to the then bishop, Soter. I cannot do better than quote the passage in which he commends the custom observed at Rome down to the persecution of our own day:

From the start it has been your custom to treat all Christians with unfailing kindness, and to send contributions to many churches in every city, sometimes alleviating the distress of those in need, sometimes providing for your brothers in the mines by the contributions you have sent from the start. Thus you Romans have observed the ancestral Roman custom, which your revered Bishop Soter has not only maintained but enlarged, by generously providing the abundant supplies distributed among God's people, and by encouraging with inspired words fellow-Christians who come to the city, as an affectionate father encourages his children.[3]

1. Marcion, who came from Pontus, had forbidden marriage.
2. Matt. xxiii. 4 and Acts xv. 28.
3. I Thess. ii. 11.

In the same letter he refers to Clement's *Epistle to the Corinthians*, proving that from the very first it had been customary to read it in church. He says:

Today being the Lord's Day, we kept it as a holy day and read your epistle, which we shall read frequently for its valuable advice, like the earlier epistle which Clement wrote on your behalf.[1]

Dionysius tells us that his own epistles had been tampered with:

When my fellow-Christians invited me to write letters to them I did so. These the devil's apostles have filled with tares,[2] taking away some things and adding others. For them the woe is reserved.[3] Small wonder then if some have dared to tamper even with the word of the Lord Himself, when they have conspired to mutilate my own humble efforts.

In addition to these there is an extant letter of Dionysius to Chrysophora, a devoted Christian woman. He writes most appropriately, and imparts to her the spiritual nourishment that she requires.

That is the complete list of Dionysius's writings.

Bishop Theophilus of Antioch

24. From the pen of Theophilus, already mentioned as Bishop of Antioch, three rudimentary treatises *To Autolycus* are extant, as is another with the title *The Heresy of Hermogenes Answered*, in which he draws on the Revelation of John. Some *Manuals of Elementary Instruction* have also survived. At that time heretics were as busy as ever spoiling like tares the pure seed of the apostolic teaching; so the pastors of the churches everywhere, as though driving away savage beasts from Christ's sheep, strove to keep them at bay, now by warnings and admonitions to their congregations, now by more militant action, by subjecting the heretics to oral

1. Dionysius is addressing the whole Roman Church.
2. Matt. xiii. 25.   3. Rev. xxii. 18-19.

direct questioning and confutation, and finally by written polemics in which they employed the most unanswerable proofs to demolish their erroneous ideas. That Theophilus took the field against them with the others is plain from an admirable work which he wrote in answer to Marcion, and which has been preserved till now along with the others I have named.

He was succeeded as Bishop of Antioch by Maximin, the seventh from the apostles.

Philip and Modestus: Melito and the contents of his books

25. Philip, whom we met in Dionysius's letter as Bishop of Gortyna, was author of another most effective answer to Marcion, as were Irenaeus and Modestus,[1] who was more successful than anyone in pinpointing the man's errors and making them crystal clear. There are several others whose works are still to be found on the shelves of many Christians. 26. Contemporary with them were Bishop Melito of Sardis and Bishop Apolinarius of Hierapolis, who were at the peak of their fame, and who without reference to each other addressed defences of the faith to the Roman emperor of the time.[2] Of their works the following have come to my knowledge.

By Melito: *The Easter Festival*, Books I and II, *Prophets and the Christian Way of Life*, *The Church*, and *The Lord's Day; The Faith of Man*, *Creation*, *Obedience to the Faith*, and *The Senses; Soul and Body*, and *Baptism*, *Truth*, *Faith, and the Birth of Christ;* his *Book of Prophecy*, *Soul and Body*, *Hospitality*, *The Key*, *The Devil*, *The Revelation of John*, and *God in Bodily Form*; and finally the *Petition to Antoninus*.[3]

1. Otherwise unknown.   2. Marcus Aurelius.
   3. Dr Lawlor suggests that these groups correspond to distinct rolls. In that case two of them may have contained *Soul and Body*, which appears twice in the list, and none of them *Extracts* (quoted below), which does not appear at all.

In *The Easter Festival* he begins by indicating the time of its composition:

When Servillius[1] Paulus was proconsul of Asia, at the time when Sagaris died a martyr's death, there was a great deal of argument at Laodicea about the Easter festival, which fell due at that time; and this essay was written.

The work is quoted by Clement of Alexandria in his own *Easter Festival*, which was composed, he says, in consequence of Melito's.

In the *Petition* to the emperor he complains of the treatment we were receiving under his rule:

What never happened before is happening now – religious people as a body are being harried and persecuted by new edicts all over Asia. Shameless informers out to fill their own pockets are taking advantage of the decrees to pillage openly, plundering inoffensive citizens night and day. . . . If this is being done by your authority, well and good: a just monarch would never follow an unjust course, and we are happy to accept the honour of such a death. But we ask you to grant this one favour: first be good enough to find out the truth about the authors of such strife, so that you can judge in accordance with the facts whether they deserve to be condemned and executed or to be acquitted and left in peace. But if you are not responsible for this policy or this new decree – which could not properly be directed even against foreign enemies – we appeal to you all the more earnestly not to leave us at the mercy of these marauding hooligans.

A little farther on he writes:

Our way of thought first sprang up in a foreign land, but it flowered among your own peoples in the glorious reign of your ancestor Augustus,[2] and became to your empire especially a portent

1. Servilius is unknown; Rufinus emends to Sergius, who was proconsul some time between A.D. 161 and 166. The name, if correct, is misspelt.

2. Christ was born in the reign of Augustus, but He did His work in that of Tiberius, and there was no organized church outside Syria and Palestine till the time of Claudius.

of good, for from then on, the power of Rome grew great and splendid. To that power you have most happily succeeded: it will remain with you and your son,[1] if you protect the way of thought that began with Augustus and has grown to full stature along with the Empire. Your ancestors respected it, as they did the other cults, and the greatest proof that the establishment of our religion at the very time when the Empire began so auspiciously was an unmixed blessing lies in this fact – from the reign of Augustus the Empire has suffered no damage, on the contrary everything has gone splendidly and gloriously, and every prayer has been answered. Of all the emperors, the only ones ever persuaded by malicious advisers to misrepresent our doctrine were Nero and Domitian, who were the source of the unreasonable custom of laying false information against the Christians. But their ignorance was corrected by your religious predecessors, who constantly rebuked in writing all who ventured to make trouble for our people. It is clear, for instance, that your grandfather Hadrian wrote to many of his representatives, in particular the proconsul Fundanus, governor of Asia; and your father,[2] while you were associated with him in the government of the world, wrote to the cities, for instance, Larissa, Thessalonica, and Athens, and to all the peoples of Greece, forbidding them to make trouble for us. You, sir, hold the same views on this matter as they did, but with much more human sympathy and philosophic insight; so we are the more convinced that you will wholeheartedly accede to our request.

The foregoing passages are taken from the *Petition*. In the *Extracts* which he wrote the same author begins his introduction with a list of the recognized books of the Old Testament, a list which it is necessary to quote at this point:

Melito to Onesimus, his brother in Christ, greeting. In your devotion to the word you have repeatedly asked for extracts from the Law and the Prophets regarding the Saviour and the whole of our Faith, and you also wished to learn the precise facts about the ancient books, particularly their number and order. I was most anxious to do this for you, knowing your devotion to the Faith and eagerness to learn about the word, and how in your yearning for God you value these things more than all else, as you strive with might and main to

1. Commodus, appointed joint-emperor in 177.   2. Antoninus Pius.

win eternal salvation. So when I visited the east and arrived at the place where it all happened and the truth was proclaimed, I obtained precise information about the Old Testament books, and made out the list which I am now sending you. Here are the names.

> Five books of Moses: Genesis, Exodus, Numbers, Leviticus, Deuteronomy;
> Joshua son of Nun, Judges, Ruth:
> Kings (four books),[1] Chronicles (two);
> The Psalms of David;
> Solomon's Proverbs (Wisdom),[2] Ecclesiastes, Song of Songs;
> Job;
> Prophets: Isaiah, Jeremiah,[3] the Twelve in a single book, Daniel, Ezekiel;
> Ezra.[4]

From these I have taken the extracts, arranged in six books.

Apolinarius and Musanus: Tatian's heresy

27. After Melito, Apolinarius. Numerous works of his are still to be found on the shelves of many persons, of which the following have come into my hands – the address to the emperor named above; *The Greeks Answered* (five books); *Truth* I and II; *The Jews Answered* I and II; and his subsequent writings against the Phrygian heresy, an innovation contrived a little later but then beginning to sprout, since Montanus with his false prophetesses was already beginning to go off the track.[5]

28. Musanus, whose name appeared in the foregoing list, has left us a very pungent criticism which he wrote and sent to some Christians who had fallen away to the sect of the

1. Including Samuel.   2. Not the Apocryphal book.
3. Including Lamentations.
4. Including Nehemiah. Note the absence of Esther, perhaps rejected because it does not mention God.
5. See pp. 217–26.

so-called Encratites, which was then beginning to spring up and was introducing an outlandish and pernicious false doctrine into the world.

29. There is evidence that the author of this error was Tatian, whose observations on 'that wonderful man Justin' I quoted a few pages back,[1] remarking that he was a disciple of the martyr. This is stated by Irenaeus in *Heresies Answered*, Book I, where, speaking of the man and his heresy, he writes:

> Borrowing from Saturninus and Marcion, the so-called Encratites preached celibacy, setting aside the original creation of God and tacitly condemning Him who made male and female for the generation of human beings.[2] They also introduced abstention from 'animate things', as they call them, showing ingratitude to God who made all things. Again, they deny the salvation of the first created man. This notion they adopted quite recently: one Tatian was the first to introduce this blasphemy. He had been a pupil of Justin, and all the time that he was with him he suggested nothing of the kind; but after Justin's martyrdom he became an apostate from the Church, and elated at the thought of being a teacher, and puffed up by the conviction of his own superiority, gave instruction on peculiar lines – he romanced about invisible aeons, like the followers of Valentinus, and repudiated marriage as being depravity and fornication, just as Marcion and Saturninus had done; his one original idea was to deny salvation to Adam.

This is what Irenaeus wrote at that time. But a little while later a man called Severus lent his weight to this sect, and in consequence its members have come to be called Severians after him. They make use of the Law, the Prophets, and the Gospels, interpreting in their own peculiar fashion the ideas contained in Holy Writ, but they ridicule Paul the Apostle, setting aside his epistles, and reject even the Acts of the Apostles. Their old leader Tatian produced a composite work by somehow combining the gospels, and called it the *Diatessaron*:[3] some people still possess copies. It is said that he was

1. p. 176.   2. Gen. i. 27.   3. Literally 'the through four'.

bold enough to alter some of the Apostle's expressions as though trying to rectify their phraseology. He has left a great many works, of which the one most generally familiar is his famous essay *The Greeks Answered*, in which he discusses primitive times, showing that all the eminent writers of Greece belong to a much later period than Moses and the Hebrew prophets. This essay is, I think, the best and most helpful of all his writings.

Bardaisan the Syrian and his extant works

30. In the same reign heretical sects abounded in Mesopotamia. Bardaisan, a most able man and a highly skilled disputant in the Syriac language, composed dialogues against the followers of Marcion and other leaders of various doctrines, and wrote them down in his own language and script along with many other works of his. These dialogues his pupils, who were very numerous in view of his powerful defence of Christian truth, have translated from Syriac into Greek. Among them is his most effective dialogue with Antoninus, entitled *Destiny*, and many other works which he is said to have written in consequence of the current persecution. At an earlier stage he had belonged to the school of Valentinus, but later he condemned it and refuted many of its fanciful ideas, satisfied in his own mind that he had changed to the right way of thinking. For all that, the taint of the old heresy stuck to him to the end.[1]

Finally, it was at that period that the death occurred of Soter, Bishop of Rome.

1. Bardaisan doubted the resurrection of the body

Book 5

MARCUS AURELIUS TO SEVERUS: THE SUCCESSION
OF BISHOPS: THEIR REFUTATION OF MARCION
AND MONTANUS: THEIR SETTLEMENT OF
THE DATE OF THE EASTER FESTIVAL

IT was in the eighth year of his rule that Bishop Soter of Rome
passed away. He was succeeded by Eleutherus, twelfth from
the apostles, it being the seventeenth year of the Emperor
Antoninus Verus.[1] At that period in some parts of the world
the persecution of the Church flared up again more fiercely,
and as the result of mob onslaughts in one city after another
countless martyrs came to their glory, as can be gathered from
what happened in a single province. Fortunately for posterity
it was all written down, and it certainly deserves a permanent
place in history. The entire document, containing a very full
account of these things, has been inserted in my *Collection of
Martyrs*.[2] It contains not only the historical record but the
lessons to be drawn from it. For the moment I will content
myself with quoting such passages as are relevant to the present work.

Other historians have confined themselves to the recording
of victories in war and triumphs over enemies, of the exploits
of commanders and the heroism of their men, stained with the
blood of the thousands they have slaughtered for the sake of
children and country and possessions; it is *peaceful* wars,
fought for the very peace of the soul, and men who in such
wars have fought manfully for truth rather than for country,
for true religion rather than for their dear ones, that my

1. A.D. 177: 'Antoninus Verus' is presumably Marcus Aurelius.
2. See p. 175.

account of God's commonwealth will inscribe on imperishable monuments; it is the unshakable determination of the champions of true religion, their courage and endurance, their triumphs over demons and victories over invisible opponents, and the crowns which all this won for them at the last, that it will make famous for all time.

Gallic martyrs of Verus's reign

1. Gaul was the country in which the arena was crowded with these people. Her capital cities, famous and held in higher repute than any in the land, are Lyons and Vienne, both situated on the River Rhône, whose broad stream flows through the whole area. A written account of the martyrs was sent by the most important churches there to those of Asia and Phrygia, relating what had happened in their midst as follows – I will quote their own words:[1]

The servants of Christ at Vienne and Lyons in Gaul to our brothers in Asia and Phrygia[2] who have the same faith and hope of redemption as we: peace, grace, and glory from God the Father and Christ Jesus our Lord.[3]

Then, after completing their introductory remarks, they begin their story thus:

The severity of our trials here, the unbridled fury of the heathen against God's people, the untold sufferings of the blessed martyrs, we are incapable of describing in detail: indeed no pen could do them

1. This document, whose authenticity need not be doubted, contains a remarkable number of open or disguised quotations from the Bible. The great majority come from the N.T., showing that within a century of its composition it had already ousted the O.T. from the affections of the Gallic Christians at least. Two disputed books, 2 Peter and Revelation, are quoted as freely as the rest. Very few of the passages quoted appear in their original form; many have been drastically reworded, perhaps through defects of memory, perhaps to give a more literary flavour to the humble N.T. Greek.

2. Most of the Gallic converts were emigrants from these areas.

3. 2 Peter i. 1–2.

justice. The adversary swooped on us with all his might, giving us now a foretaste of his advent, which undoubtedly is imminent.[1] He left no stone unturned in his efforts to train his adherents and equip them to attack the servants of God, so that not only were we debarred from houses, baths, and the forum: they actually forbade any of us to be seen in any place whatever. But against them the grace of God put itself at our head, rescuing the weak and deploying against our enemies unshakable pillars,[2] able by their endurance to draw upon themselves the whole onslaught of the evil one. These charged into the fight, standing up to every kind of abuse and punishment, and made light of their heavy load as they hastened to Christ, proving beyond a doubt that the sufferings of the present time are not to be compared with the glory that is in store for us.[3]

To begin with, they heroically endured whatever the surging crowd heaped on them, noisy abuse, blows, dragging along the ground, plundering, stoning, imprisonment, and everything that an infuriated mob normally does to hated enemies. Then they were marched into the forum and interrogated by the tribune and the city authorities before the whole population. When they confessed Christ, they were locked up in gaol to await the governor's arrival. Later, when they were taken before him and he treated them with all the cruelty he reserves for Christians, Vettius Epagathus, one of our number, full of love towards God and towards his neighbour, came forward. His life conformed so closely to the Christian ideal that, young as he was, the same tribute might be paid to him as to old Zacharias: he had scrupulously observed all the commandments and ordinances of the Lord,[4] and was untiring in service to his neighbour, utterly devoted to God,[5] and fervent in spirit.[6] As such he found the judgement so unreasonably given against us more than he could bear: boiling with indignation, he applied for permission to speak in defence of the Christians, and to prove that there was nothing godless or irreligious in our society. The crowd round the tribunal howled him down, as he was a man of influence, and the governor dismissed his perfectly reasonable application with the curt question: 'Are *you* a Christian?' In the clearest possible tones Vettius replied: 'I am.'

1. 2 Thess. ii. 7–9.   2. Gal. ii. 9 and 1 Tim. iii. 15.
3. Rom. viii. 18.   4. Luke i. 6.
5. Rom. x. 2.   6. Rom. xii. 11 and Acts xviii. 25.

And he, too, was admitted to the ranks of the martyrs. He was called the Christians' advocate, but he had in himself the Advocate,[1] the Spirit that filled Zacharias,[2] as he showed by the fullness of his love when he gladly laid down his own life in defence of his brother Christians.[3] For he was and is a true disciple of Christ, following the Lamb wherever He goes.[4]

Then the rest fell into two groups. It was clear that some were ready to be the first Gallic martyrs: they made a full confession of their testimony with the greatest eagerness. It was equally clear that others were not ready, that they had not trained and were still flabby, in no fit condition to face the strain of a struggle to the death. Of these some ten proved stillborn,[5] causing us great distress and inexpressible grief, and damping the enthusiasm of those not yet arrested. However, in spite of the agonies they were suffering, these people stayed with the martyrs and did not desert them. But at the time we were all tormented by doubts about their confessing Christ: we were not afraid of the punishments inflicted, but looking to the outcome and dreading lest anyone might fall away. But the arrests went on, and day after day those who were worthy filled up the number of the martyrs, so that from the two dioceses were collected all the active members who had done most to build up our church life. Among those arrested were some of our heathen domestics, as the governor had publicly announced that we were all to be hunted out. These were ensnared by Satan, so that fearing the tortures which they saw inflicted on God's people, at the soldiers' instigation they falsely accused us of Thyestean banquets and Oedipean incest,[6] and things we ought never to speak or think about, or even believe that such things ever happened among human beings. When these rumours spread, people all raged like wild beasts against us, so that even those who because of blood-relationship had previously exercised restraint now turned on us, grinding their teeth with fury. So was proved true the saying of our Lord: 'The time will come when whoever kills you will think he is doing a service to God.'[7] From

---

1. Paraclete: John xiv. 16.   2. Luke i. 67.
3. 1 Thess. ii. 8, 1 John iii. 16.   4. Rev. xiv. 4.
5. See p. 200.
6. Thyestes ate his sons; Oedipus had children by his mother.
7. John xvi. 2.

then on the holy martyrs endured punishments beyond all description, while Satan strove to wring even from them some of the
slanders.

The whole fury of crowd, governor, and soldiers fell with crushing force on Sanctus, the deacon from Vienne; on Maturus, very recently baptized but heroic in facing his ordeal; on Attalus, who had
always been a pillar and support[1] of the church in his native Pergamum; and on Blandina, through whom Christ proved that things
which men regard as mean, unlovely, and contemptible are by God
deemed worthy of great glory,[2] because of her love for Him shown
in power and not vaunted in appearance. When we were all afraid,
and her earthly mistress (who was herself facing the ordeal of martyrdom) was in agony lest she should be unable even to make a bold confession of Christ because of bodily weakness, Blandina was filled
with such power that those who took it in turns to subject her to
every kind of torture from morning to night were exhausted by their
efforts and confessed themselves beaten – they could think of nothing
else to do to her. They were amazed that she was still breathing, for
her whole body was mangled and her wounds gaped; they declared
that torment of any one kind was enough to part soul and body, let
alone a succession of torments of such extreme severity. But the
blessed woman, wrestling magnificently, grew in strength as she
proclaimed her faith, and found refreshment, rest, and insensibility
to her sufferings in uttering the words: 'I am a Christian: we do
nothing to be ashamed of.'

Sanctus was another who with magnificent, superhuman courage
nobly withstood the entire range of human cruelty. Wicked people
hoped that the persistence and severity of his tortures would force
him to utter something improper, but with such determination did
he stand up to their onslaughts that he would not tell them his own
name, race, and birthplace, or whether he was slave or free; to every
question he replied in Latin: 'I am a Christian.' This he proclaimed
over and over again, instead of name, birthplace, nationality, and
everything else, and not another word did the heathen hear from
him. Consequently, the governor and his torturers strained every
nerve against him, so that when they could think of nothing else to
do to him they ended by pressing red-hot copper plates against the

1. 1 Tim. iii. 15.   2. A reminiscence of 1 Cor. i. 28.

most sensitive parts of his body. These were burning, but Sanctus remained unbending and unyielding, firm in his confession of faith, bedewed and fortified by the heavenly fountain of the water of life that flows from the depths of Christ's being.[1] But his poor body was a witness to what he had suffered – it was all one wound and bruise, bent up and robbed of outward human shape, but, suffering in that body, Christ accomplished most glorious things, utterly defeating the adversary and proving as an example to the rest that where the Father's love is[2] nothing can frighten us, where Christ's glory is[3] nothing can hurt us. A few days later wicked people again put the martyr on the rack, thinking that now that his whole body was swollen and inflamed a further application of the same instruments would defeat him, unable as he was to bear even the touch of a hand; or that by dying under torture he would put fear into the rest. However, nothing of the sort happened: to their amazement his body became erect and straight as a result of these new torments, and recovered its former appearance and the use of the limbs; thus through the grace of Christ his second spell on the rack proved to be not punishment but cure.

Biblis again, one of those who had denied Christ, was handed over to punishment by the devil, who imagined that he had already devoured her[4] and hoped to damn her as a slanderer by forcing her to say wicked things about us, being – so he thought – a feeble creature, easily broken. But on the rack she came to her senses,[5] and, so to speak, awoke out of deep sleep, reminded by the brief chastisement of the eternal punishment in hell.[6] She flatly contradicted the slanderers: 'How could children be eaten by people who are not even allowed to eat the blood of brute beasts?'[7] From then on she insisted that she was a Christian, and so she joined the ranks of the martyrs.

When the tyrant's instruments of torture had been utterly defeated by Christ through the endurance of the blessed saints, the devil resorted to other devices – confinement in the darkness of a filthy prison; clamping the feet in the stocks, stretched apart to the fifth

1. A reminiscence of John vii. 38 and xix. 34.
2. A reminiscence of 1 John iv. 18.   3. 2 Cor. viii. 23.
4. 1 Peter v. 8.   5. 2 Tim. ii. 26.
6. Matt. xxv. 46.   7. Acts xv. 29.

hole; and the other agonies which warders when angry and full of
the devil are apt to inflict on helpless prisoners. Thus the majority were
suffocated in prison – those whom the Lord wished to depart in this
way, so revealing His glory.[1] Some, though tortured so cruelly that
even if they received every care it seemed impossible for them to survive, lived on in the prison, deprived of all human attention but
strengthened by the Lord and fortified in body and soul, stimulating
and encouraging the rest. But the young ones who had been recently
arrested and had not previously undergone physical torture could not
bear the burden of confinement, and died in prison.

Blessed Pothinus, who had been entrusted with the care of the
Lyons diocese, was over ninety years of age and physically very
weak. He could scarcely breathe because of his chronic physical weakness, but was strengthened by spiritual enthusiasm because of his
pressing desire for martyrdom. Even he was dragged before the tribunal, and though his body was feeble from age and disease, his life
was preserved in him, that thereby Christ might triumph. He was
conveyed to the tribunal by the soldiers, accompanied by the civil
authorities and the whole populace, who shouted and jeered at him
as though he were Christ Himself. But he bore the noble witness.[2]
When the governor asked him 'Who is the Christians' god?', he
replied: 'If you are a fit person, you shall know.' Thereupon he was
mercilessly dragged along beneath a rain of blows, those close by
assailing him viciously with hands and feet and showing no respect
for his age, and those at a distance hurling at him whatever came to
hand, and all thinking it a shocking neglect of their duty to be behind-
hand in savagery towards him, for they imagined that in this way
they would avenge their gods. Scarcely breathing, he was flung into
prison, and two days later he passed away.

Then occurred a great dispensation of God, and the infinite mercy
of Jesus was revealed to a degree rarely known in the brotherhood of
Christians, but not beyond the skill of Christ. Those who when the
first arrests took place had denied Him were gaoled with the others
and shared their sufferings: on this occasion they gained nothing by
their denial, for whereas those who declared what they were were
gaoled as Christians, no other charge being brought against them, the

1. A reminiscence of John ii. 11.
2. An allusion to 1 Tim. vi. 13.

others were further detained as foul murderers and punished twice as much as the rest. For the faithful were relieved of half their burden by the joy of martyrdom and hope of the promises, and by love towards Christ and the Spirit of the Father, but the unfaithful were tormented by their conscience, so that as they passed they could easily be picked out from the rest by the look on their faces. The faithful stepped out with a happy smile, wondrous glory and grace blended on their faces, so that even their fetters hung like beautiful ornaments around them and they resembled a bride adorned with golden lace elaborately wrought;[1] they were perfumed also with the sweet savour of Christ,[2] so that some people thought they had smeared themselves with worldly cosmetics. The unfaithful were dejected, downcast, ill-favoured, and devoid of charm; in addition they were jibed at by the heathen as contemptible cowards; they were accused of homicide, and had lost the honourable, glorious, life-giving name. The sight of this stiffened the resistance of the rest: those who were arrested unhesitatingly declared their faith without one thought for the devil's promptings. . . .

From that time on, their martyrdoms embraced death in all its forms. From flowers of every shape and colour they wove a crown to offer to the Father; and so it was fitting that the valiant champions should endure an everchanging conflict, and having triumphed gloriously should win the mighty crown of immortality. Maturus, Sanctus, Blandina, and Attalus were taken into the amphitheatre to face the wild beasts, and to furnish open proof of the inhumanity of the heathen, the day of fighting wild beasts being purposely arranged for our people. There, before the eyes of all, Maturus and Sanctus were again taken through the whole series of punishments, as if they had suffered nothing at all before, or rather as if they had already defeated their opponent in bout after bout and were now battling for the victor's crown. Again they ran the gauntlet of whips, in accordance with local custom; they were mauled by the beasts, and endured every torment that the frenzied mob on one side or the other demanded and howled for, culminating in the iron chair which roasted their flesh and suffocated them with the reek. Not even then were their tormentors satisfied: they grew more and more frenzied in their desire to overwhelm the resistance of the martyrs, but do what they

1. Ps. xlv. 13.   2. 2 Cor. ii. 15.

might they heard nothing from Sanctus beyond the words he had repeated from the beginning – the declaration of his faith.

In these two, despite their prolonged and terrible ordeal, life still lingered; but in the end they were sacrificed, after being made all day long a spectacle to the world[1] in place of the gladiatorial contest in its many forms. But Blandina was hung on a post and exposed as food for the wild beasts let loose in the arena. She looked as if she was hanging in the form of a cross, and through her ardent prayers she stimulated great enthusiasm in those undergoing their ordeal, who in their agony saw with their outward eyes in the person of their sister the One who was crucified for them, that He might convince those who believe in Him that any man who has suffered for the glory of Christ has fellowship for ever with the living God. As none of the beasts had yet touched her she was taken down from the post and returned to the gaol, to be kept for a second ordeal, that by victory in further contests she might make irrevocable the sentence passed on the crooked serpent,[2] and spur on her brother Christians – a small, weak, despised woman who had put on Christ,[3] the great invincible champion, and in bout after bout had defeated her adversary and through conflict had won the crown of immortality.

Attalus too was loudly demanded by the mob, as he was a man of note. He strode in, ready for the fray, in the strength of a clear conscience, for he had trained hard in the school of Christ and had been one of our constant witnesses to the truth. He was led round the amphitheatre preceded by a placard on which was written in Latin 'This is Attalus the Christian', while the people were bursting with fury against him. But when the governor was informed that he was a Roman, he ordered him to be put back in gaol with the others, about whom he had written to Caesar and was awaiting instructions.

Their time of respite was not idle or unfruitful:[4] through their endurance the infinite mercy of Christ was revealed; for through the living the dead were being brought back to life, and martyrs were bestowing grace on those who had failed to be martyrs, and there was great joy in the heart of the Virgin Mother,[5] who was receiving her stillborn children back alive; for by their means most of those who had denied their Master travelled once more the same road,

1. 1 Cor. iv. 9.   2. Is. xxvii. 1.   3. Gal. iii. 27.
4. 2 Peter i. 8.   5. The Church.

conceived and quickened a second time, and learnt to confess Christ.
Alive now and braced up, their ordeal sweetened by God, who does
not desire the death of the sinner but is gracious towards repentance,[1]
they advanced to the tribunal to be again interrogated by the governor. For Caesar had issued a command that they should be tortured
to death, but any who still denied Christ should be released; so at the
inauguration of the local festival, at which all the heathen congregate
in vast numbers, the governor summoned them to his tribunal, making a theatrical show of the blessed ones and displaying them to the
crowds. After re-examination, all who seemed to possess Roman
citizenship were beheaded and the rest sent to the beasts. Christ was
greatly glorified in those who had previously denied Him but now
confounded heathen expectation by confessing Him. These were in-
dividually examined with the intention that they should be released,
but they confessed Him and so joined the ranks of the martyrs. Left
outside were those who had never had any vestige of faith or notion
of the wedding-garment[2] or thought of the fear of God, but by their
very conduct brought the Way into disrepute[3] – truly the sons of
perdition.[4] But the rest were all added to the Church.[5]

During their examination, Alexander, a Phrygian by birth and a
doctor by profession, who had lived for many years in Gaul and was
known to nearly everyone for his love of God and his boldness of
speech[6] – he had a large measure of the apostolic gift – stood by the
tribunal and gestured to them to confess Christ. To those surrounding the tribunal it was plain that he was suffering birth-pangs. But
the crowds, furious that those who had hitherto denied Christ were
now confessing Him, shouted against Alexander as the person responsible. The governor made him come forward and demanded to
know who he was; when he replied 'A Christian', he lost his temper
and condemned him to the beasts. The next day he entered the arena
with Attalus, whom the governor, to gratify the mob, was again
giving to the beasts. The two men were subjected to all the instruments of torture assembled in the amphitheatre, and underwent a
supreme ordeal. In the end they were sacrificed. Alexander uttered no
cry, not so much as a groan, but communed with God in his heart,

1. A synthesis of Ez. xxxiii and 2 Peter iii. 9.   2. Matt. xxii. 11.
3. Acts xix. 9 and 2 Peter ii. 2.   4. John xvii. 12.
5. Acts ii. 47 and v.14.   6. Acts iv. 29.

while Attalus, when he was put in the iron chair and was being burnt and the reek was rising from his body, called out to the spectators in Latin: 'Look! eating men is what *you* are doing: *we* neither eat men nor indulge in any malpractices.' When asked what name God had he answered: 'God hasn't a name like a man.'

To crown all this, on the last day of the sports Blandina was again brought in, and with her Ponticus, a lad of about fifteen. Day after day they had been taken in to watch the rest being punished, and attempts were made to make them swear by the heathen idols. When they stood firm and treated these efforts with contempt, the mob was infuriated with them, so that the boy's tender age called forth no pity and the woman no respect. They subjected them to every horror and inflicted every punishment in turn, attempting again and again to make them swear, but to no purpose. Ponticus was encouraged by his sister in Christ, so that the heathen saw that she was urging him on and stiffening his resistance, and he bravely endured every punishment till he gave back his spirit to God. Last of all, like a noble mother who had encouraged her children and sent them before her in triumph to the King,[1] blessed Blandina herself passed through all the ordeals of her children and hastened to rejoin them, rejoicing and exulting at her departure as if invited to a wedding supper,[2] not thrown to the beasts. After the whips, after the beasts, after the griddle, she was finally dropped into a basket and thrown to a bull. Time after time the animal tossed her, but she was indifferent now to all that happened to her, because of her hope and sure hold on all that her faith meant, and of her communing with Christ. Then she, too, was sacrificed, while the heathen themselves admitted that never yet had they known a woman suffer so much or so long.

Not even this was enough to satisfy their insane cruelty to God's people. Goaded by a wild beast,[3] wild and barbarous tribes were incapable of stopping, and the dead bodies became the next object of their vindictiveness. Their defeat did not humble them, because they were without human understanding; rather it inflamed their bestial fury, and governor and people vented on us the same inexcusable hatred, so fulfilling the scripture: 'Let the wicked man be wicked

1. 2 Macc. vii. 21–41.   2. Rev. xix. 9.
3. The devil.

still, the righteous man righteous still.'[1] Those who had been suffocated in gaol they threw to the dogs, watching carefully night and
day to see that no one received the last offices at our hands. Then they
threw out the remains left by the beasts and the fire, some torn to
ribbons, some burnt to cinders, and set a military guard to watch
for days on end the trunks and severed heads of the rest, denying
burial to them also. Some raged and ground their teeth at them,
longing to take some further revenge on them; others laughed and
jeered, magnifying their idols and giving them credit for the punishment of their enemies; while those who were more reasonable, and
seemed to have a little human feeling, exclaimed with the utmost
scorn: 'Where is their god?[2] and what did they get for their religion,
which they preferred to their own lives?' Such were their varied
reactions, while we were greatly distressed by our inability to give
the bodies burial. Darkness did not make it possible, and they refused
all offers of payment and were deaf to entreaty; but they guarded the
remains with the greatest care, regarding it as a triumph if they could
prevent burial. . . . .

Thus the martyrs' bodies, after six days' exposure to every kind of
insult and to the open sky, were finally burnt to ashes and swept by
these wicked men into the Rhône which flows near by, that not even
a trace of them might be seen on the earth again. And this they did as
if they could defeat God and rob the dead of their rebirth,[3] 'in order,'
they said, 'that they may have no hope of resurrection – the belief
that has led them to bring into this country a new foreign cult and
treat torture with contempt, going willingly and cheerfully to their
death. Now let's see if they'll rise again, and if their god can help
them and save them from our hands.'[4]

*The martyrs' friendly aid for those fallen from grace in the
persecution*

2. Such were the experiences of the Christian churches under
Marcus Aurelius: from them one can easily guess what
happened in the other provinces of the Empire. It will be

1. Rev. xxii. 11, reworded.   2. Ps. xlii. 3.
3. Matt. xix. 28.   4. Dan. iii. 15.

worth while to add other extracts from the same document, in which the gentleness and humanity of these martyrs is described in the following words:

So eager were they to imitate Christ, who though He was in the form of God did not count it a prize to be on an equality with God,[1] that though they had won such glory and had borne a martyr's witness not once or twice but again and again, and had been brought back from the wild beasts and were covered with burns, bruises, and wounds, they neither proclaimed themselves martyrs nor allowed us to address them by this name: if any one of us by letter or word ever addressed them as martyrs he was sternly rebuked. For they gladly conceded the title of martyr to Christ, the faithful and true Martyr-witness and Firstborn of the dead and Prince of the life of God;[2] and they reminded us of the martyrs already departed: 'They indeed are martyrs, whom Christ judged worthy to be taken up as soon as they had confessed Him, sealing their martyrdom by their departure: we are nothing but humble confessors.' They implored their brother-Christians with tears, begging that earnest prayers might be offered for their fulfilment. The *power* of martyrdom they proved by their actions, showing great boldness towards the heathen, and by their endurance and dauntless courage making their nobility evident to all, but the *title* of martyr they begged their fellow-Christians not to use, filled as they were with the fear of God. . . .

They humbled themselves under the mighty hand, by which they have now been greatly exalted.[3] They defended all and accused none; they loosed all and bound none;[4] they prayed for those who treated them so cruelly, as did Stephen, the fulfilled martyr: 'Lord, do not charge them with this sin.'[5] If he pleaded for those who were stoning him, how much more for brother-Christians? . . .

This was the greatest war they fought against him through the reality of their love, that the Beast might be choked into bringing up alive those whom he thought he had swallowed already.[6] They did not crow over the fallen, but the things they themselves had in abundance they bestowed with motherly affection on those who lacked

1. Phil. ii. 6.
2. A conflation of Rev. i. 5 and iii. 14 with Acts iii. 15.
3. Peter v. 6.   4. Matt. xvi. 19.
5. Acts vii. 60.   6. 1 Peter v. 8.

5 Marcus Aurelius to Severus

them. Shedding many tears on their behalf in supplication to the
Father, they asked for life and He gave it to them.[1] This they shared
with their neighbours when triumphantly victorious they departed
to God. Peace they had ever loved; peace they commended to our
care; and with peace they went to God, leaving no sorrow to their
Mother,[2] no strife or warfare to their brothers, but joy, peace,
concord, and love.

So much may profitably be said about the affection of those
blessed ones for their brothers who had fallen from grace, in
view of the inhuman and merciless attitude of those who
later behaved so harshly towards the members of Christ's
body.[3]

The dream-vision of Attalus the martyr

3. The same record of these martyrs contains yet another
story worth repeating: there can be no objection to my
bringing it to the notice of my readers.

Among them was a certain Alcibiades, who made a practice of extreme austerity. Hitherto he had refused everything,
partaking only of bread and water, and he tried to go on like
this even in gaol. But after his first ordeal in the amphitheatre
it was revealed to Attalus that Alcibiades was not doing well
in rejecting what God had created and setting others a mis-
leading example.[4] Alcibiades saw the danger, and began to
accept everything freely and to give God thanks.[5] For they
were richly blest by the grace of God, and the Holy Spirit
was their counsellor.

It was at that very time, in Phrygia, that Montanus, Alcibiades, Theodotus, and their followers began to acquire a
widespread reputation for prophecy; for numerous other
manifestations of the miraculous gift of God, still occurring
in various churches, led many to believe that these men too

1. Ps. xxi. 4.   2. The Church.   3. The Donatists and Novatians.
4. It would encourage the gnostic heresy that matter was evil.
5. Tim. iv. 3–4

205

were prophets. When there was a difference of opinion about them, the Gallic Christians again submitted their own careful and most orthodox conclusions on the question, attaching various letters from the martyrs fulfilled in their midst – letters penned while they were still in prison to their brothers in Asia and Phrygia, and also to Eleutherus, then Bishop of Rome, in an effort to ensure peace in the churches.

Irenaeus commended in a letter from the martyrs

4. The same martyrs commended Irenaeus, already a presbyter in the Lyons diocese, to the Bishop of Rome just mentioned, paying warm tribute to his character, as is clear from their words:

> Greeting once more, Father Eleutherus: may God bless you always. We are entrusting this letter to our brother and companion[1] Irenaeus to convey to you. We are anxious that you should hold him in high regard, as a man devoted to the covenant of Christ. For if we had thought that position conferred righteousness on anyone, we should have recommended him first as a presbyter of the Church, which indeed he is.

Need I go through the list of martyrs in the document we have been considering, distinguishing those who found fulfilment in decapitation from those thrown to the beasts for food and from those who fell asleep in gaol, or enumerate the confessors still surviving at the time? Anyone who so desires may easily find out all about them by looking up the actual letter, which, as I said before, is reproduced in full in my *Collection of Martyrs*.

Rain sent from heaven in answer to Christian prayers

5. While Antoninus[2] was still on the throne, it is on record that when his brother Marcus Aurelius Caesar deployed his

1. Rev. i. 9.   2. Presumably Verus – the Lucius of p. 168.

forces for battle with the Germans and Sarmatians, his men were parched with thirst and he was in a quandary. But the soldiers of the Melitene Legion, as it is called, through faith which has never wavered from that day to this, as they faced the enemy in their lines, knelt down on the ground, our normal attitude when praying, and turned to God in supplication. The enemy were astonished at the sight, but the record goes on to say that something more astonishing followed a moment later: a thunderbolt drove the enemy to flight and destruction, while rain fell on the army which had called on the Almighty, reviving it when the entire force was on the point of perishing from thirst.

The story can be found in the works of writers remote from our way of thinking, who have undertaken to record the reign of these monarchs; it has also been told by our own. The pagan chroniclers, being aliens to the Faith, have related the astonishing occurrence, but without acknowledging that it was the result of Christian prayers:[1] our own, being lovers of truth, have described the event in a simple guileless fashion. Among these may be mentioned Apolinarius, who says that from then on the legion which by its prayers brought about the miracle received from the emperor a title appropriate to the occurrence, being called in Latin the Thundering Legion.[2] A reliable witness of these facts is Tertullian, who in addressing to the Senate his Latin *Defence of the Faith*, to which I referred in an earlier section, confirmed the story with a stronger and clearer proof. What he had to say

1. Dio Cassius and Capitolinus, who agree that the rain was an answer to prayer.

2. Inscriptions show that in Nero's time, perhaps earlier, the legion had been entitled Fulminata, 'Thunderstruck'. Some therefore conclude that Apolinarius, if correctly understood by Eusebius, was in error. But as he was writing just after the event and to Marcus Aurelius himself, this seems unlikely. Nor was Tertullian likely to misquote the Emperor's letters in writing to the Senate a little later. May it not be that Marcus changed the uncomplimentary title to Fulminatrix, 'Hurler of the thunderbolt', which is appropriate to the occurrence?

was this – letters from Marcus, the most sagacious of emperors, were still extant in which he himself testified that in Germany his army had been on the verge of destruction through lack of water, when it was saved by the Christians' prayers; and Marcus had threatened to execute any who attempted to accuse us. Tertullian continues:

> What kind of laws are these, enforced against us alone by wicked, unprincipled, and brutal men? Laws which Vespasian disregarded, though he had conquered the Jews; which Trajan to a large extent set aside, when he forbade Christian-hunting; which neither Hadrian, in spite of his obsessive interest in all that was mysterious, nor Pius ever ratified.

Everyone must make up his own mind about these matters: it is time for me to pass on to the next stage.

When Pothinus, at the age of ninety, had found fulfilment with the martyrs of Gaul, Irenaeus succeeded to the bishopric of Lyons, the diocese that had been headed by Pothinus. It appears that in his early youth he had listened to Polycarp. In Book III of his *Heresies Answered* he sets out the succession of Bishops of Rome, giving the list as far as Eleutherus, whose period I am now discussing, the period in which Irenaeus was busy writing his work. He writes as follows:

The list of Bishops of Rome

6. Having founded and built the church, the blessed apostles entrusted the episcopal office to Linus, who is mentioned by Paul in the Epistles to Timothy;[1] Linus was succeeded by Anencletus; after him, in the third place from the apostles, the bishopric fell to Clement, who had seen the blessed apostles and conversed with them, and still had their preaching ringing in his ears and their authentic tradition before his eyes. And he was not the only one: there were still many people alive who had been taught by the apostles. In Clement's time a violent

1. 2 Tim. iv. 21.

dispute broke out among the Christians at Corinth, and the church at Rome sent a very long letter to the Corinthians, bringing them together in peace and renewing their faith, and passing on to them the authentic tradition they had so recently received from the apostles. . . .

Clement was succeeded by Evarestus, Evarestus by Alexander; then Xystus was appointed, the sixth from the apostles, followed by Telesphorus, who suffered glorious martyrdom; next came Hyginus, then Pius, and after him Anicetus. Anicetus was succeeded by Soter, and now, at the twelfth stage from the apostles, the position is filled by Eleutherus. In the same order and the same succession the authentic tradition received from the apostles and passed down by the Church, and the preaching of the truth, have been handed on to us.

Miraculous powers exercised down to those times by believers

7. In accord with the accounts which I have already given, Irenaeus demonstrates these facts in the five books entitled *Refutation and Overthrow of Knowledge Falsely so Called*, and in Book II of the same work he makes it clear that right down to his own time manifestations of divine and miraculous power had continued in some churches.

But they[1] fall far short of raising the dead, as the Lord raised them, and as did the apostles through prayer, and as among later Christians, because the need was so great and the whole of the local church besought God with much fasting and supplication, the spirit of the dead man has returned and his life has been granted to the prayers of God's people. . . .

But if they suggest that the Lord has done these things only in appearance, I will refer them to the prophetic writings, and prove from them that all this had been foretold about Him and really happened, and that He alone is the Son of God. So it is that in His name those who truly are His disciples, having received grace from Him, put it to effectual use for the benefit of their fellow-men, in proportion to the gift each one has received from Him. Some drive out

1. The adherents of Simon and Carpocrates.

demons really and truly, so that often those cleansed from evil spirits believe and become members of the Church; some have foreknowledge of the future, visions, and prophetic utterances; others, by the laying-on of hands, heal the sick and restore them to health; and before now, as I said, dead men have actually been raised and have remained with us for many years. In fact, it is impossible to enumerate the gifts which throughout the world the Church has received from God and in the name of Jesus Christ crucified under Pontius Pilate, and every day puts to effectual use for the benefit of the heathen, deceiving no one and making profit out of no one: freely she received from God, and freely she ministers.[1]

Elsewhere Irenaeus writes:

Similarly, we hear of many members of the Church who have prophetic gifts and by the Spirit speak with all kinds of tongues, and bring men's secret thoughts to light for their own good, and expound the mysteries of God.[2]

This will suffice to show that diversity of gifts continued among fit persons till the time I am speaking of.

Irenaeus's comments on Holy Scripture

8. At the beginning of the work I promised, when convenient, to quote passages in which the early presbyters and historians of the Church have transmitted in writing the traditions that had come down to them regarding the canonical scriptures. One of these was Irenaeus, so without more ado I will quote his remarks, beginning with those which concern the Holy Gospels.

Matthew published a written gospel for the Hebrews in their own tongue, while Peter and Paul were preaching the gospel in Rome and founding the church there. After their passing, Mark also, the disciple and interpreter of Peter, transmitted to us in writing the things preached by Peter. Luke, the follower of Paul, set down in a book the

---

1. Adapted from Matt. x. 8.
2. Adapted from 1 Cor. xii. 7–10 and xiv. 25.

gospel preached by him. Lastly John, the disciple of the Lord, who had leant back on His breast,[1] once more set forth the gospel, while residing at Ephesus in Asia.

Such are the statements of Irenaeus in Book III of the work mentioned. In Book V he makes a definite statement about the Revelation of John and the number of the antichrist's name:

Such then is the case: this number is found in all good and early copies and confirmed by the very people who saw John face to face, and reason teaches us that the number of the Beast's name is shown according to Greek numerical usage by the letters in it. . . . I for one dare not risk making any positive assertion regarding the name of the antichrist.[2] Had there been any need for his name to be openly announced at the present time, it would have been stated by the one who saw the revelation. For it was not seen a long time back, but almost in my own lifetime, at the end of Domitian's reign.

That is what Irenaeus has to say about the Revelation. He refers also to 1 John, drawing much evidence from it, and similarly to 1 Peter. And he not only knows but accepts the 'Shepherd'.

Scripture is right in saying: 'First of all believe that God is one, the Maker and Builder of all things, etc.'

He makes use too of a few sayings from the Wisdom of Solomon, which he quotes with fair accuracy:

The vision of God is the bestower of incorruption; and incorruption brings men near to God.[3]

He refers also to short works by an apostolic presbyter, whose name he omits to mention, and quotes comments of his on Holy Writ. He has a good deal to say about Justin Martyr and Ignatius, drawing his information as usual from

1. John xxi. 20.
2. Nor should we be any more positive. The interpretation of 666 as NERO CAESAR remains the most probable – especially if, as some argue, parts of the book were written in or just after that monarch's reign.
3. Wisdom vi. 18–19.

their writings, and promises that in a special work he will refute Marcion out of his own works.

Regarding the translation by the seventy of the inspired scriptures,[1] let him speak for himself.

So God became man, and the Lord Himself saved us, giving the sign of the Virgin, but not as suggested by some who in our day venture to translate the text thus: 'Lo, the *young woman* shall be with child and bear a son', as it was translated by Theodotion of Ephesus and Aquila of Pontus, both Jewish proselytes, followed by the Ebionites, who argue that He was Joseph's child. . . . .[2]

Before the Romans established their empire, while the Macedonians still held Asia, Ptolemy son of Lagus was anxious to equip the library he had established in Alexandria with worth-while books from every quarter, so he asked the people of Jerusalem to provide him with a copy of their scriptures translated into Greek. Being at that time still subject to the Macedonians, they sent him seventy men of mature age, the most skilled they had in the scriptures and in both languages. Thus was God's purpose fulfilled. Ptolemy wished to test them in his own way, fearing that they might put their heads together and manipulate their translation to conceal the true meaning of the scriptures. So he separated them from each other, and told them they must all produce the same translation: he laid down this rule for every one of the books. When they reassembled before Ptolemy and compared their respective versions, God was glorified and the scriptures were recognized as truly divine: they had all said the same things in the same phrases and the same words from beginning to end, so that even the heathen who were present knew that the scriptures had been translated by the inspiration of God. Nor is it surprising that God made this possible, seeing that when Nebuchadnezzar took the people into captivity and the scriptures were destroyed, and then seventy years later the Jews returned to their own country, afterwards, in the reign of Artaxerxes the King of Persia, He inspired Ezra the priest of the tribe of Levi to re-create all the

    1. The Septuagint (LXX).
    2. A futile argument, though not unknown today; for while there may be doubt as to whether Isaiah was referring to a virgin birth, there can be no doubt that in quoting the passage (Is. vii. 14) Matthew was.

utterances of the old prophets and restore to the people the Law
given by Moses.[1]

Bishops of Commodus's reign: Pantaenus the philosopher

9. When the reign of Antoninus[2] had lasted nineteen years,
Commodus stepped into his shoes.[3] In his first year, Julian was
entrusted with the archbishopric of the province of Alexandria, Agrippinus having reached the end of his twelve
years ministry.

10. At that time the school for believers in Alexandria was
headed by a man with a very high reputation as a scholar, by
name Pantaenus, for it was an established custom that an
academy of sacred learning should exist among them. This
academy has lasted till our own time, and I understand that it
is directed by men of high standing and able exponents of
theology, but we know that Pantaenus was one of the most
eminent teachers of his day, being an ornament of the philosophic system known as stoicism. He is said to have shown such
warm-hearted enthusiasm for the divine word that he was
appointed to preach the gospel of Christ to the peoples of the
East, and travelled as far as India. For there were, yes, there
were even then many evangelists of the word eager to con-
tribute an inspired fervour of apostolic pattern for the increase
and building up of the divine word. Of these Pantaenus was
one: it is stated that he went as far as India, where he appears
to have found that Matthew's gospel had arrived before him
and was in the hands of some there who had come to know
Christ. Bartholomew, one of the apostles, had preached to

1. Irenaeus found this story of the origin of the seventy in the Letter of
Aristeas, said to be from the pen of a Persian noble. The statement about
Ezra is no doubt based on 2 Esdras xiv. The improbability of these stories does
not take away from the reliability of Irenaeus as a chronicler of the Christian
era.

2. Marcus Aurelius.   3. 17 March A.D. 180.

them and had left behind Matthew's account in the actual Aramaic characters,[1] and it was preserved till the time of Pantaenus's mission. He himself, after doing great work, ended up as principal of the academy in Alexandria, where both orally and in writing he revealed the treasures of the divine doctrine.

Clement of Alexandria

11. In his time Clement was noted at Alexandria for his patient study of Holy Scripture. He bore the same name as the former head of the Roman church, the pupil of the apostles. In his *Outlines* he refers by name to Pantaenus as his teacher, and it seems to me that in Book 1 of the *Miscellanies* there is a covert allusion to that scholar, After indicating the more distinguished members of the apostolic succession to which he had been admitted, he says this:

> This work is not a careful literary composition designed to impress, but notes stored up for my old age, a tonic for a bad memory, no more than a sketchy outline of those clear and vital words that I was privileged to hear, and of blessed and truly remarkable men. Of these one was in Greece (the Ionian), a second in south Italy, a third in the Lebanon, a fourth from Egypt. Others lived in the East and included one in Assyria, and one in Palestine of Hebrew origin. When I met the last – in ability, the first – by tracking him down in his Egyptian lair, I found rest. These men preserved the true tradition of the blessed teaching straight from Peter, James, John, and Paul, the holy apostles, son receiving it from father – how few are like their fathers! By the grace of God, they came right down to me, to deposit those ancestral apostolic seeds.

Bishops of Jerusalem

12. In their time there was a noted bishop in Jerusalem who even now is famous almost everywhere – Narcissus, fifteenth

1. This seems to imply that Bartholomew found a Jewish community; 'India' may mean any country east of Ethiopia.

in the succession from the time of the siege of the Jews under
Hadrian. It was then that the church there first consisted of
Gentiles, who took the place of converts from the circumcision and were headed by the first Gentile bishop, Mark, as
already explained. After him, as shown by the local succession-lists, came Bishop Cassian, followed by Publius, Maximus, Julian, Gaius, Symmachus, a second Gaius, then another Julian, followed by Capito, Valens, and Dolichian;
finally Narcissus, the thirtieth from the apostles in unbroken
succession.[1]

Rhodo and the disagreement about Marcion which he records

13. At the same period, Rhodo, an Asian by birth and, as he
himself relates, a disciple at Rome of Tatian, whose acquaintance we made earlier, composed various books, ranging himself with the others against Marcion's heretical sect. He tells
us that in his day it split into dissentient groups, describes the
people who caused the split, and effectively refutes the false-
hoods invented by each of them. Listen to what he writes:

> Consequently, they no longer agree among themselves, but
> struggle to uphold irreconcilable views. One of their herd is Apelles,
> who prides himself on his mode of life and his grey hairs. He admits
> that there is a single Source, but says that the prophecies come from a
> hostile spirit, relying on the prophecies of a demoniac girl named
> Philumene. Others, like the captain himself, Marcion, introduce two
> Sources. These include Potitus and Basilicus, who followed the Pon-
> tic wolf,[2] and failing, as he had done, to find an answer to the problem
> of evil, took the easy way out and announced two Sources, baldly
> and without proof. Others of them again plunged into still worse
> error and posited not merely two but three Natures! Their leading
> spirit is Syneros, according to those who claim membership of his
> school.

1. Eusebius has omitted two names after Capito – a second Maximus, and
Antoninus.
2. Marcion, son of a Pontic bishop.

Rhodo also states that he conversed with Apelles:

The old man Apelles, in a discussion with me, was shown to be guilty of many erroneous statements. He therefore began to suggest that it was far better not to argue about doctrine at all, and for each man to stick to his own beliefs: those who placed their hopes in the Crucified would be saved, he declared, so long as they continued in good works. The most obscure part of his teaching, as I said before, was his doctrine of God, for he spoke of a single Source, as does our doctrine.

After a full statement of Apelles's position, Rhodo continues:

When I said to him 'What is your proof of this? how can you speak of a single Source? Please explain,' he replied that the prophecies refuted themselves, as they had never once told the truth: they were inconsistent, false, and mutually destructive. As to how there was a single Source, he said he did not know but simply inclined to that opinion. Then when I adjured him to tell the truth, he swore he was absolutely sincere in saying that he did not understand how there was one uncreated God, but that was his conviction. I laughed and condemned him, because he called himself a teacher and had no idea how to establish what he taught.

In the same work, addressing himself to Callistio, Rhodo admits that he was once a disciple of Tatian at Rome. Tatian had produced a book on *Problems*. In it he had promised to set out what was obscure and puzzling in Holy Writ, so Rhodo announces that in a special work he will furnish the answers to Tatian's problems. There is also extant an essay of his on *The Six Days of Creation*.

The egregious Apelles voiced innumerable profanities about the Mosaic Law, and in treatise after treatise blasphemed the inspired words, making the most determined efforts to refute them, as he imagined, and demolish them altogether.

*The false prophets of Phrygia, and the schism of
Blastus at Rome*

14. Filled with hatred of good and love of evil the enemy of
God's Church left no trick untried in his machinations against
mankind, and did his best to make a fresh crop of heretical
sects spring up to injure the Church. Some members of these
crawled like poisonous reptiles over Asia and Phrygia, boasting of Montanus 'the Paraclete' and his female adherents
Priscilla and Maximilla, alleged to have been his prophetesses.
15. Others flourished at Rome, led by Florinus, an unfrocked
presbyter, along with Blastus who had been disgraced in the
same way. Between them they led many churchmen astray
and got them under their thumb, each trying in his own way
to pervert the truth.

Montanus and his band of false prophets

16. To counter the so-called Phrygian heresy, the Power
which fights for truth raised up an effective and invincible
weapon at Hierapolis, in the person of Apolinarius, already
referred to in these pages.[1] With him were associated many
learned men of the day, who have left us ample material for
reconstructing the history. At the beginning of his polemic
against these heretics, one of these writers first indicates that
he had also argued with them orally to refute their preten-
sions. His preface runs as follows:

My dear Abircius Marcellus,
   It is now a very long time since you invited me to write some kind
of treatise against the sect called after Miltiades, but I have been rather
hesitant until now, not from inability to refute falsehood and witness
to the truth, but as a precaution against the danger that some people
might think I was adding another paragraph or clause to the wording

1. p. 186.

of the New Covenant of the Gospel,[1] to which nothing can be added, from which nothing can be taken away, by anyone who has determined to live by the Gospel itself.[2] But a little while ago I visited Ancyra[3] in Galatia and found the local church deafened with the noise of this new craze – not prophecy, as they call it, but pseudo-prophecy, as I shall shortly prove. So far as I was able, the Lord helping me, I spoke out for days on end in the church about these matters, and replied to every argument they put forward. The church was delighted and confirmed in the truth, while the enemy were repulsed for the time being and the opposition demoralized. So I was asked by the local presbyters, with the support of my fellow-presbyter[4] Zoticus of Otrus, to leave them a summary of what I had said against the opponents of the word of truth. This I could not do, but I promised that if the Lord allowed me I would write it here and send it to them without delay.

After completing his explanation on these lines at the beginning of his book, he goes on to describe the originator of this heretical sect, as follows.

Their opposition and their recent schismatic heresy in relation to the Church originated thus. There is, it appears, a village near the Phrygian border of Mysia called Ardabau. There it is said that a recent convert[5] named Montanus, while Gratus was proconsul of Syria,[6] in his unbridled ambition to reach the top laid himself open to the adversary, was filled with spiritual excitement and suddenly fell into a kind of trance and unnatural ecstasy. He raved, and began to chatter and talk nonsense, prophesying in a way that conflicted with the practice of the Church handed down generation by generation from the beginning. Of those who listened at that time to his sham utterances some were annoyed, regarding him as possessed, a

1. Evidently the N.T. canon was already fixed. ('Testament' is of course a mistake for Covenant.)
2. Gal. iii. 15, Phil. i. 27, Rev. ii. 18–19
3. Ankara.
4. This implies that the unnamed writer was a bishop, as his authoritative manner suggests.
5. He is thought to have been a priest of Cybele.
6. Date unknown.

demoniac in the grip of a spirit of error,[1] a disturber of the masses. They rebuked him and tried to stop his chatter, remembering the distinction drawn by the Lord, and His warning to guard vigilantly against the coming of false prophets.[2] Others were elated as if by the Holy Spirit or a prophetic gift, were filled with conceit, and forgot the Lord's distinction. They welcomed a spirit that injured and deluded the mind and led the people astray: they were beguiled and deceived by it, so that it could not now be reduced to silence. By some art, or rather by methodical use of a malign artifice, the devil contrived the ruin of the disobedient, and was most undeservedly honoured by them. Then he secretly stirred up and inflamed minds closed to the true Faith, raising up in this way two others – women whom he filled with the sham spirit, so that they chattered crazily, inopportunely, and wildly, like Montanus himself. On those who were elated and exultant about him the spirit bestowed favours, swelling their heads with his extravagant promises. Sometimes it reproved them pointedly and convincingly to their faces, to avoid appearing uncritical – though few of the Phrygians were deceived. They were taught by this arrogant spirit to denigrate the entire Catholic Church throughout the world, because the spirit of pseudo-prophecy received neither honour nor admission into it; for the Asian believers repeatedly and in many parts of Asia had met for this purpose, and after investigating the recent utterances pronounced them profane and rejected the heresy. Then at last its devotees were turned out of the Church and excommunicated.

Having recorded these facts in his introduction, the author continues throughout the book to refute their error. In Book II he has this to say about their end:

They called us 'prophet-killers' because we would not receive their garrulous prophets – according to them, the ones whom the Lord promised to send to the people – so let them answer before God. Is there one person, my good sirs, among those from Montanus and the women onwards who started the chatter, who was persecuted by the Jews or killed by the wicked? Not one. Or was any one of them seized and crucified for the Name? No indeed. Very well then: was one of

1. 1 John iv. 6.   2. Matt. vii. 15.

the women ever whipped in Jewish synagogues or stoned? Never anywhere.[1] It was by a different death that Montanus and Maximilla are believed to have died. For it is thought that both of these were driven out of their minds by a spirit, and hanged themselves, at different times; and on the occasion of the death of each, it was said on all sides that this was how they died, putting an end to themselves just like the traitor Judas.[2] In the same way it is commonly asserted that Theodotus, that wonderful fellow, the first trustee, shall we say, of their 'prophecy', was once raised aloft and taken up to heaven, where he experienced an unnatural ecstasy and entrusted himself to the spirit of deception, only to be sent spinning and perish miserably. That at any rate is how they say it happened. But we must not imagine that without seeing them we know the truth about such things, my friend: it may have been in this way, it may have been in some other way, that death came to Montanus, Theodotus, and their female associate.

Later in the same book he says that the holy bishops of the time attempted to silence the spirit that was in Maximilla, but were prevented by others, who were obviously in league with the spirit:

It will not do for the spirit which spoke through Maximilla to say in the same work of Astorius Urbanus:[3] 'I am driven away like a wolf from the sheep. I am not a wolf; I am word and spirit and power.'[4] He must show clearly the power in the spirit and prove it, and by that spirit he must make himself acknowledged by those who were then present in order to test and converse with the spirit as it chattered – eminent men and bishops, Zoticus from the village of Cumane, and Julian from Apamea – who were muzzled by Themiso and his henchmen, who would not allow them to silence the lying spirit which was leading the people astray.

In the same work again, after putting forward other arguments to dispose of Maximilla's prophecies, he indicates the

1. See Matt. xxiii. 31, 34, 37 and 3 John 7.   2. Matt. xxvii. 5.
3. Otherwise unknown.   4. 1 Cor. ii. 4.

time at which he was writing this, and in the same sentence refers to her predictions, in which she foretold wars and revolutions and which he exposes as false:[1]

> Surely it is now obvious that this too is a lie? Today it is more than thirteen years since the woman's death, and there has been neither general nor local war in the world, but rather – even for Christians – continuous peace, by the mercy of God.[2]

This passage is from Book II. From Book III also I will quote short passages in which, replying to those who boasted that they too had lost many by martyrdom, he has this to say:

> When all their arguments have been disposed of and they have nothing to say, they try to take refuge in the martyrs, alleging that they have a great number and that this is a convincing proof of the power of what in their circles is called the prophetic spirit. But this seems to be as false as false can be, for some of the other heretical sects have immense numbers of martyrs, but this is surely no reason why we should approve of them or acknowledge that they have the truth. To take one instance – those who as sectaries of Marcion are called Marcionites claim an immense number of Christian martyrs, but they do not truly acknowledge Christ Himself. . . . Hence whenever members of the Church called to martyrdom for the true Faith meet any of the so-called martyrs of the Phrygian sect, they part company with them and have nothing to do with them till their own fulfilment, because they will not be associated with the spirit that spoke through Montanus and the women. That this is true, and that it occurred in our own time in Apamea on the Maeander, in the case of Gaius and Alexander and the other martyrs from Eumenia,[3] is perfectly clear.

1. Luke xxi. 9.
2. Presumably the thirteen years of Commodus's reign (A.D. 180–192).
3. In Phrygia.

Miltiades and the books which he wrote

17. In this work he also mentions Miltiades, a writer who was author of another polemic against the Montanist heresy. After quoting some of their sayings, he goes on:

> The statements which I have summarized I found in a publication of theirs attacking the work in which our brother Alcibiades[1] shows that a prophet ought not to chatter in a state of ecstasy.

Later in the same work he gives a list of those who had prophesied under the New Covenant, among whom he includes Ammia (otherwise unknown) and Quadratus.

> But the pseudo-prophet speaks in a state of unnatural ecstasy, after which all restraint is thrown to the winds. He begins with voluntary ignorance and ends in involuntary psychosis, as stated already. But they cannot point to a single one of the prophets under either the Old Covenant or the New who was moved by the Spirit in this way – not Agabus or Judas or Silas or Philip's daughters;[2] not Ammia at Philadelphia or Quadratus; nor any others they may choose to boast about though they are not of their number.... For if, as they claim, after Quadratus and Ammia at Philadelphia Montanus and his female disciples succeeded to the prophetic gift, let them tell us which of their number succeeded the followers of Montanus and the women. For the prophetic gift must continue in the whole Church until the final coming, as the apostle insists.[3] But they point to no one, though this is the fourteenth year since Maximilla's death.

Let us turn now to Miltiades, who was referred to in one of these passages. He, too, has left us reminders of his own zeal for the oracles of God, in the works that he composed, *The Greeks Answered* and *The Jews Answered*, each subject being discussed separately in two books. In addition, he wrote a *Defence before the Rulers of this World* of the philosophy which he followed.

1. Presumably a slip for 'Miltiades'.
2. Acts xi. 28, xv. 32, xxi. 8–10.
3. Reference doubtful.

*Apollonius's refutation of the Phrygians: his personal comments
on some of them*

18. While the so-called Phrygian sect was still flourishing in
Phrygia itself, an orthodox writer named Apollonius embarked on a refutation, and produced a special polemic
against them, proving point by point the fraudulent character
of their 'prophecies' and revealing the sort of life lived by the
leaders of the sect. Listen to his actual words about Montanus:

What sort of person this upstart teacher is, his own actions and
teaching show. This is the man who taught the dissolution of mar-
riages, who laid down the law on fasting,[1] who renamed Pepuza and
Tymion, insignificant towns in Phrygia, as Jerusalem, in the hope of
persuading people in every district to gather there;[2] who appointed
agents to collect money, who contrived to make the gifts roll in
under the name of 'offerings', and who has subsidized those who
preach his message, in order that gluttony may provide an incentive
for teaching it.

This is his summing-up of Montanus. A little farther on he
has this to say of his prophetesses:

It is thus evident that these prophetesses, from the time they were
filled with the spirit, were the very first to leave their husbands. How
then could they lie so blatantly as to call Priscilla a virgin?

Next he goes on to say:

Don't you agree that all scripture debars a prophet from accepting
gifts and money?[3] When I see that a prophetess has accepted gold and
silver and expensive clothing, am I not justified in keeping her at
arm's length?

1. Though our Lord fasted, He never urged His followers to do so. The
adjurations in A.V. are spurious.
2. In order to be among the saved at the Second Advent, which according
to Montanus was imminent.
3. No such prohibition can be found in the Bible. The writer may be
alluding to the *Teaching of the Twelve Apostles*.

Still farther on, he has this to say about one of their confessors:

Then there is Themiso, who is wrapped up in plausible covetousness, and who failed to raise aloft the standard of confession and bought his release by a heavy bribe. This ought to have made him feel small, but instead he vaunted himself as a martyr, and, copying the apostle, had the impudence to compose a 'general epistle' in which he instructed better Christians than himself, fought his battle with empty trumpetings, and blasphemed the Lord, the apostles, and Holy Church.

Again, about another of those whom they honour as martyrs he writes:

To confine ourselves to a single instance, let the prophetess tell us about Alexander, who calls himself a martyr, with whom she feasts, and whom many treat with profound respect. His robberies, and the other crimes for which he has been punished, there is no need for me to retail; they are filed in the record office. Who pardons whose sins? Does the prophet forgive the martyr's robberies, or the martyr the prophet's covetousness?[1] The Lord said: 'Do not provide yourselves with gold or silver or two coats',[2] but these people have done the exact opposite – they have transgressed by providing themselves with these forbidden things. I can prove that their so-called prophets and martyrs rake in the shekels not only from the rich but from poor people, orphans, and widows. If they have the courage of their convictions, let them take their stand on this and settle the question, on this condition, that if convicted they will for the future refrain from transgressing, for the fruits of the prophet must be carefully examined, for from the fruit the tree is known.[3]

For the benefit of those interested in the history of Alexander – he was tried by Aemilius Frontinus, the proconsul at Ephesus, not because of the Name but because of his impudent robberies: there had been previous convictions. Then by a lying appeal to the name of the Lord he secured his release, having deceived the faithful there, but his own diocese from which he came would not receive him, because he was a

1. An obvious allusion to sacramental absolution.
2. Matt. x. 9–10.   3. Matt. xii. 33.

robber. Any who want to know about him have the public archives of Asia to refer to. The prophet lived with him for years, and knows nothing about him, but I have exposed him, and in doing so have exposed the character of the prophet. I can show the same thing in the case of many others: if they dare, let them stand up to the exposure.

Again, elsewhere in the book he has this to say about their vaunted prophets:

If they deny that their prophets have accepted gifts, they will surely admit this, that if they are proved to have accepted them they are no prophets: I can provide endless proof of this. All the fruits of a prophet must be submitted to examination. Tell me, does a prophet dye his hair? Does a prophet paint his eyelids? Does a prophet love ornaments? Does a prophet visit the gaming tables and play dice? Does a prophet do business as a moneylender? Let them say plainly whether these things are permissible or not, and I will prove that they have been going on in their circles.

In the same work Apollonius informs us that he is writing it thirty-nine years after Montanus embarked on his career of spurious prophecy. He further states that while Maximilla was pretending to prophesy in Pepuza, Zoticus – who was mentioned by the previous writer – planted himself in front of her and tried to silence the spirit at work in her, but was prevented by her partisans. He also mentions one Thraseas as among the martyrs of that time. Furthermore, he states on the authority of tradition that the Saviour commanded His apostles not to leave Jerusalem for twelve years. He also makes use of evidences taken from the Revelation of John; and he relates how by divine power a dead man was raised by John himself at Ephesus. He makes other statements too, by which he has ably and fully demonstrated the error of the heresy under discussion. There we may leave Apollonius.

Serapion on the Phrygian heresy

19. The polemics of Apolinarius against the Phrygian heresy
are referred to by Serapion, who, we have good reason to
believe, was Bishop of Antioch in succession to Maximin in
the period under discussion. He mentions him in a personal
letter to Caricus and Pontius, in which he gives his own
answer to the same heresy, and adds this:

> In order that you may know this, that the working of the so-called
> New Prophecy of this fraudulent organization is held in detestation
> by the whole brotherhood throughout the world, I am sending you
> the writings of Claudius Apolinarius, Bishop of Hierapolis in Asia, of
> most blessed memory.

In this letter of Serapion's are preserved the signatures of
various bishops, one of whom signed himself thus:

> I, Aurelius Quirinius, a martyr, pray for your welfare.

Another, in this way:

> I, Aelius Publius Julius, from Develtum, a colony in Thrace,
> Bishop. As God in heaven lives, blessed Sotas of Anchialus wished to
> drive out Priscilla's demon, and the hypocrites would not permit him.

The autograph signatures of several other bishops, who were
of the same opinion, are preserved in the document we are
discussing. And there we will leave them.

The correspondence of Irenaeus with the schismatics at Rome

20. In opposition to those at Rome who were falsifying the
sound precepts of the Church, Irenaeus composed various
letters, entitling one *To Blastus, on Schism*, another *To Flori-*
nus, on Sole Sovereignty, or God is not the Author of Evil – a
notion which Florinus seemed to be defending. Again, when
Florinus was inveigled by the error of Valentinus, Irenaeus

composed his masterpiece *The Octet*,[1] in which he also makes it clear that he himself was in the unbroken succession from the apostles. At the end of this work I have found a most graceful note of his which I cannot refrain from including in this book. Here it is:

If, dear reader, you should transcribe this little book, I adjure you by the Lord Jesus Christ and by His glorious advent, when He comes to judge the living and the dead,[2] to compare your transcript and correct it carefully by this copy, from which you have made your transcript. This adjuration likewise you must transcribe and include in your copy.

May it prove salutary that these words were spoken by him and are here recorded by me, so that we may keep those truly saintly men of an earlier generation in mind, as a splendid example of meticulous accuracy.

In the letter *To Florinus* already mentioned, Irenaeus refers once more to his associations with Polycarp:

Such notions, Florinus, to put it mildly, do not indicate a sound judgement. Such notions are out of harmony with the Church, and involve those who accept them in beliefs well-nigh blasphemous. Such notions not even the heretics outside the Church have ever dared to propound. Such notions the presbyters of an earlier generation, those taught by the apostles themselves, did not transmit to you. When I was still a boy I saw you in Lower Asia in Polycarp's company, when you were cutting a fine figure at the imperial court and wanted to be in favour with him. I have a clearer recollection of events at that time than of recent happenings – what we learn in childhood develops along with the mind and becomes a part of it – so that I can describe the place where blessed Polycarp sat and talked, his goings out and comings in, the character of his life, his personal appearance, his addresses to crowded congregations. I remember how he spoke of his intercourse with John and with the others who had seen the Lord; how he repeated their words from memory; and how the things that he had heard them say about the

1. The eight aeons believed in by Valentinus.   2. 2 Tim. iv. 1.

Lord, His miracles and His teaching, things that he had heard direct from the eye-witnesses of the Word of Life,[1] were proclaimed by Polycarp in complete harmony with Scripture. To these things I listened eagerly at that time, by the mercy of God shown to me, not committing them to writing but learning them by heart. By God's grace, I constantly and conscientiously ruminate on them, and I can bear witness before God that if any such suggestion had come to the ears of that blessed and apostolic presbyter he would have cried out and stopped his ears, exclaiming characteristically: 'Dear God, for what times Thou hast preserved me, that I should endure this!' And he would have fled from the very place where he had been sitting or standing when he heard such words. The letters he sent either to the neighbouring churches to stiffen them, or to individual Christians to advise and stimulate them, furnish additional proof of this.

Apollonius martyred at Rome

21. During the same period – the reign of Commodus – our situation became easier, and by God's grace peace came to the churches throughout the world. Then, too, the message of salvation began to lead every soul of every race of men towards the devout worship of the God of the universe, so that now many in Rome itself who enjoyed the advantages of birth and wealth were moving with all their household and kindred towards their own salvation. Needless to say, the demon, who hates what is good and is envious by nature, found this beyond endurance. Once more he stripped for the fight, and manifold were the devices he invented to destroy us. At Rome he dragged into court Apollonius, one of the most distinguished for learning and philosophy of the Christians of the time, having induced one of his servants – fit men for the task – to accuse him. But the wretched man brought the case at just the wrong time, for by an imperial decree those who informed on such matters were not allowed to live. His legs were at once broken, this sentence being passed on him by the

1. 1 John i. 1.

judge Perennius. But God's most beloved martyr, when the judge pleaded with him long and earnestly, and pressed him to speak up for himself before the Senate, made before them all a most eloquent defence of the faith to which he was testifying, and by decree of the Senate found fulfilment in decapitation: under an old statute that still held good[1] no other verdict was possible in the case of those who were once brought into court and refused to change their plea. Anyone who wishes to know what Apollonius said in court, the answers he gave when questioned by Perennius, and the whole of his defence to the Senate, will find it all in the register I have compiled of the early martyrs.

Notable bishops of the period

22. In the tenth year of Commodus's reign,[2] after thirteen years service as bishop, Eleutherus was succeeded by Victor. At the same time, Julian having completed his tenth year, responsibility for the Alexandrian province was entrusted to Demetrius. Contemporary with them was the Serapion already mentioned, eighth from the apostles as Bishop of Antioch, and quite outstanding. Caesarea in Palestine was headed by Theophilus, while Narcissus, already referred to in this book,[3] was still responsible for the Jerusalem diocese. Other contemporary bishops were those of Corinth in Greece (Bacchyllus) and of the diocese of Ephesus (Polycrates). No doubt a great many others were prominent at the time: naturally it is those of whose orthodoxy I have found written proof that I have listed by name.

The controversy about the Easter festival

23. It was at that stage that a controversy of great significance took place, because all the Asian dioceses thought that in

1. 'It is unlawful for Christians to exist.'
2. A.D. 189.   3. p. 214.

accordance with ancient tradition they ought to observe the fourteenth day of the lunar month[1] as the beginning of the Paschal festival – the day on which the Jews had been commanded to sacrifice the lamb: on that day, no matter which day of the week it might be, they must without fail bring the fast to an end. But nowhere else in the world was it customary to arrange their celebrations in that way: in accordance with apostolic tradition, they preserved the view which still prevails, that it was improper to end the fast on any day other than that of our Saviour's resurrection. So synods and conferences of bishops were convened, and without a dissentient voice, drew up a decree of the Church, in the form of letters addressed to Christians everywhere, that never on any day other than the Lord's Day should the mystery of the Lord's resurrection from the dead be celebrated,[2] and that on that day alone we should observe the end of the Paschal fast. There is extant to this day a letter from those who attended a conference in Palestine presided over by Bishop Theophilus of Caesarea and Narcissus of Jerusalem; and from those at Rome a similar one, arising out of the same controversy, which names Victor as bishop. There are others from the Pontic bishops, presided over by Palmas as the senior; from the Gallic province, of which Irenaeus was archbishop, and from the bishops in Osrhoene and the cities of that region. There are also personal letters from Bishop Bacchyllus of Corinth and very many more, who voiced one and the same opinion and judgement and gave the same vote. All these laid down one single rule – the rule already stated.

24. The Asian bishops who insisted that they must observe the custom transmitted to them long ago were headed by Polycrates, who in the letter which he wrote to Victor and the

1. 14 Nisan, the day of the Passover full moon.
2. i.e. that Easter must be celebrated on a particular day of the week, not of the month.

Roman church sets out in the following terms the tradition
that he had received:

We for our part keep the day scrupulously, without addition or
subtraction. For in Asia great luminaries sleep who shall rise again on
the day of the Lord's advent, when He is coming with glory from
heaven and shall search out all His saints – such as Philip, one of the
twelve apostles, who sleeps in Hierapolis with two of his daughters,
who remained unmarried to the end of their days, while his other
daughter lived in the Holy Spirit and rests in Ephesus. Again there is
John, who leant back on the Lord's breast, and who became a sacrificing priest wearing the mitre, a martyr, and a teacher; he too sleeps
in Ephesus. Then in Smyrna there is Polycarp, bishop and martyr;
and Thraseas, the bishop and martyr from Eumenia, who also sleeps
in Smyrna. Need I mention Sagaris, bishop and martyr, who sleeps in
Laodicea, or blessed Papirius, or Melito the eunuch,[1] who lived
entirely in the Holy Spirit, and who lies in Sardis waiting for the
visitation from heaven when he shall rise from the dead? All of
these kept the fourteenth day of the month as the beginning of the
Paschal festival, in accordance with the Gospel,[2] not deviating in the
least but following the rule of the Faith. Last of all I too, Polycrates,
the least of you all, act according to the tradition of my family, some
members of which I have actually followed; for seven of them were
bishops and I am the eighth, and my family have always kept the day
when the people put away the leaven. So I, my friends, after spending
sixty-five years in the Lord's service[3] and conversing with Christians
from all parts of the world, and going carefully through all Holy
Scripture, am not scared of threats. Better people than I have said:
'We must obey God rather than men.'[4]

Referring to the bishops who were with him when he
wrote, and shared his opinion, he adds:

I could have mentioned the bishops who are with me and whom I
summoned in response to your request. If I write their names, the
list will be very long. But though they know what an insignificant

1. or 'celibate'.
2. John xii. 1 and 12 show that the Crucifixion took place on Passover Day,
which was always 14 Nisan.
3 Presumably since baptism.   4. Acts v. 29.

person I am, they approve my letter, knowing that I have not frittered away my long life but have spent it in the service of Christ Jesus.

Thereupon Victor, head of the Roman church, attempted at one stroke to cut off from the common unity all the Asian dioceses, together with the neighbouring churches, on the ground of heterodoxy, and pilloried them in letters in which he announced the total excommunication of all his fellow-Christians there. But this was not to the taste of all the bishops: they replied with a request that he would turn his mind to the things that make for peace[1] and for unity and love towards his neighbours. We still possess the words of these men, who very sternly rebuked Victor. Among them was Irenaeus, who wrote on behalf of the Christians for whom he was responsible in Gaul. While supporting the view that only on the Lord's Day might the mystery of the Lord's resurrection be celebrated, he gave Victor a great deal of excellent advice, in particular that he should not cut off entire churches of God because they observed the unbroken tradition of their predecessors. This is how he goes on:

The dispute is not only about the day, but also about the actual character of the fast. Some think that they ought to fast for one day, some for two, others for still more; some make their 'day' last forty hours on end.[2] Such variation in the observance did not originate in our own day, but very much earlier, in the time of our forefathers, who – apparently disregarding strict accuracy – in their naïve simplicity kept up a practice which they fixed for the time to come. In spite of that, they all lived in peace with one another, and so do we: the divergency in the fast emphasizes the unanimity of our faith.

This argument he illustrates with two anecdotes which I may with advantage quote:

Among these were the presbyters before Soter, who were in charge of the church of which you are the present leader – I mean

1. Rom. xiv. 19.
2. A round figure, no doubt, but very close to the actual time from Christ's death to the finding of the empty tomb.

Anicetus, Pius, Hyginus, Telesphorus, and Xystus. They did not keep it¹ themselves or allow those under their wing to do so. But in spite of their not keeping it, they lived in peace with those who came to them from the dioceses in which it was kept, though to keep it² was more objectionable to those who did not. Never was this made a ground for repulsing anyone, but the presbyters before you, even though they did not keep it, used to send the Eucharist to Christians from dioceses which did. And when Blessed Polycarp paid a visit to Rome in Anicetus's time, though they had minor differences on other matters too, they at once made peace, having no desire to quarrel on this point. Anicetus could not persuade Polycarp not to keep the day, since he had always kept it with John the disciple of our Lord and the other apostles with whom he had been familiar; nor did Polycarp persuade Anicetus to keep it: Anicetus said that he must stick to the practice of the presbyters before him. Though the position was such, they remained in communion with each other, and in church Anicetus made way for Polycarp to celebrate the Eucharist – out of respect, obviously. They parted company in peace, and the whole Church was at peace, both those who kept the day and those who did not.

Irenaeus, whose name means 'peaceable' and who by temperament was a peacemaker, pleaded and negotiated thus for the peace of the churches. He corresponded by letter not only with Victor but with very many other heads of churches, setting out both sides of the question under discussion.

Unanimous decision on the question of Easter

25. The Palestinian bishops of whom I spoke a little while ago, Narcissus and Theophilus, with Bishop Cassius of Tyre, Clarus of Ptolemais, and the others assembled with them, composed a lengthy review of the tradition about the Easter

1. Presumably the Quartodeciman Easter.
2. In Rome itself.

festival which had come down to them without a break from the apostles, at the end of which they add this appeal:

Try to send a copy of our letter to every diocese, so that we may not fail in our duty to those who readily deceive their own souls. We may point out to you that in Alexandria they keep the feast on the same day as we do, for we send letters to them and they to us, to ensure that we keep the holy day in harmony and at the same time.

The admirably written works of Irenaeus which have come into my hands

26. In addition to the letters and other works of Irenaeus already quoted, there is extant a very succinct and highly convincing essay directed against the Greeks and entitled *Scientific Knowledge*; another, dedicated to a fellow-Christian named Marcian, on the *Exposition of the Apostolic Preaching*; and a collection of addresses on various subjects, in which he mentions the Epistle to the Hebrews and the 'Wisdom of Solomon', quoting several passages from them. That completes the list of works by Irenaeus that have come to my cognizance.

After thirteen years, Commodus reached the end of his reign and Severus took office as emperor, Pertinax having occupied the position for something less than six months following the death of Commodus.[1]

The extant works of Irenaeus's contemporaries

27. Large numbers of short works composed with commendable zeal by churchmen of that early time are still preserved in many libraries. Those that I have read myself include Heraclitus on *The Epistles of Paul*; Maximus on the question so much discussed among the heretics, *The Origin of Evil*, and on *Matter the Result of a Creative Act*; Candidus on *The Six Days of Creation*; Apion on the same subject; also Sextus on

---

1. Pertinax reigned for three months and Julian for just over two.

The Resurrection; and an essay by Arabianus; and works by many other authors – lack of evidence make it impossible to give their dates or shed any light on their history. Finally, there are a number of others whom I cannot even name, whose writings have come into my hands – orthodox churchmen, as is clear from their respective interpretations of Holy Writ, but unknown to us all the same, as they are not named in their writings.

Propagators of Artemon's heresy, their character, their impudent corruption of Holy Scripture

28. In a polemic composed by one of these against Artemon's heresy, which again in my own day Paul of Samosata has tried to revive, there is extant a discussion pertinent to the historical period under review.[1] For the assertion of the heresy in question, that the Saviour was merely human, is exposed in this book as a recent invention, because those who introduced it were anxious to represent it as ancient and therefore respectable. After adducing many other arguments to refute their blasphemous falsehood, the writer continues:

They claim that all earlier generations, and the apostles themselves, received and taught the things they say themselves, and that the true teaching was preserved till the times of Victor, the thirteenth Bishop of Rome after Peter: from the time of his successor Zephyrinus the truth was deliberately perverted. This suggestion might perhaps have been credible if in the first place Holy Scripture had not presented a very different picture; and there are also works by Christian writers published before Victor's time, written to defend the truth against both pagan criticism and current heresies – I mean works by Justin, Miltiades, Tatian, Clement, and many more. In every one of these Christ is spoken of as God. For who does not know the books of Irenaeus, Melito, and the rest, which proclaim Christ as God and

1. We know from another source that the work referred to was known as *The Little Labyrinth*. The author's name is uncertain; Lightfoot suggested Hippolytus.

man, and all the psalms and hymns written from the beginning by faithful brethren, which sing of Christ as the Word of God and address Him as God? How then can it be true that when the mind of the Church had been proclaimed for so many years, Christians up to the time of Victor preached as these people say they did? And are they not ashamed to slander Victor in this way, knowing perfectly well that it was Victor who excommunicated Theodotus the shoemaker, the prime mover and father of this God-denying apostasy, when he became the first to declare that Christ was merely human? If Victor regarded their views in the way their slanderous statements suggest, how could he have thrown out Theodotus, the inventor of this heresy?

That is all I have to say about the events in Victor's time. When he had held office for ten years, Zephyrinus was appointed to succeed him, about the ninth year of Severus's reign.[1]

The writer of the book just quoted about the founder of the heresy under discussion describes a further incident, which occurred in Zephyrinus's time. Here is the actual passage:

I will remind many of my brother-Christians of an event which occurred in my time and which I think, had it happened in Sodom,[2] would perhaps have warned even them. There was a confessor named Natalius, who lived not a long time ago but in my own lifetime. He was led astray by Asclepiodotus and by a second Theodotus, a banker. These two were disciples of Theodotus the shoemaker, the first to be excommunicated for thinking in this way – or rather for failing to think – by Victor, who as I said was bishop at the time. They persuaded Natalius to be known as bishop of this heretical sect, in return for a stipend which he was to receive from them of £25 a month.[3] After joining them, he was repeatedly warned by the Lord in visions; for our compassionate God and Lord, Jesus Christ, did not desire one who had witnessed to His own sufferings to perish outside the Church. He paid little attention to the visions, ensnared by his pre-eminence among them and by the love of ill-gotten gain

---

1. A.D. 201.   2. Matt. xi. 23.
3. The present-day equivalent of 150 denarii.

that corrupts so many; but he was finally whipped all night long by holy angels, and suffered severely, so that he got up early, put on sackcloth, sprinkled himself with ashes, and without a moment's delay prostrated himself in tears before Bishop Zephyrinus, rolling at the feet not only of the clergy but of the laity as well, and moving with his tears the compassionate Church of the merciful Christ. But though he begged and besought them and displayed the weals left by the blows he had received, it was only after much hesitation that he was readmitted to communion.

To this I will add some further comments on the same persons from the same writer:

They have not hesitated to corrupt the word of God; they have treated the standard of the primitive faith with contempt; they have not known Christ. Instead of asking what Holy Scripture says, they strain every nerve to find a syllogistic figure to bolster up their godlessness. If anyone challenges them with a text from Divine Scripture, they examine it to see whether it can be turned into a conjunctive or disjunctive syllogistic figure. They put aside the sacred word of God, and devote themselves to geometry – earth-measurement – because they are from the earth and speak from the earth, and do not know the One who comes from above.[1] Some of them give all their energies to the study of Euclidean geometry, and treat Aristotle and Theophrastus[2] with reverent awe; to some of them Galen[3] is almost an object of worship. When people avail themselves of the arts of unbelievers to lend colour to their heretical views, and with godless rascality corrupt the simple Faith of Holy Writ, it is obvious that they are nowhere near the Faith. So it was that they laid hands unblushingly on the Holy Scriptures, claiming to have corrected them.

In saying this I am not slandering them, as anybody who wishes can soon find out. If anyone will take the trouble to collect their several copies and compare them, he will discover frequent divergencies; for example, Asclepiades's copies do not agree with Theodotus's. A large number are obtainable, thanks to the emulous energy with which disciples copied the 'emendations' or rather perversions

1. John iii. 31.   2. Aristotle's successor.
3. The famous physician of A.D. 130–c. 201.

of the text by their respective masters. Nor do these agree with Hermophilus's copies. As for Apolloniades, his cannot even be harmonized with each other; it is possible to collate the ones which his disciples made first with those that have undergone further manipulation, and to find endless discrepancies. The impertinence of this misconduct can hardly be unknown even to the copyists. Either they do not believe that the inspired Scriptures were spoken by the Holy Spirit – if so, they are unbelievers; or they imagine that they are wiser than He – if so, can they be other than possessed? They cannot deny that the impertinence is their own, seeing that the copies are in their own handwriting, that they did not receive the Scriptures in such a condition from their first teachers, and that they cannot produce any originals to justify their copies. Some of them have not even deigned to falsify the text, but have simply repudiated both Law and Prophets, and so under cover of a wicked, godless teaching have plunged into the lowest depths of destruction.

And there we will leave that subject.

Book 6

The persecution under Severus

1. When Severus, in his turn, was instigating persecution of the churches, the champions of true religion achieved glorious martyrdoms in every land. These were most numerous at Alexandria, to which, as to a huge arena, God's noble champions were conducted from the whole of Egypt and the Thebaid. There, by their heroic endurance of every kind of torture and every form of death, they were wreathed with the crowns laid up with God. Among them was Leonides (usually referred to as the father of Origen), who was beheaded, leaving his son quite young. How devoted to the word of God Origen was from the start it will not be inappropriate to describe in brief, especially in view of the story about him that has received such wide publicity. 2. There would be a great deal to say if one tried to give a full-length account of his life in writing: the record of his doings would fill a whole book. However, for the present I shall cut down most parts of the story to the fewest possible words, and mention only a few features of his career. The facts here set forth are drawn from some of his letters and from the recollections of those of his friends who have lived on till my own time.

Origen's boyhood training; his early success as a preacher

Origen's story deserves, I think, to be told right from the cradle. It was the tenth year of Severus's reign; the governor

of Alexandria and the rest of Egypt was Laetus; and as archbishop of that province Julian had just been succeeded by
Demetrius. When the flames of persecution were fanned to a
great blaze and untold numbers were being wreathed with
martyrs' crowns, such a longing for martyrdom possessed the
soul of Origen, boy as he was, that his one ambition was to
come to grips with danger and charge headlong into the conflict. Indeed, he was within a hair's breadth of arriving at the
end of his days, when for the benefit of mankind the providence of Almighty God used his mother to defeat his ambition.
She first appealed to him in words, begging him to spare his
mother's feelings for him; then, when the news that his father
had been arrested and imprisoned filled his whole being with
a craving for martyrdom, and she saw that he was more determined than ever, she hid all his clothing and compelled
him to stay at home. He, in the grip of an ambition extraordinary in one so young, could not remain silent: he did the
only thing possible, and sent his father a letter pressing him
strongly on the subject of martyrdom, and advising him exactly in these words: 'Mind you don't change your mind on
our account.'

This may serve as the first evidence of Origen's boyish
sagacity and the perfect sincerity of his devotion to God. For
already he had laid firm foundations for the understanding of
the Faith, trained as he was from early childhood in the divine
Scriptures. He had toiled at these assiduously, his father insisting that in addition to the normal curriculum he should pursue
the study of Holy Writ with equal vigour. He constantly
urged him not to give any time to secular subjects till he had
steeped himself in religious studies, and every day required
him to learn passages by heart and repeat them aloud. This
was not at all distasteful to the boy: indeed, he gave himself
up too completely to these tasks and, not content to read the
sacred words in their simple and natural sense, looked for
something more, and young as he was devoted himself to

profounder investigation; so that he worried his father with
questions as to the meaning and intention that underlay the
inspired Scripture. His father would make a show of scolding
him to his face, advising him not to look for anything beyond
his understanding, or any meaning other than the obvious
one, but in private he was delighted and profoundly grateful
to God, the Author of all good things, who had deemed him
worthy to father such a son. It is said that often when the boy
was asleep he would bend over him and bare his breast, and
as if it was the temple of a divine spirit would kiss it reverently
and count himself blest in his promising child. These stories
and others like them are told of Origen as a boy.

But when his father had found fulfilment in martyrdom he
was left destitute with his mother and as many as six younger
brothers while still in his seventeenth year. His father's property had been seized for the imperial treasury, so that he and
the rest of his family now lacked even the necessities of life.
But being deemed worthy of God's loving care, he was received into the comfortable house of a lady who was extremely wealthy and very distinguished in other ways; she
was, however, a devotee of a notorious heretic, one of those
then flourishing at Alexandria. An Antiochene by birth, he
was the adopted son of the lady in question, who kept him at
her house and was utterly devoted to him. Origen could not
help associating with him, but from the start he gave clear
proofs of his doctrinal orthodoxy. Crowds of heretics, and of
our own people too, might gather to hear Paul, as the man
was called, because his arguments seemed so convincing:
never once was Origen induced to join with him in prayer,
keeping from his earliest years the rule of the Church and
'abominating' – the very word he uses somewhere himself –
all heretical teachings. Thanks to his father, he had made good
progress in secular subjects: after his father's death he devoted himself entirely and with growing enthusiasm to the
humanities, so that he acquired considerable ability as a

literary man; in fact, his father had not long found fulfilment, before his devotion to these studies enabled him to
enjoy a standard of life beyond the means of most young
men.

3. At Alexandria there was no one dedicated to elementary
Christian teaching, as everyone had fled the threatened persecution. So while Origen was given up to his studies, as he
himself tells us somewhere in his writings, he was approached
by some pagans who wished to hear the word of God. Of
these the first to be named is Plutarch, whose noble life was
crowned with divine martyrdom. The second was Plutarch's
brother Heraclas, who by his own efforts furnished a remarkable example of the philosophic life[1] and discipline, and was
chosen Bishop of Alexandria in succession to Demetrius.
Origen was seventeen when he became principal of the school
of elementary instruction: at the same period he came to the
fore during the persecutions under Aquila the governor of
Alexandria, when he won a resounding reputation among all
adherents of the Faith by his eagerness to lend a helping hand to
all the holy martyrs, known or unknown. For not only when
they were in prison, or were being cross-examined, up to the
final sentence, but even when they were afterwards led away
to execution, he was at the side of the holy martyrs, displaying astonishing fearlessness and meeting danger face to face.
As he boldly approached and fearlessly greeted the martyrs
with a kiss, again and again the maddened crowd of pagans
that surrounded him were on the point of stoning him, had
he not found the right hand of God ever ready to help him,
so that he escaped when it seemed impossible.

The same divine and heavenly grace protected him again
and again on other occasions too many to count; for because

1. This account of Origen and his pupils contains a number of recurrent
words employed in an unusual sense, and so indicating that these pages have
been copied or adapted from some special source. One such word is 'philosophic' in the sense of 'ascetic'.

of his fearlessness and extreme enthusiasm for the word of
Christ he was at that time the target of plotters. So bitter was
the hostility of unbelievers to him that they actually collected
groups of soldiers and posted them round the house where he
was living, because of the number of those whom he was in-
structing in the rudiments of the Holy Faith. Thus the persecution directed against him grew daily hotter, so that there
no longer was room for him anywhere in the city. He moved
from house to house, driven from pillar to post, in revenge for
the number of those whom he had brought to hear his religious teaching. For in a quite amazing way his actions displayed to the full the fruits of the most genuine philosophy.
His deeds matched his words, as the saying goes, and his
words his deeds.[1] That was the chief reason why, aided by the
power of God, he led men in thousands to share his enthusiasm.

Responsibility for elementary instruction had been entrusted by Demetrius, prelate of the church, to Origen alone,
who soon saw pupils coming to him in increasing numbers.
He decided, however, that the teaching of literature did not
harmonize with training in theology, and promptly broke off
his lectures on literature, as useless and a hindrance to sacred
studies. Then, with the worthy object of making himself
independent of other people's assistance, he parted with all the
volumes of ancient literature which had hitherto been his most
cherished possessions, and if the purchaser brought him two
shillings a day he was satisfied.[2]

For very many years he persisted in this philosophic way of
life, putting away from him all inducements to youthful lusts,
and at all times of the day disciplining himself by performing
strenuous tasks, while he devoted most of the night to the
study of Holy Scripture. He went to the limit in practising a
life given up to philosophy; sometimes he trained himself by
periods of fasting, sometimes by restricting the hours of sleep,

1. A Greek proverb derived from Plato.   2. Hire purchase?

243

which he insisted on taking never in bed, always on the floor.
Above all, he felt that he must keep the gospel sayings of the
Saviour urging us not to carry two coats or wear shoes[1] and
never to be worried by anxiety about the future.[2] He displayed an enthusiasm beyond his years, and patiently enduring cold and nakedness[3] went to the furthest limit of poverty,
to the utter amazement of his pupils and the distress of the
countless friends, who begged him to share their possessions
in recognition of the labours that they saw him bestow on his
religious teaching. Not once did his determination weaken;
it is said that for several years he went about on foot without
any shoes at all, and for a much longer period abstained from
wine and all else beyond the minimum of food, so that he ran
the risk of upsetting and even ruining his constitution.

Pupils who became martyrs; Potamiaena

By setting such an example of the philosophic life to those
who saw him he naturally kindled a similar enthusiasm in
many of his pupils, so that even among pagan unbelievers and
those who had been to schools and colleges there were persons of distinction who were won over by his teaching. Thanks
to him, men like this with all their heart honestly embraced
faith in the word of God, and came into prominence in the
persecution that broke out at that time, some of them being
arrested and finding fulfilment in martyrdom.

4. The first of these was Plutarch, to whom I referred a little
while ago. As he was on the way to execution, the subject of
these pages stayed with him to the end, and again barely
escaped lynching at the hands of the martyr's fellow-citizens,
as being obviously to blame for his death, but on that
occasion, too, God's will kept him safe. After Plutarch, the
second of Origen's pupils to be revealed as a martyr was

1. Matt. x. 10. 2. Matt. vi. 34. 3. 2 Cor. xi. 27.

Serenus, who gave proof by fire of the faith he had received. From the same school the third to be martyred was Heraclides, who was still under instruction, and the fourth Hero, lately baptized: both were beheaded. In addition to these, a fifth member of the school was proclaimed a champion of true religion: a second Serenus, who – after showing the greatest patience under torture – died, there is reason to believe, under the axe. Of the women, Herais – still under instruction – received, as Origen himself records somewhere, the baptism of fire, and so departed this life.

5. Seventh among them must be reckoned Basilides, who led the renowned Potamiaena to execution. The praises of this woman are even today loudly sung by her own people. Endless the struggle that in defence of her chastity and virginity, which were beyond reproach, she maintained against lovers, for her beauty – of body as of mind – was in full flower. Endless her sufferings, till after tortures too horrible to describe she and her mother Marcella found fulfilment in fire. It is said that the judge, Aquila, subjected her whole body to dreadful agonies, and finally threatened to hand her over to the gladiators for bodily insult. She reflected for a moment, and when asked what she intended to do, gave an answer which offended their religious prejudices. She had hardly spoken when she heard sentence pronounced, and Basilides, a member of the armed forces, seized her arm and led her away to execution. As the crowd tried to plague her and insult her with obscene jests, Basilides thrust them back and drove them away, showing the utmost pity and kindness towards her. Potamiaena accepted his sympathy for her and gave him encouragement: when she had gone away she would ask her Lord for him, and it would not be long before she repaid him for all he had done for her. This said, she faced her end with noble courage – slowly, drop by drop, boiling pitch was poured over different parts of her body, from her toes to the

crown of her head. Such was the battle won by this splendid girl.

Not long afterwards Basilides was for some reason asked by his fellow-soldiers to take an oath, but he insisted that he was unable to swear in any circumstances,[1] as he was a Christian and made no secret of the fact. At first they thought he was joking, but when he stuck doggedly to his assertion he was brought before the magistrate, who, as he made no attempt to hide his convictions, committed him to prison. When his brothers in God visited him and asked the reason for this amazing impulse and determination, he is said to have declared that three days after her martyrdom Potamiaena stood before him in the night, put a wreath about his head, and said that she had prayed for him to the Lord, had obtained her request, and before long would place him by her side. At this the brethren bestowed on him the seal of the Lord,[2] and the next day, nobly witnessing for his Lord, he was beheaded. The records state that at this period many other citizens of Alexandria accepted the teaching of Christ in a body, as Potamiaena appeared to them in dreams and called them.

Clement of Alexandria: Jude the author

6. Pantaenus was succeeded by Clement, who remained principal of the school of instruction at Alexandria long enough to include Origen among his pupils. Observe that when he put together his *Miscellanies*, Clement set out a chronological table in Volume I, making the death of Commodus[3] a key date. It is clear then that he composed the work in the reign of Severus, whose times are the subject of these pages.

7. At the same period Jude, another author, wrote a treatise on Daniel's seventy weeks, bringing his account to an end in the

---

1. Matt. v. 34.   2. Baptism.   3. The last day of A.D. 192.

tenth year of Severus.[1] He believed that the much talked-of advent of antichrist would take place at any moment – so completely had the persecution set in motion against us at that time thrown many off their balance.

Origen's headstrong act

8. About the same time, while responsible for the instruction at Alexandria, Origen did a thing that provided the fullest proof of a mind youthful and immature, but at the same time of faith and self-mastery. The saying 'there are eunuchs who made themselves eunuchs for the kingdom of heaven's sake' he took in an absurdly literal sense,[2] and he was eager both to fulfil the Saviour's words and at the same time to rule out any suspicion of vile imputations on the part of unbelievers. For in spite of his youth he discussed religious problems before a mixed audience. So he lost no time in carrying out the Saviour's words, endeavouring to do it unnoticed by the bulk of his pupils. But however much he might wish it, he could not possibly conceal such an act, and it was not long before it came to the knowledge of Demetrius, as head of the diocese. He was amazed at Origen's headstrong act, but approving his enthusiasm and the genuineness of his faith he told him not to worry, and urged him to devote himself more keenly than ever to the work of instruction.

That was the line he took at the time, but when a little later the same worthy saw him prosperous, great, eminent, and universally esteemed, he yielded to human weakness and wrote to the bishops throughout the world in an attempt to make Origen's action appear outrageous, just when the most respected and outstanding bishops of Palestine, those of Caesarea and Jerusalem, judged him worthy of position in the Church and of the highest honour, and ordained him presbyter. As he had thus attained to a great name and reputation,

1. A.D. 202–3.   2. Which he afterwards repudiated.

and everyone everywhere esteemed him highly for his virtues and wisdom, Demetrius, for want of any other charge to bring against him, slandered him viciously for what he had done years before as a boy, and even dared to extend his accusations to those who had advanced him to the presbyterate.

This incident occurred somewhat later.[1] At the time we are speaking of, Origen was busy at Alexandria with the work of imparting religious knowledge to all without exception who came to him, night and day, and devoted the whole of his time unsparingly to religious teaching and the demands of his pupils.

Narcissus and Alexander

After eighteen years as master of the Empire, Severus was succeeded by his son Antoninus.[2] It was at this time that Alexander – one of those who faced persecution so manfully and openly confessed the Faith, yet by the providence of God were kept safe – was rewarded for his bold confessions of Christ by being appointed Bishop of the Jerusalem church, as recorded a few pages back. The appointment was made while his predecessor Narcissus was still alive.

9. Many stories of miracles wrought by Narcissus, handed down by generations of Christians, are told by members of the community. Among these they narrate the following tale of wonder. Once during the great all-night-long vigil of Easter, the deacons ran out of oil. The whole congregation was deeply distressed, so Narcissus told those responsible for the lights to draw water and bring it to him, and they obeyed him instantly. Then he said a prayer over the water, and instructed them to pour it into the lamps with absolute faith in the Lord. They again obeyed him, and, in defiance of natural

1. A.D. 231.   2. A.D. 211: Antoninus is better known as Caracalla.

law, by the miraculous power of God the substance of the
liquid was physically changed from water into oil. All the
years from that day to our own a large body of Christians
there have preserved a little of it, as proof of that wonderful
event.

Among the many interesting anecdotes from the life of
Narcissus is recorded the following. His energy and con-
scientiousness were more than some insignificant nonentities
could bear. Knowing themselves guilty of a long series of
misdemeanours, they were afraid that conviction and
punishment awaited them. To avoid this, they devised an
intrigue against him and smirched him with a horrid
slander. Then, to convince their hearers, they bolstered up
their accusations with oaths. One swore: 'If it isn't true, may
I be burnt to death!' Another: 'May my body be wasted by
a foul disease!' A third: 'May I lose my sight!' But no
amount of swearing made any of the faithful take any notice,
for no one could fail to see the unshakable integrity and
blameless character of Narcissus. But he himself was greatly
distressed by their dastardly allegations, and in addition he
had long ago embraced the philosophic life; so, turning his
back on the church community, he fled into a remote and
desert area, where he remained in hiding for many years.
However, the great eye of Justice did not remain unmoved
by these events, but very soon brought upon those perjured
scoundrels the curses with which they had bound themselves.
The first saw the house which he occupied ablaze from top to
bottom for no other cause whatever than a tiny spark that
settled on the roof in the night, and he and all his family were
burnt to ashes; the second felt his entire body from head to
toe permeated by the very disease he had named as his penalty;
the third, seeing the fate of the others and dreading the inescapable judgement of all-seeing God, publicly confessed his
share in the intrigue, but in his remorse he wore himself out
with so many lamentations, and poured out such a flood of

tears, that he lost the sight of both eyes. Such was the price these men paid for their lies.

10. As Narcissus had withdrawn, and there was no knowledge of his whereabouts, the heads of the neighbouring churches decided to proceed to the appointment of a new bishop. Dius was his name. After a short time as prelate, he was followed by Germanion, and he by Gordius. In his time Narcissus appeared from nowhere, as if restored to life, and was invited by the brethren to resume his prelateship, for he was admired by all even more than before because of his withdrawal and philosophic life – above all because of the judgement by which God had vindicated him.

11. When he had reached such an advanced age that he could no longer carry out his duties, the Alexander already mentioned, then holder of another bishopric, by the providence of God was summoned to share the duties with Narcissus, by means of a revelation given to him at night in a vision. Thereupon, as if in accordance with an oracle, he journeyed from Cappadocia, his original see, to Jerusalem, in order to worship there and to examine the historic sites. The Christian community welcomed him most warmly and would not let him return home again, for they, too, had received a revelation in the night, proclaiming a single unambiguous message to the most devout among them. It bade them go outside the city gates to welcome the man already chosen by God to be their bishop. This done, they forced him to remain, with the unanimous approval of the bishops who had charge of the churches round about. Alexander himself, in a personal letter to the Antinoites, which is still in my possession, mentions Narcissus as sharing the episcopal throne with him, using these exact words at the end of the letter:

Narcissus, who preceded me as bishop of this diocese, and now at the age of 116 shares my responsibility for public worship, wishes to be remembered to you. He is as anxious as I am that you should agree among yourselves.

Serapion and his extant works

Turning now to Antioch, we note that when Serapion entered into rest he was succeeded as bishop by Asclepiades, who confessed his Lord with equal boldness during the persecution. His appointment, too, is mentioned by Alexander in a letter to the Antiochenes:

Alexander, a servant and prisoner of Jesus Christ, to the blessed church of Antioch, greeting in the Lord.[1] The Lord made my fetters light and easy to bear, when news reached me in my cell that by God's providence the bishopric of your holy church of Antioch had been entrusted to Asclepiades, an excellent choice in view of his wonderful faith.

This letter was conveyed by Clement, as is shown by the final sentences:

I am sending you these lines, my dear brothers, by Clement the blessed presbyter, whom you have already heard of and will now get to know. The providence of the Master has so ordered it that during his stay with us this virtuous and estimable man has both strengthened and enlarged the Church of the Lord.

12. It is probable that other short works from Serapion's pen are in the keeping of other people: none has come into my hands but those addressed to Domnus, a man who at the time of the persecution had fallen away from faith in Christ to Jewish will-worship,[2] and to the churchmen Pontius and Caricus, together with letters to other people and a pamphlet of his composition entitled *The So-called Gospel of Peter*.[3] This

1. This opening, so like those of St Paul, cannot be modernized.
2. See Col. ii. 23.
3. A second-century apocryphal work rediscovered in 1886.

he wrote to refute the lies in that document, which had induced some members of the Christian community at Rhossus[1]
to go astray into heterodox teachings. It will be worth while
to quote from this work a few sentences which explain his
attitude to the book:

We, my brothers, receive Peter and all the apostles as we receive
Christ, but the writings falsely attributed to them we are experienced
enough to reject, knowing that nothing of the sort has been handed
down to us. When I visited you, I assumed that you all clung to the
true Faith; so without going through the 'gospel' alleged by them
to be Peter's, I said: 'If this is the only thing that apparently puts childish notions into your heads, read it by all means.' But as, from information received, I now know that their mind had been ensnared by
some heresy, I will make every effort to visit you again; so expect me in
the near future. It was obvious to me what kind of heresy Marcian[2]
upheld, though he contradicted himself through not knowing what he
was talking about, as you will gather from this letter. But others have
studied this same 'gospel', viz. the successors of those who originated it, known to us as Docetae[3] and from whose teaching the ideas
are mostly derived. With their comments in mind, I have been able
to go through the book and draw the conclusion that while most of it
accorded with the authentic teaching of the Saviour, some passages
were spurious additions. These I am appending to my letter.

The works of Clement

13. Of Clement's works the *Miscellanies*,[4] all eight books, are
in my possession, bearing the title he chose for them – *Titus
Flavius Clemens's Miscellanies: Gnostic Publications in the Light
of the True Philosophy*. There are eight volumes again of the
work he entitled *Outlines*, in which he names Pantaenus as his
teacher. In these he has expounded his own interpretations of

1. Thirty miles from Antioch.   2. Otherwise unknown.
3. Heretics who denied that Jesus had a real body that could feel pain.
Serapion's statement about the 'gospel' is correct.
4. Still extant.

Scripture alongside the traditional. There is also a work of his addressed to the Greeks – the *Exhortation*; the three volumes of the work entitled *The Tutor; The Rich Man who finds Salvation*, as another work of his is entitled; the monograph on *The Easter Festival*; the discourses on *Fasting* and on *Slander*; the *Exhortation to Patience, or For the Newly Baptized*; and the work entitled *Canon of the Church, or An Answer to the Judaizers*, dedicated to Alexander, the bishop already mentioned.

In the *Miscellanies* he has woven a tapestry combining Holy Writ with anything that he considered helpful in secular literature. He includes any view generally accepted, expounding those of Greeks and non-Greeks alike, and even correcting the false doctrines of the heresiarchs, and explains a great deal of history, providing us with a work of immense erudition. With all these strands he has blended the arguments of philosophers, so that the work completely justifies the title *Miscellanies*. In it he has made use also of evidence drawn from the Disputed Writings – the 'Wisdom of Solomon', the 'Wisdom of Jesus the son of Sirach', the Epistle to the Hebrews, and those of Barnabas, Clement, and Jude; and he refers to Tatian's *Against the Greeks* and to Cassian, the compiler of another *Chronological Record* – also to Philo and Aristobulus, Josephus, Demetrius, and Eupolemus, Jewish authors whose writings all helped to prove that the first appearance of the Greeks did not go back as far as Moses and the Jewish people. Choice passages from many other writers fill the pages of this work. In Book 1 he shows that he himself was almost an immediate successor of the apostles: farther on he promises to write a commentary on Genesis.

In his work *The Easter Festival* he declares that his friends insisted on his transmitting to later generations in writing the oral traditions that had come down to him from the earliest authorities of the Church; he refers also to Melito,[1] Irenaeus, and some others, whose statements he has reproduced.

1. See pp. 186–7.

14. In the *Outlines*, to put it briefly, he has summarized all canonical Scripture, even including the Disputed Books, namely the Epistle of Jude and the other Catholic Epistles, the Epistle of Barnabas, and the 'Revelation of Peter'. The Epistle to the Hebrews he attributes to Paul, but says that it was written for Hebrews in their own language, and then accurately translated by Luke and published for Greek readers. Hence, in the Greek version of this epistle we find the same stylistic colour as in the Acts. The usual opening – 'Paul, an apostle' – was omitted, with good reason. As Clement says:

> In writing to Hebrews already prejudiced against him and sus-picious of him, he was far too sensible to put them off at the start by naming himself. . . . Now, as the blessed presbyter[1] used to say, the Lord, the apostle of the Almighty, was sent to the Hebrews; so through modesty Paul, knowing that he had been sent to the Gen-tiles, does not describe himself as an apostle of the Hebrews, first be-cause he so reverenced the Lord, and secondly because he was going outside his province in writing to the Hebrews too, when he was an ambassador and apostle of the Gentiles.[2]

In the same volumes Clement has found room for a tradi-tion of the primitive authorities of the Church regarding the order of the gospels. It is this. He used to say that the earliest gospels were those containing the genealogies,[3] while Mark's originated as follows. When, at Rome, Peter had openly preached the word and by the spirit had proclaimed the gospel, the large audience urged Mark, who had followed him for a long time and remembered what had been said, to write it all down. This he did, making his gospel available to all who wanted it. When Peter heard about this, he made no objection and gave no special encouragement. Last of all, aware that the

1. Probably the author's teacher, Pantaenus.
2. Clement seems to have made two wild guesses: the epistle is certainly not Pauline.
3. In spite of the evidence of Clement, Origen, and Eusebius himself, most modern scholars regard Mark's gospel as the first.

physical facts had been recorded in the gospels, encouraged by his pupils and irresistibly moved by the Spirit, John wrote a spiritual gospel.

So much for Clement's writings. Clement himself is mentioned, along with Pantaenus, in a letter to Origen written by the Alexander referred to above, who knew them both. He writes as follows:

> This, as you know, is indeed God's will, that the friendship we have inherited from our forbears should not wane, but rather grow warmer and more enduring. For we have found true fathers in those blessed ones who trod the road before us, with whom we shall soon be reunited – Pantaenus, my truly blessed friend, and holy Clement, my friend and helper, and others like them. Through them I came to know you, who are in every way my best friend and brother.

Origen's labours on Holy Writ: Symmachus the translator

When Zephyrinus was head of the Roman church, Adamantius – hitherto referred to as Origen – states in one of his writings that he himself visited Rome, anxious, as he says, to see the ancient Roman church. After a short stay in Rome he went back to Alexandria and took up again with enthusiasm his work of instruction there, as the bishop of the diocese, Demetrius, still pressed and almost begged him to continue unabated his efforts to assist the brethren.   15. But he saw that he could not find time himself for the more profound study of theology and the scrutiny and translation of sacred documents if he continued to instruct those who came to him and allowed him no time to breathe, batch after batch thronging his school from dawn to dusk. He therefore divided them up, and picking out Heraclas from his pupils, a keen theologian and in addition very well informed and a promising philosopher, gave him a share in the instruction. The introductory lessons for the beginners he entrusted to Heraclas: the higher education of the advanced pupils he reserved to himself.

16. So meticulous was the scrutiny to which Origen subjected the Scriptural books that he even mastered the Hebrew language, and secured for himself a copy, in the actual Hebrew script, of the original documents circulating among the Jews. Moreover, he hunted out the published translations of Holy Writ other than the Septuagint, and in addition to the versions in common use – those of Aquila, Symmachus, and Theodotion – he discovered several alternative translations. These had been lost for many years – I don't know where – but he hunted them out of their hiding-places and brought them to light. These were wrapped in mystery, and he had no idea who wrote them: the only thing he could say was that he had found one at Nicopolis near Actium and the other at some similar place. Anyway, in his *Sixfold Edition*[1] of the Psalms, after the four familiar versions he placed in parallel columns not only a fifth but a sixth and seventh translation; in the case of one, he has added a note that it was found at Jericho in a jar during the reign of Antoninus, the son of Severus. All these he combined in one volume, breaking them up into clauses and setting them side by side in parallel columns, along with the original Hebrew text. Thus he has left us the copies of the *Sixfold Edition*, as it is called. In a separate publication he put the versions of Aquila, Symmachus, and Theodotion alongside the Septuagint, in his *Fourfold Edition*.[2]

17. Of these translators it should be observed that Symmachus was an Ebionite. The adherents of what is known as the Ebionite heresy assert that Christ was the son of Joseph and Mary, and regard Him as no more than a man. They insist also that the law ought to be kept more in the Jewish manner, as I mentioned earlier in this history.[3] Pamphlets also by Symmachus are still extant, in which he inveighs against the

1. The *Hexapla*, of which only a fragment survives.
2. The *Tetrapla*.   3. p. 137.

Gospel according to Matthew, apparently in order to bolster up his heresy. These, together with other comments on Scripture by Symmachus, Origen states that he received from a woman called Juliana, on whom, he says, Symmachus had himself bestowed them.

Ambrose

18. At the same period, Ambrose – who shared the heretical opinions of Valentinus[1] – was refuted by the truth which Origen expounded, and, as if light had dawned on his mind, accepted the orthodox teaching of the Church. Many other educated people were so impressed by Origen's universal renown that they came to his school to benefit by his skill in biblical exegesis; while innumerable heretics and a considerable number of the most eminent philosophers listened to him with close attention, as he instructed them not only in theology but to some extent in secular philosophy too, for he introduced any pupils in whom he detected natural ability to philosophic studies as well. First he taught them geometry, arithmetic, and the other preparatory subjects; then he led them on to the systems of the philosophers, discussing their published theories and examining and criticizing those of the different schools, with the result that the Greeks themselves acknowledged his greatness as a philosopher. He found time also to give many less gifted persons a general grounding, declaring that it would stand them in very good stead for the examination and study of Holy Writ. He therefore thought it most important that he himself should be skilled in secular and philosophic studies.

References to Origen

19. Testimony to his success in these endeavours is paid by the Greek philosophers who flourished in his time, in whose

1. A second-century gnostic: see p. 163.

writings I have found many references to him. Sometimes they dedicated their works to him, sometimes they submitted their own labours to him, as to a master, for criticism. Far more significant is the case of Porphyry,[1] who in my own time settled in Sicily and in an attempt to traduce the Holy Scriptures published a long treatise[2] attacking us, in which he refers to those who have interpreted them. He finds it quite impossible to bring any damaging accusation against our doctrines, so for lack of arguments he turns to abuse and traduces the interpreters. His special target is Origen, whom he claims to have known as a young man and attempts to traduce, little knowing that he is actually commending him. When he cannot help it, he tells the truth; when he thinks he will not be found out, he tells lies. Sometimes he accuses him as a Christian, sometimes he enlarges on his addiction to philosophic studies. Listen to his actual words:

In their eagerness to find, not a way to reject the depravity of the Jewish Scriptures, but a means of explaining it away, they resorted to interpretations which cannot be reconciled or harmonized with those scriptures, and which provide not so much a defence of the original authors as a fulsome advertisement for the interpreters. 'Enigmas' is the pompous name they give to the perfectly plain statements of Moses, glorifying them as oracles full of hidden mysteries, and bewitching the critical faculty by their extravagant nonsense. . . . This absurd method must be attributed to a man whom I met while I was still quite young, who enjoyed a great reputation and thanks to the works he has left behind him, enjoys it still. I refer to Origen, whose fame among teachers of these theories is widespread. He was a pupil of Ammonius,[3] the most distinguished philosopher of our time. Theoretical knowledge in plenty he acquired with the help of his master, but in choosing the right way to live he went in the opposite direction. For Ammonius was a Christian, brought up in Christian ways by his parents, but when he began to

1. A neo-platonist from Tyre, who was twenty-two when Origen died.
2. Fifteen books, all lost.
3. An Alexandrian who taught Porphyry's masters, Longinus and Plotinus.

think philosophically he promptly changed to a law-abiding way of
life. Origen on the other hand, a Greek schooled in Greek thought,
plunged headlong into un-Greek recklessness; immersed in this, he
peddled himself and his skill in argument. In his life he behaved like
a Christian, defying the law: in his metaphysical and theological
ideas he played the Greek, giving a Greek twist to foreign tales. He
associated himself at all times with Plato, and was at home among the
writings of Numenius and Cronius, Apollophanes, Longinus, and
Moderatus, Nichomachus, and the more eminent followers of Pythagoras. He made use, too, of the books of Chaeremon the Stoic and
Cornutus, which taught him the allegorical method of interpreting
the Greek mysteries, a method he applied to the Jewish Scriptures.

Such are the allegations made by Porphyry in the third
book of his treatise against the Christians. He tells the truth
about Origen's teaching and wide learning, but plainly lies –
for opponents of Christianity are quite unscrupulous – when
he says that he came over from the Greek camp, and that
Ammonius lapsed from the service of God into paganism.
For Origen clung firmly to the Christian principles his parents had taught him, as this record has already shown; and
Ammonius's inspired philosophy remained pure and intact
to the very end of his life.[1] To this, surely, his literary labours
bear witness, for the works that he bequeathed to posterity
have won him a very wide reputation – for instance the book
entitled *The Harmony of Moses and Jesus*, and the many other
works treasured by discriminating readers.

These facts suffice to prove the untruthfulness of Origen's
calumniator and his own perfect familiarity with Greek
learning. Defending himself against critics who condemned
his pre-occupation with such studies, he writes thus in one of
his letters:

When I was giving all my time to the word, accounts of my ability
went about, and brought sometimes heretics, sometimes men who
had been trained in Greek learning, particularly philosophy; so I

1. This has been questioned.

decided to examine the notions of the heretics, and also the supposed qualifications of philosophers for speaking about truth. In doing this I followed in the footsteps of one who helped many before my time – Pantaenus, a real expert in these questions; and of one who now has a seat in the presbytery at Alexandria – Heraclas, whom I found with the director of philosophical studies. He had already stayed with him five years before I attended my first lecture on the subject, and because of him he put off the normal dress he had hitherto worn, and donned a philosopher's garb, which he retains to this very day, while he devotes himself unceasingly and enthusiastically to the study of Greek literature.

That is what he says in defence of his Greek training. But at this period, when he was resident in Alexandria, one of the military arrived with letters from the ruler of Arabia to Demetrius, the bishop of the diocese, and to the governor of Egypt, asking them to send Origen at the earliest possible moment to confer with him. He did in fact visit Arabia, but he soon completed his business there and returned to Alexandria. Some time later a violent campaign blazed up in the city;[1] so he slipped out of Alexandria and went to Palestine, where he settled in Caesarea. There he gave public lectures to the church on biblical exegesis, at the invitation of the bishops of the province, though not yet ordained to the presbyterate. The truth of this is evident from what Alexander and Theoctistus, bishops of Jerusalem and Caesarea, in writing about Demetrius, say in their own defence:

He included in his letter a statement that it was an unheard-of, unprecedented thing that where bishops were present laymen should preach – a statement that is glaringly untrue. In cases where persons are found duly qualified to assist the clergy, they are called on by the holy bishops to preach to the laity; e.g. in Laranda, Euelpius; in Iconium, Paulinus; in Synnada, Theodore were called on respectively by Neon, Celsus, and Atticus, our blessed brother-bishops. Probably there are other places too where this happens, unknown to us.

1. Presumably Caracalla's massacre in 215.

Such was the respect paid to Origen while still a young man, not only by his own countrymen but even by the bishops in another land. But when Demetrius sent first a letter recalling him, then deacons of the church to hasten his return to Alexandria, back he came and resumed his labours with all his old enthusiasm.

Works of the period: notable bishops

20. Prominent at that period were a number of learned churchmen, who penned to each other letters still surviving and easy of access, as they have been preserved to our own time in the library established at Aelia by the man who then presided over the church there, Alexander – the library from which I myself have been able to bring together the materials for the work now in hand. Of these writers Beryllus, Bishop of the Arabians at Bostra, in addition to letters left us compositions of the highest literary merit, as did Hippolytus – a prelate like Beryllus, though his see is unknown. I have also read a dialogue which Gaius, a man of the greatest learning, published at Rome in Zephyrinus's time as an answer to Proclus, the champion of the Phrygian heresy. In this, while reining in the audacity of his opponents in compiling new scriptures, he refers to only thirteen of the epistles of the holy Apostle, not including that to the Hebrews with the rest; for then as now there were some at Rome who did not think that it was the Apostle's.

21. When Antoninus had reigned seven years six months, he was succeeded by Macrinus.[1] Macrinus having lasted only a year, the Roman Empire was next entrusted to another Antoninus.[2] In his first year, the Bishop of Rome, Zephyrinus,

1. A.D. 217. The combined reigns of Antoninus and Macrinus totalled seven years four months.
2. Elagabalus.

departed this life, after holding office eighteen years in all. After him Callistus took over the episcopate, but survived him by only five years, leaving his office to Urban. Alexander was the next to become sole ruler of the Roman Empire, Antoninus having lasted no more than four years. It was at this time that in the church of Antioch Asclepiades was succeeded by Philetus.

The emperor's mother Mammaea was one of the most religious and high-principled of women, and when the fame of Origen spread so far that it came to her ears, she set her heart on securing an interview with him and testing his universally admired skill as a theologian. By good luck she was staying in Antioch, so she sent a bodyguard of soldiers to fetch him. He stayed with her for some time, revealing to her many things to the glory of the Lord and of the virtue of the divine message. Then he hurried back to his ordinary duties.

22. At that same period Hippolytus, author of many other short works, composed the essay *The Easter Festival*, in which he works out a system of dates and suggests a scheme for a sixteen-year cycle for Easter, relating his dates to the first year of Alexander's reign. Of his other essays I am acquainted with *The Six Days*,[1] *The Sequel to the Six Days*, *An Answer to Marcion*, *The Song*, *Parts of Ezekiel*, *The Easter Festival*, and *An Answer to all the Heresies*. Many others are probably to be found in various private collections.

Origen's enthusiasm: his call to the presbyterate

23. It was at this period that Origen started work on his *Commentaries on Holy Scripture*, at the urgent request of Ambrose, who not only exerted verbal pressure and every kind of persuasion, but supplied him in abundance with everything

1. i.e. of creation.

needful. Shorthand-writers more than seven in number were
available when he dictated, relieving each other regularly,
and at least as many copyists, as well as girls trained in pen-
manship, all of them provided most generously with everything needful at Ambrose's expense. And not only that: in the
devoted study of the divine teaching he brought to Origen his
own immeasurable enthusiasm, the most powerful induce-
ment to the composition of the *Commentaries*.

Meanwhile, after eight years as Bishop of the Roman
Church, Urban was succeeded by Pontian, and at Antioch
Philetus's place was filled by Zebinnus. During their episcopate, the necessity of settling questions affecting the Church
forced Origen to set out for Greece via Palestine. In Caesarea
he was ordained presbyter by the Palestinian bishops. This
made him the subject of an agitation on which the prelates of
the churches passed judgement; but like the impact which,
having reached his prime, he made in other ways on the exposition of God's word, these matters deserve a book to
themselves; so in the second volume of my *Defence of Origen*
I have dealt with them at some length.

Commentaries written by him at Alexandria; references to the canonical Scriptures

24. To this I must add that in the sixth book of his *Commentary
on John's Gospel* he mentions that he wrote the first five while
still at Alexandria, but of his work on the whole of this same
gospel only twenty-two books have come into my hands.
And in the ninth book of his *Commentary on Genesis* – there
are twelve altogether – he makes it clear that at Alexandria he
wrote not only the first eight but also his *Commentary on
Psalms i–xxv*, as well as the *Commentary on Lamentations*, of
which I possess five books. In these he refers to his *Resurrection*,
a work in two books. In addition he wrote his *Origins* before
leaving Alexandria, and compiled the ten volumes entitled

Miscellanies in the same city, while Alexander was on the throne, as is proved by the notes prefixed to them by the author himself.

25. In his commentary on Psalm i he wrote out a list of the Old Testament books, in the following terms:

It should be noted that the Canonical Books, according to Hebrew tradition, number twenty-two, like the letters of their alphabet.... The twenty-two books of the Hebrew canon are these:

> GENESIS, as we call it:[1] the Hebrews (from the opening word) call it BRESITH (i.e. *in the beginning*)
>
> EXODUS – OUELESMOTH (i.e. *these are the names*)
>
> LEVITICUS – OUIKRA (*and he called*)
>
> NUMBERS – AMMESPHEKODEIM
>
> DEUTERONOMY – HELEADDEBARIM (*these are the words*)
>
> JESUS SON OF NAVE – JOSHUA BEN NUN
>
> JUDGES, RUTH – with the Hebrews, one book, SOPHETIM
>
> KINGS I and 2 – with them a single book, SAMUEL (*the called of God*)
>
> KINGS 3 and 4 – one book, OUAMMELCH DAVID (i.e. *the kingdom of David*)
>
> THE OMITTED BOOKS I and 2[2] – one book, DABREIAMIN (i.e. *accounts of days*)
>
> ESDRAS I and 2[3] – one book, EZRA (i.e. *helper*)
>
> BOOK OF PSALMS – SPHARTHELLIM
>
> PROVERBS OF SOLOMON – MELOTH
>
> ECCLESIASTES – KOELTH
>
> SONG OF SONGS (not, as sometimes thought, *Songs* of Songs) – SIR ASSIRIM
>
> ESAIAS – IESSIA
>
> JEREMIAS, with LAMENTATIONS and THE LETTER[4] in one book – JEREMIAH
>
> DANIEL– DANIEL

1. In the Septuagint.	2. Chronicles.
3. Ezra, Nehemiah, and Esdras 3.	4. Baruch vi.

EZEKIEL – EZEKIEL
JOB – JOB
ESTHER – ESTHER
Excluded from the list is MACCABEES, entitled SARBETH
SABANAIEL.[1]

These statements he inserted in the treatise referred to above.
In the first part of his *Commentary on Matthew*, when defending the canon of the Church, he testifies that he knows four
gospels only. This is what he says:

I accept the traditional view of the four gospels which alone
are undeniably authentic in the Church of God on earth. First to be
written was that of the one-time exciseman who became an apostle
of Jesus Christ – Matthew; it was published for believers of Jewish
origin, and was composed in Aramaic. Next came that of Mark, who
followed Peter's instructions in writing it, and who in Peter's general
epistle was acknowledged as his son: 'Greetings to you from the
church in Babylon, chosen like yourselves, and from my son Mark.'[2]
Next came that of Luke, who wrote for Gentile converts the gospel
praised by Paul. Last of all came John's.

In Book v of his *Commentary on John's Gospel* Origen has
this to say about the epistles of the apostles:

The man who was enabled to become a minister of the New
Covenant, not of the letter but of the spirit, Paul, proclaimed the
gospel from Jerusalem, in a wide sweep as far as Illyricum.[3] But he
did not write to all the churches he had taught; and to those to which
he did write he sent only a few lines. Peter, on whom is built Christ's
Church, over which the gates of Hades shall have no power,[4] left
us one acknowledged epistle, possibly two – though this is doubtful.
Need I say anything about the man who leant back on Jesus's breast,
John? He left a single gospel, though he confessed that he could write
so many that the whole world would not hold them.[5] He also wrote
the Revelation, but was ordered to remain silent and not write the

---

1. Meaning doubtful.   2. 1 Peter i. 13.   3. Rom. xv. 19.
4. The Fathers of the Church did not all interpret Matt. xvi. 18 thus.
5. John xxi. 25.

utterances of the seven thunders.[1] In addition, he left an epistle of a very few lines, and possibly two more, though their authenticity is denied by some. Anyway, they do not total a hundred lines between them.

Again, in his *Homilies on the Epistle to the Hebrews* he makes this comment:

In the epistle entitled *To the Hebrews* the diction does not exhibit the characteristic roughness of speech or phraseology admitted by the Apostle himself;[2] the construction of the sentences is closer to Greek usage, as anyone capable of recognizing differences of style would agree. On the other hand the matter of the epistle is wonderful, and quite equal to the Apostle's acknowledged writings: the truth of this would be admitted by anyone who has read the Apostle carefully. . . . If I were asked my personal opinion, I would say that the matter is the Apostle's but the phraseology and construction are those of someone who remembered the Apostle's teaching and wrote his own interpretation of what his master had said. So if any church regards this epistle as Paul's, it should be commended for so doing, for the primitive Church had every justification for handing it down as his. Who wrote the epistle is known to God alone: the accounts that have reached us suggest that it was either Clement, who became Bishop of Rome, or Luke, who wrote the gospel and the Acts.

Heraclas Bishop of Alexandria: what the bishops thought of Origen

26. It was in the tenth year of Alexander's reign that Origen made the move from Alexandria to Caesarea, leaving to Heraclas the school of elementary instruction for those in the city. Not long afterwards Demetrius, Bishop of the Alexandrian church, died, having completed forty-three years in that office; he was succeeded by Heraclas.

27. At this time Firmilian, Bishop of Caesarea in Cappadocia, paid a remarkable tribute to Origen, showing such admira-

---

1. Rev. x. 3-4.   2. 2 Cor. xi. 6.

tion for him that at one time he would invite him to his own
region to assist his churches, at another he would go all the
way to Judaea to see him and spend some time with him, in
order to deepen his own spiritual life. In the same way the
head of the Jerusalem church, Alexander, and Theoctistus of
Caesarea listened attentively to him at all times as their only
teacher, leaving to him the interpretation of Holy Writ and
all other branches of religious instruction.

Persecution under Maximin

28. When after reigning thirteen years the Roman emperor
Alexander died, Maximin Caesar succeeded him. Through
rancour against Alexander's house, which consisted mainly of
believers, he instigated a persecution and ordered the leaders
of the churches alone, as being responsible for the teaching of
the gospel, to be destroyed. It was then that Origen composed
his *Martyrdom*, dedicating his treatise to Ambrose and Protoc-
tetus, a presbyter of the Caesarean diocese, both of whom had
had a terrible time in the persecution, a time in which it is on
record that they were fearless in the confession of their faith
throughout Maximin's reign of three years only. This time
for the duration of the persecution was noted by Origen in
Section xxii of his *Commentary on John's Gospel*, and in
various letters.

Fabian miraculously designated by God as Bishop of Rome

29. Gordian having succeeded Maximin as Roman emperor,
Pontian, after six years as Bishop of the Roman church, was
succeeded by Anteros, and he, after filling the office for a
month, by Fabian. It is said that after Anteros's death Fabian
came with a party from the country and paid a visit to Rome,
where by a miracle of divine and heavenly grace he was
chosen to fill the place. When the brethren had all assembled

267

with the intention of electing a successor to the bishopric, and a large number of eminent and distinguished men were in the thoughts of most, Fabian, who was present, came into no one's mind. But suddenly out of the blue a dove fluttered down and perched on his head (the story goes on), plainly following the example of the descent upon the Saviour of the Holy Spirit in the form of a dove. At this, as if moved by one divine inspiration, with the utmost enthusiasm and complete unanimity the whole meeting shouted that he was the man, and then and there seized him and set him on the bishop's throne.

At about the same time, Zebinnus, Bishop of Antioch, departed this life, and Babylas succeeded to his position; while at Alexandria – where, following Demetrius, Heraclas had been appointed to the office – the school of elementary instruction was taken over by Dionysius, another of Origen's old pupils.

Men who became Origen's pupils

30. While Origen was performing his normal tasks at Caesarea, his services were in constant demand not only by the local people but also by innumerable foreign students who had left their own countries. The most distinguished names known to me are those of Theodore – who was none other than that illustrious bishop of my own day, Gregory – and his brother Athenodore. They were passionately devoted to Greek and Roman studies, but he implanted in them a love of true philosophy and induced them to exchange their old enthusiasm for a theological training. Five whole years they spent with him, making such remarkable progress in theology that while still young both were chosen to be bishops of 'e churches in Pontus.

Africanus

31. At this time, Africanus – author of the work entitled
Cesti[1] – was another eminent writer. A letter which he wrote
to Origen has survived. In it he cast the gravest doubt on the
authenticity of the story of Susanna in Daniel.[2] Origen wrote
a very full reply. From the same author there has also come
into my hands a five-volume *Dictionary of Dates*, compiled
with unsparing devotion to accuracy. In it he says that he
made a special journey to Alexandria, in view of the great
reputation of Heraclas, who – as already stated – after showing himself an outstanding exponent of philosophy and other
secular studies, had been elevated to the bishopric of the
church there. Another of his letters has survived: it is addressed to Aristides, and deals with the alleged discrepancy
between Matthew and Luke on the subject of Christ's genealogy. In it he demonstrates the harmony of the evangelists
most convincingly, from an account which has come down
to him and which I have found it convenient to reproduce
earlier, in Book 1 of the present work.[3]

Commentaries written by Origen at Caesarea

32. Origen himself was busy at that time putting together his
Commentary on Isaiah, and at the same time that on *Ezekiel*.
On the third section of Isaiah, as far as the vision of the beasts
in the desert,[4] thirty books have come into my hands, and on
Ezekiel twenty-five, covering the entire book. It was during
a visit to Athens at that stage that he completed the *Commentary on Ezekiel* and began that on the *Song of Songs*, getting

1. Meaning either 'embroidered girdles' or 'boxing gloves'. For Africanus,
see p. 51 n.
2. In the Septuagint the story is part of Daniel: not being found in the
Hebrew, it is in our Bibles consigned to the Apocrypha.
3. pp. 53–6.   4. Is. xxx. 6.

as far as Book v before leaving Athens and returning to Caesarea, where he wrote the remaining five books. But this is not the time to give a detailed list of all his works, which would be a task in itself. I have already included one in my *Life of Pamphilus*, the holy martyr of my own day, in which, to show the intensity of his devotion to theology, I mentioned the list of books in the library he had built up of the works of Origen and the other Church writers. From these anyone who wishes can learn all about the extant works of Origen. But now I must go on to the next stage in the story.

The deviation of Beryllus

33. Beryllus, who was mentioned some pages back as Bishop of Bostra in Arabia, perverted the true doctrine of the Church and tried to bring in ideas alien to the Faith, actually asserting that our Saviour and Lord did not pre-exist in His own form of being before He made His home among men, and had no divinity of His own but only the Father's dwelling in Him. Accordingly, a large number of bishops questioned and argued with him; then Origen was sent for, with several others. He began by getting into conversation with him, to find out what his ideas were. Then, having acquainted himself with his assertions, he straightened out his unorthodox ideas, and argued so convincingly that he set him on the right doctrinal path and brought him back to his former sound opinion. We still possess accounts of Beryllus and the synod that he made necessary; these, in addition to the questions put to him by Origen and the discussions held in his own see, record everything done at that time.

A great many other traditions about Origen have been passed on orally by the older men of our day, but I think I will omit them, as irrelevant to the present work. All that it is important to know about him can be gathered from the *Defence of Origen* written by myself and that holy martyr of

our time, Pamphilus – a joint effort, a labour of love undertaken as an answer to carping critics.

The reign of Philip: Heraclas succeeded by Dionysius

34. After six years as Roman emperor Gordian died, and
Philip along with a son of the same name succeeded him. He,
there is reason to believe, was a Christian, and on the day of
the last Easter vigil he wished to share in the prayers of the
Church along with the people; but the prelate of the time
would not let him come in until he made open confession and
attached himself to those who were held to be in a state of sin
and were occupying the place for penitents. Otherwise, if he
had not done so, he would never have been received by him
in view of the many accusations brought against him. It is
said that he obeyed gladly, showing by his actions the genuine
piety of his attitude towards the fear of God.

35. It was in Philip's third year that Heraclas departed this
life, after presiding for sixteen years over the Alexandrian
province, and Dionysius took office as bishop.

Other works written by Origen

36. At this period of rapid expansion of the Faith, when our
message was being boldly proclaimed on every side, it was
natural that Origen, now over sixty and with his abilities fully
developed by years of practice, should, as we are told, have
allowed his lectures to be taken down by shorthand-writers,
though he had never before agreed to this. During the same
period, he wrote his eight pamphlets to refute the attack made
on us by Celsus the Epicurean in his *Truth Established*; also
the twenty-five books of his *Commentary on Matthew's Gospel*,
and his *Commentary on the Minor Prophets*, of which I have
laid my hand on twenty-five books only. We possess also a

letter of his to the Emperor Philip himself, another to his consort Severa, and others to various other persons. These have been preserved here and there by various persons: all that I have succeeded in collecting I have stored methodically in separate bundles, to prevent them from being dispersed again. He also wrote to Bishop Fabian of Rome and to the heads of many other churches about his orthodoxy. You will find all this set out in Book VI of my *Defence of Origen*.

Unorthodox beliefs in Arabia: the Helkesaite heresy

37. While he was thus engaged, a new group appeared on the Arabian scene, originators of a doctrine far removed from the truth, namely, that at the end of our life here the human soul dies for a time along with our bodies and perishes with them; later, when one day the resurrection comes, it will return with them to life. At this crisis, a synod was convoked on a large scale, and Origen was again invited. On arrival he opened a public debate on the question at issue, and argued so forcibly that he compelled those who had previously gone astray to change their views.

38. At the same time another distorted idea was started by the 'Helkesaite' sect, but it was no sooner started than it was extinguished. It is referred to in a published sermon by Origen on Psalm lxxxii:

A man has recently come forward who prides himself on his ability to uphold a blasphemous and most impious theory – known as that of the Helkesaites – which has lately reared its head against the churches. The pernicious suggestions of that theory I will make clear to you, for fear you may be carried away by it. It rejects parts of every book of the Bible, though it makes use of passages from every Old Testament book and every gospel: the Apostle it rejects altogether. It says that to deny the truth does not matter, and that in case of need the sensible man will deny it with his lips but not in his heart.

They produce a book, alleging that it fell from heaven: anyone who hears it read and believes will receive forgiveness for his sins – forgiveness other than that which Jesus Christ won for us.

What happened under Decius

39. Philip, after a reign of seven[1] years, was succeeded by Decius. Through hatred of Philip he started a persecution against the churches, in which Fabian found fulfilment in martyrdom at Rome, where Cornelius succeeded him as bishop.

In Palestine, Alexander, Bishop of the Jerusalem church, was again brought before the governor's court at Caesarea, and as for the second time he boldly confessed the Faith, he endured imprisonment, though crowned with ripe old age and venerable white hairs. After bearing splendid and glorious witness in the governor's court, he fell asleep in his cell, and Mazabanes was named as successor to the Jerusalem bishopric. Alexander's fate was not unique, for at Antioch Babylas confessed the Faith and departed this life in prison, Fabius being made head of the church there.

As for Origen, the terrible sufferings that befell him in the persecution, and how they ended, when the evil demon, bent on his destruction, brought all the weapons in his armoury to bear and fought him with every device and expedient, attacking him with more determination than anyone he was fighting at that time – the dreadful cruelties he endured for the word of Christ, chains and bodily torments, agony in iron and the darkness of his cell; how for days on end his legs were pulled four paces apart in the torturer's stocks – the courage with which he bore threats of fire and every torture devised by his enemies – the way his maltreatment ended, when the judge had striven with might and main at all costs to avoid sentencing him to execution[2] – the messages he left us after

---

1. Apparently a mistake for five.   2. Origen survived the persecution.

all this, messages full of help for those in need of comfort – of all these things a truthful and detailed account will be found in his own lengthy correspondence.

What happened to Dionysius

40. What happened to Dionysius I will make clear by quoting his letter directed against Germanus, in which he gives this account of himself:

I speak as in the presence of God, who knows whether I am lying. I did *not* act on my own judgement or without God when I made my escape; but even before that, when Decius announced his persecution, Sabinus then and there dispatched a *frumentarius*[1] to hunt me out, and I stayed at home four days waiting for him to arrive. But though he went round searching every spot – roads, rivers, fields – where he guessed I was hiding or walking, he was smitten with blindness and did not find the house; he never imagined that when an object of persecution I should stay at home! It was only after four days, when God commanded me to go elsewhere, and by a miracle made it possible, that I set out along with the boys[2] and many of the brethren. That this was indeed the work of divine providence was proved by what followed, when perhaps we were of use to some.

After dealing with various other matters, he describes what happened to him after the flight:

About sunset, my companions and I were caught by the soldiers and taken to Taposiris;[3] but by the purpose of God it happened that Timothy was absent and was not caught. When he arrived later, he found the house empty except for a guard of servants, and learnt that we had been captured without hope of release. . . . And how was God's wonderful mercy shown? You shall hear the truth. As Timothy fled distracted, he was met by one of the villagers on his way to attend a wedding-feast – which in those parts meant an all-night celebration – who asked why he was in such a hurry. He told the

1. A military policeman.   2. Sons? Or servants?
3. Thirty miles south-west of Alexandria.

truth without hesitation, whereupon the other went in and informed the guests as they reclined at table.[1] With one accord, as if at a signal, they all sprang to their feet, came as fast as their legs would carry them, and burst in where we were with such terrifying shouts that the soldiers guarding us instantly took to their heels. Then they stood over us, as we lay on bare mattresses. At first, God knows, I thought they were bandits who had come to plunder and steal, so I stayed on the bed. I had nothing on but a linen shirt; my other clothes that were lying near I held out to them. But they told me to get up and make a bolt for it. Then I realized what they had come for, and called out, begging and beseeching them to go away and let us be. If they wanted to do me a good turn, they had better forestall my captors and cut off my head themselves. While I shouted like this, they pulled me up by force, as the companions who shared all my adventures know. I let myself fall on my back on the floor, but they grasped me by hands and feet and dragged me out, followed by those who witnessed the whole scene, Gaius, Faustus, Peter, and Paul, who picked me up and carried me out of the village, set me on a donkey bareback, and led me away.

This is the account Dionysius gives us of his adventure.

Martyrs who suffered at Alexandria and elsewhere

41. In his letter to Bishop Fabius of Antioch, he gives this account of the ordeals of those who were martyred at Alexandria under Decius:

It was not the imperial edict that set the persecution in motion against us: it had already been going on for a whole year, and the nameless prophet and worker of mischief for this city[2] was the first to stir up and incite the heathen masses against us, fanning the flames of their local superstition and working them up, till they seized on every available authority for their unholy deeds and convinced themselves that the only true religion was this demon-worship – thirst for our blood.

First they seized an old man named Metras, and ordered him to

---

1. At Marea, several miles away: see p. 297.   2. Unidentified.

utter blasphemous words; when he refused, they beat him with
cudgels, drove pointed reeds into his face and eyes, took him to the
suburbs, and stoned him to death. Next they took a female convert
named Quinta to the idol's temple and tried to make her worship.
When she turned her back in disgust they tied her feet and dragged
her right through the city over the rough paved road, bumping her
on the great stones and beating her as they went, till they arrived at
the same place, where they stoned her to death. Then they all ran in
a body to the houses of the Christians, charged in by groups on those
they knew as neighbours, raided, plundered, and looted. The more
valuable of their possessions they purloined; the cheaper wooden
things they threw about, or they made a bonfire of them in the streets,
making the city look as if it had been captured by enemies. The Christians retired and gradually withdrew; like those to whom Paul paid
tribute, they took with cheerfulness the plundering of their belongings.[1] I do not know of anyone, except possibly one man who fell
into their clutches, who up to now has denied the Lord.

Next they seized the wonderful old lady Apollonia, battered her
till they knocked out all her teeth, built a pyre in front of the city,
and threatened to burn her alive unless she repeated after them their
heathen incantations. She asked for a breathing-space, and when they
released her, jumped without hesitation into the fire and was burnt to
ashes.

Serapion they arrested in his own house. They racked him with
horrible tortures and broke all his limbs, then threw him down head
first from the upper floor.

No road, no highway, no alley was open to us, either by night or
by day; always and everywhere, everybody was shouting that anyone
who did not join in their blasphemous chants must at once be dragged
away and burnt. For a long time the terror remained intense, but the
wretched men were suddenly plunged into faction and civil war,
which turned the savagery of which we had been the victims against
its authors. For a little while we breathed again, as they were too
busy to vent their rage on us, but very soon the change from the
reign that had been kinder to us became generally known, and the
threat to our safety filled us with horrible foreboding. And the edict indeed arrived, almost exactly as foretold by our Lord in His truly terrify-

1. Dionysius evidently accepted the Pauline authorship of Hebrews.

ing words: 'So as, if possible, to trip up even the elect.'[1] Anyway, terror
was universal, and of many public figures some at once came forward
through fear, others who were in state employment were induced by
professional reasons, others were dragged forward by the mob.
Summoned by name, they approached the unclean, unholy sacrifices.
Some came white-faced and trembling, as if they were not going to
sacrifice but to be sacrificed themselves as victims to the idols, so that
the large crowd of spectators heaped scorn upon them and it was
obvious that they were utter cowards, afraid to die and afraid to
sacrifice. Others ran more readily towards the altars, trying to prove
by their fearlessness that they had never been Christians. Of these, the
Lord had declared long before with complete truth that they would
be saved with difficulty.[2] Of the rest, some followed each of these
groups, others tried to get away; some were caught, and of these
some allowed themselves to be chained and imprisoned (in some
cases remaining confined for weeks), and then, even before coming
into court, renounced their faith, while others held out for a time under torture but in the end gave up.

But the unbending, blessed pillars of the Lord, strengthened by
Him and receiving power and endurance deservedly and in proportion to the vigorous faith that was in them, proved wonderful martyr-
witnesses of His kingdom. Of these the first was Julian, a sufferer
from gout, unable to stand or walk, who was brought to trial with
two others to bear him. One of the two at once denied his Master;
the other, Cronion by name but nicknamed Goodfellow, and the
aged Julian himself, confessed the Lord and were taken right through
the city, which as you all know is immense, mounted on camels and
whipped while perched aloft. Finally, while the whole population
milled around, they were burnt up with quicklime. A soldier who
was standing by as they were led away protested at the insults, and
roused the mob to fury: he was brought to trial, Besas the gallant
warrior of God, and having fought like a hero in the great war for
the Faith, was beheaded. Another man, of Libyan stock, true both
to his name Macar[3] and to the Beatitude, in spite of all the efforts of
the judge to make him deny the Faith, stood firm and was burnt alive.

1. A slight misquotation of Matt. xxiv. 24.
2. An allusion to Matt. xix. 23.
3. A variant form of the first word of each Beatitude.

After these came Epimachus and Alexander, who after remaining in prison a long time endured numberless agonies from scrapers and whips, and like the others were destroyed with quicklime.

With them were four women.[1] Ammonarion, a most respectable young woman, in spite of the savage and prolonged torture inflicted on her by the judge because she had already made it clear beforehand that she would never say any of the things he ordered her to say, kept true to her promise and was led away. The others were Mercuria, a very dignified old lady, and Dionysia, the mother of a large family but just as devoted to her Lord. The governor was ashamed to go on torturing without result and to be defeated by women, so they died by the sword without being put to any further test by torture: this Ammonarion, foremost in the fight, had taken on herself for them all.

Three Egyptians, Hero, Ater, and Isidore, together with a boy of about fifteen called Dioscorus, were informed against. The judge began with the lad, trying to trick his unformed character with words, and to break down his feeble resistance by torture, but Dioscorus would neither obey nor give in. The others he tore in pieces with the utmost savagery, and when they held out they too were consigned to the flames. But Dioscorus behaved so splendidly in public, and gave such wise answers when questioned in private, that he astonished the judge, who let him go, saying that in view of his youth he would allow him time to come to his senses. And the saintly Dioscorus is with us still, having survived for a more prolonged ordeal and a more lasting conflict.

Nemesion, another Egyptian, was falsely reported to be in league with bandits. No sooner had he cleared himself before the centurion of such an absurd accusation than he was denounced as a Christian, and brought in chains before the governor. He, with gross injustice, subjected him to twice the tortures and floggings inflicted on the bandits, and burnt him between them, honouring him – blest indeed! – with a resemblance to Christ.

A whole squad of soldiers, Ammon, Zeus, Ptolemy, and Ingenuus, with an old man, Theophilus, were standing in court. When a man accused of being a Christian was on the point of denying Christ, they ground their teeth as they stood by, grimaced, stretched out their

1. One name is missing

hands, and gestured with their bodies. All eyes were turned towards them, but before anyone could stop them they made a dash for the dock, saying that they were Christians. The governor and his fellow-judges were filled with alarm; in contrast to the panic on the bench, the accused all showed a complete disregard of the sufferings to come; they marched out of the court in triumph, proud of their witness, their fame gloriously spread abroad by God.   42. Many others in cities and villages were torn to pieces by the heathen. One example will suffice. Ischyrion was the salaried agent of one of the magistrates. His employer ordered him to sacrifice. When he refused, he insulted him; and when he persisted, he heaped abuse on him. Having failed to shift him, he took a stout stick, drove it through his bowels and internal organs, and so killed him.

Need I speak of the vast number who wandered over deserts and mountains[1] till hunger, thirst, cold, sickness, bandits, or wild beasts destroyed them? The survivors pay tribute to those chosen to be victors, but one incident I must bring to your notice as showing what kind of men they were. Chaeremon, the very aged Bishop of Nilopolis, fled with his wife[2] to the mountain region of Arabia. He never came back, and despite a thorough search, the brethren failed to find either them or their remains. In that same mountain region very many were enslaved by the half-civilized Saracens.[3] Some of them with difficulty and at great cost were ransomed; others never to this day.

This long account, brother, I have given in no idle spirit, but in order that you may know the extent of the terror to which we have been subjected. Those more deeply involved could tell you more about it. . . .

Thus even the divine martyrs among us, who now sit by Christ's side as partners in His kingdom, share His authority, and are His fellow-judges, opened their arms to their fallen brethren who faced the charge of sacrificing. Seeing their conversion and repentance, they were sure that it would be acceptable to Him who does not in the least desire the death of a sinner, but rather his repentance; so they received them, admitted them to the congregation as 'bystanders',[4]

1. A reminiscence of Hebrews xi. 38.
2. Bishops were not required to be celibate.
3. Here first mentioned in literature.
4. Favoured penitents.

279

and allowed them to take part in services and feasts. What then, brothers, is your advice to us in this matter? What must we do? Shall we take our stand in full agreement with them, uphold their merciful decision, and deal gently with those they pitied? Or shall we condemn their decision as improper, and set ourselves up as judges of their attitude, wound their gentleness, and turn their practice upside down?

Novatus, his character and his heresy

43. Dionysius had good reason to argue thus, bringing up the question of those who had shown weakness at the time of the persecution, for Novatus[1] a presbyter of the Roman church, regarded them with lofty contempt: there was no hope of salvation for them now, even if they did everything in their power to prove their conversion sincere and their confession wholehearted. So he set himself up as leader of a new sect, whose members in the pride of their hearts entitled themselves Puritans. To deal with the situation a synod on the largest scale was convened at Rome, and was attended by sixty bishops and a still greater number of presbyters and deacons, while in the other provinces of the Empire the local pastors considered separately what was to be done. The result was a unanimous decree that Novatus, his companions in presumption, and any who thought fit to approve his attitude of hatred and inhumanity to brother-Christians, should be regarded as outside the Church, but that those brothers who had had the misfortune to fall should be treated and cured with the medicine of repentance.

I have had access to a letter from Bishop Cornelius of Rome to Bishop Fabius of Antioch, giving an account of the Synod of Rome and the decisions reached by the representatives of Italy, Africa,[2] and the neighbouring regions; and another, written in Latin, from Cyprian and his companions in Africa, making it clear that they too agreed that those who had

1. i.e. Novatian-Novatus was another person.   2. Now Tunisia.

been tempted should be helped, and that it was right and fair to expel from the Catholic Church the leader of the sect and to deal in the same way with all who had erred with him. Attached to these was a second letter from Cornelius, about the resolutions of the synod, and yet a third, about the conduct of Novatus; from this I will quote certain passages to enable readers of this book to know the facts about him. Enlightening Fabius as to the character of Novatus, Cornelius writes thus:[1]

It is essential that you should know that years ago this fine fellow set his heart on becoming a bishop, and kept this consuming ambition of his bottled up inside, cloaking his crazy notion with the support that from the start the Confessors[2] had given him. Maximus, one of our own presbyters, and Urban, who by confessing their faith had twice won the highest renown; Sidonius; and Celerius, a man who by the mercy of God had endured torture of every kind with unshakable determination, fortifying the weakness of the flesh by the strength of his faith, and had crushingly defeated the adversary – these four men observed him, and detecting his unscrupulousness and shiftiness, his perjuries and prevarications, his self-centredness and hollow pretence of friendship, returned to Holy Church. All the artifices and dirty tricks that he had long kept out of sight they revealed publicly in the presence of several bishops and presbyters and a crowd of laymen, weeping penitently for their folly in listening to this treacherous, malignant beast and for a time deserting the Church. . . .
It is remarkable, dear brother, what a complete transformation we saw in him a little while later. This admirable person, who swore terrible oaths to convince us that to be a bishop was the last thing he desired, suddenly appears as a bishop as if he had been catapulted into our midst. For this doctrinal purist, this champion of the Church's teaching, in his attempt to grab and filch the bishopric not given to him from above, chose as his accessories two men who had renounced their own salvation, and sent them to an obscure corner of Italy to

---

1. We know enough about Novatian from other sources to say that this spiteful letter gives a most unfair portrait of him.
2. Eight men who were persecuted at Rome.

deceive three bishops[1] of the region, uneducated and simple-minded men, and trick them into coming. He declared emphatically that their presence in Rome was urgently necessary, on the ground that the difference of opinion that had occurred might be completely resolved by their mediation, with the help of other bishops. As already stated, they were too simple-minded to cope with the schemes of unscrupulous rogues, so on their arrival they were shut up by some men as disorderly as himself, and in the late afternoon, when they were hopelessly drunk, he forcibly compelled them to make him a bishop, by a counterfeit and invalid consecration, so acquiring by craft and rascality an office not his by right. Not long afterwards one of the three returned to the Church, frankly and tearfully confessing his fault. We admitted him as a layman, since all the laity present pleaded for him. As for the other two, we appointed successors and sent them to occupy the vacant positions.

Thus the vindicator of the gospel was unaware that there can be only one bishop in a Catholic church, in which, as he knew perfectly well, there are forty-six presbyters, seven deacons, seven sub-deacons, forty-two acolytes, fifty-two exorcists, readers, and doorkeepers, and more than fifteen hundred widows and distressed persons.[2] All these are supported by the Master's grace and love for men. But this vast community, so necessary to the church, a number by the providence of God both rich and growing, together with laymen too numerous to count, did not suffice to turn him from such a hopeless, crazy ambition and recall him to the Church. . . .

Well now, I had better say next what activities or policies emboldened him to claim the episcopate. Did he make this claim because from the start he had spent his life in the Church, had endured many ordeals on her behalf, and had often been in the greatest danger for the sake of his religion? Not at all. The occasion of his becoming a believer came from Satan, who entered into him and stayed within him for a considerable time. While the exorcists were trying to help him he fell desperately ill, and since he was thought to be on the point of death, there as he lay in bed he received baptism by affusion – if it can be called baptism in the case of such a man. And when he

---

1. Cornelius himself had been consecrated by sixteen.

2. On the strength of this figure the number of Christians in Rome has been reckoned as between 30,000 and 50,000.

recovered he did not receive the other things of which one should partake according to the rule of the Church, in particular the sealing by a bishop.[1] Without receiving these how could he receive the Holy Ghost? . . .

The man who through cowardice and love of life at the time of the persecution denied that he was a presbyter! The deacons begged and besought him to come out of the chamber in which he had shut himself, and to help his brothers, in danger and in need of assistance, in every way right and possible for a presbyter; but so far was he from answering the deacons' appeal that he actually went right away in a rage, declaring that he did not want to be a presbyter any longer: he was in love with a different way of thought. . . .

This fine fellow left the Church of God, in which after becoming a believer he was accepted for the presbyterate, by favour of the bishop who ordained him to presbyter's orders. The whole clerical body, and many laymen too, objected that the rules did not permit anyone baptized in bed by affusion owing to illness, as in the present case, to receive any orders, so the bishop asked leave to lay hands on this man only.

Now we come to something else, the vilest of the man's misdemeanours:

When he has made the offerings and is distributing to each his share and handing it over, he compels the unfortunate worshippers to take an oath instead of praising God. He takes the hands of those who have received in both his own, and does not let go until they take this oath – I quote his own words: 'Swear to me by the Blood and Body of the Lord Jesus Christ never to desert me and turn to Cornelius.' And the wretched man does not taste unless he first calls down a curse on his own head, and instead of saying Amen as he receives that Bread, he says: 'I will not go back to Cornelius.' . . .

You will be glad to learn that now he has been stripped of support and left by himself, as every day Christian people are deserting him and coming back into the Church. And when Moses, the blessed martyr who so recently bore noble and wonderful witness while yet in the world, saw his crazy impudence, he broke off all contact with

---

1. Confirmation.

him, and with the five presbyters who like him had cut themselves
off from the Church.

At the end of the letter he has listed the bishops who met at
Rome and condemned the fatuity of Novatus, indicating
both their names and their respective sees. Those who were
absent from the Rome meeting but assented in writing to the
decision of those already mentioned are also named, along
with the cities from which they severally wrote. All this information was included in the letter from Cornelius to Bishop
Fabius of Antioch.

Dionysius's story about Serapion

44. Fabius, who inclined a little towards the schism, received
another communication – this time from Dionysius of
Alexandria, who in his letter to him wrote a great deal about
repentance, and described with particular care the ordeals of
those recently martyred in Alexandria. In the course of his
story he describes a quite amazing incident, which I must on
no account omit:

> I will tell you of one instance that occurred here. Among our
> number was an old believer named Serapion, whose conduct for
> most of his life had been beyond reproach, but who had lapsed when
> trial came. Again and again he pleaded, but no one listened – he had
> sacrificed. He fell sick, and for three days on end remained speechless
> and unconscious, but on the fourth day he was a little better, and
> called his grandson to his bedside. 'How long, child,' he asked, 'are
> you all determined to keep me alive? Do please hurry, and let
> me go quickly! You go yourself, and bring me one of the presbyters.'
> After saying this, he became speechless again. The boy ran to fetch
> the presbyter. But it was night time, and he was unwell and unable to
> come. I had, however, given instructions that those departing this
> life, if they desired it, and especially if they happened to have pleaded
> before, should be absolved, so that they could depart in sure hope;
> so he gave a portion of the Eucharist[1] to the little boy, telling him to

1. Presumably the Reserved Sacrament.

soak it and let it fall drop by drop into the old man's mouth. The boy returned with it to the house, but before he could enter, Serapion rallied again and said: 'Is that you, child? The presbyter could not come, but you must do as he told you, and let me depart.' The boy soaked it, and poured it into the mouth of the old man, who after swallowing a little immediately died. Was he not plainly preserved and kept alive until he was released and, his sin blotted out, could be honoured for his many good deeds?

Letters of Dionysius to Novatus and others

45. Now let us see the sort of letter the same Dionysius in-dited to Novatus at the time when he was upsetting the Roman brotherhood. When Novatus blamed his apostasy and schism on some of his fellow-Christians on the ground that they had coerced him into behaving thus, this is how Dionysius writes to him:

My dear Novatian,[1]

If, as you say, you were led on unwillingly, you can prove it by retracing your steps willingly. You ought to have been ready to suffer anything whatever rather than split the Church of God, and martyr-dom to avoid schism would have brought you as much honour as martyrdom to escape idolatry – I should say, more. For in the latter case a man is martyred to save his own single soul, in the former to save the whole Church. Even now, if you were to persuade or coerce your fellow-Christians into unanimity, your fall would count for less than your recovery – the first will be forgotten, the second applauded. If they will not listen, and there is nothing you can do, by all means save your own soul.

Hold fast to peace in the Lord, and may every blessing be yours.

46. To the Egyptians he wrote a letter on repentance, in which he explained his views on those who had fallen into sin, distinguishing degrees of guilt. To Bishop Colon of Hermopolis he sent a personal letter, still extant, on repen-tance; another, calling for a change of heart, to his own flock

1. Dionysius gets the name right.

at Alexandria. The surviving letters include the one to Origen on martyrdom. To the Christians of Laodicea[1] under their bishop Thelymidres, and to those of Armenia, whose bishop was Meruzanes, he wrote further letters on repentance. In addition to all these, he wrote to Cornelius of Rome, after receiving his letter against Novatus. In this answer he made it plain that he had been invited by Bishop Helenus of Tarsus in Cilicia, and the others with him – Firmilian in Cappadocia and Theoctistus in Palestine – to attend the Antioch Synod, at which an attempt was being made to strengthen the schism of Novatus. He further stated that he had been informed that Fabius had fallen asleep, and that Demetrian had been chosen to succeed him as Bishop of Antioch. He also referred to the Bishop of Jerusalem, in the following terms:

> That wonderful man Alexander was put in prison, and is now at rest with the blessed.

Next to this there is another extant letter, a helpful letter from Dionysius to the Romans, written on his behalf by Hippolytus. To the same church he addressed a second on peace, and a third on repentance. He also sent one to the confessors there while they still adhered to the views of Novatus. This was followed by two more after their return to the Church. He communicated similarly by letter with many others, leaving a rich reward to those who still study his writing with attention.

1. In Syria.

Book 7

GALLUS TO GALLIENUS: THE WORK OF CYPRIAN
AND DIONYSIUS: THE HERESIES OF
SABELLIUS, NOVATUS, NEPOS,
PAUL, AND THE MANICHEES

IN writing Book 7 of my *History of the Church* I shall again enjoy the cooperation of the great Bishop of Alexandria, Dionysius, who in the letters that he left behind furnished an account in his own words of the whole course of events in his time. From that starting-point I will begin my narrative.

The criminal folly of Decius and Gallus

1. Decius had reigned rather less than two years, when he was murdered, together with his sons, and was succeeded by Gallus. It was at this time that Origen, now in his seventieth year, died.[1] Writing to Hermammon Dionysius has this to say about Gallus:

Nor did Gallus realize Decius's mistake or guard against what caused his fall, but tripped over the same stone with his eyes open. When his reign was proceeding smoothly and things were going to his liking, he drove away the holy men who were praying God to grant him peace and health. In banishing them, he banished their supplications on his behalf.

Bishops of Rome: the question of baptism for penitent heretics: Sabellianism

2. In the city of Rome the episcopate of Cornelius lasted about three years. Lucius was chosen to succeed him, but after serving

1. It is now thought that Origen died in the next reign.

in this ministry for less than eight months, he died, passing on his office to Stephen. To him Dionysius addressed the first of his letters on baptism, for a lively controversy had arisen at that time as to whether those who abandoned a heresy of any kind ought to be cleansed by baptism. There was un-doubtedly an old-established custom that in such cases all that was necessary was prayer combined with the laying on of hands [3] and Cyprian, pastor of the see of Carthage, was the first man of his time to maintain that only when cleansed by baptism ought they to be readmitted. But Stephen thought it wrong to introduce any innovation in defiance of the tradi-tion established from the beginning, and protested vigorously. 4. So Dionysius communicated with him about this question in a very long letter, at the close of which he pointed out that now that the persecution had abated, the churches every-where had turned their backs on the innovation of Novatus and resumed peace among themselves:

5. Now let me assure you, brother, that all the previously divided churches in the East and still farther away have been united, and all their prelates everywhere are at one, overjoyed at the unexpected return of peace – Demetrian at Antioch, Theoctistus at Caesarea, Mazabanes at Aelia, Marinus at Tyre (since Alexander fell asleep), Heliodorus at Laodicea (since Thelymidres went to his rest), Helenus at Tarsus with all the Cilician churches, Firmilian with all Cappadocia. I have named the more distinguished bishops only, for fear of making my letter too long and its contents wearisome. However, the whole of Syria and Arabia, which you assist at every opportunity and have now communicated with; Mesopotamia; Pontus; and Bithynia – in a word, everyone everywhere is delighted at the new spirit of har-mony and brotherly love, and thankful to God.

When Stephen had fulfilled his ministry for two years, he was succeeded by Xystus.[1] To him Dionysius indited a second letter on baptism, making clear the views held and expressed

1. Usually known as Sixtus II.

by Stephen and the other bishops, and speaking of Stephen as
follows:

He had written previously with reference to Helenus, Firmilian,
and all who came from Cilicia, Cappadocia, and of course Galatia
and all the neighbouring countries, saying that he would have nothing to do with them, for this reason – they rebaptized heretics. Try to
realize the seriousness of the situation. For it is a fact that resolutions
about this question have been passed in the largest synods of bishops,
if my information is correct, to the effect that those who come over
from heresies are first instructed, then washed and cleansed afresh
from the filth of the old unclean leaven. So I wrote appealing to him
on all these questions. . . . I also wrote two letters – the first brief,
the second longer – to my dear fellow-presbyters Dionysius and
Philemon, who at one time shared Stephen's view and wrote to me
about this question.

6. In the same letter he mentions the Sabellian heretics, making it clear that they were numerous in his time:

The doctrine now being propagated at Ptolemais in Pentapolis[1]
is an impious one, characterized by shocking blasphemy against
Almighty God, Father of our Lord Jesus Christ; utter disbelief in
His only-begotten Son, the Firstborn of all creation, the Word made
man; and indifference to the Holy Ghost. From both sides there came
to me first manifestos, then adherents prepared to argue the question;
so I wrote letters as well as I could, with God's help, dealing with the
question in a rather professorial manner. I enclose copies of them for
you.

*The heretics' disgusting error: the rule of the Church: the
heterodoxy of Novatus*

7. In Dionysius's third letter on baptism, written to Philemon
the Roman presbyter, we find the following story:

I myself studied the writings and teachings of the heretics, pollut-
ing my soul for a time with their disgusting ideas, but gaining this

1. In Cyrenaica.

benefit from them that I disproved them for myself, and greatly increased my loathing. A brother-presbyter, indeed, tried to deter and frighten me from floundering in the mire of their wickedness, since I should harm my own soul. He was right, as I realized. But a vision sent by God came to strengthen me, and I heard a commanding voice say these very words: 'Study anything you lay your hand on; you are competent to examine and test everything – this gift was from the start the reason for your faith.' I accepted the vision, as agreeing with the apostolic precept directed to the more able: 'Prove yourselves sound bankers.'[1]

Then, commenting on all the heresies, he continues.

This is the rule and principle I took over from our blessed pope[2] Heraclas. Those who came over from the heretical sects had seceded from the Church. ('Seceded' is not the right word – they were still regarded as members of the congregation when they were reported as regular pupils of some heterodox teacher.) So he expelled them from the Church, shutting his ears to all pleas until they publicly confessed all that they had heard from our militant opponents.[3] Then he readmitted them without requiring them to be baptized again, as they had previously received holy baptism at his hands.

After dealing with the question at great length, he goes on:

I have learnt this too, that the practice is not of recent origin in Africa; a long while back, in the time of my episcopal predecessors, it was adopted in the most populous dioceses and in Church synods, at Iconium, Synnada, and many other places. I would not think of upsetting their arrangements and involving them in strife and contention. 'You shall not move your neighbour's boundaries, which were fixed by your ancestors.'[4]

The fourth of his letters on baptism was written to Dionysius of Rome, who had recently been ordained presbyter and was shortly to be consecrated bishop of the diocese. From its

1. Other early writers attribute this saying to our Lord.
2. This title, identical with our own 'papa', was not reserved for the Bishop of Rome, to whom we first find it applied two generations later.
3. 2 Tim. ii. 25.   4. Deut. xix. 14.

pages we can learn of the tribute paid to the learning and high character of this man too by Dionysius of Alexandria. After dealing with other matters, he refers to the business of Novatus thus:

8. Naturally, I feel bitter against Novatian. He has split the Church and drawn some of our brothers into profanity and blasphemy; he has brought in the most unholy teaching about God; he impudently suggests that our most kind Lord Jesus Christ was devoid of pity; and as if all this was not enough, he makes light of holy baptism, does away with the faith and confession that precede it, and even when there was some hope that the Holy Spirit would remain or even return to them, he banishes Him completely.

The heretics' perversion of baptism

9. His fifth letter was written to the Bishop of Rome, Xystus. In it he brings many charges against the heretics, and relates the following incident from his experience:

My dear brother,
I really do need your advice, and I want you to give me your opinion about a problem I am faced with, for fear I am acting mistakenly. In the congregation there is a man regarded for a long time as a faithful Christian, whose membership goes back beyond my election, and I think beyond the appointment of the blessed Heraclas. After attending a recent baptism, and listening to the questions and answers, he came to me weeping, lamenting, and falling at my feet; confessing and protesting that the baptism he had received from the heretics was not like ours and had nothing in common with it: it was full of profanity and blasphemy. Now he was cut to the heart, and did not even dare to raise his eyes to God, after starting with such unholy words and ceremonies. And so he was anxious to receive this unalloyed cleansing and acceptance and grace. I could not presume to do this; I told him that his prolonged communion with us made it unnecessary. He had listened to the Eucharistic prayers and joined in the Amen; he had stood by the table and held out his hands to receive the holy food; he had received it, partaking of the body and blood of

our Lord for long enough: I could not presume to rebuild him from the foundations. So I urged him to put his fears away, and with strong faith and confident hope to come forward and partake of the holy things. But he goes on grieving, and is too frightened to approach the table, and in spite of my invitation he can scarcely bring himself to join the 'bystanders' at the services.[1]

In addition to the letters already mentioned as extant, there is another of his on baptism addressed by him and his diocese to Xystus and the Roman church. In it he discusses the subject in question with elaborate arguments and at great length. Another extant letter of his, sent to Dionysius of Rome, deals with Lucian.[2]

Valerian and the persecution in his time

10. When Gallus and his associates had held sway for less than two years they disappeared from the scene, and Valerian with his son Gallienus took over the government. What Dionysius has to say about Valerian may be gathered from his letter to Hermammon, in which we find the following account:

John received a similar revelation. 'He was given,' says the writer, 'a mouth uttering boasts and blasphemy; he was given authority and forty-two months.'[3]
Both phases of Valerian's rule are astonishing, the first being especially remarkable in character: he was so wonderfully friendly and gentle to the people of God. Not one of the emperors before him – not even those who were supposed to have been avowed Christians – was so kindly and sympathetic in his attitude to them as was Valerian at first, when he received them publicly with all friendship and affection and filled his whole palace with godfearing people, making it a church of God. But what a change when he was induced to get rid

1. See p. 279 n. 2. Identity unknown.
3. Rev. xiii. 5, slightly misquoted: Dionysius is thinking of the three and a half years of Valerian's persecution.

of them by the teacher and guild-leader of the magicians from
Egypt,[1] who urged him to kill or persecute pure and saintly men as
rivals who hindered his own foul, disgusting incantations! For they
are and were able, by being present and seen, and simply by breathing
on them and speaking boldly, to frustrate the schemes of the wicked
demons. He also induced him to perform devilish rites, loathsome
tricks, and unholy sacrifices, to cut the throats of unfortunate boys,
use the children of unhappy parents as sacrificial victims, and tear out
the vitals of newborn babies, cutting up and mincing God's handi-
work, as if these things would bring them happiness. . . .

They[2] must have been delighted with the thank-offerings Macrian
brought them for his hoped-for empire. At first he held office as
accountant to the whole[3] imperial exchequer, but left Catholic principles wholly out of account. Now he has fallen under the prophetic
curse: 'Woe to those who prophesy from the heart and do not see
the whole.'[4] For he had no idea of the catholicity of providence, and
no suspicion of the judgement of One who is before all and through
all and over all.[5] So he has made himself the enemy of His Catholic
Church, and alienated and estranged himself from the mercy of God,
and banished himself as far as he could from his own salvation, proving thus how well his name fits him![6] ... Led by him into such
courses, Valerian was subjected to insults and abuse,[7] as was said to
Isaiah: 'These have chosen their own ways and their own abominations; their soul delighted in them. I will choose their delusions, and
for their sins I will repay them.'[8]

Macrian, mad to become emperor though quite unqualified, and
unable to fit the imperial robes on his crippled body, put forward his
two sons, who inherited their father's sins. For the prophecy uttered
by God was unmistakably true of them: 'Visiting the fathers' sins
on the children down to the third or fourth generation of those who
hate me.'[9] In heaping his own evil ambitions – which came to noth-

1. Macrian, as below.   2. The demons.
3. Greek 'catholic'; one of a series of puns.
4. A misreading of Ez. xiii. 3.
5. A conflation of Eph. iv. 6 and Col. i. 17.
6. Macrian somewhat resembles a Greek word for 'far off'.
7. He was captured and ill-treated by the Persian King Shapur.
8. Is. lxvi. 3–4.   9. Ex. xx. 5.

ing – on the heads of his sons, he wiped off on them his own wickedness and hatred of God.

How Dionysius and others fared under Valerian

11. As regards the persecution that raged so fiercely in his time, what Dionysius and others underwent because of their devotion to the God of the universe is vividly protrayed in the lengthy account that he directed against Germanus, a bishop of his time who was trying to blacken his character:

> I am in danger of falling head first into utter silliness and stupidity, as I am compelled to recount God's amazing kindness to me. But as we are told that it is good to keep the secret of a king but honourable to reveal the works of God,[1] I will meet Germanus's attack.
>
> I came before Aemilian, not alone but followed by my fellow-presbyter Maximus and the deacons Faustus, Eusebius, and Chaeremon; and one of the Christians from Rome came in with us. Aemilian did not open the proceedings by saying to me: 'You are not to hold meetings.' That would have been a waste of breath – the last thing he would say, when he was going back to the beginning. He did not talk about not holding meetings, but about not being Christians ourselves: he ordered me to abandon my beliefs, thinking that if I changed the rest would follow me. I gave a reasonable reply, on the lines of 'We must obey God rather than men.'[2] I told him outright that I worship the only God and no other, and would never change or cease to be a Christian. At that he ordered me to go right away to a village near the desert, called Cephro.
>
> Perhaps you would care to hear the speeches on both sides, as they appear in the official records.
>
> 'When Dionysius, Faustus, Maximus, Marcellus, and Chaeremon were brought into court, Aemilian the acting governor said: "In an interview I spoke to you of the generosity our masters have shown you; they have given you a chance to go scot-free, if you are prepared to turn to what is natural and worship the gods who preserve their throne, and to forget those who are unnatural. What do you

1. Tobit xii. 7.   2. Acts v. 29.

say to this? I suppose you will not be ungrateful for their generosity, as they are advising you for your own good."

'Dionysius: "Not all men worship all gods; each worships some – those he believes in. We believe in the one God and Creator of all things, who entrusted the throne to His most beloved emperors, Valerian and Gallienus; Him we both worship and adore, and to Him we continually pray that their throne may remain unshaken."

'Aemilian, the acting governor: "Who prevents you from worshipping him too, if he is a god, as well as the natural gods? You were ordered to worship gods, and gods known to all."

'Dionysius: "We worship no one else."

'Aemilian, the acting governor: "I see you are both ungrateful and blind to the leniency of our emperors; therefore you shall not stay in this city, but remove yourselves to Libya and remain in a place called Cephro. This is the place I have selected, by command of our emperors. On no account will you or anyone else be permitted either to hold assemblies or to enter the cemeteries, as you call them.[1] If anyone is shown not to have gone to the place I have named, or is found at any meeting, he will get himself into serious trouble. For you will be under careful and constant observation. You will therefore go at once to the place appointed."'

Even though I was ill he hurried me away, refusing to grant a single day's grace. So what time had I left to hold a meeting or anything else? . . .

But we did not refrain even from openly meeting together with the Lord, but I tried all the harder to bring together the Christians in the city as if I were with them – absent in body, as the Apostle said, but present in spirit.[2] At Cephro a large church formed itself round us, some following us from the city, others coming from various parts of Egypt. And there God opened to us a door for the word.[3] At first we were persecuted and stoned, but later quite a number of the heathen left their idols and turned to God. Never before had they received the word, but now at last through us it was sown among them. Surely it was for this purpose that God brought us to them, and when we had completed our mission took us away again.

1. 'Sleeping-places', a word used only by Christians. The Romans did not wish martyrs' graves to be rallying-points.
2. 1 Cor. v. 3.   3. Col. iv. 3.

Aemilian decided to remove us to what he thought rougher and more typically Libyan places, and ordered the Christians from every side to be concentrated in the district of Marea, allotting different villages in the area to the various groups. For us he chose a place closer to the road, so that we should be the first to be captured. Obviously, he was managing and arranging it so that whenever he decided to seize us he should find us easy to catch. In my own case, when I was ordered to go to Cephro I had no idea on which side the place lay – I had scarcely heard even the name before; however, I set off in good heart and made no fuss. But when I was told that I must go right away to the Colluthion district, those who were present know how badly I took it, for here I shall take myself to task. At first I was annoyed and very angry. It was true that these places happened to be better known and more familiar to me, but I was informed that there were no Christians or reputable people in the area, where travellers were exposed to annoyance and to bandit raids. But I felt happier when my friends reminded me that it was nearer the city, and that while Cephro allowed us to see a good deal of our friends from Egypt, so that our church was more broadly based, our new home was so much nearer to the city that we should have more opportunities to enjoy the sight of those we cared for most, our nearest and dearest. They would come and stay for a time, and as in the outer suburbs, there would be local meetings. And so it proved.

After giving further details of his adventures, he goes on as follows:

No doubt Germanus prides himself on a great many confessions of faith, and can tell of a great many things that he has had to bear; all the things he can list in my own case – court sentences, confiscations, proscriptions, plundering of property, relinquishing of privileges, contempt for worldly glory, indifference to praise or the reverse from governors and councils, patience in face of threats, outcries, dangers, persecutions, homelessness, distress, affliction of every kind; all of which were my lot under Decius and Sabinus, and are still my lot under Aemilian. But where did Germanus come in? What was said about him? But I must not make an utter fool of myself because of Germanus, so I will refrain from giving a detailed account of what occurred to friends who know about it already.

In his letter to Domitius and Didymus he again refers to the events of the persecution:

To give all the names of our people, who are so numerous and quite unknown to you, would be a waste of time, but I must tell you that men and women, youngsters and greybeards, girls and old women, soldiers and civilians, every race and every age, some the victims of scourges and the stake, others of the sword, came through their ordeal triumphantly and have received their crowns. In the case of others, not even a very long time sufficed for them to appear acceptable to the Lord, as indeed in my own case hitherto. No doubt I have been reserved for the proper time, known to Him who said: 'At an acceptable time I heard you, and in a day of salvation I succoured you.'[1] You ask about our affairs and want to know how we live. Well, you have heard of course that when we were being taken away as prisoners by a centurion and magistrates and the soldiers and servants with them – Gaius, Faustus, Peter, Paul, and myself – we were surprised by a party from Marea, who when we objected and refused to go with them dragged us off by force and carried us away. Now only Gaius, Peter, and I, bereft of our friends, are confined in a barren, parched spot in Libya, three days journey from Paraetonium. . . .

In the city four presbyters – Maximus, Dioscurus, Demetrius, and Lucius – have gone underground and secretly visit the Christians there. Those who are better known in the world, Faustinus and Aquila, are wandering about Egypt. Deacons who survived those who died on the island are Faustus, Eusebius, and Chaeremon – the Eusebius whom from the very first God inspired and equipped to attend so energetically to the needs of the confessors who were in prison, and perform the dangerous duty of laying out the bodies of the fulfilled and blessed martyrs. For even now the governor, as I said before, is relentlessly putting to a cruel death some of those who are brought before him; some he mangles on the rack; others he leaves to languish fettered in prison, forbidding anyone to come near them and watching to see if anyone is caught doing so. However, through the determination and perseverance of fellow-Christians God gives a breathing-space to the hard-pressed.

1. 2 Cor. vi. 2, quoted from Is. xlix. 8.

It should be noted that Eusebius, whom Dionysius here calls a deacon, a little later was appointed Bishop of Laodicea in Syria; while Maximus, to whom he refers as a presbyter at that time, succeeded Dionysius himself as head of the Alexandrian church; but that Faustus, who then made as noble a confession of faith as Dionysius himself, was preserved till the persecution of my own time, when in the evening of a very long life he found fulfilment as a martyr, in my own lifetime, by the headsman's axe.

Martyrdoms at Caesarea in Palestine

12. During the same persecution of Valerian three men who at Caesarea in Palestine made a glorious confession of Christ were crowned with a divine martyrdom, becoming food for beasts. One was called Priscus and one Malchus, while the name of the third was Alexander. It is said that these men, while living in the country, at first accused themselves of apathy and indifference: they scorned the prizes which the times offered to those who craved for them with a heavenly longing, instead of grasping the martyr's crown with both hands. So when they had talked it over, they set out for Caesarea, where they presented themselves before the judge and met the end already described. It is also on record that in addition to these a woman, during the same persecution and in the same city, battled through a similar ordeal. But she is thought to have belonged to Marcion's sect.

The peace under Gallienus: contemporary bishops

13. Not long afterwards Valerian became the slave of the Persians.[1] His son, who now found himself sole ruler, showed more prudence in his conduct of affairs. One of his first acts was to issue edicts ending the persecution against us. To those

1. A.D. 261.

responsible for the word he granted freedom to perform their normal duties. This is the wording of the decree:

The Emperor Caesar Publius Licinius Gallienus Pius Felix Augustus to Dionysius, Pinnas, Demetrius, and the other bishops. The benefit of my bounty I have ordered to be proclaimed throughout the world. All places of worship shall be restored to their owners; you bishops, therefore, may avail yourselves of the provisions of this decree to protect you from any interference. The complete liberty of action which you now possess has long been granted by me; accordingly Aurelius Quirinius, my chief minister, will enforce the ordinance given by me.

To make the meaning clearer, the decree here quoted has been translated from the original Latin. We also possess another enactment of the same emperor addressed to other bishops, permitting them to recover the ground occupied by 'cemeteries'.

14. At that time the Roman church was still headed by Xystus,[1] the Antioch church by Fabius's successor Demetrian, the church of Cappadocian Caesarea by Firmilian, and the Pontic churches by Gregory and his brother Athenodore, pupils of Origen. At Palestinian Caesarea, when Theoctistus died Domnus succeeded him as bishop; but Domnus lasted only a short time, and Theotecnus, my own contemporary, was chosen as his successor. He too came from Origen's school. Lastly at Jerusalem, when Mazabanes had gone to his rest, his throne was filled by Hymenaeus, who was prominent for so many years of my own lifetime.

Martyrdom of Marinus at Caesarea: the story of Astyrius

15. In their time the churches everywhere enjoyed peace; nevertheless at Caesarea in Palestine Marinus, who had served in the army with great distinction and was a man of good

1. An error: Xystus had been martyred in A.D. 258. See p. 313 n.

birth and great wealth, was beheaded for his witness to Christ. It came about thus. Among the Romans the vine-switch is a mark of honour, and those who win it, we are told, become centurions. A vacancy occurred, and by order of seniority Marinus was entitled to be promoted to fill it. But when he was about to receive the honour, another man advanced to the tribune and declared that Marinus was debarred by old-established laws from holding rank in the Roman army, as he was a Christian and did not sacrifice to the emperors; so the office fell to himself. Reacting to this, the judge – his name was Achaeus – first asked what opinions Marinus held; when he saw that he stubbornly declared himself a Christian, he allowed him three hours to think it over.

As soon as he left the court, Theotecnus, the bishop of the diocese, came to him through the crowd, drew him aside, took him by the hand, and led him to the church. Inside, he placed him right in front of the altar, and drawing aside his cloak a little way pointed to the sword at his side. Then he fetched the book containing the divine gospels, placed it before him, and invited him to choose whichever of the two he preferred. Without a moment's hesitation, he put out his hand and took the divine book. 'Hold fast then,' said Theotecnus. 'Hold fast to God. May you obtain what you have chosen, inspired by Him. Go in peace.' No sooner had Marinus gone back than an usher called on him to present himself before the court; the period of grace was now over. He stood erect before the judge and displayed still greater devotion to the Faith. Instantly, just as he was, he was taken to execution and thus found fulfilment.

16. It was at Caesarea also that Astyrius is remembered for the boldness by which he delighted the heart of God. A member of the Roman Senate, and highly esteemed by emperors, he was in the public eye because of his birth and affluence. He was present when the martyr found fulfilment, and, shoulder-

ing the mortal remains, he placed them on a magnificent costly robe, laid them out in the most expensive fashion, and gave them fitting burial.

Many other stories are told about this man by acquaintances of his, who have survived to my own time. They include the following miraculous incident.

17. Near Caesarea Philippi, called Paneas by the Phoenicians, on the skirts of the mountain called Paneum, they point to springs believed to be the source of the Jordan.[1] Into these they say that on a certain feast day a victim is thrown, and that by the demon's power it disappears from sight miraculously. This occurrence strikes the onlookers as a marvel to be talked of everywhere. One day Astyrius was there while this was going on, and when he saw that the business amazed the crowd he pitied their delusion, and looking up to heaven pleaded through Christ with God who is over all to refute the demon who was deluding the people and stop them from being deceived. When he had offered this prayer, it is said that the sacrifice instantly came to the surface of the water. Thus their miracle was gone, and nothing marvellous ever again happened at that spot.

The statue of the woman with a haemorrhage

18. As I have mentioned this city, I do not think I ought to omit a story that deserves to be remembered by those who will follow us. The woman with a haemorrhage, who as we learn from the holy gospels was cured of her trouble by our Saviour,[2] was stated to have come from here. Her house was pointed out in the city, and a wonderful memorial of the benefit the Saviour conferred upon her was still there. On a tall stone base at the gates of her house stood a bronze statue of a woman, resting on one knee and resembling a suppliant

1. See Josephus: *Jewish War*, p. 382.   2. Mark v. 25–34.

with arms outstretched. Facing this was another of the same material, an upright figure of a man with a double cloak neatly draped over his shoulders and his hand stretched out to the woman. Near his feet on the stone slab grew an exotic plant, which climbed up to the hem of the bronze cloak and served as a remedy for illnesses of every kind. This statue, which was said to resemble the features of Jesus, was still there in my own time, so that I saw it with my own eyes when I resided in the city.[1] It is not at all surprising that Gentiles who long ago received such benefits from our Saviour should have expressed their gratitude thus, for the features of His apostles Paul and Peter, and indeed of Christ Himself, have been preserved in coloured portraits which I have examined. How could it be otherwise, when the ancients habitually followed their own Gentile custom of honouring them as saviours[2] in this uninhibited way?

The throne of Bishop James

19. The throne of James – who was the first to receive from the Saviour and His apostles the episcopacy of the Jerusalem church, and was called Christ's brother, as the sacred books show – has been preserved to this day. The Christians there, who in their turn look after it with such loving care, make clear to all the veneration in which saintly men high in the favour of God were regarded in time past and are regarded to this day.

Letters of Dionysius on the Easter festival and on events in Alexandria

20. In addition to the letters already quoted, Dionysius wrote at that time the 'festival letters', in which he expresses him-

1. The statue is mentioned by three other writers, two of whom had seen it.
2. Caesarea was a mainly Gentile city; there would be no objection to statuary.

self with unusual solemnity on the subject of the Easter festival. One letter is addressed to Flavius, another to Domitius
and Didymus. In the latter he propounds a rule based on an
eight-year cycle, and demonstrates that at no time other than
after the spring equinox is it legitimate to celebrate Easter.
Besides these, he indited another to his fellow-presbyters at
Alexandria and to others at the same time in various places,
These he wrote while the persecution was still going on.

21. When peace was almost established, he returned to Alexandria; but when faction fighting broke out there anew, it
was impossible for him to keep a fatherly eye on all the Christians in the city, divided as they were between the two war-
ring camps. So when Easter came he was again forced, like
someone in a foreign country, to communicate with them by
letter from Alexandria itself. Then to Hierax, a bishop in
Egypt, he wrote another festival letter, in which he speaks as
follows of the current dissension in Alexandria:

In my own case, is there any wonder if it is difficult to communicate even by letter with those living at a distance, when it has become
almost beyond me even to converse with myself or think things over
in my own mind? I am most anxious to send letters to those who
mean so much to me, the brothers who belong to the same family,
who are of the same mind, who are members of the same church;
but to get such letters through to them seems impossible. It would be
easier to make one's way, not merely into a foreign land but from
farthest east to farthest west, than to reach Alexandria from Alexandria itself. The great trackless desert that took Israel two generations to
cross was less difficult and impassable than the street through the very
middle of the city! The sea which divided and formed a wall on
either side providing them with a carriage way, a high road on which
the Egyptians disappeared under the water, foreshadowed only too
clearly our calm and waveless harbours, which from the murders
committed in them have so often resembled a Red Sea. The river that
flows past the city at one time appeared drier than the waterless desert,
more parched than the one in crossing which Israel was so thirsty

that Moses cried out, and from the only Doer of wonders drink poured for them out of the flinty rock. At another time it rose so high that it flooded the whole neighbourhood, roads and fields alike, threatening us with the rush of water that occurred in Noah's time. At all times it flows polluted with blood and murders and drownings, such as under the hand of Moses it became for Pharaoh, when it changed to blood and stank. What other water could there be to cleanse the water that cleanses everything? How could the mighty ocean impassable to man, if poured over it, clear the filth from this dreadful sea? How could the great river that flows out of Eden, if it channelled the four heads into which it divides into one, the Gihon,[1] wash away the filthy gore? When would the air, fouled by the poisonous exhalations rising on every side, be purified? Such vapours are given off from the land, such winds from the sea, such breezes from the rivers, such mists from the harbours, that it is the discharges from dead bodies rotting in all their component parts that form the dew. And then people are surprised and puzzled as to the source of the continual epidemics, the serious illnesses, the variety of pestilences, the changing forms and high rate of human mortality, and unable to see why this immense city no longer contains as big a number of inhabitants, from infant children to those of extreme age, as it used to support of those described as hale old men. As for those from forty to seventy, they were then so much more numerous that their total is not reached now, though we have counted and registered as entitled to the public food ration all from fourteen to eighty; and those who look the youngest are now reckoned as equal in age to the oldest men of our earlier generation. Men see the human race upon earth constantly shrinking and wasting thus, yet they do not turn a hair, while its complete destruction comes daily nearer.

22. Later, when a severe epidemic followed the war just as the festival was approaching, he again communicated in writing with the Christian community, revealing the horrors of the disaster:

Other people would not think this a time for festival: they do not so regard this or any other time, even if, so far from being a time of

1. Gen. ii. 10–14; the Fathers identified Gihon with the Nile.

distress, it is a time of unimaginable joy. Now, alas! all is lamentation, everyone in mourning, and the city resounds with weeping because of the numbers that have died and are dying every day. As
Scripture says of the firstborn of the Egyptians, so now there has been
a great cry: there is not a house in which there is not one dead – how I
wish it had been only one!

Many terrible things had happened to us even before this. First
we were set on and surrounded by persecutors and murderers, yet
we were the only ones to keep festival even then. Every spot where
we were attacked became for us a place for celebrations, whether
field, desert, ship, inn, or prison. The most brilliant festival of all was
kept by the fulfilled martyrs, who were feasted in heaven. After that
came war and famine, which struck at Christian and heathen alike.
We alone had to bear the injuries they did us, but we profited by
what they did to each other and suffered at each other's hands; so yet
again we found joy in the peace which Christ has given to us alone.
But when both we and they had been allowed a tiny breathing-space,
out of the blue came this disease, a thing more terrifying to them than
any terror, more frightful than any disaster whatever, and as a historian of their own[1] once wrote: 'the only thing of all that surpassed
expectation'. To us it was not that, but a schooling and testing as valuable as all our earlier trials; for it did not pass over us, though its full
impact fell on the heathen. . . .

Most of our brother-Christians showed unbounded love and
loyalty, never sparing themselves and thinking only of one another.
Heedless of the danger, they took charge of the sick, attending to
their every need and ministering to them in Christ, and with them
departed this life serenely happy; for they were infected by others
with the disease, drawing on themselves the sickness of their neighbours and cheerfully accepting their pains. Many, in nursing and
curing others, transferred their death to themselves and died in their
stead, turning the common formula that is normally an empty cour-
tesy into a reality: 'Your humble servant bids you good-bye.' The
best of our brothers lost their lives in this manner, a number of presbyters, deacons, and laymen winning high commendation, so that
death in this form, the result of great piety and strong faith, seems in
every way the equal of martyrdom. With willing hands they raised

1. Thucydides, describing the plague of Athens.

the bodies of the saints to their bosoms; they closed their eyes and mouths, carried them on their shoulders, and laid them out; they clung to them, embraced them, washed them, and wrapped them in grave-clothes. Very soon the same services were done for them, since those left behind were constantly following those gone before.

The heathen behaved in the very opposite way. At the first onset of the disease, they pushed the sufferers away and fled from their dearest, throwing them into the roads before they were dead and treating unburied corpses as dirt, hoping thereby to avert the spread and contagion of the fatal disease; but do what they might, they found it difficult to escape.

After this letter, when the people in the city were at peace, he again sent a festival letter to the Egyptian community, following it up with several others. A letter of his on the Sabbath and another on religious training have also been preserved.

The reign of Gallienus

Communicating again by letter with Hermammon and the Egyptian community, he has much to say about the criminal folly of Decius and his successors, and recalls the peace under Gallienus.   23. It will be worthwhile to hear what he has to say about these things:

Macrian, after goading one of his emperors and attacking the other, suddenly disappeared root and branch with his whole family, and Gallienus was proclaimed and recognized by all. He was both an old emperor and a new: he both preceded and followed them. For, in accordance with the message given to the prophet Isaiah: 'See, the earliest things have come about, and new things shall now arise.'[1] You know how a cloud sweeps under the sun's rays and for a time screens and darkens it and is seen in its place; then when the cloud has gone by or melted, the sun reappears, shining as it did before. In the same way Macrian, after pushing himself forward and insinuating himself into the imperial prerogatives of Gallienus, is no more (he never was!), while Gallienus is just as he was before, and as if it had

1. Is. xlii. 9.

cast off its old age and purged away its former dross, the monarchy flourishes now as never before, is seen and heard over a wider sweep, and spreads in all directions.

He goes on to indicate the time at which he wrote this:

> It occurs to me to take another look at the length of the various reigns. I observe that the wicked emperors who once were famous have been quickly forgotten, while the one who became more religious and devoted to God has passed the seven-year mark and is now completing a ninth year, in which we may indeed keep festival.

Nepos and his schism

24. Beside all this letter writing, he found time to produce the two pamphlets *On Promises*. These were occasioned by Nepos, one of the Egyptian bishops, who taught that the promises made to the saints in holy scripture would be fulfilled more in accordance with Jewish ideas, and suggested that there would be a millennium of bodily indulgence on this earth. Thinking that he could draw on the Revelation of John to prove his peculiar notion, he wrote a book on the subject and entitled it *The Allegorists Refuted*.[1] To this Dionysius replied in his two pamphlets: in the first he expounds his own opinion about the doctrine; in the second he discusses the Revelation of John, after referring to Nepos at the start in the following terms:

> They put forward a treatise by Nepos, on which they rely completely as proving incontrovertibly that Christ's kingdom will be on earth. Now in general I respect and love Nepos for his faith and industry, his careful study of the Scriptures, and his rich hymnody, which is still a source of comfort to many of our fellow-Christians, and I am most unwilling to criticize him, especially now that he has gone to his rest. But more than anything we must love and reverence truth, and while it is right to give ungrudging praise and approval to every statement that is correct, it is our duty to examine and criticize

1. See p. 309.

any piece of writing that appears unsound. If Nepos were here now and putting forward his ideas in speech alone, conversation with nothing in writing would suffice, using question and answer as means to persuade and win over our militant opponents.[1] But a work has been published which some people find most convincing, and certain teachers regard the Law and the Prophets as worthless, discourage the following of the gospels, make light of the apostolic[2] epistles, and make extravagant claims for the teaching of this treatise as if it was some great and hidden mystery. They do not allow our simpler brethren to have lofty noble thoughts, either about the glorious and truly divine epiphany of our Lord or about our own resurrection from the dead, when we shall be gathered together and made like Him;[3] they persuade them to expect in the kingdom of God what is trifling and mortal and like the present. How then can we do otherwise than thrash the matter out as if our brother Nepos were here with us? ...

When I arrived in the district of Arsinoe,[4] where as you know this notion had long been widely held, so that schisms and secessions of entire churches had taken place, I called a meeting of the presbyters and teachers of the village congregations, with any laymen who wished to attend, and urged them to thrash out the question in public. So they brought me this book as positive and irrefutable proof, and I sat with them for three days on end from dawn to dusk, criticizing its contents point by point. In the process I was immensely impressed by the essential soundness, complete sincerity, logical grasp, and mental clarity shown by these good people, as we methodically and good-temperedly dealt with questions, objections, and points of agreement. We refused to cling with pig-headed determination to opinions once held even if proved wrong. There was no shirking of difficulties, but to the limit of our powers we tried to grapple with the problems and master them; nor were we too proud, if worsted in argument, to abandon our position and admit defeat: conscientiously, honestly, and with simple-minded trust in God, we accepted the conclusions to be drawn from the proofs and teachings of Holy Writ. In the end, the author and originator of this doctrine, Coracion by name, in the hearing of all present assured and promised us that for

1. 2 Tim. ii. 25.   2. i.e. Pauline.
3. Mark xiii. 27 and 1 John iii. 2.   4. The Fayyum.

the future he would not adhere to it, argue about it, mention it, or teach it, as he was completely convinced by the arguments on the other side. Of the rest, some were delighted with the discussion, and with the all-round spirit of accommodation and concord.

The Revelation of John

Farther on he has this to say about the Revelation of John:

25. Some of our predecessors rejected the book and pulled it entirely to pieces, criticizing it chapter by chapter, pronouncing it unintelligible and illogical and the title false. They say it is not John's and is not a revelation at all, since it is heavily veiled by its thick curtain of incomprehensibility: so far from being one of the apostles, the author of the book was not even one of the saints, or a member of the Church, but Cerinthus, the founder of the sect called Cerinthian after him, who wished to attach a name commanding respect to his own creation. This, they say, was the doctrine he taught – that Christ's kingdom would be on earth; and the things he lusted after himself, being the slave of his body and sensual through and through, filled the heaven of his dreams – unlimited indulgence in gluttony and lechery at banquets, drinking-bouts, and wedding feasts, or (to call these things by what he thought more respectable names) festivals, sacrifices, and the immolation of victims. But I myself would never dare to reject the book, of which many good Christians have a very high opinion, but realizing that my mental powers are inadequate to judge it properly, I take the view that the interpretation of the various sections is largely a mystery, something too wonderful for our comprehension. I do not understand it, but I suspect that some deeper meaning is concealed in the words; I do not measure and judge these things by my own reason, but put more reliance on faith, and so I have concluded that they are too high to be grasped by me; I do not condemn as valueless what I have not taken in at a glance, but rather am puzzled that I have not taken it in.

After examining the whole book of the Revelation and proving the impossibility of understanding it in the literal sense, he goes on:

On arriving almost at the end of his prophecy, the prophet blesses those who observe it, and indeed himself too: 'Blessed is the man who keeps the words of the prophecy in this book, and I John, the man who saw and heard these things.'[1] That he was called John, and that this work is John's, I shall therefore not deny, for I agree that it is from the pen of a holy and inspired writer. But I am not prepared to admit that he was the apostle, the son of Zebedee and brother of James, who wrote the gospel entitled According to John and the general epistle. On the character of each, on the linguistic style, and on the general tone, as it is called, of Revelation, I base my opinion that the author was not the same. The evangelist nowhere includes his name or announces himself in either the gospel or the epistle . . . but John nowhere, in either first or third person; whereas the writer of the Revelation puts himself forward at the very beginning: 'The Revelation of Jesus Christ, which He gave Him to show to His servants at once; and He sent and signified it by His angel to His servant John, who testified to the word of God and to His testimony, to everything that he saw.'[2] Next he writes a letter: 'John to the seven churches in Asia: grace to you and peace.'[3] But the evangelist did not prefix his name to the general epistle either, but without any preliminaries began with the solemn mystery of the divine revelation: 'What was from the beginning; what we have heard, what we have seen with our own eyes.'[4] It was on this revelation that the Lord congratulated Peter: 'Blessed are you, Simon Bar-Jonah; for flesh and blood have not revealed it to you, but my Father in heaven.'[5] Nor again in the second and third extant epistles of John, though they are so short, is John named: he is mentioned anonymously as 'the presbyter'. But this writer did not even think it enough, after naming himself once for all, to go on with his story, but goes back to it again: 'I John, your brother and partner in the oppression and kingdom and in the patience of Jesus, was in the island called Patmos because of the word of God and the testimony of Jesus.'[6] Again, at the

1. Rev. xxii. 7–8, which Dionysius has misunderstood. See R.V., where verse 8 begins a new paragraph and reads, 'And I John am he that . . .' It must be borne in mind that Greek MSS. are not punctuated. The argument as to authorship is unaffected.

2. Rev. i. 1–2; by several small omissions, Dionysius has obscured the meaning.

3. Rev. i. 4.　　4. 1 John i. 1.　　5. Matt. xvi. 17.　　6. Rev. i. 9.

end he speaks thus: 'Blessed is the man who keeps the words of the prophecy in this book, and I John, the man who saw and heard these things.'

That the writer was John he himself states, and we must believe him. But which John? He does not say here, as so often in the gospel, that he was the disciple loved by the Lord, the one who leant back on His breast, the brother of James, the eyewitness and earwitness of the Lord. He would surely have used one of these descriptions, had he wished to reveal his identity. But he uses none of them, merely calling himself our brother and partner, a witness of Jesus, blessed in seeing and hearing the revelations. Many, I imagine, have had the same name as John the apostle, men who because they loved, admired, and esteemed him so greatly, and wished to be loved as he was by the Lord, were more than glad to be called after him, just as Paul and Peter are favourite names for the children of believers. We find, too, another John in the Acts of the Apostles, John surnamed Mark, whom Barnabas and Paul took with them,[1] and who is referred to again in the words: 'They had John as their attendant.'[2] Was he the writer? I should say not. For he did not go as far as Asia with them, as the record shows: 'Setting sail from Paphos, Paul and his companions came to Perga in Pamphylia; but John left them and went back to Jerusalem.'[3] I think there was another John among the Christians of Asia, as there are said to have been two tombs at Ephesus, each reputed to be John's.

From the ideas too, and from the words used and the way they are put together, we shall readily conclude that this writer was different from the other. There is complete harmony between the gospel and the epistle, and they begin alike. The one says 'In the beginning was the Word', the other 'What was from the beginning'. The one says: 'And the Word became flesh and made His home in our midst: and we gazed on His glory, glory such as an only son receives from his father.' The other, the same thing in slightly different words: 'What we have heard, what we have seen with our own eyes; what we gazed on and our hands touched, concerning the Word of life – the life was manifested.' The reason for this prelude is, as he shows in what follows, that his target is those who declare that the Lord has not come in the flesh. So he carefully added: 'We have seen and bear

1. Acts xii. 25.   2. Acts xiii. 5.   3. Acts xiii. 13.

witness and proclaim to you the eternal life, which was with the
Father and was manifested to us; what we have seen and heard we
proclaim to you also.' He is consistent and adheres to his plan, setting
out everything under the same headings and in the same language. I
will give some brief examples.

The careful reader will find in both books again and again the Life,
the Light, Turning away from darkness, Truth, Grace,[1] Joy, the Flesh
and the Blood of the Lord, Judgement, Forgiveness of sins,[2] God's
love for us, the Commandment 'love one another', the obligation to
keep all the Commandments; the Convicting of the world, the devil,
antichrist; the promise of the Holy Ghost; the Adoption[3] of sons by
God; the Belief[4] that is constantly required of us; the Father and the
Son (*passim*). To sum up, anyone who examines their characteristics
throughout will inevitably see that Gospel and Epistle have one and
the same colour. But there is no resemblance or similarity whatever
between them and the Revelation; it has no connexion, no relationship with them; it has hardly a syllable in common with them.[5] Nor
shall we find any mention or notion of the Revelation in the Epistle
(let alone the Gospel), or of the Epistle in the Revelation. How different from Paul, who in his epistles gives us a glimpse of his revelations,[6]
which he did not write down by themselves.

By the phraseology also we can measure the difference between
the Gospel and Epistle and the Revelation. The first two are written
not only without any blunders in the use of Greek, but with remarkable skill as regards diction, logical thought, and orderly expression.
It is impossible to find in them one barbarous word or solecism, or
any kind of vulgarism. For, by the grace of the Lord, it seems their

1. No: the word is used in Rev. but not in 1 John; it is very much com-
moner in the writings of Peter, Paul, and Luke.

2. Not to be found in any Johannine book.

3. The word is used five times by Paul, never by John; but the idea will be
found in John i. 12, 1 John iii. 1-2, and elsewhere.

4. This noun, used very frequently by all other N.T. writers, and translated
'faith', is used only once by John; but the corresponding verb 'believe' is
used by him constantly.

5. On the contrary, there are many resemblances between Rev. and the
fourth gospel. As to the vocabulary, there are hundreds of words used in both
these books but not in the epistle. Does this prove anything about authorship?

6. 2 Cor. xii. 1-4, Eph. iii. 3, and Col. i. 26.

author possessed both things, the gift[1] of knowledge and the gift of speech. That the other saw revelations and received knowledge and prophecy I will not deny; but I observe that his language and style are not really Greek: he uses barbarous idioms, and is sometimes guilty of solecisms. There is no need to pick these out now; for I have not said these things in order to pour scorn on him – do not imagine it – but solely to prove the dissimilarity between these books.

The letters of Dionysius

26. In addition to these letters of Dionysius, many others are preserved, e.g. those denouncing Sabellius, sent to Ammon, Bishop of Bernice, Telesphorus, Euphranor, Ammon again, and Euporus. He was also the author of four pamphlets on the same subject addressed to his namesake at Rome. Many more letters of his are in my collection, as well as lengthy documents in letter form, e.g. those on Nature addressed to his boy[2] Timothy, and the one on temptation dedicated to the same Euphranor. Besides these, when writing to Basilides, Primate of Pentapolis, he says that he has written a commentary on the beginning of Ecclesiastes, and he has left us various other letters to the same correspondent.

Paul of Samosata starts a heresy at Antioch

Now let us pass on to another subject, and describe for the benefit of future generations the character of our own.

27. When Xystus had been head of the Roman church for eleven years[3] he was succeeded by the Bishop of Alexandria's namesake, Dionysius. At the same period Demetrian departed this life at Antioch, and the bishopric went to Paul of Samosata. As he held low, degraded opinions about Christ, in defiance of the Church's teaching, regarding Him as in His

1. Literally 'word'.   2. See p. 274 n.   3. Probably a slip for 'months'.

nature just an ordinary man, Dionysius of Alexandria was invited to attend the synod; but, excusing himself on the ground of both age and sickness, he put off his coming and sent a letter expressing his own view of the question. The other pastors of the churches, however, gathered from every direction to deal with this destroyer of Christ's flock, all hastening to Antioch.

Famous bishops of the time

28. Pre-eminent among these was Firmilian, Bishop of Cappadocian Caesarea; the brothers Gregory and Athenodore, pastors of the Pontic communities; Helenus, Bishop of Tarsus, and Nicomas, Bishop of Iconium; and of course Hymenaeus of the Jerusalem church and Theotecnus of its neighbour, my own church of Caesarea. I must name one more – Maximus, who was shepherding the Christians of Bostra with such distinction. It would be easy to reckon up many, many more, together with presbyters and deacons, who assembled in Antioch for the same purpose, but the most eminent were those I have named. They all met on many different occasions, and at every meeting questions were raised and arguments put forward, Paul and his friends endeavouring all the time to hide and cover up his heterodox ideas, while the others did all they could to lay bare and bring into the open his heresy and blasphemy against Christ.

Meanwhile Dionysius died, in the twelfth year of Gallienus,[1] after being head of the Alexandrian church for seventeen years. His successor was Maximus. When Gallienus had completed fifteen years as emperor, he was succeeded by Claudius, who at the termination of his second year left his throne to Aurelian.

I. A.D. 264–5.

Paul excommunicated; the bishops' letter condemning him

29. During his reign a final meeting of the synod was held, attended by a very large number of bishops,[1] who exposed and at last, explicitly and unanimously, condemned for heterodoxy the originator of the Antioch heresy, who was excommunicated from the Catholic Church throughout the world. The person who did most to call him to account and to pin him down, wriggle as he might, was Malchion, a man of great learning who was principal of a school of rhetoric, one of the centres of Hellenic education at Antioch, and in view of the utter genuineness of his faith in Christ had been appointed presbyter of that community. He arranged for shorthand writers to take notes as he embarked on an argument with Paul which we know to be extant to this day; he and he alone succeeded in exposing the crafty dissembler.

30. Accordingly, a single letter expressing their united judgement was drafted by the assembled pastors: nominally addressed to Bishop Dionysius of Rome and Maximus of Alexandria, it was sent out to all the provinces of the Empire. In it they made clear to all the trouble they had taken, the perverse heterodoxy of Paul, and the arguments and questions they had put to him; they also gave a survey of his whole life and character. To make sure that the facts are not forgotten, it would be well at this point to reproduce what they said:

Helenus, Hymenaeus, Theophilus, Theotecnus, Maximus, Proclus, Nicomas, Aelian, Paul, Bolanus, Protogenes, Hierax, Eutychius, Theodore, Malchion, Lucius, and all the other members of our communities in the neighbouring cities and countries – bishops, presbyters, deacons, and Christian congregations – to their beloved brothers in the Lord, Dionysius, Maximus, and all our fellow-ministers in every land – bishops, presbyters, and deacons – and to the entire Catholic Church throughout the world – greeting. . . .

1. Variously given as 70–80.

We sent invitations to many even of the more distant bishops to join in putting right this deadly teaching, for instance Dionysius at Alexandria and Firmilian of Cappadocia, both of blessed memory. Dionysius wrote to Antioch, disregarding the existence of the originator of the error, and addressing his letter not to him but to the diocese as a whole: we enclose a copy. Firmilian, who actually came twice, condemned Paul's modernistic notions, a fact for which we who were present can vouch, and which is known to many others; but when Paul promised to change, Firmilian, trusting and believing that without any reproach to the word the matter would be happily settled, adjourned the proceedings, duped by a man who denied his God and Lord and had abandoned the belief that he himself had previously held. And Firmilian was on the point of crossing to Antioch a third time, and had got as far as Tarsus, having seen too much of the God-denying wickedness of this man. But meanwhile, when we had met together and were sending for him and waiting till he arrived, he reached the end of his days.

Farther on they describe the tenor of his life:

Whereas he has forsaken the canon and deviated to spurious and bastard doctrines, there is no need to judge the actions of one who is outside the Church, even in the case of a man who once was nearly penniless, having neither inherited a competence from his forbears nor acquired one by the labour of hand or brain, but who now has amassed immense wealth by committing illegalities, robbing churches, and blackmailing his fellow-Christians. He deprives the injured of their rights, promising them help if they will pay for it but breaking his word to them, and makes easy money out of the readiness of those entangled in court proceedings to buy relief from their persecutors. In fact, he regards religion as a way of making money.[1]

Nor need we judge him because he is ambitious and arrogant, decking himself out with worldly honours and anxious to be called *ducenarius*[2] rather than bishop, and swaggers in city squares,[3] reading letters aloud or dictating them as he walks in public surrounded by a numerous bodyguard, some in front and some behind. The result

1. 1 Tim. vi. 5.
2. A procurator earning the exceptionally high salary of 200 sestertia, worth about £10,000.
3. A reminiscence of Demosthenes.

is that the Faith is regarded with distaste and hatred because of his self-importance and inflated pride.

Nor need we judge the way this charlatan juggles with church assemblies, courting popularity and putting on a show to win the admiration of simple souls, as he sits on the dais and lofty throne he has had constructed for him (how unlike a disciple of Christ!) or in the *secretum*,[1] as he calls it, which he occupies in imitation of the rulers of the world. He slaps his thigh and stamps on the dais. Some do not applaud and wave their handkerchiefs as in a theatre, or shout and spring to their feet like his circle of partisans, male and female, who form such a badly behaved audience: they listen, as in God's house, in a reverent and orderly manner. These he scolds and insults. Those who have departed this life, but once preached the word, he assails in a drunken, vulgar fashion in public, while he boasts about himself as if he were not a bishop but a trickster and mountebank.[2]

All hymns to our Lord Jesus Christ he has banned as modern compositions of modern writers, but he arranges for women to sing hymns to himself in the middle of the church on the great day of the Easter festival: one would shudder to hear them! And he allows the fawning bishops of the neighbouring districts and towns, and presbyters too, to talk in the same way when preaching to the people. He will not admit that the Son of God came down from heaven – as we shall explain more fully later, not merely stating the fact but proving it from passage after passage of the attached notes, especially where he says that Jesus Christ is 'from below'. Yet those who sing hymns and praises to him in the congregation say that their blasphemous teacher is an angel come down from heaven; and he allows this to go on even when he is there to hear, such is his vanity. And what of his 'spiritual brides', as the Antioch people call them? and those of his presbyters and deacons, with whom he joins in concealing this and their other incurable sins, though he knows all about them, so as to have them under his thumb, too frightened on their own account to accuse him of his offences in word and deed? He has even enriched them, thus securing the loyalty and admiration of those who are the same way inclined.

But why should we put these things in writing? We know, dear brothers, that the bishop and entire priesthood ought to be an

1. A magistrate's private room.   2. Demosthenes again.

example to the people of all good works; we are aware also how many through taking 'spiritual brides' have fallen, while others have become suspect. Even if we grant that he does nothing licentious, he should at least have taken care to avoid the suspicion to which such practices give rise, so as not to lead someone else astray and make others imitate him. How could he reprove another man, or advise him not to associate any longer with a 'bride', for fear of a slip – as Scripture warns us[1] – when he has dismissed one already and now has two in his house, both young and pretty, whom he takes round with him whenever he leaves home, living, I may add, in luxury and surfeiting? Small wonder that all weep and groan in secret; for so frightened are they of his tyrannical power that they dare not accuse him. Yet, as we said before, a man could be called to account for these things, if only he had a catholic mind and was one of our number.[2] But when he burlesqued the mystery[3] and paraded with the filthy sect of Artemas[4] (it is our unpleasant duty to name his father),[5] we do not feel called upon to ask for an explanation of all this. . . .

We were therefore obliged, as he ranged himself against God and would not yield, to excommunicate him and appoint another bishop in his place for the Catholic Church. By the providence of God, as we feel sure, we chose Domnus, the son of Demetrian of blessed memory[6] who once presided with such distinction over the same diocese. He possesses all the excellent qualities required in a bishop, and we are informing you of his appointment in order that you may write to him and receive from him a letter establishing communion. But this fellow had better write to Artemas, then Artemas and his gang can be in communion with him.[7]

When Paul had lost both the orthodoxy of his faith and his bishopric, Domnus, as already stated, took over the ministry

1. Eccles. ix. 8–9.　　　2. Acts i. 17.
3. A reminiscence of Lucian.　　4. On p. 235, 'Artemon'.
5. An allusion to John viii.　　6. Another married bishop; see p. 279 n.
7. We may well accept the statement of Jerome that this letter was the work of Malchion, the learned headmaster. Apart from the borrowings from Demosthenes and Lucian and the use of two Latin words, it reeks of rhetoric, with its abuse, its pretended unwillingness to accuse, and its immensely long and involved sentences, one of which (with a single main verb) stretches to 330 words.

of the Antioch church. But Paul absolutely refused to hand over the church building; so the Emperor Aurelian was appealed to, and he gave a perfectly just decision on the course to be followed: he ordered the building to be assigned to those to whom the bishops of the religion in Italy and Rome addressed a letter. In this way the man in question was thrown out of the church in the most ignominious manner by the secular authority.

Such was the treatment we received from Aurelian at that time. But as his reign went on, he changed his attitude towards us and was now pressed by some of his advisers to instigate a persecution against us, and this became the subject of much comment on every side. But when he was on the point of doing so and was almost in the act of signing the decrees against us, divine justice struck, seizing him in an iron grip to frustrate the attempt – clear proof for all to see that it would never be easy for the rulers of this world to resist the churches of Christ, unless the protecting hand, as a divine and heavenly judgement to chasten and reform us, should at times of its own choosing allow this to be done. Anyway, Aurelian had reigned only six years when he was succeeded by Probus,[1] who held sway for about as long and was followed by Carus, in association with his sons Carinus and Numerian. They lasted less than three years, and the government next fell to Diocletian[2] and those later co-opted. Under them the persecution of my own time took place, and with it the destruction of the churches.

Shortly before this the Bishop of Rome, Dionysius, after holding this office for nine years, was succeeded by Felix.

The heterodox deviation of the Manichees, then starting

31. Meanwhile, the maniac whose name[3] reflected his demon-inspired heresy was arming himself with mental

1. Two short reigns omitted.   2. A.D. 284.   3. Mani.

derangement, since the demon, God's adversary Satan himself, had put him forward for the ruin of many. A barbarian in mode of life, as his speech and manners showed, and by nature demonic and manic, he acted accordingly, and tried to pose as Christ: at one time he announced himself as the Paraclete, the Holy Ghost himself, being a maniac and a boaster too; at another he imitated Christ, and chose twelve disciples as partners of his crazy ideas. Bringing together false and blasphemous doctrines from the innumerable long-extinct blasphemous heresies, he made a patchwork of them, and brought from Persia a deadly poison with which he infected our own world. From him came the unholy name of Manichee, which is still in common use. Such then is the basis of this Knowledge falsely so called, which grew up at the period mentioned.

Distinguished churchmen of my own time

32. At that period too, Felix, head of the Roman church for five years, was succeeded by Eutychian. He lasted less than ten months[1] and left his office to Gaius, my own contemporary, who governed the see for about fifteen years. Marcellinus was chosen to succeed him, but has since fallen victim to the persecution.[2]

In their time the bishopric of Antioch passed from Domnus to Timaeus, who was succeeded by my contemporary Cyril. In his time I made the acquaintance of Dorotheus, a learned man who had been ordained to the presbyterate at Antioch. Enraptured with the study of divinity, he mastered the Hebrew language so thoroughly that he was able to read and understand the precious Hebrew scriptures; he was equally at home in the most liberal studies and Greek elementary education. He was however a natural eunuch, having been such from birth: the emperor, seeing in this a kind of miracle, honoured him with his friendship and graciously appointed

1. A mistake for years.   2. Of Diocletian.

him manager of the dye-works at Tyre. I heard him expounding the Scriptures in church very sensibly.

After Cyril, Tyrannus succeeded to the bishopric of Antioch: it was in his day that the attack on the churches reached
its peak.

As head of the diocese of Laodicea, Socrates was followed
by Eusebius, who came from Alexandria. The reason for his
move was the question of Paul. On his account he came to
Syria, where eager students of divinity detained him. He was
one of the most lovely examples of true religion in my time,
as may easily be seen from the remarks of Dionysius already
quoted.[1] Anatolius was appointed his successor, one good man
following another, as the saying goes. Anatolius was by
birth an Alexandrian, and for his learning, secular studies,
and philososophy was in the first rank of the most eminent
men of my time; indeed in arithmetic, geometry, astronomy,
and the other sciences, physical or metaphysical, and in the
speaker's art too, he had climbed to the summit. It was apparently on this account that he was invited by the citizens
there to found the school of the Aristotelian succession at
Alexandria. Countless exploits of his during the siege of the
Pirucheum at Alexandria are recorded: a unique privilege
among the officials was unanimously conferred on him. I shall
mention one incident only. It is said that when the defenders
had run out of wheat, so that now the enemy without were
less terrible than hunger within, our hero devised the following scheme.

The other half of the city was fighting on the Roman side
and so was not besieged. Eusebius, who was still there before
his move to Syria, was in this half, and had won such fame
and such an outstanding reputation that even the Roman
commander was impressed. Anatolius sent to Eusebius a full
account of the starving victims of the siege. On receiving it,
he asked the Roman general as an act of the greatest kindness

1. See p. 297.

to promise immunity to deserters from the enemy: having obtained his request, he informed Anatolius. When the promise reached him, Anatolius at once convened a council of Alexandrians and began by appealing to them all to give the right hand of friendship to the Romans. When he saw that they were angered by the suggestion, he went on: 'Well, I don't think you would say no if I advised you to allow those who are superfluous and of no use to us, old men and women and young children, to go outside the gates whichever way they like. Why do we hold on to these people to no purpose, when they are on the point of death? Why do we let the maimed and crippled die of starvation, when we ought to support only men and youths and ration our precious wheat to those capable of defending the city?'

With arguments on these lines he convinced the meeting, and was the first to stand up and give his vote that the whole mass of men and women incapable of military service should be free to leave the city, because if they continued to stay there uselessly they could not hope to survive, as hunger would destroy them. When the whole council agreed to this proposal, he succeeded in saving nearly everyone inside the gates. He saw to it that first the members of the Church, and then the rest of those in the city, whatever their age, should escape, not only those covered by the vote but countless others pretending to be so, who disguised themselves in women's clothing and in accordance with his plan slipped out of the gates and hurried towards the Roman lines. There they were all welcomed by Eusebius, who like a father and a doctor looked after them, much the worse for the long siege, with every care and attention. Such were the two pastors whom the church of Laodicea was privileged to have in succession: by divine providence they had come there from Alexandria after the war described above. No very great number of works came from Anatolius's pen, but enough have come into my hands to demonstrate his learning and varied knowledge. In these he presents in particular his views on the Easter festival. It will be desirable at this point to quote the following:

FROM THE CANONS OF ANATOLIUS ON THE EASTER FESTIVAL

It has therefore in the first year the new moon of the first month, which begins the whole nineteen-year cycle – according to the Egyptians on 26 Phamenoth, according to the Macedonian calendar 22 Dystrus, by Roman reckoning 22 March. On this day the sun is found not only to have reached the first sign of the Zodiac, but to be already passing through the fourth day within it. This sign is generally known as the first of the twelve, the equinoctial sign, the beginning of months, head of the cycle, and start of the planetary course. But the sign before that is the last of the months, the twelfth sign, last stage, and end of the planetary circuit. For this reason I am convinced that those who place the first month in it, and fix the Paschal 'fourteenth day'[1] accordingly,[2] make a great and indeed an extraordinary mistake. This is not my own suggestion: the Jews were aware of the fact long ago, even before Christ's time, and observed it carefully. We can learn it from the statements of Philo, Josephus, and Musaeus, and not them only but still earlier writers, the two Agathobuli, famous as the teachers of Aristobulus the Great. He was one of the Seventy who translated the sacred and inspired Hebrew Scriptures for Ptolemy Philadelphus and his father; he also dedicated commentaries on the Mosaic Law to the same kings. These authorities, in explaining the problems of the Exodus, state that the Passover ought invariably to be sacrificed after the spring equinox, at the middle of the first month; and that this occurs when the sun is passing through the first sign of the solar, or as some of them call it, the zodiacal cycle. Aristobulus adds that it is necessary at the Passover Festival that not only the sun but the moon as well should be passing through an equinoctial sign. There are two of these signs, one in spring, one in autumn, diametrically opposite each other, and the day of the Passover is assigned to the fourteenth of the month, after sunset; so the moon will occupy the position diametrically opposite the sun, as we

1. See p. 230.
2. Dr Oulton's conjecture: the Greek seems untranslatable.

can see when the moon is full: the sun will be in the sign of the spring equinox, the moon inevitably in that of the autumnal. I am familiar with many other of their statements, in some cases probable, in others claimed as final proofs, by which they try to show that the festival of the Passover and Unleavened Bread ought always to be kept after the equinox. But I decline to demand such a structure of proof from those from whom has been removed the veil on the Law of Moses; for them it remains now with face unveiled at all times to reflect like a mirror Christ and the life of Christ,[1] His lessons and sufferings.[2] That the first month according to the Hebrews includes the equinox can be shown also by reference to Enoch.[3]

Anatolius has also left us an *Elements of Arithmetic*, complete in ten parts, as well as evidences of his lifelong study of divinity. He had first been consecrated bishop by Theotecnus, Bishop of Palestinian Caesarea, who was anxious to secure him as his successor in his own diocese after his death, and indeed for some little time they both administered the same church. But he was summoned to Antioch by the synod that dealt with Paul, and as he passed through Laodicea the Christians there took possession of him, Eusebius having fallen asleep.

When Anatolius too departed this life, his episcopate passed to Stephen, the last bishop before the persecution. For his attainments in philosophy and other secular studies he was widely admired; but he was not equally devoted to the divine Faith, as was shown in the course of the persecution, in which he stood revealed as a dissembler and a spiritless coward rather than a true philosopher. However, the church was not to be ruined because of him; she was set on her feet again by one whom God Himself, the universal Saviour, at once chose to be bishop of that diocese – Theodotus, who by his very acts proved his own name[4] and that of bishop true. In the science of bodily healing he was very highly qualified; in the curing

1. See 2 Cor. iii. 15–18.   2. Heb. v. 8.
3. The uncanonical book quoted in Jude 14.
4. *Theodotus* means 'God-given'.

of souls he was without a rival, such were his kindness, genuine
sympathy, and active interest in those who asked him for
help; he also put a great deal of effort into the study of divinity. Such was his character in a nutshell.

At Caesarea in Palestine Theotecnus, after carrying out his
episcopal duties most conscientiously, was succeeded by
Agapius. I know that he too worked very hard, and showed
a most genuine regard for the welfare of his people, ministering with a generous hand to the poor most of all. In his time
I made the acquaintance of a most remarkable man, a true
philosopher in his life, who was chosen for the presbyterate
in that diocese – Pamphilus. To discuss his background and
character would be too big an undertaking; all the details of
his life, the school he founded, his ordeals in successive confessions of his faith during the persecution, and the crown of
martyrdom which he won at last, I have recorded in a work
devoted to him alone. He was the most wonderful of the
people there, but among the men of my time there were certainly two of the rarest merit – one of the Alexandrian presbyters, Pierius, and Meletius, Primate of the Pontic province.
Pierius had been noted for his life of absolute poverty and for
his philosophical studies. He was exceptionally well versed
in the science and exposition of theology, and was a first-rate
popular preacher. Meletius – Mellifluous,[1] as the learned called
him – was the sort of man who might be described as the
complete all-round scholar. His excellence as an orator cannot be sufficiently admired, though it might be said that this
came to him as a gift from nature. But who could rival his
excellence as a lifelong and profound scholar? You had only
to meet him to discover that in every kind of intellectual
activity he was the most accomplished and well informed
person alive. No less remarkable was the excellence of his
character. I observed him at the time of the persecution, when
he was chased all over Palestine for seven years.

1. Greek 'the honey (*meli*) of Attica'.

In the Jerusalem church, following Hymenaeus, the bishop mentioned a little while back, Zabdas took over the ministry. Very soon he fell asleep, and Hermo, last of the bishops up to the persecution of my time, ascended the apostolic throne preserved there to this day.[1]

At Alexandria Maximus, who for eighteen years after the death of Dionysius had been bishop, was succeeded by Theonas. In his time Achillas was ordained to the presbyterate at Alexandria, along with Priscus, and was greatly esteemed. The school of the holy Faith was entrusted to his hands, for he had shown unusual and unrivalled abilities as a philosopher, and a character in true accord with the gospel way of life. When Theonas had done his utmost for nineteen years, he was succeeded in the diocese of Alexandria by Peter, who in his turn did splendid work for twelve years. He administered the church for not quite three years before the persecution; for the rest of his life he subjected himself to a harsher discipline, and his care for the common good of the churches was evident to all. The result was that in the ninth year of the persecution he was beheaded, and so was honoured with the crown of martyrdom.

In these books I have dealt fully with the subject of the successions from our Saviour's birth to the destruction of our places of worship, a story covering 305 years.[2] Well now, for the information of future generations, I had better next record the continual and terrible ordeals of those who in my time fought so manfully for true religion.

1. See p. 302.   2. 3 B.C. to A.D. 303. See p. 49 n.

Book 8

DIOCLETIAN TO MAXIMIAN: PERSECUTIONS: THE IMPERIAL RECANTATION

HAVING dealt fully with the apostolic succession in seven books, in this eighth section it is surely a matter of the highest importance that for the enlightenment of future generations I should set down the events of my own day, calling as they do for a most careful record. That shall be the starting-point for my account.

Events before the persecution of my time

1. How great, how unique were the honour, and liberty too, which before the persecution of my time were granted by all men, Greeks and non-Greeks alike, to the message given through Christ to the world, of true reverence for the God of the universe! It is beyond me to describe it as it deserves. Witness the goodwill so often shown by potentates to our people; they even put into their hands the government of the provinces,[1] releasing them from the agonizing question of sacrificing, in view of the friendliness with which they regarded their teaching. What need I say about those in the imperial palaces and about the supreme rulers? Did they not permit the members of their households – consorts, children, and servants[2] – to embrace boldly before their eyes the divine message and way of life, hardly minding even if they boasted of the liberty granted to the Faith? Did they not hold them in special esteem, and favour them more than their fellow

1. See pp. 338, 341.
2. Including, till the persecution began, Diocletian's wife and daughter.

servants? I might instance the famous Dorotheus, the most
devoted and loyal of their servants, and on that account much
more honoured than the holders of offices and governorships.
With him I couple the celebrated Gorgonius, and all who because of God's word were held in the same honour as these
two. And what approbation the rulers in every church unmistakably won from all procurators and governors! How
could one describe those mass meetings, the enormous
gatherings in every city, and the remarkable congregations in
places of worship? No longer satisfied with the old buildings,
they raised from the foundations in all the cities churches
spacious in plan. These things went forward with the times
and expanded at a daily increasing rate, so that no envy
stopped them nor could any evil spirit bewitch them or
check them by means of human schemes, as long as the divine
and heavenly hand sheltered and protected its own people, as
being worthy.

But increasing freedom transformed our character to
arrogance and sloth; we began envying and abusing each
other, cutting our own throats, as occasion offered, with
weapons of sharp-edged words; rulers hurled themselves at
rulers and laymen waged party fights against laymen, and
unspeakable hypocrisy and dissimulation were carried to the
limit of wickedness. At last, while the gatherings were still
crowded, divine judgement, with its wonted mercy, gently
and gradually began to order things its own way, and with
the Christians in the army the persecution began. But alas!
realizing nothing, we made not the slightest effort to render
the Deity kindly and propitious; and as if we had been a lot
of atheists, we imagined that our doings went unnoticed and
unregarded, and went from wickedness to wickedness. Those
of us who were supposed to be pastors cast off the restraining
influence of the fear of God and quarrelled heatedly with
each other, engaged solely in swelling the disputes, threats,
envy, and mutual hostility and hate, frantically demanding

the despotic power they coveted. Then, then it was that in accordance with the words of Jeremiah, the Lord in His anger covered the daughter of Zion with a cloud, and cast down from Heaven the glory of Israel; He remembered not the footstool of His feet in the day of His anger, but the Lord also drowned in the sea all the beauty of Israel, and broke down all his fences.[1] So also, as foretold in the Psalms, He overthrew the covenant of His bondservant and profaned to the ground (through the destruction of the churches) his sanctuary and broke down all his fences; He made his strongholds cowardice. All that passed by the way despoiled the multitudes of the people; moreover, he became a reproach to his neighbours. For He exalted the right hand of his enemies, and turned back the aid of his sword and did not assist him in the war. But He also cut him off from cleansing and threw down his throne to the ground, and shortened the days of his time, and finally covered him with shame.[2]

The destruction of the churches

2. Everything indeed has been fulfilled in my time; I saw with my own eyes the places of worship thrown down from top to bottom, to the very foundations, the inspired holy Scriptures committed to the flames in the middle of the public squares, and the pastors of the churches hiding disgracefully in one place or another, while others suffered the indignity of being held up to ridicule by their enemies – a reminder of another prophetic saying: for contempt was poured on rulers, and He made them wander in a trackless land where there was no road.[3] But it is not for me to describe their wretched misfortunes in the event: nor is it my business to leave on record their quarrels and inhumanity to

1. A conflation of parts of Lam. ii. 1–2 with Ps. lxxxix. 40.
2. A free adaptation of Ps. lxxxix. 39–45.
3. Ps. cvii. 40.

each other before the persecutions, so I have made up my mind to relate no more about them than enough to justify the divine judgement. I am determined therefore to say nothing even about those who have been tempted by the persecution or have made complete shipwreck of their salvation[1] and of their own accord flung themselves into the depths of the stormy sea; I shall include in my overall account only those things by which first we ourselves, then later generations, may benefit. Let me therefore proceed from this point to describe in outline the hallowed ordeals of the martyrs of God's word.

It was the nineteenth year of Diocletian's reign and the month Dystrus, called March by the Romans, and the festival of the Saviour's Passion was approaching, when an imperial decree was published everywhere, ordering the churches to be razed to the ground and the Scriptures destroyed by fire, and giving notice that those in places of honour would lose their places, and domestic staff, if they continued to profess Christianity, would be deprived of their liberty. Such was the first edict against us. Soon afterwards other decrees arrived in rapid succession, ordering that the presidents of the churches in every place should all be first committed to prison and then coerced by every possible means into offering sacrifice.

Ordeals endured in the persecution: God's glorious martyrs

3. Then, then it was that many rulers of the churches bore up heroically under horrible torments, an object lesson in the endurance of fearful ordeals; while countless others, their souls already numbed with cowardice, promptly succumbed to the first onslaught. Of the rest, each was subjected to a series of different tortures, one flogged unmercifully with the whip, another racked and scraped beyond endurance, so that the lives of some came to a most miserable end. But differ-

1. A reminiscence of 1 Tim. i. 19.

ent people came through the ordeal very differently: one
man would be forcibly propelled by others and brought to
the disgusting, unholy sacrifices, and dismissed as if he had
sacrificed, even if he had done no such thing; another, who
had not even approached any abomination, much less
touched it, but was said by others to have sacrificed, would go
away without attempting to repudiate the baseless charge.
Another would be picked up half dead, and thrown away as
if already a corpse; and again a man lying on the ground
might be dragged a long way by his feet, though included
among the willing sacrificers. One man would announce at
the top of his voice his determination not to sacrifice,
another would shout that he was a Christian, exulting in the
confession of the Saviour's Name, while yet another insisted
that he had never sacrificed and never would. These were
struck on the mouth and silenced by a formidable body of
soldiers lined up for the purpose: their faces and cheeks were
battered and they were forcibly removed. It was the one
object in life of the enemies of true religion to gain credit for
having finished the job.

But no such methods could enable them to dispose of the
holy martyrs. What could I say that would do full justice to
them?   4. I could tell of thousands who showed magnificent
enthusiasm for the worship of the God of the universe, not
only from the beginning of the general persecution, but much
earlier when peace was still secure. For at long last the one
who had received the authority[1] was as it were awaking from
the deepest sleep, after making attempts – as yet secret and
surreptitious – against the churches, in the interval that followed Decius and Valerian. He did not make his preparations
all at once for the war against us, but for the time being took
action only against members of the legions. In this way he
thought that the rest would easily be mastered if he joined

1 Presumably Galerius, who forced Diocletian to agree to persecute. Others
suggest the devil.

battle with these and emerged victorious. Now could be seen
large numbers of serving soldiers most happy to embrace
civil life, in order to avoid having to repudiate their loyalty
to the Architect of the universe. The commander-in-chief,
whoever he was,[1] was now first setting about persecuting the
soldiery, classifying and sorting those serving in the legions,
and allowing them to choose either to obey orders and retain
their present rank, or alternatively to be stripped of it if they
disobeyed the enactment. But a great many soldiers of Christ's
kingdom without hesitation or question chose to confess Him
rather than cling to the outward glory and prosperity they
enjoyed. Already here and there one or two of them were
suffering not only loss of position but even death as the reward
of their unshakable devotion: for the time being the man behind the plot was acting cautiously and going as far as bloodshed[2] in a few cases only; he was apparently afraid of the
number of believers, and shrank from launching out into war
with them all at once. But when he stripped more thoroughly
for battle, words are inadequate to depict the host of God's
noble martyrs whom the people of every city and every
region were privileged to see with their own eyes.

Martyrs in Nicomedia and in the imperial palaces

5. When the edict against the churches was issued at Nicomedia and posted up in a conspicuous public place, a well-
known person,[3] by worldly standards of pre-eminence a man
of the greatest distinction, was so stirred by religious enthusiasm and carried away by burning faith that he promptly
seized it and tore it to shreds, as something unholy and utterly
profane – and that, when two emperors were there in the
same city, the most senior of them all and the one who held

1. Veturius, as Eusebius states elsewhere.
2. Reminiscent of Heb. xii. 4.
3. Euethius, put to death the same day.

the fourth place in the government.[1] But he was only the first
of many who at that time distinguished themselves in this way
and suffered the natural consequences of such bold conduct,
preserving a cheerful, confident bearing to their very last
breath. 6. Of all those who have at any time been praised in
song for their virtues and lauded for their courage, among
Greeks and non-Greeks alike, none was ever more remarkable
than the divine martyrs produced by this occasion – Dorotheus and the imperial servants who followed his lead. They
had been most highly honoured by their imperial masters
and treated by them as if they had been their own children,
but they accounted reproaches and sufferings for religion, and
the many kinds of death invented against them, as in truth
greater riches than worldly fame and luxury.[2] I shall describe
the death that one of them met, and leave it to my readers to
infer from that case what happened in the others.

In the city named above, the rulers in question brought a
certain man into a public place and commanded him to
sacrifice. When he refused, he was ordered to be stripped,
hoisted up naked, and his whole body torn with loaded
whips till he gave in and carried out the command, however
unwillingly. When in spite of these torments he remained as
obstinate as ever, they next mixed vinegar with salt and
poured it over the lacerated parts of his body, where the bones
were already exposed. When he treated these agonies too with
scorn a lighted brazier was then brought forward, and as if it
were edible meat for the table, what was left of his body was
consumed by the fire, not all at once, for fear his release
should come too soon, but a little at a time; and those who
placed him on the pyre were not permitted to stop till after
such treatment he should signify his readiness to obey. But
he stuck immovably to his determination, and victorious in
the midst of his tortures, breathed his last. Such was the

1. Diocletian and Galerius.
2. Freely adapted from Heb. xi. 26.

martyrdom of one of the imperial servants, a martyrdom worthy of the name he bore – it was Peter.

The heroism of the others was just as great, but to preserve the proportions of this book I shall pass it over, only recording that Dorotheus and Gorgonius, with many more of the imperial household, went through a succession of ordeals and finally were put to death by strangling, carrying off the prizes of their inspired victory.

It was at that period that Anthimus, then head of the Nicomedian church, bore witness to Christ and was beheaded. He was followed by a number of martyrs at once, for somehow or other at that very time there was a conflagration in the palace at Nicomedia, and through a groundless suspicion word went round that our people were responsible.[1] By imperial command God's worshippers there perished wholesale and in heaps, some butchered with the sword, others fulfilled by fire; it is on record that with an inspired and mystical fervour men and women alike leapt on to the pyre. A number of others were bound by the public executioners, dumped in small boats, and thrown into the depths of the sea. As for the imperial servants already dead and committed to the ground with fitting ceremony, they were dug up by their so-called masters, who thought it advisable to start again and throw them too into the sea, with the absurd notion that as they lay in their graves some people would worship them in the belief that they were gods!

Such was the state of affairs at Nicomedia in the early stages of the persecution. But when a little later, in the district of Melitene[2] and all over Syria as well, attempts were being made to attack the empire, an imperial decree was circulated that the heads of the churches everywhere should be

1. An interesting parallel to the burning of Rome: the Christians were blamed, but according to Lactantius, who was there, the fire was the work of the Emperor Galerius. Readers will also be reminded of the burning of the Reichstag.

2. In Armenia Minor.

fettered and imprisoned. The spectacle of what happened after this beggars description: in every town great numbers were locked up, and everywhere the gaols built long before for homicides and grave-robbers were crowded with bishops, presbyters and deacons, readers and exorcists, so that now there was no room in them for those convicted of crimes.

It was not long before the first decree was followed by another, in which it was laid down that if the prisoners offered sacrifice they should be allowed to go free, but if they refused they should be mutilated by endless tortures. Now once more, how could one count the number of martyrs in every province of the Empire, especially those in Africa and Mauretania, in the Thebais and Egypt? From Egypt at this time some went off to other cities and provinces, where they showed their worth by martyrdom.

Egyptian martyrs in Phoenicia, in Egypt itself, and in the Thebais

7. At any rate we know those of them who became shining lights in Palestine, and we know those at Tyre in Phoenicia. Did any man see them without being amazed at the merciless floggings and the endurance displayed under them by these truly astounding champions of pure religion; at the ordeal with man-eating beasts which came directly after the floggings, when they were attacked by panthers, bears of different kinds, wild boars, and bulls goaded with red-hot irons; at the unflinching courage of these noble people in the face of every one of the beasts? When these things were going on I was there myself, and there I witnessed the ever-present divine power of Him to whom they testified, our Saviour Jesus Christ Himself, visibly manifesting itself to the martyrs. For some time the man-eaters did not dare to touch or even approach the bodies of God's beloved, but rushed at the

others who apparently were irritating and provoking them from outside; only the holy champions, as they stood naked, and in accordance with their instructions waved their hands to attract the animals to themselves, were left quite unmolested: sometimes when the beasts did start towards them, they were stopped short as if by some divine power, and retreated to their starting-point. When this went on for a long time it astounded the spectators, so that in view of the ineffectiveness of the first a second and third beast were set on to one and the same martyr.

Nothing could be more amazing than the fearless courage of these saints under such duress, the stubborn, inflexible endurance in youthful bodies. You would see a youngster not yet twenty standing without fetters, spreading out his arms in the form of a cross, and with a mind unafraid and unshakable occupying himself in the most unhurried prayers to the Almighty; not budging in the least and not retreating an inch from the spot where he stood, though bears and panthers breathing fury and death almost touched his very flesh. Yet by some supernatural, mysterious power their mouths were stopped, and they ran back again to the rear. Again you would have seen others – there were five altogether – thrown to an infuriated bull. When others approached from outside he tossed them with his horns into the air and mangled them, leaving them to be picked up half-dead; but when in his fury he rushed head down at the lonely group of holy martyrs, he could not even get near them, but stamped his feet and pushed with his horns in all directions. Provoked by the hot irons he breathed rage and threats, but divine providence dragged him back. So, as he too did his intended victims no harm whatever, other beasts were set on them. At last, when these animals had launched their terrible varied assaults, the martyrs were one and all butchered with the sword, and instead of being buried in the earth were given to the waves of the sea.

8. Such was the ordeal of the Egyptians who championed the faith so gloriously at Tyre. But we should feel equal admiration for those of them who were martyred in their own country, where immense numbers of men, women, and children, despising this transient life, faced death in all its forms for the sake of our Saviour's teaching. Some were scraped, racked, mercilessly flogged, subjected to countless other torments too terrible to describe in endless variety, and finally given to the flames; some were submerged in the sea; others cheerfully stretched out their necks to the headsman's axe; some died under torture; others were starved to death; others again were crucified, some as criminals usually are, some with still greater cruelty nailed the other way up, head down, and kept alive till they starved to death on the very cross.

9. But words cannot describe the outrageous agonies endured by the martyrs in the Thebais. They were torn to bits from head to foot with potsherds like claws till death released them. Women were tied by one foot and hoisted high in the air, head downwards, their bodies completely naked without a morsel of clothing, presenting thus the most shameful, brutal, and inhuman of all spectacles to everyone watching. Others again were tied to trees and stumps and died horribly; for with the aid of machinery they drew together the very stoutest boughs, fastened one of the martyr's legs to each, and then let the boughs fly back to their normal position; thus they managed to tear apart the limbs of their victims in a moment. In this way they carried on, not for a few days or weeks, but year after year. Sometimes ten or more, sometimes over twenty were put to death, at other times at least thirty, and at yet others not far short of sixty; and there were occasions when on a single day a hundred men as well as women and little children were killed, condemned to a succession of ever-changing punishments.

I was in these places, and saw many of the executions for

myself. Some of the victims suffered death by beheading, others punishment by fire. So many were killed on a single day that the axe, blunted and worn out by the slaughter, was broken in pieces, while the exhausted executioners had to be periodically relieved. All the time I observed a most wonderful eagerness and a truly divine power and enthusiasm in those who had put their trust in the Christ of God. No sooner had the first batch been sentenced, than others from every side would jump on to the platform in front of the judge and proclaim themselves Christians. They paid no heed to torture in all its terrifying forms, but undaunted spoke boldly of their devotion to the God of the universe and with joy, laughter, and gaiety received the final sentence of death: they sang and sent up hymns of thanksgiving to the God of the universe till their very last breath.

Wonderful as these were, far, far more wonderful were those who were conspicuous for their wealth, birth, and reputation, and for learning and philosophy, yet put everything second to true religion and faith in our Saviour and Lord Jesus Christ. One was Philoromus, who had been entrusted with an important office in the imperial administration at Alexandria, and with his authority and Roman rank had a military bodyguard and conducted judicial investigations every day. Another was Phileas, Bishop of Thmuis,[1] a man esteemed for his patriotic activities and public services, and for his work as a philosopher. Great numbers of relations and friends implored them, as did prominent officials, and the judge himself appealed to them to pity themselves and spare their wives and children; yet all this was not enough to make them yield to love of life and despise our Saviour's warning about confessing and denying Him. So with manly and philosophic determination, or rather with heartfelt devotion and love of God, they stood like rocks against all the judge's threats and insults, and were both beheaded.

1. In Lower Egypt.

Phileas the martyr's written account of events at Alexandria

10. Since I have said that Phileas made his mark by his secular learning too, let him come forward as his own witness, to make clear what sort of man he was and at the same time to describe, more accurately than I could and in his own words, the martyrdoms that took place at Alexandria in his day.

EXCERPT FROM THE LETTER OF PHILEAS TO THE THMUITES

With all these examples and precedents and trustworthy signposts before their eyes in the inspired and holy Scriptures, the blessed martyrs among us did not hesitate, but directing the eye of the soul[1] with all earnestness towards the Almighty, and resolved to die for their faith, they clung firmly to their vocation, aware that our Lord Jesus Christ became man for our sakes, in order to destroy every kind of sin and make it possible for us to enter into eternal life. For He did not regard it as a prize to be on an equality with God, but emptied Himself, taking the form of a bondservant, and appearing in human shape submitted humbly to death, and death on the cross.[2] So, eagerly desiring the greater gifts,[3] the Christ-bearing martyrs endured every kind of suffering and every outrage that iniquity could invent, not once but twice in some cases; and when their armed guards competed not only in making all sorts of threats against them, but also in carrying them out, they never wavered, because perfect love casts out fear.[4]

What words would suffice to recount their heroic courage under every torture? Liberty was given to all who wished to insult them, and some struck them with cudgels, some with sticks, some with whips, others with straps, and yet others with rope-ends. The spectacle of these outrages was constantly changing and abominable through and through. Some, with their hands tied behind them, were hung from the gibbet and all their limbs were pulled apart by machines; then the torturers were ordered to get to work on every part of their helpless bodies, not as with murderers applying their instruments of correction to sides alone, but even to belly, legs, and

1. A reminiscence of Plato's *Republic*?   2. Phil. ii. 6–8, slightly abridged.
3. I Cor. xii. 31.   4. I John iv. 18.

cheeks. Others were hung by one hand from the porch and hauled up: no agony could have been so horrible as the stretching of their joints and limbs. Others were bound to pillars, facing inwards, with their feet off the ground and the weight of the body drawing the ropes tighter and tighter. This they endured, not while the governor was busy haranguing them, but almost all day long. Whenever he went on to another group, he left subordinate officials to keep an eye on the first, in case anyone succumbed to the tortures and seemed to be giving in. He instructed them to add unsparingly to their bonds,[1] and then when they were at the last gasp to cut them down and drag them away. They were not to show the least consideration for us but to regard us and treat us as if we no longer existed, this being the second torture devised by our adversaries in addition to the floggings. Some, even after these outrageous sufferings, were put in the stocks with their feet stretched out all four holes apart, so that they were forced to lie on their backs, incapacitated by the open wounds with which the blows had covered their entire bodies. Others were hurled to the ground and lay helpless, as a result of the concentrated onslaught of the torturers, presenting to the spectators a sight more horrible than the torture itself, as they bore in their bodies marks of the elaborate and unlimited ingenuity of the torturers.

In this state of affairs some died under their tortures, shaming their adversary by their unshakeable determination; others were locked up in prison half dead, and a few days later were overcome by their agonies and so found fulfilment; the rest responded to treatment and time, and their stay in prison restored their confidence. So when the order was given, they were invited to choose between touching the abominable sacrifice (in which case they would go unmolested, receiving from their persecutors the freedom that brought a curse with it) and refusing to sacrifice and so incurring the supreme penalty. Without hesitating a moment, they went gladly to their death, knowing what Holy Scripture has laid down for us: 'He who sacrifices to other gods shall be utterly destroyed',[2] and 'You shall have no gods other than Me'.[3]

Such was the message that the martyr, truly both lover of wisdom and lover of God, sent to the Christians of his

1. Reading doubtful.   2. Ex. xxii. 20.   3. Ex. xx. 3.

diocese before the final sentence, while he was still undergoing imprisonment, explaining his own situation and at the same time urging them on to hold firmly, even after his approaching fulfilment, to true religion in Christ.

Martyrs in Phrygia; various ordeals of many others of both
sexes

But why need I tell a long story, piling up examples of the victories won by devoted martyrs all over the world, especially those who were attacked now not under common law but as enemies in war? 11. For example a little Christian town in Phrygia was encircled by legionaries, who set it on fire and completely destroyed it, along with the entire population – men, women, and children – as they called on Almighty God. And why? Because all the inhabitants of the town without exception – the Mayor himself and the magistrates, with all the officials and the whole populace – declared themselves Christians and absolutely refused to obey the command to commit idolatry.

There was also a man whom the Romans had raised to high office, Adauctus by name. He came from a distinguished Italian family, and had progressed through all the offices tenable under the emperors, giving complete satisfaction in the general administration of what the Romans call *magistratus* or the ministry of finance. As in addition to all this he set a shining example by the splendid things he did in his religious fervour, and by his bold confession of the Christ of God, he was adorned with the crown of martyrdom: he was still serving as finance minister when he faced his ordeal for his religion's sake.

12. Need I now mention the rest by name, or count all the men, or depict the constantly changing outrages suffered by the amazing martyrs? Sometimes they were killed with the

axe, as happened to those in Arabia; sometimes their legs were broken – the fate of those in Cappadocia. Sometimes they were hung up by the feet head down over a slow fire, so that the smoke rising from the burning wood choked them, as was done to those in Mesopotamia; sometimes noses, ears, and hands were severed, and the other parts and portions of the body cut up like meat – the procedure at Alexandria.

Need I rekindle the memory of the martyrs at Antioch, who were roasted over lighted braziers, not roasted to death but subjected to prolonged torture? Or of others who plunged their hands right into the fire sooner than touch the abominable sacrifice? Some of them were unable to face such a trial, and before they were caught and came into the hands of their would-be destroyers, threw themselves down from the roofs of tall houses, regarding death as a prize snatched from the scheming hands of God's enemies.

At Antioch there was a saintly person[1] whose woman's body housed an indomitable spirit. Universally respected for wealth, birth, and good judgement, she had brought up on religious principles a couple of unmarried daughters in the full flower of their girlish charm. These aroused a great deal of envy: as a result every effort was made to track them to their hiding-place; and when it was discovered that they were living abroad they were purposely summoned to Antioch, and were at the mercy of the soldiers. Seeing that her daughters and herself were in dire peril she opened their eyes to the dreadful things they must expect at human hands, and of all dreadful things the most unbearable – the threat to their chastity. She impressed on the girls and herself too the necessity of shutting their ears to any such suggestion, declaring that to surrender their souls to be enslaved by demons was worse than any death and any destruction, and putting it to them that the only way to escape from it all was to take refuge with the Lord. All three agreed on this, so they arranged

1. Domnina.

their garments neatly about them, and when they had travelled exactly half way they modestly requested the guards to excuse them a moment, and threw themselves into a river that flowed by.

These three made away with themselves. But there was another couple of girls, again at Antioch, Christians in every respect and sisters indeed, aristocratic by birth, splendid in their lives, young in years, charming in appearance, serious in their outlook, religious in their conduct, admirable in their devotion; but as if such perfection was too much for the earth to support, they were thrown into the sea by command of the demon's devotees.

Things that would make the hearer shudder were done to others in Pontus. Pointed reeds were driven into the fingers of both hands under the ends of the nails; in other cases lead was melted over a fire and the boiling seething mass poured down their backs, roasting the vital parts of the body; others endured in their private parts and bowels sufferings shameful, merciless, and unmentionable, which the noble judges, upholders of the law, showing off their brutality as proof of their cleverness, most ingeniously devised: by constantly inventing new outrages, as if they were taking part in a prize competition, they tried their hardest to put each other in the shade.

These miseries came to an end when, worn out at last by their ghastly wickedness, tired of killing, satiated and surfeited with bloodshed, they turned to what seemed to them kindness and humanity: they thought they were no longer doing us any harm. It was not in good taste, they said, to pollute the city with the blood of people of their own race, or to lay the highest levels of government open to the charge of cruelty, a government mild and gentle to all; rather ought the beneficence of the humane imperial authority to be extended to everybody, no one henceforth being punished with death: they had already ceased to impose this penalty on us, thanks

343

to the emperor's humanity. Orders were then issued that eyes
should be gouged out and one leg maimed. That is what they
meant by 'humanity' and 'the lightest of punishments' inflicted on us. As a result of this 'humanity' shown by God's
enemies, it is no longer possible to count the enormous
number of people who first had the right eye hacked out with
a sword and cauterized with fire, and the left foot rendered
useless by branding-irons applied to the joints, and then were
condemned to the province's copper mines, not so much to
secure their services as to subject them to ill-treatment and
physical hardship, to say nothing of the various other ordeals
that befell them and were too numerous to list, for their
heroic achievements went beyond all reckoning.

In these trials the splendid martyrs of Christ let their light
so shine over the whole world that they everywhere astounded
the eyewitnesses of their courage – and small wonder: they
furnished in themselves unmistakable proof of our Saviour's
truly divine and ineffable power. To mention each one by
name would be a lengthy task – nay, an impossibility.

*Church leaders who by their blood proved the religion they
preached genuine*

13. Of leading churchmen martyred in important cities the
first whose name we must blazon on monuments to God's
faithful servants as a martyr of Christ's kingdom was Bishop
Anthimus of Nicomedia, who was beheaded. Of the martyrs
at Antioch the one who was noblest throughout his life was a
local presbyter, Lucian, who at Nicomedia, when the emperor himself was there, had proclaimed the heavenly kingdom of Christ, first by a spoken defence of the Faith, then by
deeds as well. Of the martyrs in Phoenicia the most famous
are surely God's altogether beloved pastors of the spiritual
nurslings of Christ – Tyrannion, bishop of the church at
Tyre, Zenobius, presbyter of the church at Sidon, and

Silvanus, Bishop of Emesa and the neighbouring churches. Silvanus became food for beasts with others at Emesa itself, and was taken up into the choirs of martyrs; the other two glorified the word of God in Antioch by enduring to the last. One of them, the bishop, was thrown into the depths of the sea, while Zenobius, the best of physicians, died bravely under the torments applied to his sides. Of the martyrs in Palestine, Silvanus, Bishop of Gaza and the neighbouring churches, was beheaded at the copper mines in Phaeno, with thirty-nine others. There also two Egyptian bishops, Peleus and Nilus, with several others, were burnt at the stake.

And now also mention must be made of the chief glory of the Caesarean community, Pamphilus, a presbyter and the most wonderful man of my time, the marvel of whose heroic achievements I shall describe when the moment is opportune. Of those at Alexandria and throughout the Thebais and the rest of Egypt who found glorious fulfilment, I must mention first Peter, Bishop of Alexandria itself, a splendid example of the teachers of true religion in Christ; of the presbyters with him, Faustus, Dius, and Ammonius, fulfilled martyrs of Christ; and Phileas, Hesychius, Pachymius, and Theodore, bishops of the Egyptian churches. Besides these there were countless other prominent persons who are commemorated by the churches in their area and locality.

To commit to writing the ordeals of those who battled all over the world for the true worship of the Deity, and to set out in detail everything that happened to them, are no tasks for me: they are surely reserved for those who saw the events with their own eyes. But the struggles I myself witnessed I shall put on record, for the benefit of future generations, in another work.[1] However, in the present book I shall follow up my record with the recantation of the measures taken against us and all the events that followed the opening of the persecution, matters of very great moment to my readers.

1. Presumably *The Martyrs of Palestine.*

As regards the state of the Roman government before the war against us, in every period when the emperors were friendly to us and peaceably disposed, it is beyond the power of words to describe the harvest and abundance of good things that it enjoyed, when the supreme rulers of the world-wide empire, on reaching their tenth and twentieth year, spent their time in festivities and public gatherings, in the gayest of banquets and jollifications, with complete and stable peace. But as there was no obstacle to the growth of their authority, which daily became more inflated, they suddenly abandoned their peaceful attitude to us and launched an implacable campaign. The second year of this kind of activity had not yet run its course, when a shock at the centre of affairs turned the whole system upside down. An unfortunate illness struck down the most senior of the four emperors,[1] resulting in mental derangement; so, together with the one next to him in order of precedence,[2] he returned to normal private life. And this had not yet come about when the whole empire was split in two,[3] a thing that had never happened before, if memory serves.

Not very long afterwards the Emperor Constantius, who throughout his life showed a gentle and kindly spirit towards his subjects and a friendly attitude to the divine teaching, after appointing his lawful son Constantine Emperor and Augustus in his place, paid his debt to nature,[4] and so became the first of the four to be proclaimed one of the gods by the Romans, the recipient of every posthumous honour that could be bestowed on an emperor, and the kindest and mildest of emperors. He was the only one in my time who spent the whole of his reign in a manner worthy of his exalted position. In all ways he showed himself most considerate and benevolent

---

1. Diocletian.   2. Maximian.
3. A colourful way of saying that Christians were differently treated in east and west.
4. A.D. 306.

towards everyone: above all he took no part in the campaign against us – indeed he saved God's servants among his subjects from injury and ill-usage, and he neither pulled down church buildings nor caused us any other mischief. So he achieved a conclusion to his life that was happy and supremely blest; for he alone while still emperor died in an atmosphere of goodwill and glory, to be succeeded by a lawful son in every way most prudent and most religious.

His son Constantine was immediately proclaimed Absolute Ruler[1] and Augustus by the legions – and long before them by the Supreme Ruler,[2] God Himself; and he determined to emulate his father's reverent attitude to our teaching.

Later Licinius, by common vote of the princes, was declared Emperor and Augustus. This was a bitter blow to Maximin, who was everywhere still entitled only Caesar. So, being a tyrant to the marrow, he impudently usurped the honour and became a self-appointed Augustus. Meanwhile, it was discovered that a plot to kill Constantine had been hatched by the man who, as already explained, had abdicated and then resumed office, and he died a most ignominious death:[3] he was the first whose complimentary inscriptions and statues, and everything else that it is customary to set up, were thrown down as being reminders of a foul monster.

The conduct of the enemies of true religion

14. His son Maxentius, who assumed autocratic power in Rome, began by making a pretence of our faith in order to gratify and flatter the citizens. He commanded his subjects to cease persecuting the Christians, putting on the guise of religion and trying to appear considerate and much gentler than

----

1. and 2. The word *basileus*, meaning either 'king' or 'emperor', defies satisfactory translation. Cf. John xix. 15.
3. Maximian strangled himself.

his predecessors. But what people hoped he would be was very different from what he turned out to be. He plunged into every kind of depravity, and there was not one filthy, dissolute act of which he was innocent, given up as he was to adultery and sexual corruption in all its forms. He would take respectable married women away from their husbands, insult and grossly dishonour them, and send them back to their husbands; and he took care not to victimize unknown or obscure persons, but to make the most outstanding of the senior members of the Roman Senate the chief recipients of his besotted attentions. The whole city cowered before him, common people and magistrates, well known and unknown, worn down by his cruel tyranny: not even when they stayed quiet and made doormats of themselves was there any escape from the tyrant's bloodthirsty cruelty. With a trivial excuse he once handed the people over to be massacred by his bodyguard, and thousands of Roman citizens were killed in the heart of the city, not by Scythians or other foreigners, but by their fellow-citizens in full military array. How many senators were massacred because of designs on their property cannot possibly be determined: for one fabricated reason or other hundreds were put to death. The culmination of the tyrant's crimes was his resort to witchcraft: full of magical notions, he sometimes ripped up pregnant women, sometimes scrutinized the entrails of new-born babies, slaughtered lions, and invented unspeakable rites to call up demons and avert the threat of war; for in these practices lay all his hope of emerging victorious.

What this man did while lording it at Rome to enslave his subjects defies description: they were reduced to such desperate straits for lack of even essential food as my contemporaries inform me have never once been known at Rome.

The eastern despot Maximin, as if he were tarred with the same brush, made a secret alliance with Maxentius in Rome, and for a long time imagined that no one was any the wiser.

(Actually he was later found out and paid the penalty he deserved.[1]) It was wonderful what blood-brothers in crime the two of them appeared, or rather how Maximin robbed his opposite number of the first prize for villainy. Quacks and impostors held the highest place in his esteem; terrified at every sound, and horribly superstitious, he was at the mercy of his illusions about idols and demons. Without divinations and oracles he could not bring himself to move a hair's breadth. The result was that he devoted himself to the persecution against us with more vehemence and determination than his predecessors, ordering temples to be built in every city and the sacred precincts which had gone to ruin with the lapse of time to be carefully restored; he appointed priests of idols in every locality and city, and over these a high priest of every province chosen from the public servants of the first rank and distinguished in every branch of civic life, with a bodyguard of armed soldiers; and with utter recklessness he rewarded all impostors, as the pious darlings of the gods, with governorships and the highest privileges.

From that time on he tortured and oppressed not one city or district, but the provinces under him, whole and complete, by exactions of gold and silver and goods without stint, and by very heavy impositions and a variety of judicial penalties. Robbing the wealthy of the property their ancestors had bequeathed to them he lavished unbounded wealth and mountains of goods on his circle of flatterers. His drunken orgies he carried to such a pitch that in his cups he went crazy and out of his mind, and issued orders when drunk which he regretted next day when sober. In debauchery and wild self-indulgence he brooked no rival, appointing himself a teacher of wickedness to those round him, both rulers and ruled. He induced the army to grow soft through utter self-indulgence and wantonness, and invited governors and army commanders to ruin their subjects with plundering and extortion, as if they were his

1. See p. 377.

co-tyrants. Need I recall his crimes of lust, or count the host of women he seduced? He was incapable of passing through a town without leaving a trail of dishonoured wives and ravished maidens. These things went as he wanted with all except Christians, who laughed at death and snapped their fingers at his vile tyranny. The men endured fire and sword and crucifixion; wild beasts and submersion in the sea; severance of limbs and branding; stabbing and gouging out of eyes; mutilation of the entire body; and, in addition, starvation, fetters, and the mines – they were prepared to endure anything for religion's sake, rather than give to idols the reverence due to God. As for the women, schooled by the divine word, they showed themselves as manly as the men. Some underwent the same ordeals as the men, and shared with them the prize of valour; others, when dragged away to dishonour, gave up their souls to death rather than their bodies to that dishonour. Alone among those whom the tyrant tried to seduce at Alexandria, a Christian woman of the greatest eminence and distinction[1] won the victory by her heroic spirit over the lustful and wanton soul of Maximin. Famed for her wealth, birth, and education, she put everything second to modesty. In spite of his constant advances and her willingness to die, he could not put her to death, because desire was stronger than anger; but he exiled her as a punishment, and appropriated all her possessions. Numberless others were assailed by provincial governors, but refusing even to listen to a threat of sexual relations, underwent every kind of punishment: they were racked and tortured till they died.

Wonderful as were these, the palm goes to a woman at Rome[2] – like them a Christian – who was quite the noblest and most modest of all the intended victims of the besotted tyrant there, Maxentius, whose conduct was only too like Maximin's. When she was told that the tyrant's pandars were at her door, and that her husband – a Roman prefect

1. Dorothea.   2. Sophronia.

at that – through fear had given them leave to seize her and take her away, she begged to be excused a moment, as if to dress herself for the occasion. Then she went into her own room, shut the door, and stabbed herself to the heart, dying instantly. Her dead body she left to the emperor's pimps; but by deeds that spoke more loudly than any words she proclaimed to all men then living or yet to come that the only unconquerable and indestructible possession was a Christian's virtue. So far could vileness be carried, as practised at one and the same time by the two tyrants who had divided east and west between them. Would anyone who sought the reason for these crimes fail to put his finger on the persecution against us? Particularly as this appalling state of confusion did not come to an end until Christians got back their freedom.

What happened to those outside the Church

15. Throughout the ten-year period of the persecution, their plotting and campaigning against each other continued without intermission. The seas were unnavigable, and wherever people sailed from they could not avoid being subjected to outrages of every sort: they were racked, and had their sides torn open, and were interrogated with the aid of an endless variety of tortures, on the pretext that they might be enemy agents; finally they were subjected to crucifixion or to punishment by fire. Then again the manufacture of shields and breastplates, and the preparation of javelins, spears, and other munitions of war, not to mention warships and naval equipment, went on apace everywhere, and no one could look for anything but an enemy attack any day. On them, too, fell the famine and pestilence that followed. I shall give the necessary details at the proper time.

The change for the better

16. Such were the conditions that persisted throughout the persecution, which in the tenth year by the grace of God came to a complete end, having begun to die down after the eighth. For when it became evident that we were in the kindly, beneficent keeping of divine and heavenly grace, an amazing thing happened – our rulers, the very people who had long been the driving force behind the campaign against us, changed their minds in a most astonishing manner and solemnly recanted, extinguishing by means of decrees sympathetic to us and ordinances of the mildest character the fire of persecution which had raged so fiercely. It was no human initiative that brought this about – no pity, as might be suggested, or humanity on the part of the rulers. Anything but that: they were from the start daily devising against us still further measures yet more drastic; by multifarious and constantly changing schemes they were for ever inventing new ways of outraging us. It was a manifest visitation of divine providence, which became reconciled to the common people but took action against the perpetrator of these crimes,[1] indignant with him as being primarily responsible for the whole iniquitous persecution. It was indeed inevitable that these things should come about as a divine judgement, but 'Woe', the Scripture says, 'to the man through whom the stumbling-block comes'.[2] He was pursued by a divinely ordained punishment, which began with his flesh and went on to his soul. Without warning, suppurative inflammation broke out round the middle of his genitals, then a deep-seated fistular ulcer: these ate their way incurably into his inmost bowels. From them came a teeming indescribable mass of worms, and a sickening smell was given off; for the whole of his hulking body, thanks to over-eating, had been transformed even before his illness into a huge lump of flabby fat, which then decomposed and pre-

1. Galerius.   2. Paraphrased from Luke xvii. 1.

sented those who came near with a revolting and horrifying sight. Of the doctors, some were unable to endure the over-powering and extraordinary stench, and were executed on the spot; others, unable to be of any assistance now that the entire mass had swollen up and deteriorated beyond hope of recovery, were put to death without mercy.[1]

The recantation of the emperors

17. As he wrestled with this terrible sickness, he was filled with remorse for his cruel treatment of God's servants. So he pulled himself together, and after first making open confession to the God of the universe, he called his court officials and ordered them to lose no time in stopping the persecution of Christians, and by an imperial law and decree to stimulate the building of churches and the performance of the customary rites, with the addition of prayers for the Emperor's Majesty. Action immediately followed the word, and imperial ordin-ances were published in all the cities, setting forth in the fol-lowing terms the recantation by the emperors of our time:

The Emperor Caesar Galerius Valerius Maximianus Invictus Augustus, Pontifex Maximus, Germanicus Maximus, Egyptiacus Maximus, Thebaicus Maximus, Sarmaticus Maximus five times, Persicus Maximus twice, Carpicus Maximus six times, Armeniacus Maximus, Medicus Maximus, Adiabenicus Maximus, Holder of Tri-bunician Authority for the twentieth time, Imperator for the nine-teenth, Consul for the eighth, Pater Patriae, Proconsul;[2] the Emperor Caesar Flavius Valerius Constantinus Pius Felix Invictus Augustus, Pontifex Maximus, Holder of Tribunician Authority, Imperator for the fifth time, Consul, Pater Patriae, Proconsul; and the Emperor

1. Four other potentates had died similar deaths – Herod the Great (Josephus: *Jewish War*, p. 110), Herod Agrippa I (Acts xii. 20–3 and Josephus *Ant.*), Antiochus I (2 Maccabees), and Sulla (Plutarch's *Lives*) – to be followed cen-turies later by Philip II of Spain.

2. Maximin's name is thought to have dropped out here; but see the first paragraph of Book 9.

Caesar Valerius Licinianus Licinius Pius Felix Invictus Augustus, Pontifex Maximus, Holder of Tribunician Authority for the fourth time,
Imperator for the third, Consul, Pater Patriae, Proconsul – to the
people of their several provinces, greeting.

Among the other steps that we are taking for the advantage and
benefit of the nation, we have desired hitherto that every deficiency
should be made good, in accordance with the established law and
public order of Rome; and we made provision for this – that the
Christians who had abandoned the convictions of their own forefathers should return to sound ideas. For through some perverse
reasoning such arrogance and folly had seized and possessed them that
they refused to follow the path trodden by earlier generations (and
perhaps blazed long ago by their own ancestors), and made their own
laws to suit their own ideas and individual tastes and observed these;
and held various meetings in various places.

Consequently, when we issued an order to the effect that they were
to go back to the practices established by the ancients, many of them
found themselves in great danger, and many were proceeded against
and punished with death in many forms. Most of them indeed persisted in the same folly, and we saw that they were neither paying to
the gods in heaven the worship that is their due nor giving any
honour to the god of the Christians.[1] So in view of our benevolence
and the established custom by which we invariably grant pardon to
all men, we have thought proper in this matter also to extend our
clemency most gladly, so that Christians may again exist and rebuild
the houses in which they used to meet, on condition that they do
nothing contrary to public order. In a further letter we shall explain
to the justices what principles they are to follow. Therefore, in view
of this our clemency, they are in duty bound to beseech their own god
for our security, and that of the state and of themselves, in order that
in every way the state may be preserved in health and they may be
able to live free from anxiety in their own homes.

So ran the edict in the original Latin, which I have turned
into Greek to the best of my ability. What happened subsequently it is now time to consider.

1. Because meetings were forbidden.

APPENDIX[1]

The author of the edict had no sooner made this confession, than he was released from his bodily torments; but in a very little while he was dead. It is on record that he had been the prime mover in the calamitous persecution, for long before the other emperors made a move he had used physical violence to pervert the Christians in the armed forces, after starting with the members of his own household. Some he had deprived of their military rank, some he had insulted most shamefully, others he had actually threatened with death. Finally, he had incited the fellow-emperors to undertake a worldwide persecution.

It would not be proper to pass over the deaths of these men in silence. Of the four who had shared worldwide rule, the two who were senior in years and status[2] abdicated less than two years after the start of the persecution, as I have already explained, and after passing the rest of their lifetimes like any ordinary citizens, met their end as follows. The one who had reached first place in status and years[3] succumbed to a prolonged and very painful physical disease. The one who held second place strangled himself, thereby fulfilling a demon-inspired prediction, for he had been guilty of innumerable atrocities. Of the junior pair, the occupant of the last place,[4] who as already stated was the person behind the whole persecution, suffered the fate described above, but his immediate superior, the kindest and mildest of emperors, Constantius, spent the whole of his reign in a manner worthy of his exalted position. In all ways he showed himself most considerate and benevolent towards everyone; above all, he stayed outside the campaign against us and saved God's servants among his subjects from injury and ill-usage, and he neither pulled

1. Found in about two thirds of the M ss., this appendix is undoubtedly the work of Eusebius, though not properly integrated into his book.

2. Diocletian and Maximian.

3. Diocletian.   4. Galerius.

down church buildings nor caused us any other mischief whatever. So he truly achieved a conclusion to his life that was happy and supremely blest; for he alone while still emperor died in an atmosphere of goodwill and glory, to be succeeded on the throne by a lawful son in every way most prudent and religious. He was immediately proclaimed Absolute Ruler and Augustus by the legions, and he determined to emulate his father's reverent attitude to our teaching.

Such were the ways in which, one by one, the lives of the four men of whom I have written above came to an end. Last of them to survive was the man of whom I wrote a little way back.[1] He, with those later admitted to the highest office,[2] in the document reproduced above published for all to read the confession which I have described.

1. Galerius, see p. 352.
2. Maximin, Constantine, and Licinius.

Book 9

The pretence of relaxation

1. The recantation of the imperial will set forth above was published up and down the whole of Asia and in the adjoining provinces of the empire. When this task had been accomplished, Maximin, tyrant in the east – a bitter enemy of religion if ever a man was, and most hostile to the worship of the God of the universe – found what was written little to his liking; instead of circulating the letter set forth above, he gave oral instructions to his subordinate officials to relax the campaign against us. As he could find no other way to reverse the decision of his superiors, he put on one side the ordinance set forth above, and making sure that in the areas under his control it should never be brought to light, he issued verbal instructions to his subordinate officials to relax the persecution against us. They put the order in writing for each other's information. For example, the man they had honoured with the title of His Excellency the Prefect, Sabinus, informed the provincial governors of the emperor's wishes in a letter written in Latin, the translation of which is as follows:

With the most shining and dedicated zeal the Divinity of our most divine masters, the Emperors, has long been resolved to lead the thoughts of all men to the holy and right way of life, in order that even those who apparently follow customs alien to the Romans might render to the immortal gods the worship that is their due. But the opposition and fierce resistance of some was so extreme that the sound logic of the order failed to shake their fixed purpose, and the

357

threatened punishment had no terrors for them. Since therefore the result of such behaviour was that many were involving themselves in danger, the Divinity of our masters, the most mighty potentates, in accordance with the habitual grandeur of their devotion to the gods, deeming it alien to their own most divine purpose that for such a cause they should involve the men in so great danger, issued a command that through my Dedicatedness your Sagacity should be informed in writing that if any of the Christians were found practising the religion of his own people, you must safeguard him from molestation and from danger, and must not on these grounds hold any man guilty of a punishable offence, inasmuch as in the course of so long a time it has become evident that it is impossible to persuade them by any means whatever to abandon their determined opposition. It is therefore your Vigilance's duty to write to the sheriffs, magistrates, and *praepositi*[1] of every urban district, in order that they may realize that it is incumbent on them to take no action that goes beyond what is here laid down.[2]

Thereupon the provincial governors, having decided that the recommendations in the letter they had received were genuine, wrote to the sheriffs, magistrates, and rural commissioners explaining the imperial decision. It was not only in writing that they gave effect to this policy, but much more by action. To make sure that the imperial will was carried out, they saw to it that all whom they were keeping shut up in prison because of their confession of the Deity were brought out and set free; indeed, they released those prisoners who as a punishment were shackled in the mines – for in their innocence they believed this to be what the emperor really intended.

When these recommendations had been carried out, it was as if all at once a light had shone out of a dark night. In every town could be seen crowded churches, overflowing congregations, and the appropriate ceremonies duly performed. This dumbfounded all the unconverted heathen, who were astonished at the miracle of this transformation and loudly proclaimed that the Christians' God was alone great and

1. Senior officials.   2. See p. 364 n.

true. Of our own people, those who had faithfully and manfully fought through the ordeal of the persecutions again held
their heads high in the sight of all; those whose faith had been
sickly and their souls storm-tossed made earnest efforts to be
made well, begging and imploring those who had stood firm
to hold out the right hand of deliverance, and beseeching God
to be merciful to them. Then, too, the gallant champions of
true religion were released from the misery of the mines and
allowed to return to their homes, exulting and beaming as
they passed through every town, full of unspeakable joy and a
confidence beyond description. Long columns of men and
women went on their way, singing psalms and hymns of
praise to God in the middle of the highways and city squares.
Those who a little while ago had been prisoners, driven from
their homeland and punished most cruelly, could be seen with
happy, smiling faces regaining their own hearths, so that even
those who had earlier been athirst for our blood, when they
saw this marvellous thing, so utterly unexpected, shared our
joy at what had happened.

The subsequent change for the worse: the idol at Antioch: resolutions attacking us: the forged 'Memoranda'

2. All this was more than could be borne by the tyrant who as
I have said ruled the eastern region, for everything noble was
hateful to him and all good men were objects of his enmity;
in fact, he did not tolerate this state of affairs for as long as
six months. He did all he could think of to overthrow the peace.
First, he found a pretext for trying to stop us from meeting
in the cemeteries;[1] then, through the agency of a number of
scoundrels, he sent embassies to himself to appeal against us,
having instigated the citizens of Antioch to ask him to grant
them a very great favour by absolutely forbidding any
Christian to live in their country, and to work it so that others

1. See p. 295 n.

suggested the same thing. The man behind all this belonged to Antioch itself – one Theotecnus, a clever unprincipled trickster who belied his name.[1] Apparently he was the city sheriff.

3. Time after time this man campaigned against us. He left no method untried in his determination to hunt our people out of hiding-places as if they were thieving scoundrels; he employed every device to defame and calumniate us; he engineered the deaths of thousands; finally he set up an image of Zeus the Friendly, with tricks and illusions; invented devilish rites, unholy initiations, and loathsome purifications;[2] and even in the emperor's presence displayed his magic arts by spurious oracular utterances. In fact, by subtle flattery of the emperor, this man aroused the demon against the Christians: the god, he said, had commanded 'the emperor's enemies', to be cleared right out of the city and its neighbourhood.

4. This man was the first to follow his bent, but all the other authorities in the cities under the same rule lost no time in following his lead: the provincial governors had seen at once that the emperor approved of such a course, and they had advised their subjects to act in this very way. The tyrant was most happy to approve their resolutions, by means of a rescript; so the persecution against us blazed up all over again.

Priests, if you please, were appointed in every town by Maximin himself – priests of the images, and high priests too[3] – men of the greatest note in political life and continuously in the public eye, who were filled with enthusiasm for the worship of the gods they served. The absurd superstition of the emperor, in short, was inducing all under him, rulers and ruled alike, to seek his favour by an all-out attack on us. This was the greatest favour that they could bestow on him, in

---

1. *Theotecnus* means 'God's child'.
2. Eusebius has found Dionysius's rich vocabulary very useful. See p. 293.
3. In imitation of bishops and archbishops.

return for the benefits they expected at his hands – to thirst
for our blood and show their spite against us in novel ways.

5. They actually forged *Memoranda* of Pilate and our Saviour,
full of every kind of blasphemy against Christ.[1] These, with
the approval of their superior, they sent to every district under
his command, announcing in edicts that they were to be
publicly displayed in every place, whether hamlet or city, for
all to see, and that they should be given to children by their
teachers instead of lessons, to study and learn by heart.[2]
   While these steps were being put into effect, an army officer
– called *dux* by the Romans – at Damascus in Phoenicia arranged
for some disreputable women to be removed by force from
the city square, and threatened to torture them. In this way
he compelled them to sign a statement to the effect that they
had once been Christians and were aware of breaches of the
law by Christians, who in their very churches were guilty of
immoral practices and everything else he wished the women
to say in defamation of the Faith. What they said he set down in
a report which he passed to the emperor, and at his command
he published the document in every city and district.   6. But
not long afterwards he, the officer, committed suicide and so
paid the penalty of his malignity.

Martyrdoms at this time

For us there was a resumption of banishments and harsh
persecution, and of bitter attacks on us by all the provincial
governors. As a result, some of the most notable preachers of
the word were sentenced to death, with no right of appeal.
Three of these in Emesa, a Phoenician town, confessed themselves Christians and were given to wild beasts as food. Among
them was a bishop, Silvanus, a very old man who had filled

1. See p. 60 n.
2. Indoctrination was not a twentieth-century invention.

this office for forty years. At the same time Peter, who had presided over the Alexandrian churches most admirably – a splendid example of a bishop in the nobility of his life and his intimate knowledge of Holy Scripture – was suddenly arrested for no reason and without warning, marched off then and there without explanation, and beheaded, as if by Maximin's command. With him many other Egyptian bishops suffered the same fate.

Lucian, a man of the highest character, self-disciplined and steeped in divinity, a presbyter of the Antioch diocese, was taken to Nicomedia, where the emperor then happened to be staying. Before the ruler he put forward his defence of the doctrine he upheld, and was sent to prison and to death.

So swift an onslaught did Maximin, in his hatred of all that is good, direct against us, that the earlier persecution seemed trifling in comparison with this.   7. In the middle of the cities – an unheard of thing – resolutions from cities attacking us, and rescripts embodying imperial decisions on the questions raised, were engraved on bronze tablets and posted up; and the children in the schools daily repeated the names of Jesus and Pilate and the insolent forged *Memoranda*.

Here I find it necessary to insert the actual document set up on tablets by Maximin, in order that the swaggering, arrogant presumption of this enemy of God may be clear to all, and with it the divine justice following hard on his heels with its unsleeping detestation of evil in the wicked. This it was that soon afterwards drove him to treat us in exactly the opposite way, and publish written laws declaring his policy.

COPY OF A TRANSLATION OF MAXIMIN'S RESCRIPT IN
REPLY TO THE RESOLUTIONS ATTACKING US, TAKEN FROM
THE TABLET IN TYRE

At last the feeble presumption of the human mind has succeeded in shaking off and scattering all the black fog of error that till now had wrapped the senses of men not so much wicked as unfortunate in the fatal darkness of ignorance, and was still assailing them; at last it has realized that the beneficent providence of the almighty gods governs it and keeps it secure. It is beyond me to express my extreme gratitude, pleasure, and delight at the magnificent proof you have given of your devout disposition; for even before this no one was unaware of the wonderful reverence and piety you always showed towards the immortal gods, evincing not a faith of bare and empty words but a constant and astonishing flow of notable deeds. And therefore your city deserves to be called the temple and abode of the immortal gods: there are many evidences to prove that it is the residence there of the celestial gods that causes it to flourish.

So it is that your city completely disregarded its private interests and did not press its earlier requests with reference to its own affairs, and when it saw that the adherents of that damnable folly were again beginning to spread – like a neglected and smouldering pyre which when it burns up again becomes a huge blazing mass – instantly and without a moment's delay it fled for refuge to our piety as to a mother-city of all religious feelings, appealing for some remedy and assistance. This salutary thought was undoubtedly planted in you by the gods because of the faith shown by your devotion to them. He therefore it was, he the most high and mighty Jupiter, the guardian of your most glorious city, the protector of your ancestral gods, of your women and children, of your hearth and homes, from all destruction and decay, who inspired your breasts with this wholesome resolve, clearly revealing how wonderful and glorious and salutary it is with due reverence to approach the worship and sacred ceremonies of the immortal gods.

Who could be found so stupid or devoid of all sense as not to see that it is thanks to the beneficent activity of the gods that the soil does not refuse the seeds committed to it and disappoint the hopes and expectations of the farmer? and that the form of impious war does not rise up irresistibly upon the earth while the balmy air of heaven grows foul and men's bodies covered with filth are dragged off to death? and that the sea does not rage and swell under the blasts of the squally winds? and that typhoons do not burst without warning, bringing destruction in their wake? and again that the earth, nurse and mother of all, does not sink down from her deepest hollows with

363

a frightful tremor and the mountains that rise from her face disappear into the chasms thus formed? All these things, and things more terrible still, have in days gone by happened over and over again, as we all know. And all of them happened at once as a result of the fatal error implicit in the empty folly of these immoral people, when it enslaved their minds and by its shameful deeds came near to making the entire world suffer. . . .

Let them cast their eyes on the wide plains, where already the crops are ripe with waving ears of corn, and the meadows, thanks to abundance of rain, are bright with flowering plants, and the weather we enjoy is temperate and very mild. Let them rejoice also, every one of them, that through our piety, our sacrifices, and our adoration, the power of the most mighty and most unyielding air has been propitiated; and let them therefore rejoice that they benefit by the most tranquil peace in security and repose. As for all those who have been brought safely out of the blind error in which they wandered, and restored to a right and satisfactory state of mind, let them the more rejoice, as if they had been rescued from a sudden tempest or from a grave illness and were henceforth gathering from life a rich harvest. But if they persist in their damnable folly, let them be thrown out as you requested, and driven right away from your city and neighbourhood, in order that thereby, in accordance with your praiseworthy enthusiasm in this matter, your city may be purged of all contamination and impiety, and in pursuit of its set purpose may with due reverence give itself to the regular worship of the immortal gods.

That you may know how welcome your request in this matter has been to us, and how anxious our mind is, apart from resolutions and entreaties, and of its own accord, to exercise beneficence, we permit your Dedicatedness to ask whatever munificence you wish in return for this your devout purpose. Make up your minds now to do this and receive your reward: it will be yours without the least delay. The fact of its being granted to your city will provide evidence for all time of your devoted piety towards the immortal gods.[1]

---

1. With this flowery effusion compare the absurd pomposity of the document quoted on p. 357. Readers who think of the Romans as simple, practical, and matter-of-fact people who wrote with brevity, sanity, and clarity may well be astonished. Of the addiction of the later emperors to the accumulation of names and titles we had a striking instance on p. 353.

This attack on us was engraved on tablets in every province of the Empire, depriving us of any hope, humanly speaking, so that in full accordance with the divine saying, if possible these things should trip up even the elect.[1] Indeed, generally speaking, in the majority expectation was fainting,[2] when all at once, while those in charge of the document attacking us were on their way, with a few miles still to go in some districts, God, the Defender of His own Church, curbing the loud boasting of the tyrant against us, revealed Himself as our ally in heaven.

Famine, pestilence, and war

8. It was the winter season, and the usual rains and showers were withholding their normal downpour, when without warning famine struck, followed by pestilence and an outbreak of a different disease – a malignant pustule, which because of its fiery appearance was known as a carbuncle. This spread over the entire body, causing great danger to the sufferers; but the eyes were the chief target for attack, and hundreds of men, women, and children lost their sight through it.

Besides this, the tyrant had to cope with the war against the Armenians, people who from a very early date had been friends and allies of Rome. They were Christians and zealous adherents of the Deity; so the God-hater attempted to force them to sacrifice to idols and demons, thereby turning them from friends into foes and from allies into enemies.

The conjunction of all these things at one and the same time disproved the presumptuous tyrant's loud boasting against the Deity, for he had had the effrontery to declare that his devotion to the idols and his attack on us prevented any famine or plague or even war from occurring in his time.

1. Quoted from Matt. xxiv. 24, with the same inaccuracy as on p. 277.
2. A very free paraphrase of Luke xxi. 26.

These things, coming on him together and at the same time, formed the prelude to his own downfall. In the Armenian war the emperor was worn out as completely as his legions: the rest of the people in the cities under his rule were so horribly wasted by famine and pestilence that a single measure of wheat fetched 2,500 Attic drachmas.[1] Hundreds were dying in the cities, still more in the country villages, so that the rural registers which once contained so many names now suffered almost complete obliteration; for at one stroke food shortage and epidemic disease destroyed nearly all the inhabitants. Some, indeed, thought fit to sell their most precious possessions to those who were better off, in return for a tiny quantity of food; others parted with their treasures one at a time till they were driven by want to desperate straits; while some ruined their bodily health by chewing small fragments of cattle fodder and recklessly swallowing poisonous plants, with fatal results. As for the women, some leaders of city society were driven by their straits to such shameless necessity that they went out to beg in the public squares, showing signs of their gentle nurture in their shy looks and the care with which they were dressed.

Some people, shrunken like ghosts and at death's door, tottered and slipped about in all directions till, unable to stand, they fell to the ground; and as they lay face down in the middle of the streets, they implored passers-by to hand them a tiny scrap of bread, and with their life at its last gasp they called out that they were hungry – anything else than this anguished cry was beyond their strength. Others – men classed as well-to-do – were astounded by the number of beggars, and after giving to scores, they adopted for the future a hard and merciless attitude, in the expectation that very soon they themselves would be no better off; so that in the middle of public squares and narrow streets dead and naked bodies lay about unburied for days on end, furnishing a most distressing

1. Equivalent in purchasing power to £500 in the 1960s.

sight to all who saw them. Indeed some even became food
for dogs, and it was mainly for this reason that the survivors
turned to killing the dogs, for fear they might go mad and
begin devouring human flesh. No less terrible was the pestilence which consumed every household, particularly those
which were so well off for food that famine could not wipe
them out. Men of great wealth, rulers, governors, and numberless officials, left by the famine to the epidemic disease as
if on purpose, met a sudden and very swift end. Lamentations
filled the air on every side, and in all the lanes, squares, and
streets there was nothing to be seen except processions of
mourners with the usual flute-playing and beating of breasts.
In this way death waged war with these two weapons of
pestilence and famine, swallowing whole families in a few
moments, so that two or three dead bodies could be seen
carried to the graveyard by a single group of mourners.

Such was the reward for Maximin's loud boasts and the
cities' resolutions against us, while the fruits of the Christians'
limitless enthusiasm and devotion became evident to all the
heathen. Alone in the midst of this terrible calamity they
proved by visible deeds their sympathy and humanity. All
day long some continued without rest to tend the dying and
bury them – the number was immense, and there was no one
to see to them; others rounded up the huge number who had
been reduced to scarecrows all over the city and distributed
loaves to them all, so that their praises were sung on every
side, and all men glorified the God of the Christians and
owned that they alone were pious and truly religious: did
not their actions speak for themselves?

At the end of all this, when God, the great and heavenly
Defender of Christians, had by such means displayed his
wrath as a warning to all men in return for the cruel wrongs
they had done us, He again restored to us the kindly, cheering
radiance of His providence towards us. As if in black darkness, He most wonderfully illumined us with the light of

peace from Himself, making it plain to all that God himself had been watching over us throughout: at first He had scourged His people, and by severe trials had in due time corrected them; then again, after sufficient chastisement, He had shown Himself gracious and kind to all whose hopes were fixed on Him.

The victory of God's beloved emperors

9. Thus Constantine, an emperor and son of an emperor, a religious man and son of a most religious man, most prudent in every way, as stated above – and Licinius the next in rank, both of them honoured for their wise and religious outlook, two men dear to God – were roused by the King of kings, God of the universe, and Saviour against the two most irreligious tyrants and declared war on them. God came to their aid in a most marvellous way, so that at Rome Maxentius fell at the hands of Constantine, and the ruler of the East[1] survived him only a short time and himself came to a most shameful end at the hands of Licinius, who at that time was still sane.

The senior in imperial rank and position, Constantine, was the first to feel pity for the victims of tyranny at Rome. Calling in prayer on God in heaven and on His Word, Jesus Christ Himself, the Saviour of all, to come to his aid, he advanced at the head of all his forces, intent on recovering for the Romans the liberty of their ancestors. Maxentius, for his part, pinned his faith more to the wiles of a trickster than to the goodwill of his subjects, and could not pluck up courage to go an inch beyond the city gates. Instead he employed a vast host of heavy infantry and countless centuries of legionaries to garrison every region, district, or city, in the neighbourhood of Rome or anywhere in Italy, that he had reduced to slavery. The emperor who clung to God for aid attacked the first, second, and

1. Maximin.

third of the tyrant's concentrations, completely defeated them all, overran a great part of Italy, and arrived almost at the gates of Rome. Then, to save him from the necessity of fighting Romans because of the tyrant, God Himself as it were dragged the tyrant with chains a long way from the city gates; and the words enshrined long ago in Holy Writ as a warning to the wicked – words regarded as mythical by most and disbelieved, but to believers worthy of all belief – by their unmistakable truth compelled the belief of practically everyone, believer or unbeliever, when he saw the miracle before his eyes. In the time of Moses himself and the godfearing nation of the ancient Hebrews,

> The chariots of Pharaoh and his hosts He hurled into the sea;
> His picked horsemen, his captains, He swallowed up in the Red Sea;
> With the deep He covered them.

In just the same way Maxentius and his bodyguard of infantry and pikemen

> Went down into the depths like a stone[1]

when he turned back before the God-given might of Constantine, and began to cross the river in his path, having himself constructed a perfectly sound bridge of boats from one bank to the other, contriving thus an instrument for his own destruction. And so we might say

> He made a pit and dug it,
> And shall fall into the ditch that he fashioned.
> His labour shall return on to his own head,
> And on his own crown shall his unrighteousness come down.[2]

In this way, through the breaking of the floating bridge, the crossing collapsed, and in a moment the boats, men and all, went to the bottom, and first the prime villain, then his

---

1. Ex. xv. 4–5.   2. Ps. vii. 15–16.

bodyguard of picked men, in the way foretold by the inspired sayings

Sank like lead in the mighty waters.[1]

Thus, if not in words at any rate in deeds, like the great servant Moses and his companions, the men who with God's help had won the victory might well sing the same hymn as was sung about the villainous tyrant of old:

Let us sing to the Lord, for gloriously has He been glorified:
Horse and rider He threw into the Sea.
The Lord became my helper and protector, to my salvation.[2]

And

Who is like Thee among the gods, Lord? who is like Thee?
Glorified among saints, marvellous in praises, doing wonders?[3]

These things, and many others akin to them and just like them, Constantine by his very deeds sang as a hymn to the universal Lord, the author of his triumph, God. Then he rode into Rome with songs of victory, and together with women and tiny children, all the members of the Senate and citizens of the highest distinction in other spheres, and the whole populace of Rome, turned out in force and with shining eyes and all their heart welcomed him as deliverer, saviour, and benefactor, singing his praises with insatiate joy. But he, as if he possessed an innate reverence for God, was not in the least excited by their shouts or elated by their plaudits, fully aware that his help came from God: at once he ordered a trophy of the Saviour's Passion to be set up under the hand of his own statue – indeed, he ordered them to place him in the most frequented spot in Rome, holding the sign of the Saviour in his right hand, and to engrave this inscription in Latin. I reproduce it exactly:

By this saving sign, the true proof of courage, I saved your city from the yoke of the tyrant and set her free; furthermore I freed the

1. Ex. xv. 10.　　2. Ex. xv. 1–2.　　3. Ex. xv. 11.

Senate and People of Rome and restored them to their ancient renown and splendour.

After this, Constantine himself and with him the Emperor
Licinius – whose mind was not yet unhinged by the mania
which later took possession of him – first made things right
with God, the author of all their successes; then both with
one will and intent formulated on behalf of the Christians a
most thoroughgoing law in the fullest terms. Next, an account of the wonders that God had performed for them, of
their triumph over the tyrant, and of the law itself, was sent
to Maximin, who was still master of the eastern provinces
and posing as their friend. He, tyrant that he was, was very
upset by what he learnt. He did not wish it to appear that he
was giving way to others; on the other hand, he dared not
suppress the order, for fear of those who had issued it. So, as
if on his own initiative, he perforce indited to the governors
under him this first missive on behalf of the Christians; in it he
lays claim to actions he had never yet taken, lying about himself.

COPY OF A TRANSLATION OF THE TYRANT'S LETTER

Jovius Maximinus Augustus to Sabinus. I am satisfied that it is obvious to Your Steadfastness and to everybody else that our masters
Diocletian and Maximian, our fathers, when they realized that nearly
everyone had abandoned the worship of the gods and associated himself with the people known as Christians, were justified in giving
orders that all who withdrew from the worship of their own immortal gods should by public correction and punishment be recalled
to the worship of the gods. But when I first arrived so auspiciously in
the east I was informed that in some localities a great number of
people capable of service to the community were for the reason
already given being deported by judges, so I gave instructions to each
of the judges that for the future none of them was to treat the provincials harshly, but rather by coaxing and persuasion recall them to
the worship of the gods. The immediate result was that in conformity with my order the judges carried out their instructions and no one

371

in the eastern region was either deported or interfered with, but rather as a result of the leniency with which they were treated they were recalled to the worship of the gods.

Later, however, when last year I paid an auspicious visit to Nicomedia and was staying there, some of the citizens presented themselves before me, bringing images of the gods and earnestly requesting that in no circumstances should such people be allowed to live in their city. But when I was informed that large numbers of men who practised that same religion lived in that very region, I gave them this answer: I thanked them heartily for their request, but saw that it was by no means unanimous. So, if there were some who persisted in the same superstition, each must keep to his purpose in accordance with his own choice, and if they wished they could acknowledge the worship of the gods. Notwithstanding, to the people of Nicomedia and the other cities which with such enthusiasm have made the same request to me – that none of the Christians should live in their cities – I had no option but to give a friendly answer; for this very principle had been maintained by all my predecessors from the beginning, and the gods themselves, without whom all mankind and the whole administration of the Empire would perish, willed that such a request, put forward on behalf of the worship of their Deity, should be confirmed by me.

The position therefore is this. Particular instructions have in the past been sent in writing to Your Dedicatedness, and express commands have similarly laid it down that provincials who have made up their mind to adhere to such a custom must be treated not harshly, but with forbearance and restraint. Nevertheless, to prevent their suffering insults or blackmail at the hands of *beneficiarii*[1] or anyone else, I have thought it desirable to send this further letter to draw the attention of Your Steadfastness to the advantages of coaxing and persuading the provincials into a proper regard for the gods. If therefore anyone decides by his own choice that the worship of the gods must be acknowledged, such persons may appropriately be welcomed; but if some choose to follow their own worship, you will please leave them free to do so.

My final recommendation to Your Dedicatedness is that you adhere to these instructions, and that you give no one authority to sub-

---

1. Privileged soldiers or officials.

ject our provincials to insults and blackmail; for, as already stated, it
is by persuasion and coaxing that our provincials can more appropriately be recalled to the worship of the gods. And in order that this
our command may come to the knowledge of all our provincials you
are requested to issue an edict of your own, and so give publicity to
what we have commanded.

As it was under the compulsion of necessity and not in
accordance with his own wishes that he sent out these commands, it was now universally recognized that he was neither
truthful nor trustworthy, for already on a previous occasion,
after making a similar concession, his attitude had been inconsistent and hypocritical. So none of our people ventured to hold
a meeting or appear in public, because not even this was allowed him by the letter, which merely permitted us to be
protected from deliberate cruelty, and gave no encouragement to the holding of meetings or building of churches or
performance of any of our normal practices. And yet the
advocates of peace and true religion had sent him written
instructions to allow these very things, and by laws and
decrees had conceded them to all their subjects. But this
unprincipled scoundrel had made up his mind not to budge an
inch – till he found himself in the grip of divine Justice and
at long last driven willy-nilly to give way.

Close of the tyrant's lives

10. His downfall was brought about by the following circumstance. The burden of the government with which he had so
undeservedly been entrusted was too heavy for his shoulders,
and for want of a prudent and imperial mentality he was
clumsy in his handling of affairs; above all, he was senselessly
elated by arrogance and boastfulness, even at the expense of
his colleagues in the Empire, who were vastly superior to him
in birth, upbringing, and education, in character and intellect,

and in the most important thing of all – prudence and reverence for the true God. He began to display presumption and
effrontery, publicly proclaiming himself first in rank. Then,
pushing his madness to the point of utter dementia, he broke
the treaty he had made with Licinius and brought about a war
to the death. It was not long before he had produced universal
confusion and set every city in a turmoil. He concentrated all
available forces, forming an army of immense size, and set
out in battle array to challenge Licinius, pinning his hopes to
demons whom, if you please, he regarded as gods, and
supremely confident, in view of the immense numbers of his
infantry forces.

When the armies met,[1] he found himself deprived of God's
assistance, and it was to his rival, who was still on the throne,
that the one and only God of all Himself assigned the victory.
First to perish was the heavy infantry on which he had placed
such reliance; then his personal bodyguard deserted him,
leaving him utterly defenceless, and went over to his con-
queror. So the wretched man lost no time in stripping off the
imperial insignia, of which he was so unworthy,[2] and un-
manly, craven coward as he was, slipped unnoticed into the
crowd. Then he ran this way and that, hiding in fields and
villages. But though he tried so hard to save his skin, he only
just succeeded in eluding his pursuers, proving by his own
straits the absolute trustworthiness and truth of the inspired
sayings:

> No king is saved by great power,
> And a giant will not be saved by the fulness of his strength;
> Vain is a horse for safety,
> And by the fulness of his power he will not be saved.
> Lo, the eyes of the Lord are on those that fear Him,
> Those that hope in His mercy,
> To deliver their souls from death.[3]

1. At Campus Serenus in Thrace on 30 April 313.
2. Like Pompey at Pharsalus.   3. Ps. xxxiii. 16–19.

In this very way the tyrant, full of shame, reached his own territory.[1] There in his insane fury he began by seizing many priests and prophets of the gods whom he had once so revered and whose oracles had inflamed his warlike ardour, and – on the ground that they had tricked and deceived him, and above all that they had betrayed his safety – he put them to death. Next, he paid tribute to the Christians' God, and to safeguard their freedom drew up a law that went the whole way to meet their case. But the sands had run out, and in a few days his life came to a miserable end.

The law issued by him was as follows:

COPY OF THE TYRANT'S ORDINANCE IN FAVOUR OF THE CHRISTIANS, TRANSLATED FROM LATIN INTO GREEK

The Emperor Caesar Gaius Valerius Maximinus, Germanicus Sarmaticus, Pius Felix Invictus Augustus. That in every way we devote our constant attention to the benefit of our provincials, and desire to furnish them with those things by which the advantage of all is most fully secured, with all such things as are to the advantage and benefit of the community as a whole, tending to the public advantage and meeting the wishes of each individual, is a truth of which all are aware, for everyone who looks at the facts themselves must realize without a shadow of doubt that it is so – of that I am convinced. Whereas therefore before this it has come to our knowledge that with the excuse that orders had been given by Diocletian and Maximian, our most divine fathers, that Christian assemblies were prohibited, blackmail and robbery had been practised on a large scale by public employees, and that with the passage of time this was causing increasing hurt to our provincials – whose interests we strongly desire to be carefully considered – as their own personal possessions were being whittled away: we have sent letters to the governors of each province in the past year, decreeing that if any man chose to follow such a custom or the same form of worship, he might without hindrance hold on to his purpose and be hindered or prevented by none, and that they should have freedom, without any fear or suspicion, to

1. Cilicia.

do exactly as each man pleased. But even so it has not escaped our notice that some of the judges have been disregarding our commands and causing our people to feel doubts about our instruction, making them more hesitant to participate in those facts of worship that accorded with their desires.

In order therefore that for the future all suspicion or doubt due to fear may be done away, we have decreed that this ordinance shall be promulgated, making it clear to all that everyone who chooses to follow this sect and form of worship may, in accordance with this our indulgence and in fulfilment of his own choice and desire, participate in such acts of worship as he was accustomed and wishful to practise. Permission to build 'the Lord's houses',[1] as they call them, has also been accorded. Moreover, in order that our indulgence may be yet greater, we have thought it good to make this further decree: if any houses and lands which before this were the legal property of the Christians have through the command of our predecessors passed into the ownership of the Treasury, or been confiscated by any city council – whether these have been publicly auctioned or bestowed as a favour on an individual – all these shall by our command be restored to their former legal owners, the Christians, in order that in this also our piety and loving care may be apparent to all.

These were the tyrant's words, coming less than a year after the posting on tablets of his anti-Christian ordinances. The very man by whom such a little while before we had been judged impious and godless and ruinous to public life – so that we were not permitted to live in the country or the desert, much less in a city – was now drawing up pro-Christian ordinances and decrees; and those who so recently were being destroyed by fire and sword and given as food for beasts and birds before his eyes, and were undergoing every kind of punishment and torture and death – as if, poor wretches, they were godless and impious – are now allowed by the same man to practise their form of worship and per-

1. This is the first appearance in literature of the word *kyriakon*, which we have corrupted into 'kirk' and 'church'. Everywhere else in this work the word *ekklesia* is used, meaning 'church' in any sense.

mitted to rebuild the Lord's houses; and the tyrant himself allows that they have legal rights!

When he had allowed all this he received a reward, of a sort, for doing so; at any rate, he got a great deal less than his deserts when he was struck all at once by God's scourge, and in the second encounter of the war met his end. The character of his end was not such as befalls the general at the head of his army, who for the sake of his friends and the right again and again plays the man and fearlessly meets a glorious fate in battle, but like an impious enemy of God, while his army still held its position on the field he stayed at home in hiding, till he paid the penalty that fitted his crimes. All at once he was struck by God's scourge over his whole body, so that he was plagued with terrible, agonizing pains and fell prone; he was wasted by hunger, and the whole of his flesh was consumed by an invisible fire sent from God, so that all the contours of his former shape disintegrated and disappeared, and nothing but a collection of dry bones, like a phantom reduced by long years to a skeleton, was left, so that the onlookers could imagine nothing else than that his body had become the grave of his soul, which was interred in what was already a corpse and completely disintegrated. As the fever that consumed him blazed up ever more fiercely from the depths of his marrow, his eyes stood out of his head and fell from their sockets, leaving him blind. But even in this condition he could still breathe, and made open confession to the Lord, begging for death. So at long last he acknowledged that he deserved these torments because of his furious onslaught on Christ, and all was over.

Final destruction of the enemies of true religion

11. The way had now been left clear by Maximin, the last survivor of the enemies of true religion and unmistakably the worst. So the re-establishment of the churches from the

foundations was by the grace of Almighty God taken in hand, and the message of Christ, making itself clearly heard to the glory of the God of the universe, was preached with greater freedom than before, while the anti-religious activities of the enemies of true religion were covered with the utmost shame and dishonour. For Maximin had been the first to be pro-claimed by the supreme rulers a common enemy of all and posted in public notices as a most anti-religious, abominable, and God-hated tyrant. Of the portraits set up in every city in his honour and his children's, some were flung from a height to the ground and smashed, others had their faces blacked out with dark paint and were damaged beyond repair. The many statues, too, that had been erected in his honour were similarly thrown down and smashed, and lay there an object of jesting and horseplay to all who wished to insult and abuse them.

The next step was to strip the other enemies of true religion of all their honours, and to execute all Maximin's sympathizers especially those in government circles who had held office under him, and as a sop to him had poured violent and irre-sponsible abuse on our teaching. Such was the man who was higher in his favour and more respected than anyone else, the most trustworthy of his friends, Peucetius, consul a second and a third time and by Maximin's appointment chief finance minister; another was Culcianus, who had held every office in turn, a man who had prided himself on the murder of innumerable Christians in Egypt; to say nothing of many others who had been chief contributors to the strengthening and extending of Maximin's tyranny.

Theotecnus[1] too was called to account, for justice was determined that what he had done to the Christians should never pass into oblivion. For when he set up the idol at Antioch he had seemed to be on top of the world, and indeed was rewarded with a governorship by Maximin, but when Licinius arrived at Antioch, he hunted out the impostors and

1. See p. 360.

tortured the prophets and priests of the newly made idol, to
find out the means by which they perpetrated their frauds.
When these tortures made it impossible to hide the truth, and
they revealed that the whole mystery was a fraud contrived by
the arts of Theotecnus, Licinius gave all of them their deserts:
first Theotecnus himself and then his partners in imposture
were subjected to elaborate tortures and handed over to the
executioner.

To these were added the sons of Maximin, who had already
made them partners in his imperial honours, with their
features publicly displayed in painted portraits. Those who
hitherto had vaunted their kinship with the tyrant and arro-
gantly attempted to lord it over all and sundry suffered the
same fate, with every circumstance of shame; for they did not
receive correction[1] or know or understand the precept in the
inspired books:

> Put not your trust in princes,
> In the sons of men, in whom is no salvation.
> His breath shall go forth and he shall return to his earth;
> In that day shall perish all their thoughts.[2]

Thus the wicked were purged away, and the imperial
powers that had been theirs were preserved stable and undisputed for Constantine and Licinius and for them alone. They
made it their first duty to purge the world of enmity towards
God, and recognizing the blessings He had lavished upon
them, they showed their high purpose and love of God, their
devotion and gratitude to the Deity, by their decree in favour
of the Christians.

1. A reminiscence of Zeph. iii. 2.   2. Ps. cxlvi. 3–4.

Book 10

The peace bestowed on us by God

1. Thanks be to God, the Almighty, the King of the universe, for all His mercies; and heartfelt thanks to the Saviour and Redeemer of our souls, Jesus Christ, through whom we pray that peace from troubles outside and troubles in the heart may be kept for us stable and unshaken for ever.

Together with my prayers I now add Book 10 of the *History of the Church* to its predecessors. This I shall dedicate to you, my most worshipful Paulinus, calling on you to set the seal on the entire work; and it is appropriate that in a perfect number I should here set out the perfect account in celebration of the re-establishment of the churches, obeying the Divine Spirit when He exhorts us thus:

> Sing to the Lord a new song, for He has done marvellous things;
> His right hand and His holy arm have wrought salvation for Him.
> The Lord has made known His salvation;
> In the sight of the heathen He has revealed His righteousness.[1]

As these inspired lines command me, let me now obediently sing aloud the new song, because after those terrifying darksome sights and stories I was now privileged to see and celebrate such things as in truth many righteous men and martyrs of God before us desired to see on earth and did not see, and to hear and did not hear.[2] But they, hastening with all speed,

---

1. Ps. xcviii. 1–2.   2. Adapted from Matt. xiii. 17.

attained far better things in the heavens, caught up in a paradise of divine pleasure;[1] whereas I, acknowledging that even
my present lot is better than I deserve, have been more than
amazed at the bountiful grace of its Author, and am duly
filled with wonder, worshipping Him with my whole soul's
strength, and testifying to the truth of the written prophecies
which declare:

> Come hither and behold the works of the Lord,
> What wonders He has wrought in the world,
> Making wars cease to the ends of the world:
> The bow He will break and will shatter the weapon,
> And the shields He will burn up with fire.[2]

Happy that all this has been clearly fulfilled in my own time
let me proceed with the next part of my story.

Destruction, in the way described, had overtaken the whole
brood of God's enemies, and at one stroke had blotted them
out from human sight. Thus yet another inspired saying had
been fulfilled:

> I saw the wicked high exalted,
> And lifted up like the cedars of Lebanon.
> And I passed by, and lo, he was not;
> And I sought his place, and it was not found.[3]

From that time on a day bright and radiant, with no cloud
overshadowing it, shone down with shafts of heavenly light
on the churches of Christ throughout the world, nor was
there any reluctance to grant even those outside our community the enjoyment, if not of equal blessings, at least of an
effluence from and a share in the things that God had bestowed on us.

1. See 2 Cor. xii. 4.   2. Ps. xlvi. 8–9.   3. Ps. xxxvii. 33–6.

Re-establishment of the churches

2. Thus all men living were free from oppression by the
tyrants; and released from their former miseries, they all in
their various ways acknowledged as the only true God the
Defender of the godly. Above all for us who had fixed our
hopes on the Christ of God there was unspeakable happiness,
and a divine joy blossomed in all hearts as we saw that every
place which a little while before had been reduced to dust by
the tyrants' wickedness was now, as if from a prolonged and
deadly stranglehold, coming back to life; and that cathedrals
were again rising from their foundations high into the air, and
far surpassing in magnificence those previously destroyed by
the enemy.

Emperors too, the most exalted, by a succession of ordinances in favour of the Christians, confirmed still further and
more surely the blessings that God showered upon us; and a
stream of personal letters from the emperor reached the
bishops, accompanied by honours and gifts of money. I shall
take the opportunity at the proper place in my account to
inscribe in this book as on a sacred tablet these communica-
tions, translated from Latin into Greek, in order that all who
come after us may bear them in remembrance.

Dedication ceremonies everywhere

3. The next stage was the spectacle prayed and longed for
by us all – dedication festivals in the cities and consecrations
of the newly built places of worship, convocations of bishops,
gatherings of representatives from far distant lands, friendly
intercourse between congregation and congregation, uni-
fication[1] of the members of Christ's body conjoint in one
harmony. In accordance with a prophet's prediction, which
mystically signified beforehand what was to be, there came

1. A familiar word – *enosis*.

together bone to bone[1] and joint to joint, and all that in riddling oracles the scripture infallibly foretold. There was one power of the divine Spirit coursing through all the members, one soul in them all,[2] the same enthusiasm for the faith, one hymn of praise on all their lips. Yes, and our leaders performed ceremonies with full pomp, and ordained priests the sacraments and majestic rites of the Church, here with the singing of psalms and intoning of the prayers given us from God, there with the carrying out of divine and mystical ministrations; while over all were the ineffable symbols of the Saviour's Passion. And together, the people of every age, male and female alike, with all their powers of mind, rejoicing in heart and soul, gave glory through prayers and thanksgiving to the Author of their happiness, God Himself.

Every one of the dignitaries of the Church present delivered a public oration according to his ability, inspiring the great audience. 4. One of the moderately capable[3] came forward into their midst with a prepared discourse. It was a church assembly, and the many pastors present gave him a quiet and orderly hearing. Addressing himself personally to a single bishop, an admirable man and one dear to God, through whose initiative and enthusiasm the most magnificent cathedral in Phoenicia had been built at Tyre, he delivered the following address.

FESTIVAL ORATION ON THE BUILDING OF THE CHURCHES,
ADDRESSED TO PAULINUS, BISHOP OF TYRE

Friends of God, and priests[4] clothed with the sacred vestment and the heavenly crown of glory, the divine unction and priestly garments of the Holy Spirit; and you, so young yet the pride of the holy temple

1. Ez. xxxvii. 7. Eusebius has added the 'joints' to secure the play upon words.
2. Acts iv. 32.   3. One may guess who.
4. Eusebius here writes not *presbyteroi* but *hiereis*, equivalent to Latin *sacerdotes*; he uses the corresponding adjective just below.

of God, honoured with ripe wisdom from God yet renowned for the precious works and deeds of virtue in its youthful prime, on whom the God who holds the entire universe in His hand has Himself bestowed the supreme honour of building His house upon earth and re-establishing it for Christ, His only begotten and firstborn Word, and for Christ's holy and majestic bride – shall I call you a new Bezalel,[1] the master builder of a divine tabernacle, or a Solomon, king of a new and far nobler Jerusalem, or a new Zerubbabel, who adorned the temple of God with the glory that was far greater than the old?[2] And you too, nurslings of the sacred flock of Christ, home of good words, school of self-discipline, and university of true religion, earnest and dear to God.

Long ago, as the inspired records of miraculous signs from God and the wonders performed by the Lord in the service of men were read aloud in our hearing, we might well send up hymns and songs to God; for we were taught to say:

O God, with our ears have we heard, our fathers have told us,
The work which Thou didst in their days, in ancient days.[3]

But now it is no longer by hearing the spoken word that men learn of the uplifted arm and the heavenly right hand of our God, All-gracious and King of all; but by deeds, if we may put it so, and with our very eyes we see that the traditions of an earlier age were trustworthy and true. And so we may raise our voices in a second hymn of victory and cry aloud:

As we have heard, so also we have seen
In the city of the Lord of Hosts, in the city of our God.[4]

And in what city but this new-made city built by God? It is the Church of the Living God, the pillar and basis of truth,[5] and of it another inspired saying joyously declares:

Glorious things have been spoken of thee,
O city of God.[6]

1. Ex. xxxv. 30.   2. Hag. ii. 9.   3. Ps. xliv. 1.
4. Ps. xlviii. 8.   5. 1 Tim. iii. 15.   6. Ps. lxxxvii. 3.

And since in this city God the All-Gracious has brought us together
through the grace of His Only-begotten, let each of the invited guests
sing, nay shout,

> I was glad when they said to me
> 'Into the house of the Lord we will go'

and

> Lord, I have loved the beauty of Thy house,
> And the dwelling-place of Thy glory.[1]

It is not only for each by himself, but for all of us together with
one spirit and one soul, to give glory and praise, saying:

> Great is the Lord and highly to be praised
> In the city of our God, in His holy mountain.[2]

For great He is in truth, and great is His house, lofty and stretching
far, and lovely in beauty beyond the sons of men.[3] Great is the Lord,
who alone does wondrous things; great is He who does things great
and unsearchable, glorious and marvellous things of which there is
no number;[4] great is He who changes times and seasons, removing
kings and setting them up, raising the poor man from the ground and
from the dunghill lifting up the needy.[5] He has pulled down princes
from their thrones and exalted the humble from the ground; the
hungry He has filled with good things and the arms of the proud He
has broken.[6] Not only for believers but also for unbelievers has He
proved true the record of the ancient narratives, He the Doer of
wonders, the Doer of great things, the Master of the universe, the
Fashioner of the whole world, the Almighty, the All-Gracious, the
one and only God. To Him then let us sing the new song with this
as the background to our thought:

> To Him who alone does wondrous things
> (For everlasting is His mercy);
> To Him who smote great kings,
> And slew mighty kings
> (For everlasting is His mercy).
> For in our low estate He remembered us,
> And redeemed us from our adversaries.[7]

1. Ps. cxxii. 1 and xxvi. 8.   2. Ps. xlviii. 1.
3. Baruch iii. 24 and Ps. xlv. 2.   4. Ps. lxxii. 18 and Job ix. 10.
5. Dan. ii. 21 and Ps. cxiii. 7.   6. Luke i. 52–3 and Job xxxviii. 15.
7. Ps. cxxxvi. 4, 17–18, 23–4.

The Father of the universe may we praise aloud in such strains without ceasing. The second source of our blessings, our Guide to the knowledge of God, the Teacher of true religion, the Destroyer of the wicked, the Tyrannicide, the Reformer of our life, our Deliverer from despair, Jesus, let us glorify, His name ever on our lips. For He alone, being an All-Gracious Father's unique, All-Gracious Son, in fulfilment of His Father's love for man, most willingly put on the nature of us men who lay far below, doomed to perish. A devoted physician, to save the lives of the sick, sees the horrible danger yet touches the infected place, and in treating another man's troubles brings suffering on himself:[1] but we were not merely sick, or afflicted with horrible ulcers and wounds already festering, but actually lying among the dead, when He by his own efforts saved us from the very abyss of death, because no one else in heaven was strong enough to minister unscathed to the salvation of so many. Alone He took hold of our most painful perishing nature; alone endured our sorrows; alone He took upon Him the retribution for our sins.[2] When we were not half dead, but lying in tombs and graves and by now altogether foul and stinking,[3] He raised us up; and as He did long ago, so now in His eager love for men He surpasses all the hopes of ourselves or anyone else, saving us and giving us His Father's blessings without stint – He the Lifegiver, the Lightbringer, our great Physician and King and Lord, the Christ of God. Then, once for all, seeing that the entire human race was buried in gloomy night and deep darkness through the deceitfulness of wicked demons and the activities of accursed spirits, by nothing but His appearing He tore asunder – as easily as the sun's rays melt wax – the imprisoning bonds of our sins.

And now, as a result of this wonderful grace and bounty, the envy that hates good, the demon that loves evil, bursting with rage, lined up all his lethal forces against us. At first he was like a mad dog that closes his jaws on the stones thrown at him and vents on the inanimate missiles his fury against those who are trying to keep him away: he directed his ferocious madness against the stones of the places of worship and the inanimate timbers of the buildings, bringing, as he himself imagined, ruin on the churches. Then he uttered terrible hissings

1. Quoted from Hippocrates, *Flatulence.*
2. Adapted from Is. liii. 4–5.
3. A reminiscence of John v. 28 and xi. 39.

and his own serpent-like sounds, at one time in the threats of godless tyrants, at another in the blasphemous decrees of impious rulers. Again, he vomited forth his own deadly venom, and by his noxious, soul-destroying poisons he paralysed the souls enslaved to him, almost annihilating them by his death-bringing sacrifices to dead idols, and letting loose against us every beast in human shape and every kind of savagery.

But once again the Angel of great counsel, God's great Commander-in-Chief,[1] after the thoroughgoing training of which the greatest soldiers in His kingdom gave proof by their patience and endurance in all trials, appeared suddenly and thereby swept all that was hostile and inimical into oblivion and nothingness, so that its very existence was forgotten. But all that was near and dear to Him He advanced beyond glory in the sight of all, not men only but the heavenly powers as well – sun, moon, and stars, and the entire heaven and earth. So now as never before the most exalted emperors of all, aware of the honour they have been privileged to receive from Him, spit in the faces of dead idols, trample on the lawless rites of demons, and laugh at the old lies handed down by their fathers. But as the one only God they recognize the common Benefactor of themselves and all men, and Christ they acknowledge as Son of God and sovereign Lord of the universe, naming Him 'Saviour' on monuments, and inscribing in royal characters in the middle of the city that is queen of the cities on earth an indelible record of His triumphs and His victories over the wicked. So it is that alone since time began Jesus Christ our Saviour is not acknowledged as an ordinary human king – even by the most exalted on earth – but worshipped as the true Son of the God of the universe and as Himself God.

And no wonder. For which of the kings who ever lived achieved such greatness as to fill the ears and mouths of all men on earth with his name? What king established laws so just and impartial, and was strong enough to have them proclaimed in the hearing of all mankind from the ends of the earth and to the furthest limit of the entire world? Who made the barbarous, uncivilized customs of uncivilized races give place to his own civilized and most humane laws? Who was for whole ages attacked on every side, yet displayed such superhuman greatness as to be for ever in his prime and to remain young

1. Joshua v. 14.

throughout his life? Who so firmly established a people unheard-of from the beginning of time that it is not hidden in some corner of the earth but is found in every place under the sun? Who so armed his soldiers with the weapons of true religion that their souls proved tougher than steel in their battles with their opponents? Which of the kings wields such power, leads his armies after death, sets up trophies over his enemies, and fills every place, district, and city, Greek or non-Greek, with votive offerings – his own royal houses and sacred temples, like this cathedral with its exquisite ornaments and offerings?

These things are indeed awe-inspiring and overwhelming, astonishing and amazing, and serve as clear proofs that our Saviour is King; for now too

> He spoke, and they were made;
> He commanded, and they were created.[1]

What indeed could withstand the will of the sovereign Lord and Ruler, the Word of God Himself? These things, again, call for a lengthy exposition of their own, if we are to examine them carefully and interpret them. But less importance attaches to the efforts of those who have laboured, in the eyes of Him whom we name God, when He looks at the live temple consisting of us all, and views the house of living and immovable stones,[2] well and securely based on the foundation of the apostles and prophets, Jesus Christ Himself being the chief cornerstone.[3] This stone was rejected by the master builders not only of that old building which no longer exists, but also of the building that still stands and consists of most of mankind – bad builders of bad buildings. But it was accepted by the Father, who laid it then to be for all time the head of the corner of this our common Church. This temple built of you yourselves, a living temple of a living God, the greatest truly majestic sanctuary, I say, whose innermost shrines are hidden from the mass of men and are in truth a Holy Place and a Holy of Holies, who would dare to examine and describe? Who could ever look inside the surrounding temple buildings, except the Great High Priest of the universe, who alone is permitted to search out the secrets of every rational soul?

But perhaps there is one other for whom, alone among equals, it is possible to take the second place after Him. I mean the commander at

1. Ps. xxxiii. 9 and cxlviii. 5.   2. 1 Peter ii. 4.   3. Eph. ii. 20–1.

the head of this army, whom the first and great High Priest[1] Himself has honoured with second place in the priestly offices here performed, the shepherd of your spiritual flock, who by the allotment
and judgement of the Father was set over your people, as if He had
Himself appointed him His votary and interpreter, the new Aaron or
Melchizedek, made like the Son of God,[2] abiding and guarded by
Him continually through the common prayers of you all. Let him
then be permitted alone after the first and greatest High Priest, if not
in the first place at any rate in the second, to see and examine the
innermost recesses of your souls; for through long experience he has
made a thorough test of every man, and by his enthusiasm and atten-
tiveness he has disposed you all in the order and teaching of true religion; and of all men he is best able to give an account to match his
deeds of all that by divine power he has accomplished.

Our first and great High Priest tells us that whatever He sees the
Father doing, that the Son does likewise.[3] This one looks to the First
as to a teacher, with the pure eyes of the mind, and whatever he sees
Him doing, that he takes as an archetype and pattern, and like an
artist he has moulded its image, to the best of his ability, into the
closest likeness. In no respect is he inferior to that Bezalel whom God
Himself filled with a spirit of wisdom and understanding, and with
technical and scientific knowledge, and chose to be architect of the
temples that symbolized the heavenly types. In the same way this
man, having the whole Christ, the Word, the Wisdom, the Light,
impressed upon his soul, has built this magnificent shrine for God
Most High, resembling in its essence the pattern of the better one as
the visible resembles the invisible. Words cannot do justice to his
generosity, to his liberal hand, so insatiable in its determination, or
to the eagerness of you all, to the generous scale of your contributions, as in splendid rivalry you strove to be in no way behind him in
this same purpose.

This site, to put first things first, which by the machinations of
our opponents had been buried under a heap of filthy rubbish, he did
not disregard or abandon to the malignity of those responsible,
though he could have gone to any of the innumerable sites that
abounded in the city, and so found an easy solution of the problem
and a means of avoiding trouble. Instead, he first braced himself to

1. Heb. iv. 14.   2. Heb. vii. 1, 3.   3. John v. 19.

his task, then roused all Christian people by his enthusiasm, gathered them all together in one great body, and launched his first campaign; for he felt that the church which had been assailed by her enemies, which had suffered before the rest and had endured the same persecutions as we, but before they came to us, and which was like a mother bereft of her children, should be the first to share the enjoyment of the All-Gracious God's munificence. For when the Great Shepherd [1] had driven away the wild beasts and wolves and every kind of savage creature, and had, as the word of God declares, broken the teeth of the lions,[2] deeming it good that His sons should again come together, it was most proper that he should erect the fold of the flock, in order to shame the enemy and avenger and publicly condemn the crimes of the sacrilegious enemies of God.

Now these men no longer exist, these enemies of God – in fact they never did; for after bringing distress on other people and on themselves too, they paid to justice a penalty not to be laughed at, utterly ruining themselves, their friends, and their families. Thus the predictions inscribed so long ago on sacred tablets have been proved trustworthy by events. In them the voice of God speaks the truth throughout, but listen to these declarations about them.

> A sword have the wicked drawn, they have bent their bow,
> To cast down the poor and needy,
> To slay the upright in heart.
> May their sword enter their own hearts,
> And may their bows be broken.[3]

And again:

> Their memorial has perished with a resounding crash,
> And their name Thou hast blotted out for ever and for ever and
> ever.[4]

For indeed, when they were in trouble,

> They cried, and there was none to save;
> To the Lord, and He did not listen to them.
> They were bound hand and foot and fell;
> But we have risen and have been set upright.[5]

1. Heb. xiii. 20.   2. Ps. lviii. 6.   3. Ps. xxxvii. 13–14.
4. Ps. ix. 6, 5.   5. Ps. xviii. 41, xx. 8.

And listen to this prophecy:

> Lord, in Thy city Thou shalt set their image at nought.[1]

The truth of that statement has been established for all to see.

These men, like the giants of old,[2] joined battle with God and have brought their lives to this miserable end. By contrast, the Church that was desolate and rejected by men has by her inspired endurance won the victory we have seen, so that the prophetic voice of Isaiah calls aloud to her thus:

> Be glad, thirsty desert;
> Let the desert rejoice, and blossom as a lily;
> The desert places shall blossom forth and rejoice.
> Be strong, weak hands and feeble knees:
> Take courage, you that are timid at heart;
> Be strong, do not fear.
> Lo, our God dispenses justice and will dispense;
> He will come and save us.
> For (says he) in the desert water broke out,
> And a channel in thirsty soil;
> And the dry ground shall become lush meadows,
> And on the thirsty soil shall be a spring of water.[3]

These things were foretold in words long ago, and set down in sacred books; but the fulfilment has reached us no longer by hearsay but in fact. This desert, this dry ground, this defenceless widow – they cut down her gates with axes as in a thicket of trees, together breaking her down with hatchet and stonemason's hammer; they destroyed her books and set on fire the sanctuary of God; they profaned to the ground the dwelling-place of His name; all that passed by the way plucked her fruit, having first broken down her fences; the boar from the thicket ravaged her and the solitary wild beast devoured her – yet by the miraculous power of Christ, now when He wills it, she has become like a lily. At that time by His command, as of a father who cares, she was disciplined:

> For whom the Lord loves, He disciplines,
> And He whips every son whom He acknowledges.[4]

1. Ps. lxxiii. 20.
3. Is. xxxv. 1–7.
2. A reference to the Greek legend.
4. Prov. iii. 12 and Heb. xii. 6.

In moderation, then, she was suitably corrected; and now once more she is commanded to rejoice again, and she blossoms like a lily and breathes her sweet divine odour on all mankind; for, as the Scripture says, in the desert water broke out, the stream of the divine regeneration by the saving baptism; and now what a little while ago was desert has become lush meadows, and on the thirsty soil has gushed a spring of living water. Strength has indeed come to hands that before were weak; and to the strength of those hands these great and splendid works bear witness. The once diseased and sagging knees have recovered their normal movement, and march straight forward along the road to the knowledge of God, in haste to rejoin the flock of the All-Gracious Shepherd. If the tyrants' threats have reduced some souls to torpor, even they are not passed over by the Saving Word as incurable: to them He freely gives the healing medicine, urging them on towards the divine comfort:

> Take courage, you that are timid at heart;
> Be strong, do not fear.

The word which foretold that she whom God had allowed to become desolate should enjoy these blessings was heard and readily understood by this new and splendid Zerubbabel of ours, after that bitter captivity and the abomination of desolation.[1] He did not pass the body over as dead, but he made it his very first task, by means of entreaties and prayers, to propitiate the Father, with the warm approval of you all. Taking the only Quickener of the dead as ally and co-worker, he raised up the fallen church, after first cleansing her and curing her sickness; and he clothed her with a garment – not the old one she had had from the first, but one that accorded with the further instructions of the divine oracles which emphatically declare: 'The final glory of this house shall be greater than the former.'[2]

1. Dan. xii. 11 and Matt. xxiv. 15.
2. Hag. ii. 9. The next six paragraphs contain the earliest extant description of a Christian church. If the reader finds it hard to visualize the building, he must remember that Eusebius is not writing an architectural specification for the information of posterity, but voicing the emotions of a mass meeting at the wonderful new birth of the Church, which he sees figured and presented in concrete form in the magnificent cathedral at Tyre, of which every feature has for him a symbolical meaning.

Accordingly, the whole area that he took in was much larger, and he gave the outer enclosure the protection of a wall surrounding the whole, to provide the maximum safety for the entire structure. Then he opened up a gateway, wide and towering high, to receive the rays of the rising sun, thus providing even those who stood outside the sacred precincts with an unlimited view of the interior, and as it were turning the eyes even of strangers to the Faith towards the first entrances, so that no one should hurry past without being profoundly moved by the thought of the former desolation and the miraculous transformation now: he hoped that perhaps emotion at the mere sight would turn people and propel them towards the entrance.

He does not permit a man who has passed inside the gates to go at once with unhallowed and unwashed feet into the holy places within; he has left a very wide space between the church proper and the first entrances, adorning it all round with four colonnades at right angles, so that the outer walls turn the site into a quadrangle and pillars rise on every side. The space between these he has filled with wooden screens of trellis work to a proportionate height. In the middle he left a clear space where the sky can be seen, so that the air is bright and open to the sun's rays. There he placed symbols of sacred purifications, constructing fountains exactly in front of the cathedral: these with their ample flow of fresh water enable those who are proceeding towards the centre of the sacred precincts to purify themselves. For all who enter, this is the first stopping-place, lending beauty and splendour to the whole and at the same time providing those still in need of elementary instruction with the station they require.

Passing beyond this wonderful sight, he opened passages to the cathedral through still more numerous gateways inside the court. In the full blaze of the sun once more, he sited three gates on one side: the centre one he dignified with height and breadth far exceeding those of the outside pair, and by providing bronze plates[1] bound with iron, and elaborate reliefs, he gave it breathtaking loveliness, so that it looks like a queen between two humble bodyguards. In the same way he determined the number of the gateways to the colonnades along both sides of the whole edifice: over the colonnades, to admit still more light, he designed separate openings into the buildings; and these he ornamented elaborately with exquisite wood-carvings.

1. Meaning doubtful: possibly 'almanacs'.

The basilica itself[1] he built solidly of still richer materials in abundance, never for a moment counting the cost. This is not, I think, the time to state the precise measurements of the building, or to describe in full its dazzling beauty, the incredible vastness, the brilliant appearance of the workmanship, the towering walls that reach for the sky, and the costly cedars of Lebanon that form the ceiling. Even about them the inspired word has something to tell us.

> The trees of the Lord shall be glad,
> The cedars of Lebanon which He planted.[2]

I need not go into details now about the perfection of the overall design and the superlative beauty of the individual parts, for the evidence of our eyes makes instruction through the ears unnecessary. But I will say this: after completing the great building I have described, he furnished it with thrones high up, to accord with the dignity of the prelates, and also with benches arranged conveniently throughout. In addition to all this, he placed in the middle the Holy of Holies – the altar – excluding the general public from this part too by surrounding it with wooden trellis-work wrought by the craftsmen with exquisite artistry, a marvellous sight for all who see it.

Not even the floor was overlooked by him. This he made bright with marble laid in wonderful patterns, going on next to the outside of the building, where he constructed halls and chambers along both sides on a great scale, skilfully uniting them with the fabric of the basilica so that they share the openings that let light into the central building. These, too, were provided for those still in need of cleansing and sprinkling with water and the Holy Ghost, and were the work of our most peaceful Solomon, who built the temple of God, so that the prophecy I quoted earlier is no longer mere words but plain fact; for the final glory of this house has become and now in truth is greater than the former.

It was natural and right that – as her Shepherd and Lord had once for all accepted death on her behalf, and after His Passion had changed the foul body which for her sake He had put on into His dazzling glorious body, and brought the very flesh that was dissolved from

1. Churches of this period followed the design of the public buildings in the Roman forum.
2. Ps. civ. 16.

perishability to imperishability[1] – so in her turn the Church should reap the benefit of the Saviour's labours. For having received from Him the promise of much better things than these,[2] she longs to receive permanently and for all time the much greater glory of the regeneration in the resurrection of an imperishable body, with the choir of the angels of light in the kingdom of God beyond the skies, and with Christ Jesus Himself, the great Benefactor and Saviour. Meanwhile, in the present she who was once widowed and desolate has by God's grace been wreathed with these blossoms, and has become in truth like a lily, as the prophecy declares; and having donned her bridal dress and put on the garland of loveliness, she is taught by Isaiah to dance, so to speak, offering her thanks to God the King in words of praise. Listen to what she says:

Let my soul rejoice in the Lord;
For He has clothed me with the mantle of salvation and the tunic of
    gladness;
He has wreathed me like a bridegroom with a chaplet,
And like a bride He has adorned me with ornaments,
And like the ground that grows its blossom,
And as a garden will cause what is sown in it to spring up,
So the Lord, the LORD, has caused righteousness and rejoicing to
    spring up before all the heathen.[3]

With such words on her lips she dances. And how does the Bridegroom, the heavenly Word, Jesus Christ Himself, answer her? Listen to His words:

Do not fear because you have been put to shame,
Or tremble because you have been reproached;
For your everlasting shame you will forget,
And the reproach of your widowhood you will remember no more.
Not as a wife forsaken and without hope has the Lord called you,
Nor as a woman hated from her youth, says your God.
For a little while I forsook you,
And with great mercy will I comfort you.

1. 1 Cor. xv. 42.
2. An allusion to Heb. xi. 39–40.
3. Is. lxi. 10–11.

With a little wrath I turned my face from you,
And with everlasting mercy will I comfort you,
Says your Deliverer, the Lord.
Awake, awake!
You who have drunk from the hand of the Lord the cup of His
    wrath;
For the cup of staggering, the bowl of my wrath, you have drained
    and emptied.
There was none to comfort you out of all the children whom you
    bore,
And there was none to take your hand.
Lo, I have taken from your hand the cup of staggering, the bowl
    of my wrath;
And never again shall you drink it:
I will put it into the hands of those who wronged you and humbled
    you.
Awake, awake! put on your strength, put on your glory:
Shake off the dust and stand up.
Sit down: loose the band from your neck.
Raise your eyes and look about you, and see your children gathered
    together:
Lo, they are gathered together and have come to you.
As I live, says the Lord, you will put them all on as an ornament,
And wrap them about you like the ornaments of a bride.
For your desolate, destroyed, and ruined places will be too narrow
    for your inhabitants,
And those who swallow you up will be removed far from you.
For the sons you have lost will say in your ears,
'The place is too narrow for me: give me a place where I may dwell.'
And you will say in your heart, 'Who has begotten me these?
I am childless and a widow: who has brought these up for me?
I was left alone: these my children, whence came they?'[1]

These things Isaiah foretold, these things had long ago been set
down about us in sacred books, but it was necessary, was it not, that
their truth should one day be shown by facts. And since this is the
way in which the Bridegroom, the Word, speaks to His Bride, the

1. Is. liv. 4–8, li. 17–23, lii. 1–2, xlix. 18–21.

Sacred and Holy Church, it was with good reason that this escort of
the Bride stretched out *your* hands in the common prayers of you all,
and woke and raised up the desolate one who lay dead, despaired of
by men, by the will of God the universal King and by the manifestation of the power of Jesus Christ; and when he had raised her he made
her such as the precepts of the sacred oracles taught him she should
be.

This cathedral is a marvel of beauty, utterly breathtaking, especially to those who have eyes only for the appearance of material things.
But all marvels pale before the archetypes, the metaphysical proto-
types and heavenly patterns of material things – I mean the re-establishment of the divine spiritual edifice in our souls. This edifice the
Son of God Himself created in His own image, and in every way and
in every respect He endowed it with the divine likeness, an imperishable nature, a non-physical spiritual essence, remote from any earthly
matter and actively intelligent. Once for all, at the first He transformed it from non-existence to existence, making it a holy bride
and a most sacred temple for Himself and the Father. This He Himself plainly reveals in this confession:

> I will dwell in them and walk in them;
> And I will be their God, and they shall be my people.[1]

Such is the perfect and cleansed soul, begotten from the beginning
so as to bear the image of the heavenly Word.

But when, through the envy and jealousy of the demon that loves
evil, she became by her own free choice a lover of sensuality and
evil, the Deity withdrew from her, and bereft of a protector, she was
soon captured, proving an easy prey to the inveiglements of those
so long bitter against her. Overthrown by the battering-rams and
engines of her unseen and spiritual foes, she came crashing to the
ground, so that not even one stone of her virtue remained standing
on another in her; she lay full length on the ground dead, her natural
thoughts about God gone without trace. As she lay prostrate, made
as she was in the image of God,[2] she was ravaged not by that boar out
of the wood[3] visible to us, but by some destroying demon and
spiritual beasts of the field, who inflamed her with sensual passions

---

1. 2 Cor. vi. 16; a conflation of Lev. xxvi. 12 and Ez. xxxvii. 27.
2. Gen. i. 27.   3. Ps. lxxx. 13.

as if with blazing arrows of their own wickedness,¹ and set on fire
the truly divine sanctuary of God, profaning to the ground the
dwelling-place of His name.² Then they buried the unfortunate under
a great heap of earth, and robbed her of the last hope of salvation.

But when she had paid the just penalty of her sins, the Protector,
the Word, the divinely bright and saving One, restored her once
more, obedient to the benevolent spirit of His Father, the All-
Gracious. First He chose the souls of the supreme emperors, most dear
to Him, and by their means He purged the whole world of all the
wicked and pernicious people, and of the terrible God-hating tyrants
themselves. Then He brought out into the open His own disciples,
who all their lives had been dedicated to Him but, as in a storm of
evils, secretly concealed under His sheltering wings, and with His
Father's munificence He gave them a worthy reward. Again by their
means He purged the souls which a little while before were fouled
and heaped with rubbish of every sort and the debris of impious decrees: He cleansed them with pickaxes and two-pronged hoes – the
penetrating lessons that He taught; and when He had made the place
of the understanding of you all bright and shining, thenceforth He
entrusted it to this leader, so wise and dear to God. An acute and discriminating judge of other matters, he is well able to appreciate and
evaluate the character of the souls entrusted to his care; and from almost the first day he has never yet ceased to build, finding the right
place, now for the shining gold, now for the tested, pure silver and
the precious, costly stones among you all. So once more a sacred,
mystic prophecy is fulfilled in what he has done for you – the prophecy that says:

> Lo, I prepare for you the carbuncle for your stone,
> And for your foundations the sapphire,
> And for your battlements the jasper,
> And for your gates stones of crystal,
> And for your enclosing wall choice stones,
> And all your sons taught of God,
> And in perfect peace your children;
> And in righteousness shall you be built.³

1. A reminiscence of Eph. vi. 16.
2. Ps. lxxiv. 7.   3. Is. liv. 11–14.

Building truly in righteousness, he equitably divided the whole people in accordance with their powers. With some, he walled round the outer enclosure – that was enough for them – making unwavering faith the protective barrier. This accounted for far the greater part of the people, who were not strong enough to support a greater edifice. To some he entrusted the entrances to the church proper, giving them the task of waiting at the doors to guide those entering, since he justifiably regarded them as gateways to the house of God. Others he made under-props to the first outer pillars that form a quadrangle round the court, bringing them for the first time into touch with the letter of the four gospels. Others he joined to the basilica along both sides, still under instruction and in process of advancing, but not very far removed from the divine vision that the faithful enjoy of what is innermost. From these last he chooses the undefiled souls, purified like gold by divine washing; these he makes under-props to pillars much grander than the outer ones, drawing on the innermost mystic teaching of Holy Writ, while others he illumines with openings towards the light. With one huge gateway, consisting of the praise of our Sovereign Lord, the one only God, he adorns the whole cathedral; and on both sides of the Father's supreme power he supplies the secondary beams of the light of Christ, and the Holy Ghost.[1] As to the rest, from end to end of the building he reveals in all its abundance and rich variety the clear light of the truth in every man, and everywhere and from every source he has found room for the living, securely-laid, and unshakable stones of human souls. In this way he is constructing out of them all a great and kingly house, glowing and full of light within and without, in that not only their heart and mind, but their body too, has been gloriously enriched with the many-blossomed adornment of chastity and temperance.

There are also in this shrine thrones and an infinite number of benches and seats, all the souls, on which rest the Holy Spirit's gifts, just as in olden time, they appeared to the holy apostles, and others with them, to whom were revealed dividing tongues like flames of fire, fire which rested on each one of them.[2] In the ruler of them all[3]

---

1. Eusebius intends no heresy: As Christ is begotten of, and the Holy Ghost proceeds from, the Father, the Father may not unnaturally be deemed primary.   2. Acts ii. 3.   3. Paulinus.

we may say that the entire Christ Himself has found a resting-place, and in those who take second place to him proportionately, according to each man's capacity to receive the power of Christ and the Holy Spirit divided among them.[1] The souls of some might be benches for the angels assigned to each man with a view to his instruction and protection. As to the solemn, great, and unique altar, what could it be if not the spotless Holy of Holies of the common Priest of them all – His soul? Standing beside it on the right-hand side,[2] the great High Priest of the universe,[3] Jesus Himself, the only begotten of God, receives with shining eyes and upturned hands the sweet-smelling incense of all the worshippers, and the bloodless and immaterial prayer-sacrifices, and transmits them to the Father in heaven, the God of the universe. He Himself first adores the Father, and alone renders Him the honour due; then He beseeches Him to continue favourable and propitious towards us for ever.[4]

Such is the great cathedral which throughout the whole world under the sun the great Creator of the universe, the Word, has built, Himself again fashioning this spiritual image on earth of the vaults beyond the skies, so that by the whole creation and by rational beings on earth His Father might be honoured and worshipped. As for the realm above the skies and the patterns there of things here on earth, the Jerusalem above, as it is called,[5] the heavenly Mount Zion and the celestial city of the Living God, in which countless hosts of assembled angels and the church of the first-born enrolled in heaven give glory with praises beyond our utterance or understanding to their Maker, the supreme Ruler of the universe – these things no mortal can worthily hymn; for indeed eye has not seen and ear has not heard, and into the heart of man there have not entered, these very things which God has prepared for those that love Him.[6] Of these things we have now in part been found worthy; so let us all – men, women, and children, small and great together, with one spirit and one soul – everlastingly give thanks and praise to the Author of all the blessings we enjoy. He is very merciful to all our iniquities, He cures all our diseases, He redeems our life from destruction, He crowns us with pity and compassion, He satisfies our desire with good things. He has

1. Heb. ii. 4.   2. Luke i. 11.   3. Heb. iv. 14.
4. Rom. viii. 34 and Heb. vii. 25   5. Gal. iv. 26.
6. 1 Cor. ii. 9, slightly modified.

not dealt with us according to our sins or rewarded us according to our iniquities; for as far as the east is from the west, He has removed our iniquities from us. Just as a father pities his sons, the Lord has pitied those who fear Him.[1]

Let us now and for all time to come rekindle the memory of these things; and let the Author of the present assembly and of this joyous and most glorious day, the Lord of the festival Himself, be before the eyes of our mind night and day at every hour and, may I say, at every breath. Let us love and reverence Him with all the power of our soul; and let us now stand up and with a loud voice of supplication beseech Him to shelter us in His fold and preserve us to the end, bestowing on us His own unbreakable, unshakable, and everlasting peace in Christ Jesus our Saviour, through whom be glory to Him for ever and ever. Amen.

Copies of imperial laws

5. At this point it would be well to reproduce also the imperial ordinances of Constantine and Licinius in translations from the Latin.[2]

COPY OF IMPERIAL ORDINANCES, TRANSLATED FROM
LATIN

For a long time past we have made it our aim that freedom of worship should not be denied, but that every man, according to his own inclination and wish, should be given permission to practise his religion as he chose. We had therefore given command that Christians and non-Christians alike should be allowed to keep the faith of their own religious beliefs and worship. But in view of the fact that numerous conditions of different kinds had evidently been attached to that rescript, in which such a right was granted to those very persons, it is

1. Ps. ciii. 3–5, 10–13, slightly modified.
2. The document that follows, based on the Edict of Milan, is a rescript sent to an individual governor, to whose intelligence the extraordinary repetitiveness does little credit. Eusebius's Greek is marred by several omissions and mistakes, apparently due to deficiencies in his copy of the Latin. These are here corrected from the Latin as preserved in Lactantius, *De Mortibus Persecutorum*.

possible that some of them were soon afterwards deterred from such observance.

When with happy auspices I, Constantinus Augustus, and I, Licinius Augustus, had arrived at Milan, and were enquiring into all matters that concerned the advantage and benefit of the public, among the other measures directed to the general good, or rather as questions of highest priority, we decided to establish rules by which respect and reverence for the Deity would be secured, i.e. to give the Christians and all others liberty to follow whatever form of worship they chose, so that whatsoever divine and heavenly powers exist might be enabled to show favour to us and to all who live under our authority. This therefore is the decision that we reached by sound and careful reasoning: no one whatever was to be denied the right to follow and choose the Christian observance or form of worship; and everyone was to have permission to give his mind to that form of worship which he feels to be adapted to his needs, so that the Deity might be enabled to show us in all things His customary care and generosity. It was desirable to send a rescript stating that this was our pleasure, in order that after the complete cancellation of the conditions contained in the earlier letter[1] which we sent to Your Dedicatedness about the Christians, the procedure that seemed quite unjustified and alien to our clemency should also be cancelled, and that now every individual still desirous of observing the Christian form of worship should without any interference be allowed to do so. All this we have decided to explain very fully to Your Diligence, that you may know that we have given the said Christians free and absolute permission to practise their own form of worship. When you observe that this permission has been granted by us absolutely, Your Dedicatedness will understand that permission has been given to any others who may wish to follow their own observance or form of worship – a privilege obviously consonant with the tranquillity of our times – so that every man may have permission to choose and practise whatever religion he wishes. This we have done to make it plain that we are not belittling any rite or form of worship.

With regard to the Christians, we also give this further ruling. In the letter sent earlier to Your Dedicatedness precise instructions were laid down at an earlier date with reference to their places where

---

1. The Edict of Galerius.

earlier on it was their habit to meet. We now decree that if it should appear that any persons have bought these places either from our treasury or from some other source, they must restore them to these same Christians without payment and without any demand for compensation, and there must be no negligence or hesitation. If any persons happen to have received them as a gift, they must restore the said places to the said Christians without loss of time; provided that if either those who have bought these same places or those who have received them as a gift wish to appeal to our generosity, they may apply to the prefect and judge of the region, in order that they also may benefit by our liberality. All this property is to be handed over to the Christian body immediately, by energetic action on your part, without any delay.

And since the aforesaid Christians not only possessed those places where it was their habit to meet, but are known to have possessed other places also, belonging not to individuals but to the legal estate of the whole body, i.e. of the Christians, all this property, in accordance with the law set forth above, you will order to be restored without any argument whatever to the aforesaid Christians, i.e. to their body and local associations, the provision mentioned above being of course observed, namely, that those persons who restore the same without seeking compensation, as we mentioned above, may expect to recoup their personal losses from our generosity.

In all these matters you must put all the energy you possess at the service of the aforesaid Christian body, in order that our command may be carried out with all possible speed, so that in this also our liberality may further the common and public tranquillity. For by this provision, as was mentioned above, the divine care for us of which we have been aware on many earlier occasions will remain with us unalterably for ever. And in order that the pattern of this our enactment and of our generosity may be brought to the notice of all, it is desirable that what we have written should be set forth by an edict of your own and everywhere published and brought to the notice of all, so that the enactment giving effect to this our generosity may be known to every citizen.

COPY OF A SECOND STATUTE ISSUED BY THE EMPEROR,
MAKING IT CLEAR THAT ONLY TO THE CATHOLIC CHURCH
WAS THE FAVOUR GRANTED

Greeting, Anulinus, Your Excellency.

It is in keeping with our benevolence that when things belong by right to another man we wish them not only to suffer no damage, but also to be restored, Your Excellency Anulinus. Accordingly it is our wish that when you receive this letter you will see to it that if any of the former property of the Catholic Church of the Christians in the several cities or other places is now in the possession either of citizens or of any other persons, it shall be restored forthwith to the said churches, inasmuch as we have determined that whatever the said churches formerly possessed shall be restored to its rightful owners. Since therefore Your Faithfulness sees plainly that the purport of this our command is perfectly clear, you must take energetic steps to ensure that gardens, houses, and everything else of which the said churches were the rightful owners shall in their entirety be restored to them at the earliest possible moment, so that we may be duly informed that this our command has been meticulously carried out by you. Our compliments to you, Anulinus, Your most Esteemed Excellency.

COPY OF AN IMPERIAL LETTER ORDERING AN EPISCOPAL
SYNOD TO BE HELD AT ROME WITH A VIEW TO THE
UNITY AND CONCORD OF THE CHURCHES

Constantinus Augustus to Miltiades, Bishop of Rome, and Mark.[1]

In view of the nature of the missives sent to me repeatedly by Anulinus, the Illustrious Proconsul of Africa, which convey the intelligence that Caecilian, Bishop of Carthage, is accused by some of his colleagues in Africa of numerous misdemeanours, I feel it to be a very serious matter that in those provinces which divine providence has freely entrusted to My Dedicatedness, and where the population is very large, the general public should be found persisting in the wrong course as if it were splitting in two, and the bishops divided among themselves. I have therefore decided that Caecilian himself, with ten

1. Unknown.

of the bishops who apparently are accusing him, and ten others regarded by him as essential to his case, shall sail for Rome. There in the
presence of yourselves and of Reticius, Maternus, and Marinus, your
own colleagues whom I have instructed to proceed at once to Rome
for this purpose, he will be granted a hearing in such conditions as you
will judge proper under the most sacred law. To ensure that you shall
be fully acquainted with all the circumstances of the case, I am enclos-
ing with my letter copies of the reports sent to me by Anulinus, and
am dispatching them to your colleagues named above. When you
have read them, Your Steadfastness will decide what procedure will
be most appropriate for investigating the aforementioned case and
reaching a just verdict; for, as Your Diligence is well aware, such is
the regard I pay to the lawful Catholic Church that I desire you to
leave no schism or division of any kind anywhere.

May the divine power of the great God keep you all safe for many
years, Your Excellency.

COPY OF AN IMPERIAL LETTER COMMANDING A SECOND
SYNOD TO BE HELD WITH A VIEW TO THE HEALING OF
ALL DIVISIONS BETWEEN THE BISHOPS

Constantinus Augustus to Chrestus, Bishop of Syracuse.

When on an earlier occasion base and perverted motives led certain
persons to begin creating divisions regarding the worship of the holy
and heavenly Power and the Catholic Religion, I determined to cut
short such quarrels among them. I therefore gave instructions for
certain bishops to be sent from Gaul, and for those men who had
taken sides and were engaged in persistent and unrelenting strife to
be summoned from Africa, and for the Bishop of Rome to be present
also: in this way the question which had apparently been raised would
be enabled by their presence to be thoroughly examined in all its
implications and finally settled. But as it happens, certain persons
have forgotten both their own salvation and the respect due to their
most holy religion, and have not ceased even now to keep alive their
private enmities: they refuse to accept the decision already reached,
and allege that only a few persons expressed their views and opinions,
or that without first subjecting all points that required investigation to
careful scrutiny they were in far too great a hurry to pass judgement.

In consequence of all this it has come about that the very persons who ought to display brotherly unity and concord are estranged from each other in a way that is disgraceful if not positively sickening; and to people whose minds are strangers to this most holy religion they give a pretext for mockery. It therefore became incumbent on me to provide that what ought after the judgement already passed to have been ended by voluntary agreement should now at last by the presence of many persons be terminated once and for all.

Inasmuch therefore as we have ordered a very large number of bishops from various places beyond counting to assemble at Arles by the first of August, we have decided to write specially to you. Be good enough to obtain from the Illustrious Latronian, my *corrector*[1] in Sicily, a public carriage; attach to yourself two others in presbyter's orders, chosen entirely by yourself; take with you three servants who will be able to look after your comfort on the journey; and present yourself by the appointed day at the place named above. We have likewise ordered those who are now at variance with each other to be present. When all their arguments have been heard, it will be possible for Your Steadfastness, together with the united and harmonious wisdom of the others there assembled, to see that this latest dispute – which owing to inexcusable contentions has most regrettably survived till this present time – may be transformed, however belatedly, into genuine religious feeling, faith, and brotherly concord.

May God Almighty keep you in good health for many years.

COPY OF AN IMPERIAL LETTER MAKING GRANTS OF
MONEY TO THE CHURCHES

6. Constantinus Augustus to Caecilian, Bishop of Carthage.

Inasmuch as I have resolved that in all provinces, namely, Africa, Numidia, and Mauretania, certain named ministers of the lawful and most holy Catholic Religion should receive some contribution towards expenses, I have sent a letter to Ursus, the Eminent Finance Officer of Africa, informing him that he must arrange the transfer to Your Steadfastness of 3000 *folles*[2] in cash. Your task on receipt of this

    1. A title given at this period to certain provincial governors. From it is derived the *corregidor* of old Spain.
    2. A very large sum, difficult to estimate accurately

sum of money will be to see that it is distributed among all the persons named above according to the schedule supplied to you by
Hosius.[1] If later you find that you still lack means to carry out my
intentions in this matter in respect of them all, you must not hesitate
to ask Heraclidas our treasurer for whatever you find necessary. I
have given him orders in person that if Your Steadfastness should ask
him for any sum, he is to arrange for its transfer to you without
question.

And whereas I have learnt that certain persons of unstable character desire to lead astray the laity of the most holy Catholic Church
by disreputable enticements, this is to inform you that I have given
full instructions to Anulinus the Proconsul and also to Patricius the
Prefects' *Vicarius*[2] in person, that in all matters, and particularly
in this, they are to make the appropriate arrangements and are on no
account to overlook such incidents. If therefore you observe any such
persons persisting in this insane conduct, you must without hesitation
apply to the aforementioned judges and refer the matter to them, so
that, as I have instructed them in person, they may bring pressure to
bear.

May the divine power of the great God keep you safe for many
years.

COPY OF AN IMPERIAL LETTER COMMANDING THE HEADS
OF THE CHURCHES TO BE EXEMPTED FROM ALL PUBLIC
DUTIES

7. Greeting, Anulinus, Your Excellency.

Many facts combine to prove that the sad neglect of religious observances, by which the highest reverence for the most holy, heavenly
Power is preserved, has brought great dangers upon the community,
and that the lawful restoration and preservation of the same has
conferred the greatest good fortune on the Roman name, and wonderful prosperity on all mankind – blessings conferred by divine
benevolence. I have accordingly decided that those men who with
due holiness and constant attention to this law give their services to
the conduct of divine worship shall receive the rewards of their own

1. Bishop of Corduba and religious adviser to Constantine.
2. Deputy.

labours, Anulinus, Your Excellency. So in the province entrusted to you, in the Catholic church over which Caecilian presides, I desire those who give their services to these sacred observances – the people commonly known as clergymen – once and for all to be kept entirely free from all public duties. This will ensure that by no error or sacrilegious fall from grace will they be drawn away from the worship owed to the Godhead; rather will they be completely free to serve their own law at all times. In thus rendering wholehearted service to the Deity, it is evident that they will be making an immense contribution to the welfare of the community.

Our compliments to you, Anulinus, Your Most Esteemed Excellency.

The criminal folly of Licinius, and his calamitous end

8. Such then were the boons conferred on us by the divine, heavenly grace of the manifestation of our Saviour; so great was the abundance of good things won for all men through the peace we enjoyed. And thus our new life was inaugurated with festivities and celebrations. But in the eyes of evil-minded envy and of the malignant demon the sight of what was going on was beyond endurance, and in the same way Licinius could not be brought to a sensible frame of mind by the fate of the tyrants already mentioned.[1] He had been honoured with sovereign power in time of prosperity; he had ranked next after the great Emperor Constantine, and had become brother-in-law and kinsman of the most exalted person living; yet he turned his back on the examples of good men and emulated the wickedness and criminal folly of the evil tryants; and he chose to follow the same path as those whose life he had with his own eyes seen ending in calamity, rather than remain on terms of friendship and esteem with his superior. Madly envious of the universal benefactor, he launched an unholy, all-out war against him, paying no respect to natural laws and trampling underfoot solemn pledges, ties of blood,

1. Maxentius and Maximin.

and treaties. For, like the all-gracious emperor that he was, Constantine had given him tokens of real goodwill, not grudging kinship with himself or refusing him the privilege of a brilliant marriage with his sister. Again, he honoured him with a share in his ancestral nobility and the imperial blood he had inherited, and conferred on him, as brother-in-law and joint emperor, the privilege of enjoying sovereign power, giving him an equal part of the lands under Roman sway to govern and administer.

But Licinius responded by behaving in the opposite way: he devised scheme after scheme to injure his superior, and invented plan after plan in his efforts to return evil for good. At first he attempted to conceal his intrigues, and posed as a friend, in the hope that by making constant use of trickery and deception he would most easily achieve his purpose. But in God Constantine had a true Friend, Protector, and Guardian, who brought to light the plots devised in darkness and secrecy and frustrated them: so powerful is the great weapon of godliness for the repulse of the enemy and the preservation of its own safety. Thus protected, our Emperor, God's dearly beloved, escaped the plots of this infamous twister. The latter saw that his stealthy intrigue was not going at all according to plan, for God made every trick and fraud manifest to His beloved emperor; so, being unable to remain hidden any longer, he made war openly. Having resolved to fight it out with Constantine, he was already rushing into conflict with the God of the universe too, whom he knew that his rival worshipped. So – quietly and cautiously at first – he planned an attack on the ministers of God among his subjects, though they had never yet shown the least disloyalty to his rule. The motive for this was the terrible blindness forced upon him by his inborn vileness. Thus he failed to keep before his eyes the memory either of those who had persecuted Christians before him, or of those whom he had taken it upon himself to punish and destroy because of their iniquitous activities. But he turned his back on prudence and commonsense, lost his sanity altogether, and determined to match his strength against God Himself, as Constantine's Protector, rather than against the person protected.

He began by dismissing every Christian from his household, robbing himself, poor fool, of the supplication to God for him which their fathers had taught them to make for all men.[1] Next, he ordered the soldiers, city by city, to be picked out and deprived of their rank if they did not choose to sacrifice to demons.

These were mere trifles, judged by comparison with more drastic measures. There is no need to mention one by one the separate acts of this enemy of God, and how laws that were unlawful were invented by this most lawless of men. One actually laid down that where men were languishing in prison no one might give them food as an act of humanity, or pity those who were fettered and starving to death: no one was to show any kind feeling at all, and no kind act was to be done even by those who were compelled by their own nature to show fellow-feeling for their neighbours. Among his laws one was undisguisedly shameless and most cruel, excluding every civilized sentiment: it ordained that those who showed pity should suffer the same punishment as those who aroused it, and that any who performed humane services should be fettered and flung into prison, to share the punishment of those already undergoing it. Such were the orders of Licinius.

Need I enumerate his innovations with regard to marriage, or his startling changes affecting those who departed this life? He had the impudence to rescind the ancient Roman laws, so well and wisely laid down, replacing them with barbarous, uncivilized substitutes, laws unquestionably unlawful and contrary to law. Then there were the innumerable demands that he concocted at the expense of subject peoples, the

1. 1 Tim. ii. 1.

constant exactions of gold and silver, the revaluations of land, the pocketing of fines imposed on country-dwellers no longer alive but long since departed. In addition, this hater of his fellow-men devised means of banishing persons entirely innocent, and of arresting men of good birth and high reputation, whose lawful wives he removed and handed over to filthy menials to be insulted and humiliated; while he himself, the besotted old dotard,[1] used countless married women and unwedded girls to satisfy his own unbridled lust. But why should I dwell on these things, when the extravagance of his ultimate behaviour makes the earlier seem trifling and negligible?

In the later stages of his madness he took action against the bishops. As the servants of the God who is over all, he felt them to be obstacles to his misdeeds; so he began to plot against them, not openly at first, for fear of his superior, but secretly as usual and guilefully; and enlisting the help of the governors he put the most influential of them to death. The way they were murdered was a novel one, till then unheard of. The things done at Amasea and the other Pontic cities outranged the most extravagant cruelty. Some of the churches of God there were again thrown down from roof to foundations; others were locked up, to prevent any of the regular congregation from meeting and giving to God the worship due to Him. And why? Because he did not believe that the prayers were offered on his behalf – the suggestion sprang from his guilty conscience – but was convinced that it was for the Emperor whom God loved that we did everything and made our supplications to Him. That was what brought down his wrath upon our heads. Among the governors were flatterers who – in the conviction that they were doing what the wretched man wanted – subjected some of the bishops to the penalties reserved for criminals, men completely innocent

1. He was under sixty-five when he died, but had been white-haired for years.

being arrested and executed without pretext as if they were murderers. Others suffered an even more unprecedented form of death: their bodies were hacked with a sword and carved up like butcher's meat; then, after this savage, horrifying spectacle, they were thrown into the depths of the sea to feed the fishes. This led to a new flight of the ministers of God, and once more the fields, once more the deserts, valleys, and hills became the refuge of Christ's servants.

When the evil emperor had achieved his purpose in this way also, he next turned his attention to indiscriminate persecution. His design was in his power, and there was no obstacle to its being carried out, had not the threatened danger been speedily foreseen by God, the defender of the souls that are His, who in the black darkness and utter gloom of night all at once kindled a great beacon light, a saviour for them all, with uplifted arm leading His servant Constantine to the spot. 9. On him, as the due reward of his devotion, God bestowed from heaven above the trophies of victory over the wicked; but the guilty one He threw down, with all his counsellors and friends, prone beneath Constantine's feet.

Victory of Constantine; the benefits he conferred on his subjects

When Licinius had rushed headlong to the limit of madness, this seemed no longer endurable to the emperor, God's friend, who – reasoning along sound lines and tempering the rigidity of justice with humanity – determined to rescue the tyrant's victims, and by putting a few destroyers out of the way made haste to save the bulk of the human race. He had treated Licinius with nothing but kindness hitherto, and had shown mercy where no sympathy was deserved. But Licinius grew no better: his wickedness continued unabated, and he raged more and more madly against his subject peoples; while for his victims there remained no hope of escape, with a wild beast tyrannizing over them.

And so, his love of goodness blended with a hatred of evil, the champion of the good set out with his son Crispus,[1] that most humane emperor, by his side, holding out a saving hand to all who were perishing. Then, taking God the universal King, and God's Son the Saviour of all, as Guide and Ally, father and son together divided their battle array against God's enemies on every side, and easily carried off the victory:[2] every detail of the encounter was made easy for them by God, in fulfilment of His purpose. Suddenly in less time than it takes to say it, those who a day or two before had been breathing death and threats were no more, and even their name was forgotten; their portraits and tributes were swept into merited oblivion; and the very things that Licinius with his own eyes had seen befall the wicked tyrants who preceded him he underwent himself, because he did not allow himself to be disciplined or learn wisdom from the blows that fell on his neighbours; and having pursued the same path of wickedness as they, he deservedly toppled over the identical cliff.[3]

His adversary thus finally thrown down, the mighty victor Constantine, pre-eminent in every virtue that true religion can confer, with his son Crispus, an emperor most dear to God and in every way resembling his father, won back their own eastern lands and reunited the Roman Empire into a single whole, bringing it all under their peaceful sway, in a wide circle embracing north and south alike from the east to the farthest west. Men had now lost all fear of their former oppressors; day after day they kept dazzling festival; light was everywhere, and men who once dared not look up greeted each other with smiling faces and shining eyes. They danced and sang in city and country alike, giving honour first of all to God our Sovereign Lord, as they had been instructed,

1. The eldest son, then commanding the navy but two years later executed by his father.
2. At Adrianople in July, and at Scutari in September, A.D. 324.
3. Constantine had him killed.

and then to the pious emperor with his sons, so dear to God. Old troubles were forgotten, and all irreligion passed into oblivion; good things present were enjoyed, those yet to come eagerly awaited. In every city the victorious emperor published decrees full of humanity and laws that gave proof of munificence and true piety. Thus all tyranny had been purged away, and the kingdom that was theirs was preserved securely and without question for Constantine and his sons alone. They, having made it their first task to wipe the world clean from hatred of God, rejoiced in the blessings that He had conferred upon them, and, by the things they did for all men to see, displayed love of virtue and love of God, devotion and thankfulness to the Almighty.

APPENDIXES

A. EMPERORS AND BISHOPS

BISHOPS

B.C.	Rome	Alexandria	Jerusalem	Antioch
44 Augustus				
A.D.				
14 Tiberius				
37 Gaius (Caligula)				
41 Claudius				
			James	(Peter)
54 Nero				
	(Paul, Peter)			
	Linus	Mark I		
		Annianus		Euodius
68 Galba				
69 Otho, Vespasian				
			Symeon	
79 Titus	Anencletus			
81 Domitian				
		Avilius		
	Clement			
96 Nerva				Ignatius
98 Trajan		Cerdo		
	Evarestus		Justus I	
	Alexander	Primus		
			Zacchaeus	
			Tobias	
			Benjamin	Hero (Heros)
117 Hadrian			John	
	Xystus I	Justus	Matthias	
			Philip	
			Seneca	
			Justus II	
	Telesphorus		Levi	
		Eumenes	Ephres	
			Joseph	
			Judas	
			Mark	Cornelius
138 Antoninus Pius	Hyginus			
	Pius		Cassian	

EMPERORS		BISHOPS		
A.D.	*Rome*	*Alexandria*	*Jerusalem*	*Antioch*
138 Antoninus Pius (*cont.*)		Mark II		
			Publius	
			Maximus I	
			Julian I	Eros
		Celadion	Gaius I	
	Anicetus		Symmachus	
			Gaius II	
161 Marcus Aurelius				
	Soter	Agrippinus	Julian II	Theophilus
			Capito	
			Maximus II	
			Antoninus	
	Eleutherus		Valens	Maximin
			Dolichian	
180 Commodus		Julian	Narcissus	
				Serapion
	Victor			
		Demetrius		
192 Pertinax				
193 Severus				
	Zephyrinus			
211 Caracalla			Alexander	
				Asclepiades
217 Macrinus				
218 Elagabalus	Callistus			
222 Alexander	Urban			Philetus
	Pontian			Zebinnus
		Heraclas		
235 Maximin				
238 Gordian	Anteros			
	Fabian			Babylas
244 Philip				
		Dionysius		
249 Decius	Cornelius		Mazabanes	Fabius
251 Gallus				Demetrius
	Lucius			
253 Valerian and Gallienus				
	Stephen			
	Xystus II		Hymenaeus	Paul of Samosata
261 Gallienus only	Dionysius			
		Maximus		
268 Claudius				Domnus
	Felix			

Appendix

EMPERORS		BISHOPS			
A.D.		Rome	Alexandria	Jerusalem	Antioch
270	Aurelian				
		Eutychian			
276	Probus			Zabdas	
282	Carus		Theonas		
		Gaius		Hermo	
284	Diocletian				Timaeus
286	Maximian also				
		Marcellinus			
			Peter		Cyril
305	Constantius, Galerius, and Maximin				
306	Galerius, Constantine, Maxentius, and Maximin				
308	Licinius also				
311	Galerius dies	Miltiades			
312	Maxentius dies				
313	Maximin dies				
324	Licinius dies				

B. BISHOPRICS

Region	See
Africa	Carthage, 288, 404
Arabia	Bostra, 261, 314
Armenia	At least one see, 286
Asia	Ephesus, 141, 145, 225, 229, 231
	Hierapolis, 141, 145, 186, 226
	Laodicea, 187, 231, 286–8
	Magnesia, 145
	Philadelphia, 146, 174, 222
	Sardis, 166
	Smyrna, 145–6, 167–74
	Tralles, 146
Bithynia	Amastris, 183
	Nicomedia, 183, 332–4
Cappadocia	Caesarea, 266, 314
	At least one other see, 250
Cilicia	Tarsus, 286, 314
Crete	Cnossus, 181, 184
	Gortyna, 183
Egypt	ALEXANDRIA, 89, 103, 124, 127, 154–6, 164, 181, 213, 229, 242, 266, 271, 298, 326

Appendix

Region	See
Egypt	Hermopolis, 285
	Nilopolis, 279
	Thmuis, 338
	At least five other sees, 345
Galatia	Iconium, 260, 314
	Laranda, 260
Gaul	Arles, 406
	Lyons, 193–205, 208
	Vienne, 193–205
Greece	Athens, 110, 183
	Corinth, 105, 110, 124, 181, 229
Italy	ROME, 104, 107, 110, 124, 145, 154–7, 163–4, 180, 192, 208–9, 229, 261–3, 267, 273, 287–8, 313, 319–20, 404
Libya	Bernice, 313
	Pentapolis, 313
Osrhoene	At least two sees, 230
Palestine	Caesarea, 229, 260, 267, 299, 314, 324
	Gaza, 343
	JERUSALEM, 72, 118, 123, 142, 145, 156, 181, 214–15, 248–51, 273, 299, 314, 326
Phoenicia	Ptolemais, 233
	Tyre, 233, 288, 344, 383
Phrygia	Apamea, 220
	Cumane, 220
	Eumenia, 231
	Otrus, 218
	Philomelium, 168
	Synnada, 260
Pontus	Two or more sees, 183, 299, 314, 325
Sicily	Syracuse, 405
Syria	ANTIOCH, 128, 145–7, 181, 185–6, 226, 251, 263, 268, 273, 286, 313–20
	Emesa, 345
	Laodicea, 298, 321, 324
Thrace	Anchialus, 226
	Develtum, 226

C. MARTYRDOMS

Emperor	Locality	Martyr
Tiberius	Jerusalem	Stephen, 71, 111, 204
Claudius	Jerusalem	James the Apostle, 81, 111
Nero	Jerusalem	James the Righteous, 72, 99–103, 111, 123, 181

418

Emperor	*Locality*	*Martyr*
Nero (*cont.*)	Rome	Paul and Peter, 97–9, 104–5, 107, 140
		Peter's wife, 140
Domitian	Rome	Many eminent men, 125
Trajan	Jerusalem	Symeon, 142
	Rome	Ignatius, 145–7
		Rufus and Zosimus, 147
	Many lands	'An alarming number,' 144
Antoninus Pius	Rome	Telesphorus, 163, 208
	Smyrna	Germanicus, 169
		Polycarp, 168–74, 231
		Metrodorus, 174
		Pionius, 174
		Thraseas, 231
	Pergamum	Carpus, Papylas, Agathonice, 175
Marcus Aurelius	Rome	Justin, 86, 175–7
		Ptolemy and Lucius, 178
	Athens	Publius, 188
	Laodicea	Sagaris, 187, 231
	Lyons and Vienne	Vettius Epagathus, 194–5
		Sanctus and Maturus, 196, 199–200
		Attalus, 196, 199–202, 205
		Blandina, 196, 199–202
		Biblis, 197
		Pothinus, 198, 208
		Alexander, 201
		Ponticus, 202
		Alcibiades, 205
		Many others, 193–205
Commodus	Apamea	Gaius and Alexander, 221
	Rome	Apollonius, 228–9
Severus	Alexandria	Leonides, 239–41
		Plutarch, 242–4
		Serenus (1 and 2), Heraclides, Hero, Herais, 244–5
		Potamiaena, Basilides, Marcella, 245–6
Decius	Rome	Fabian, 273
	Alexandria	Metras and Quinta, 275–6
		Apollonia, 276
		Serapion, 276
		Julian and Cronion, 279
		Besas, Macar, Epimachus, Alexander, 277–8
		Ammonarion, Mercuria, Dionysia, 278

Appendix

Emperor	Locality	Martyr
Decius (cont.)	Alexandria (cont.)	Hero, Ater, Isidore, 278
		Nemesion, 278
		Ammon, Zeus, Ptolemy, Ingenuus, Theophilus, 278–9
	Egypt	Ischyrion, 279
Valerian	Caesarea	Priscus, Malchus, Alexander, 298
Gallienus	Caesarea	Marinus, 299–300
	Rome	Marcellinus, 320
Diocletian and Galerius	Nicomedia	Euethius, 332–3
		Peter, 333–4
		Anthimus and many others, 334, 344
		Dorotheus and Gorgonius, 327–8, 333–4
	Tyre	Five Egyptians, 335–6
	Egypt and Thebais	'Immense numbers', 335–40
		Philoromus, 338
		Phileas, 338–41, 345
		Hesychius, Pachymius, Theodore, 345
	Africa and Mauretania	'Countless martyrs', 335
Maximin	Phrygia	A whole village, 341
		Adauctus, 341
	Arabia, Cappadocia, Mesopotamia	'Amazing martyrs', 341–2
	Pontus	A number of martyrs, 343
	Antioch	Woman and daughters, 342–3
		Two sisters, 343
		Tyrannion and Zenobius, 344–5
	Phaeno	Silvanus of Gaza and 39 others, 345
		Peleus and Nilus, 345
	Caesarea	Pamphilus, 270, 325, 345
	Emesa	Silvanus of Emesa and two others, 345, 361–2
	Alexandria	Peter and many bishops, 345, 361–2
	Nicomedia	Lucian, 344, 362

D. HERETICS

Groups	Rough Date	Leaders
Gnostics and Docetics	A.D. 65	Thebuthis, Simon, Cleobius, Dositheus, and Gorthaeus, 182
	70	Menander, 135–6, 158

Groups	Rough Date	Leaders
Gnostics and Docetics (cont.)	A.D. 80	Saturninus, 158
		Basilides, 158
		Carpocrates, 159–60
	90	Cerinthus, 137–9, 167
	140	Cerdo, 163
	150	Valentinus, 163–4, 167, 191, 226
		Marcus, 164
		Marcion, 163–7, 174, 186, 212, 215
	165	Apelles, 215–16
		Potitus, 215
		Basilicus, 215
		Syneros, 215
	170	Tatian, 190–1
	180	Severus, 190
	190	Bardaisan, 191
	220	Ambrose, 257
Nicolaitans	80	? Nicolaus, 139
Phrygian heretics	160	Montanus, 189, 205, 217–26
	170	Alcibiades, 295
		Theodotus, 205, 220
		Maximilla, 217–21, 225
		Priscilla, 217–19, 223
		Themiso, 224
		Alexander, 224–5
	185	Florinus and Blastus, 217, 226–8
	190	Miltiades, 217–18
	200	Proclus, 104–5, 261
Ebionites	170	Symmachus, 256–7
Adoptionists	190	Theodotus the Shoemaker, 205, 236
	210	Asclepiodotus and Theodotus the Banker, 236
		Natalius, 236–7
	225	Artemon, 235, 318
	240	Beryllus, 270
	260	Paul of Samosata, 235, 315–19
Monarchians	220	Sabellius, 289, 313
Manichees	240	Mani, 319–20
Puritans	250	Novatian, 280–6
Millennialists	250	Nepos and Coracion, 307–9

Note. The above groups overlap. Mani might be classed with the Docetics, Cerinthus and Symmachus with the Adoptionists and the Millennialists. There are sub-groups, e.g. Encratites (Tatian and Severus).

Appendix

E. SOURCES QUOTED OR SUMMARIZED

30 B.C.–A.D. 45	Philo	*Mission*, 77–9
		Contemplative Life, 89–93
A.D. 30–97	Clement of Rome	*Epistle to Corinthians*, 148–9, 208–9
37–101	Josephus	*Jewish War*, 50, 58–60, 80, 95–7, 102, 105–6, 112–21
		Antiquities, 50, 58–64, 78, 82–5, 96, 102–3, 121–2
		Against Apion, 121–2
		Life, 123
50–115	Ignatius	*Letters*, 145–7
60–135	Papias	*Sayings of the Lord*, 88, 149–53
61–113	Pliny	Letter to Trajan, 144
69–156	Polycarp	Letter to Philippians, 147
75–145	Quadratus	*Defence*, 155–6
76–138	Hadrian	Rescript, 162–3
?	?	Edessan Archives, 65–70
100–60	Aristo	Bar Cochba's Revolt, 157–8
?	Agrippa Castor	Refutation of Basilides, 159
100–65	Justin Martyr	*Defence*, 86, 136, 161–5, 175–8
		Dialogue, 179–80
		Against Marcion, 164–5, 180
100–80	Hegesippus	Acts of the Church, 99–102, 124–7, 142–3, 160–1, 181–2
110–80	Dionysius of Corinth	Letters, 105, 183–5
?	Pinytus	Letter to Dionysius, 184
115–85	Tatian	*Greeks Answered*, 176–7, 190–1
		Diatessaron, 190
115–85	Melito	*Petition*, 186–8
		Defence, 166
		Easter Festival, 187
		Extracts, 188–9
121–80	M. Aurelius	Decree, 165–6
126–200	Polycrates	Letter to Victor, 140–1, 230–2
130–200	Irenaeus	*Heresies Answered*, 86–8, 125, 128, 135–6, 147–9, 158, 163–4, 167–80, 190, 208–9
		Refutation, 209–13
		Octet, 226–7
		Letters, 227–8, 332–3
140–210	Rhodo	Against Marcion, 215–16
140–210	Serapion	Letter to Caricus and Pontius, 226
		Gospel of Peter, 251–2

?	Gallic Churches	Martyrs of Gaul, 193–205
		Letter to Eleutherus, 206
?	Anonymous	Against Miltiades, 217–22
150–215	Clement of	*Outlines*, 64, 72, 81–2, 88, 99, 253–5
	Alexandria	*Miscellanies*, 139–40, 214, 246, 252–3
		Easter Festival, 187, 253
		Rich Man Who Finds Salvation, 128–31, 253
?	Jude	Daniel, 246–7
150–220	Apollonius	Against the Montanists, 223–5
154–222	Bardaisan	Dialogues, 191
?	Smyrna Church	Martyrdom of Polycarp, 168–74
?	Unknown	*Martyrdom of Pionius*, 174–5
160–221	Tertullian	*Defence*, 75–6, 104, 127, 144, 207–8
160–230	Gaius	*Dialogue*, 104–5, 137–8, 141, 261
?	Palestinian Bps	Easter Festival, 233–4
160–230	Hippolytus	*Easter Festival*, 262
?	Alexander	Letters, 250–1, 260
170–245	Julius Africanus	*Dictionary of Dates*, 269
		Letters, 53–6, 269
185–254	Origen	*Commentaries*, 107, 262–6
		Hexapla and *Tetrapla*, 256
		Resurrection, 263
		Martyrdom, 267
		Letters, 259–60
190–264	Dionysius of	*Promises*, 138, 307–13
	Alexandria	Letters on Baptism, 288–92
		Festival Letters, 302–6
		Other letters, 273–80, 284–6, 292–7, 306–7
200–52	Cornelius	Letter to Fabius, 280–4
218–68	Gallienus	Decree, 298–9
?	Malchion	Letter to Dionysius and Maximus, 315–18
?	Unknown	Pilate's *Memoranda*, 60, 64, 361
?	Anatolius	Canons, 323–4
220–307	Phileas	Letter to Thmuites, 339–40
233–304	Porphyry	Against Christianity, 258–9
242–311	Galerius	Recantation, 253–4
?	Sabinus	Letter to Governors, 357–8
?–313	Maximin	Rescript, 362–4
		Letter to Sabinus, 371–3
		Ordinance, 375–6
288–337	Constantine	Ordinances and letters, 401–8

Note. Many of the above dates are approximate only.

Appendix

F. CANON OF THE NEW TESTAMENT

Recognised Books

Matthew, 132–4, 152, 210, 213, 254, 265
Mark, 88–9, 132–4, 152, 210, 254, 265
Luke, 109–10, 132, 210–11, 254, 265–6
John, 132–4, 210, 254–5, 265
Acts, 97, 109–10, 134, 141, 266

Thirteen Pauline Epistles, 103, 134
1 Peter, 108, 134, 211, 265
1 John, 134, 210, 266
1 Clement, 124–5, 148–9, 185

Disputed Books

Hebrews, 108, 149, 253–4, 261, 266, 276
James, 103, 134
2 Peter, 108, 134, 265

2 and 3 John, 134, 266
Jude, 103, 134, 253–4
Revelation, 139, 150, 211, 225

Rejected Books

Peter	Gospel, 108, 135, 251–2	Barnabas	Epistle, 134, 253
	Acts, 108	Apostles	Teachings, 134
	Preaching, 108	Thomas	Gospel, 135
	Revelation, 108, 134, 254	Matthias	Gospel, 135
Paul	Acts, 108, 134	?	Gospel of the Hebrews,
Hermas	Shepherd, 108, 134, 211		135–7, 153, 182
Clement	Second Epistle, 149, 253	Andrew	Acts, 135
		John	Acts, 135

INDEX

Index

426

427

Index